HOLISTIC ASTROLOGY

The Analysis of Inner and Outer Environments

By the same author:

The Horoscope as Identity

The Principles and Practice of Astrology
	in twelve volumes, for home study and college curriculum

The Guide to the Principles and Practice of Astrology
The Missing Moon

All published by Llewellyn Publications, Box 43383, St. Paul, MN 55164

HOLISTIC ASTROLOGY

The Analysis of Inner and Outer Environments

by Noel Jan Tyl

First Edition 1980

TAI Books
Box 927
McLean, Virginia 22101

Library of Congress Cataloging in Publication Data

Tyl, Noel, 1936-
  Holistic astrology.

  Bibliography: p.
  Includes index.
  1. Astrology. I. Title.
BF1708.T89   133.5   79-92421
ISBN 0-935620-00-1

Printed in the United States of America by R. R. Donnelley & Sons
    Company.
Cover Art designed and executed by Michael David Brown Inc.,
    Rockville, Maryland
Author's photo by Gary D. Landsman

PREFACE

This book is about perception, feeling, and art. It is dedicated to us all as astrologers and to the astrology of our era, to help with perception of the world in which we live, to help with feeling the patterns that condition our growth, and to help with the art of helping others.

I have tried to awaken us all to the dramatic developmental process between inner environmental needs and outer environmental prescriptions. That developmental process contains complex behavioral patterns, anchored within both environments, routinized by time, and stereotyped by any given era. Study of the process is submitted in terms of artistic analysis, to appreciate the message of the environment, the awareness of anxiety, and the process of remediation. It is designed to show the way to astrologers, not only into a horoscope in richness, but into a life in compassion and understanding and, as well, into personal appreciation of the existence we all experience together.

This book is born totally from the perception, feeling, and art of analytical experience. And to those clients who have shared their lives with me over the years, to those clients who have given permission for their lives to be shared with you in this volume, I extend my deepest appreciation.

Noel Jan Tyl
November 1979

i

"Very few physicians have exact knowledge
of diseases and their causes,
but my books are not written like those of other physicians,
merely copying the ancient authorities.
I have composed them on the basis of experience,
which is the greatest master of everything.
Look, observe, go back to the bedside;
... Proceed from reason and move on the learning of experience."
—Paracelsus.

TABLE OF CONTENTS

Part One:
THE MESSAGE OF
THE ENVIRONMENT

Chapter One
OBSERVATIONS

A long, long line of Jews led from the train depot to an inspection area. There the line was divided. The stronger went to barracks to prepare to work for the Nazi war effort; the weak went to shower chambers to prepare for a new life. It was Auschwitz 1944.

*　　*　　*

Classes were changing after the lunch break on Friday, November 22, 1963. The seventh grade class in a Junior High School in Pike County, Alabama was brought to order by the teacher. The teacher announced that the President of the United States had been shot and was thought to be dying. The class spontaneously broke into exclamations of surprise and pleasure.

After the next class, the teacher had another announcement: the President was dead. The class of seventh graders went into an uproar, applauding and yelling in happiness.

*　　*　　*

Many thousands gathered on the Capitol grounds in Washington, D.C. for four days at the end of April 1979. They gathered to act upon the environment, to champion solar energy through the Appropriate Community Technology Fair-Conference.

3

4

These three glimpses of life are true. They show us individual reactions in relation to environment. The extermination of the Jews during World War II shows us *victimization* by the environment; the seventh graders' reactions to the assassination of President Kennedy show us their *reflection* of their environment; the ACT Fair-Conference in Washington, D.C. shows individuals working together to *change* the environment.

In no way would the individual horoscopes of the millions of Jews victimized by the Nazis, of the seventh graders indoctrinated by parental politics, or of the solar energy supporters dedicated to change and improvement show reliably these specific environmental relationships. Yet the environment is continually at work, shaping individuation, channeling personality development, and guiding destiny.

In astrology, we rivet our total attention upon the horoscope. By assuming the supposed all-importance of the horoscopic environment, we tend to forget the individual's position within societal structure, to forget the societal matrix within which and from which the individual grows. All too easily, by concentrating upon the meanings of measurements within the horoscope, we ignore full assessment and appreciation of the environment. When we sense that our analyses are incomplete or shallow, we strain measurements beyond tenability; we grope to relate the individual to his or her surrounding world through the horoscope alone. To remedy this, to improve our astrology, *we must understand the roles of the environment within life development.*

With every client, we must ask ourselves about environmental influence and individual reaction to it. To what extent is the client influenced by his or her environment; what about the changes in that environment for that individual through the lifetime of development; what does the individual need from different environmental dimensions; what about the client's personalized dimensions of passive victimization, naive reflection, and willful change within the vital environmental embrace? How has the client participated in relationships within the environment; how has the client differentiated selfhood within it all?

The symbols and measurements of astrology are simply abbreviations of what we know; what we have learned about life. These symbols and measurements continuously grow in amplitude of significance as the astrologer grows in awareness. Our symbolic pantheon has incredibly more meaning for us now than, say, for astrologers in England at the turn of the century. Our lives are more complex now, more accelerated. Indeed, every era of life devises the astrology it needs to explain its texture of individual behavior and collective philosophy. Our symbolizations grow—should grow—to keep pace with the times in which we live, with the many dimensions of environment.

Instead of trying to fit an individual to the horoscope, thereby *confining* individualism to what we know and express through astrology's symbols, we should reverse the process. We should relate the horoscope to the individual. In this way, we learn more about what the symbols mean within an individual's life. This learning will then naturally include the registration of the environment within the individual's life development. Astrology will come to life.

Relating the horoscope to the individual is a very subtle but powerful concept. We abandon the paltry ego rewards of proving astrology's rigorous descriptions in order to appreciate the bloom of astrology as lived by a human being. We learn about life in the process. We fulfill what astrology is all about.

We study how the horoscope has been fulfilled by the individual. Whenever the symbolic profile of a horoscope indicates a dimension that does not appear to have manifested within the individual's life or consciousness, we must know that something in the individual's development has shifted the emphasis of growth. That "something" keys us almost invariably to environmental concerns, especially during the early developmental years.

For example, a woman is born in a small town in Oklahoma or Kansas in the early 1920's. Her horoscope shows emphasized ego strengths through an obvious Aries focus, yet the individual now in her late fifties lives a routinized, muted existence, and her past history generally shows little of the powerful Aries expression potential. We sense underachievement; we question the horoscope's accuracy; we begin to founder in our analysis.

But let us think for a moment: what were the times like in the 1920's and 1930's in that area of the country? What was a woman's position within that environment? What was the cultural ideal passed on by the family to the young girl during her developmental years? What were the environmental pressures during that extremely important early growth time? Certain Solar Arc, Progression, and/or transit activity of especially dramatic nature could be suggested within the person's first sixteen years. What would have been the individual contact with the environmental pressures at that time? How would family reorganization have affected the woman's goals for herself, her behavior patterns, her cultural profile?

Our answers would tell us much: a rural existence, probably on a farm; a depressed national economy biting strongly into the family's local economic level; probably an extended family group with several siblings, all working out individual needs and family needs together; the males would have the future and would get whatever education that would minimally suffice; the women would be expected to marry and have children, and education and other resources would not be wasted on them. Perhaps the mother died when the woman was 14, and as the eldest daughter, she was forced into taking care of the entire household. She toiled hard and uncomplainingly (thanks to the Aries energy), but privately she longed to be rescued by marriage, to be taken out of one situation and into another, very similar but less hectic and oppressed. Marriage came all to early. She was freed into another routine. Life went on. The routine was reinforced. Sameness was security. The early environmental values endured.

This environmental picture tells us so much. It is a valid demographic and cultural profile for that time and geographic area. The woman, now in her late fifties has come to the astrologer to find a new path for individual significance. She has been alerted to this need by the changing times, by the new values, by the new environment. She says it all most simply but dramatically in her wish to have been born into a different era, into a different environment.

Individuation

Philosophers have long toiled with the problems of individuation within the social environment. Giambattista Vico, an Italian social theorist and philosopher of history, wrote in the early eighteenth century that every phase of history has its own style of thought which provides it with a specific and appropriate cultural mentality. This is valid not only in the epochal view but as well in generational and regional views. Karl Marx, in his *Introduction to the*

Critique of Political Economy, stated that it is not men's consciousness which determines their existence, but on the contrary it is their social existence which determines their consciousness. Marx saw individual awareness resting on a substructure of special human relationships. Another group of thinkers, including Emile Durkheim and Karl Mannheim, saw the individual as the most likely source of error within any social mold, and society as the most reliable source of truth.—It continues to be a philosophical dilemma to reduce social facts to individual facts. Astrology solves this dilemma by knowing that the human being is the focus of *both*.

In the philosophy and practice of astrology, in the pursuit of individual identity, we must contend with all the life dimensions around us in the environment and within us in relation to the environment. We must contend with all the things that *preserve sameness* in the name of secure identity and all the things that work to *change sameness* in the name of personality growth. We must contend with those things that work societally to preserve astrological expectability within our culturally evolved symbolisms and with those things that work individually to personalize those same astrological symbolisms. We must look for environmental victimization, environmental reflection, and individual activity to affect environmental change. To understand this growth process is the challenge to the astrologer in astrological analysis of a horoscope and to the individual in living the horoscope in life. The balance clarified and achieved among these dimensions at any given moment within development measures the efficacy of the astrologer and the identity of the individual.

There are many, many forces at work within an individual's relationship to the environment, within the cross pressures to stay the same and yet to change. There is a perpetual flux in life—people age, trees shed leaves, ice melts, winds blow—and within it, within these pressures, there is the constant threat of insecurity. We affect change, and immediately we must contend with insecurity. We need to keep something the same, to cling to formative values of environmental influence, in order to minimize insecurity. This decreases the extent of change while reinforcing an earlier status quo. The flux falters; routine protects; identities stabilize. The shifting winds fill no sails.

It is no wonder then that human beings easily take the growth of identity out of the mainstream of change. Some predictable, comfortable, secure permanence of identity is needed as a base within the changing pressures of time. This is essential for human beings to meet challenges of development and not feel lost. But to what extent is sameness maintained for security in relation to challenge accepted for change?—It is no wonder that many can find comfort by living the sociological fact that individual blunder or underachievement can be neutralized or insulated by a common societal attitude. Being like the others in our cultural mentality, focusing our consciousness within our society's values, helps us please our parents and peer group, patterns our relationships, but at the same time quiets our individual voices for growth and change.

These are some of the dilemmas facing us all within the growth process. These are dimensions that are carried by electrical impulses within our brains, that are painted in colors within our dreams, that are hidden within our words, that are embraced by the symbolisms of our horoscopes. These must be the concerns of holistic astrological analysis.

A quarter century ago, Abraham Maslow startled the research world of psychology by testing human self-actualization in terms of intrinsic positivism. The novelty of his theories was that he assumed human beings had an inborn nature that was essentially good, never evil. The psychological theories of the times then assumed that human instincts and motives were bad and had to be trained through socialization. Maslow maintained that human beings became miserable, that they underachieved, *only because of the environment*. Individuals had particular needs; when they were not fulfilled in good enough measure through interaction with the environment, attitudinal negativism was born. Psychologists today are planning tests along similarly positive lines. They are working to understand and measure the concept of self in terms of love, hope, and relationship dynamics that relate to subjective identity awareness more than they do to objective behavioral performance. The shift has been to the *inner* environment and its positive values, not to ignore the outer environment but to add insight to the dynamic interaction between the two.

Similarly, our astrology has changed. We call the change an Aquarian Age influence. We have polished the analytical lens of astrology to reflect internal states of psychological awareness. We work to ban negative "old time" words from our symbological lexicons. We seek to complement knowledge of the external environment with sensitivity to the inner environment. It is all too easy to concentrate upon one without the other. Holistic astrology demands that the two be integrated, that social fact and individual fact merge within the human being, that the horoscope be related to the life as it is lived by the individual.

The holistic astrologer must appreciate the change in astrology in terms of an individual client's awareness and registration of a changed era and all its cross pressures. Every individual faces a generation transition within normal growth time. Clients born within the values of the earlier "survival society", pre-1940, now live in the expectations and values of the present "identity society." The goal oriented upbringing that has endured in the sameness maintained to preserve identity security clashes with the role oriented pressures of a changed environment. The need now is to be verified as a person instead of accepted as a function. The holistic astrologer must study this environmental metamorphosis and reflect an understanding of the dynamics within the client's awareness of it.

Values of one society or the other can not be espoused; the values of both must be embraced in terms of the client's personalized human drama. All must be considered in respect for the struggle, in appreciation of the samenesses that carry life forward with minimized insecurity, in assimilation of the differences that threaten security but promise growth. In this way, holistic astrology becomes in its revelations a living part of a dynamic learning process. In this way, the symbols of astrology grow. In this way, social facts and individual facts are recognized as merged within the individual, and the individual horoscope lives in meaning as the individual lives in life.

Maintaining Sameness

The drive within us all to maintain sameness is extremely powerful. We saw it clearly in our earlier example of the woman born in the 1920's in the rural Southwest. The drive to remain as we are or as we are expected to be serves to minimize insecurity in the challenge of change. It is so terribly important because it is activated upon birth—even organized and planned unconsciously by the parents before the birth of their facsimile—and is reinforced through the vital developmental years in the home. As we will see soon, sameness, constancy, predictability are rewarded powerfully at all times in our society. They are learned; they are the way of life. And they are the major bulwark against the dynamism of change and individuation.

We can see this phenomenon in little ways every day: stilted conversation in an elevator or with a casual acquaintance in an apartment house lobby reliably seeks to fill a societally conditioned pattern. Discussions about the weather, perfunctory inquiries about one's health, idle chit-chat about the postal service, a recent sports event or news item; all these kinds of things are "expected." Dress codes confer status; status dictates approachability and conversation content. All these observations recognize a societal rhythm. *Not* cooperating obligingly within this rhythmic pattern creates vivid tension, introduces the threat of rejection, hampers socialization. Not cooperating defies environmental relationship prescriptions and brings aloneness.

The societal rhythm is felt in deeper levels as well: we are commanded to honor father and mother; we are conditioned to curb awareness of—even apologize for—personal excellence and high personality definition; we are expected to communicate and hold opinions that are espoused by some larger group or authority.

There are serious problems when we miss a beat within this rhythm: we eventually realize that the pressures in us for individuation cause us to be different from our parents; we eventually realize that to appreciate others we must first appreciate ourselves; we eventually realize that we get a great sense of being alive when we respect our own minds.

These examples abbreviate the astrological lessons taught by the three Grand Crosses among the Houses within the horoscope. The Ascendant *squares* the parental axis (X-IV): for individual growth, we need our parents for developmental nurturance but also for contrast; the completion of this Grand Cross is when the VIIth House enters our growth awareness, when in relationships we meet others with the same individuation concerns. The IInd House symbolizing self-worth *squares* the love-given and love-received axis (V-XI): there is a developmental tension among loving one's self, giving love to others, and expecting love in return; the completion is symbolized by the VIIIth House which is the similar self-worth second of all those with whom we are in relationship. The IIIrd House symbolizing our communication and opinions *squares* the VIth House of interpersonal cooperation and the XIIth House of societal institutionalization: there is a developmental tension between communication of our selves and gaining the support of others individually and collectively. This lesson pattern is completed by introduction of the IXth House, society's laws, teachings, propaganda, and others' opinions.

In each of the configurations, we meet the same core concern in someone else in our environment. Gratefully, *we are not alone.* Therefore, through relationships of varying frequency, depth, and longevity, we learn middle-grounds, compromises. In short, we learn to maintain an approximation of sameness in order to minimize personal insecurity during growth. We do this with others who have the same problems. Always, we are linked for support with the same elements to which we are born and in which we are raised; always, we are challenged for growth by different elements. The balance becomes precarious.

We maintain sameness because the environment rewards us. The rewards are provided in terms of *environmental support and approval.* Beyond the individual support gained through relationships with others who have the exact same concerns within the growth process, we gain the approving support of the environment in various sub-wholes: our family, our neighborhood, our community, our co-workers, our government, our religion. The reward power of these areas of support and approval is enormous: many adults can look back and see that they lost identity strength, self-worth security, and mental independence by acquiescing to the demands and reward promise offered by parents and other environmental figureheads. Many adults can see it continue to happen in different ways throughout their lives. The reward of support and approval is undeniable; its power plays into human vulnerability by illuminating the way of security during the challenges of growth. In relative measures, individuals sacrifice identity to be part of environment approval.

The force is inexorable; yet the process is reasonable. We can call it the strategy of survival, keeping peace (Libra opposite Aries), rolling with the punches, fate. All human beings must maintain some sameness in order to gain environmental support, but *the degree to which different human beings participate in the process* is directly related to their individual insecurity, identity development, and maturation.

Indeed, this process is reflection of the environment. It is the middle ground between victimization by the environment and change of the environment. The seventh grade students were surprised by the announcement of assassination of the President; it was unique; there was no precedent to establish value or prescribe reaction. The youngsters behaved in a way that reflected their parents' views, their parents' expectations. The demand to react to this startling news had to be met securely, and what more secure way of reaction was there for the very young than the way their parents react!

This process of environmental reflection is very, very real. How many women marry men like their fathers; how many men marry symbols of their mothers? How vast is the majority who never leave the early home community or, if they do, move to one very similar to it? How many times do multiple marriages reflect similar conditions throughout the series to echo unresolved environmental tensions within the early home? How often do people have problems with expressing love because they had little experience with love expression in the early home?

By reflecting the environment to varying degrees during growth throughout life, human beings are minimizing insecurity by creating reliable, predictable structure. As continually nascent individuals, we work *to fulfill individualized needs* as best we can through relationships with others specifically and the environment generally. We establish personal resources, determine what resources we have, seek to make an exchange, go on to another cycle of need press, need fulfillment, and momentary stabilization. During this process, there are varying degrees of tension in relation to the press of particular needs for fulfillment and the degree of ease or difficulty in the fulfillment process. Insecurity always threatens. We need always *to confirm societal structure.*

We reflect environment to maintain some sameness, to seek support and approval from various sub-wholes of the environment. The structure we build, the structure that approves of us, reflects our past experience and is used to tell a great deal—sometimes to tell all—about who we are. It is welcome to read this thought (as if written for astrologers!) in Uriel and Edna Foa's *Societal Structures of the Mind*: "Man classifies stimuli and organizes their classes; in this process the environment acquires meaning for him and the experiences of the past enable him to understand the present and to predict the future."[1]

Even one of the extremes in our discussion, victimization by the environment, has within its dynamics a maintenance dimension, a preservation of status quo. There are many records of healthy individuals sitting down to die after learning of a Voodoo curse placed upon them. They die shortly, as if to fulfill the environmental expectation. The curse, the victimization, *is supposed to work this way*. We have the grisly record of mass cult suicide in Jonestown, Guyana. The cult members had given up personal identity to a leader in exchange for certain environmental rewards (support and approval). Acquiescence to suicide was an extension of this structure, with reward promised in another realm, to all of them all together.

In the face of victimization, we sense the irrational. It is irrational for the environment to do away with its constituency which it needs for support and maintenance. We can not project upon others similar to us that which is inconceivable to us. Therefore, the authoritative, more resourceful portion of the environment must be right! We acquiesce to the victimizing demands. We do not understand; we rationalize . . . "everything will be alright; what will be will be". . .; the mind trusts itself. Lemmings follow their kind into the sea to drown. Not knowing during the process is transient blessing; understanding later is horror.

Think of the times that parents arbitrarily ignore the needs of their child by enforcing behavioral patterns, opinions, destiny upon the child. Think of the times the child becomes a scapegoat for the parents' own frustrations. Think of the guilt that only sometimes occurs to stimulate rewards to the child in compensation. Think how these rewards actually reinforce the earlier behavior. Think of all the confusion that works its way into development. For the child, frequent acquiescence can become habitual. The child believes what is is what should be; what is comes from the environment that sometimes supports and occasionally rewards. How many people have a negative self-image, have in part died, because environmental pressures to demean them were frequent enough in development so as to instill habitual acquiescent reaction?

In the other extreme of our discussion, changing the environment, we see a group of people banding around a particular idea in order to establish a new status quo, to create a new sameness to be maintained for the common good. When the group becomes the majority, democracy hears the voice. When the group is a minority, its views are classified as dissident, threatening the status quo the majority works to maintain.

John Steinbeck has written, "It is the nature of a man as he grows older... to protest against change, particularly change for the better." This thought illuminates our entire discussion: as we grow within varying degrees of environmental reflection, we fear the insecurity presented by change. As we cross generations within lifetime, we face the altered values of changed times. We resist because of the power of all the environmental prescriptions we have accumulated. Privately, we may languish. Eventually we may try change, to release the grip on functionalism and acknowledge the grasp of new role identification.

We can acknowledge the presence of change and get rid of the tensions of confrontation by condemning the different values. In this way, we tighten our grip on who we have always been. If different values are touted as "better", we instinctively need to deny this because it tends to demean all we have represented throughout development. Yet, privately, we imagine what could be. Our defenses work overtly by denial and covertly through fantasy.

Yet, it is through the power of *reinforced fantasy* that change can be not only assimilated but accepted. On August 28, 1963, many thousands gathered in Washington, D.C. to champion the Civil Rights Movement, to reinforce a people's "fantasy", to change a reality. Millions throughout the world watched to see change emerge; millions were poised on the periphery to join up supportively when numbers and power and rewards gained enough leverage to be heard. Martin Luther King, Jr. made history *not* by proclaiming that he had a *plan*—this would have been too tangible, too deniable, too vulnerable—but by proclaiming that he had a *dream*. The minds and spirits of multitudes were fired. Dream could be held without insecurity; dream was shared by all; dream was future oriented and did not condemn the past. In the quest for change, dreams of the future have more life than history of the past.

On the particularly individual level, motivation for change must be visualized or shown somehow, by someone else, by fantasy, by dream, by hope, by some awakening. Change and growth can not be accomplished without reinforcing relationship factors of some kind. We need the approving strengths of another person for the courage of individuated self-awareness. Astrologically, we associate the symbolization of the planet Uranus with the intensification of individuation. With projected contact between Uranus and the angles of the horoscope, especially the Ascendant, we have learned empirically to expect geographic displacement. *This tells us that change of environment and abandoning accumulated sameness are concomitant with individual assertion.* "Going somewhere else" allows a fresh start. Through this observation, we see that at such times the individual becomes a majority.

Throughout development, the young organism makes continual attempts to assert itself, to risk individual assertion and, in effect, create change. The environment responds. Reward and support are given through loving guidance and appreciation, or reprimand and behavioral coercion are given through punishment or neglect. More often than not, personal needs go unfulfilled in varying measures, and negative attitudes emerge. The structure of the environment becomes dominant, and this dominance tends to displace the individual need profile. Frustration grows. The relative intensity mounts until a time of possible courage, until the time of individual majority.

Holistic astrology must be richly aware of all these concerns. They are not difficult, for two reasons: first, we are all part of the human process, and opening our awareness reveals it to us; second, the process always remains the same with only temporal and regional stereotypical dimensions articulating the structure differently. These concerns are keyed by the birth data (date and place), focused within the individual horoscope pattern, and articulated further by the presence and disclosure of the human being. These concerns establish the level of the horoscope and articulate what I call astrology's Law of Naturalness: *a horoscope works through an individual to express potentials and fulfill needs naturally, so far as the environment allows, supports, or rewards.*

Awareness of the Environment

The process of environmental interaction courses through our entire awareness of identity and life. As we have seen, it begins even before birth, possibly before fertilization, within the plans for us made by our parents; it is activated with the birth of our horoscope and develops inseparably with life development. There are continuously fluctuating periods of contentment and frustration, security and insecurity. The overall preoccupation with environmental interaction keeps us unaware of the specific dimensions of the process. Degrees of victimization emerge out of degrees of reflection and lull us into complacency. Complacency creates routinized contentment, and within it all we settle even more into unawareness. Only with reinforced awareness can the capactity for change be wakened.

Often, when driving through the wide open countryside with isolated farmhouses dotting the horizon, or past row upon row of identical homes in a neat suburban community, or past congested arcades of tenements deep in a city, I wonder about the horoscopes living within. The environment is so obvious in these scenes through its emblematic stratification. The influence of such environments upon the spirits of the inhabitants has been tested over and over again by sociologists and social psychologists, yet each human being lives his or her horoscope as instinctively naturally as the environment will allow. I wonder what the horoscopes would "say" through the environment filters, but I know that the horoscopes would *not* tell the story. *The individual human being would*, by clarifying the level and articulation of the horoscope in terms of the environmental interaction process.

The more keenly environmental stratification is established for a person, the harder it is for the person to diverge from it. The person's awareness is often defensively proud of such growth beginnings. Comedians still exploit life in New York's Lower East Side, wealthy communities in Connecticut, and "minority" sociological groups for real-life human situations. Understanding environmental stereotype is assumed; humor about these situations stimulates empathy and a subtle identification process that keep the entire environment relationship process all in the family. We know that these conditions exist and that a lot of credit is due to whoever escapes the mold. The biggest turn of plot and applause in the situation comedies shown on television always occur when a character defies expectation and proudly asserts individual will.

Divergence is something to contend with, something to be proud of. We applaud it in others and wish it for ourselves.

In 1950, during cold war tensions, Gian-Carlo Menotti's opera *The Consul* premiered at the Ethel Barrymore Theater in New York City. It won the New York Drama Critics' Circle Award for the best musical play and the Pulitzer Prize for Music. The musical drama portrays the percussive duress of bureaucracy as it hammered the heroine, Magda Sorrel, to suicide after endless attempts to leave an oppressed country and join her freedom fighting husband. Magda Sorrel wanted to leave her environment to join her husband who was trying to change it. Both were victimized by that environment.

In the waiting room of the Consul's office, there are people from several walks of life, different sub-environments, all of them wanting to see the environmental authority figure for particular personal reasons. They are thwarted at every turn. One old man absorbs the pain by hoping for tomorrow; a foreign woman trying to join her ill daughter is told to be patient; others are summarily ignored. A magician trying *to enter* the country to ply his skills is refused as well. The Consul's office works coldly to maintain environmental sameness; no one in or out.

The magician seeks to prove himself, and he hypnotizes all in the waiting room; he releases through fantasy all the pains of reality. He frees them momentarily to sing of lovely dance, the light so bright, and the music so sweet.

Magda Sorrel then makes her presentation in one of the most dramatic moments of all theatre experience. In utter frustration, she sings "To this we've come, that man be born a stranger upon God's earth, that he be chosen without a chance for choice, that he be hunted without the hope of refuge." She responds to the Consul secretary's questions: my name is woman; my age, still young; color of hair, gray; color of eyes, the color of tears; occupation, waiting.

It is not difficult to see the significance of this example within our discussion. We see the analogies between the Consul's waiting room and the life that surrounds us. We wait for "tomorrows" and trust patience. We understand Magda Sorrel's pain: her name is a number, her husband has fled, her child is dead in its cradle, her voice is unheard. Personal identification with these extreme values is immediate because of their reality, their validity. Each individual has a level of environmental awareness in relation to identity, and that level is somewhere between the security of complacency and the security of death.

It is essential in holistic analysis for the astrologer to determine a client's level of awareness of the environmental process. At the level of sociological expectancy, we have seen that this will be suggested by the date and place of birth and illuminated further by the client's personal presence and communication. The degree to which the astrologer knows the cultural profile anticipated and the degree to which the client shows congruence or divergence from the anticipated profile will begin the process of assessment productively.

We know that the planets within the horoscope symbolize needs and behavioral faculties to fulfill those needs. Through my earlier works, I have suggested this theory and that the reigning need of the personality is symbolized by the Moon, using the symbolism of the Sun for mode and energy of self-application. Continuing with the planets, I have suggested that Mercury in its sign symbolizes how a person needs to think to be efficient in fulfillment. Venus in its sign suggests the socialization needs required ideally for the person's fulfillment. Mars symbolizes the need to apply a certain kind of energy toward fulfillment. Jupiter suggests a need for a particular kind of reward, keyed by the sign it is in. Saturn indicates the needs at work to absorb the learning process, within the internalization of necessary controls. Uranus symbolizes intensification of self; Neptune, supression of self; and Pluto, an overall perspective.

The aspects between the planets symbolize need pressures, with Mars adding urgency to need fulfillment, Jupiter adding hope, Saturn adding strategic learning, Uranus adding intensification, Neptune adding visualization, and Pluto providing an adverbial function of quantity and direction.

These interplays of need pressure and behavioral potential operate within the circle of Houses, symbolizing the environmental dimensions upon which we are concentrating. A planet *within or ruling* a particular House is called the *significator* of that House. *The significator of any House guides us reliably and quickly into the corresponding area of psychodynamic interaction with environment.*

With the preliminary anticipation of sociological profile provided by the birth date and place, the astrologer seeks congruence or divergence of this anticipation within the client. To this end, it is extremely important for the astrologer to listen for word choice, conversation level, grammar, and revealing idioms during the entire consultation with the client, beginning with the moment of meeting. The astrologer must assess the client's wardrobe to infer economic and aesthetic levels. The astrologer must be alert to every clue of environmental background and level. The client has entered a new environment; the prospect of astrological study stirs up insecurity; insecurity calls into play the person's own reliable means of environmental interaction, conditioned over years of development. Under this pressure, much is revealed to prepare the analytical environment within the horoscope.

If the horoscope shows the significator(s) of the parental axis (X-IV) under aspect tension (square, opposition, strong conjunction, sesquiquadrate, semisquare), the astrologer knows that parental tensions within the developmental period of early homelife will have to be inspected in dialogue with the client. The astrologer will have to assess what the developmental tensions were, what emerged from them as the individual sought support and approval from that environment. Certain Solar Arc, Progression, and/or transit activity during those developmental years would be checked. Conversation would further illuminate the vital environmental backdrop.

If the horoscope shows the significator of the education House (IX) under strong aspect tension, the anticipation of education having been interrupted is extremely reliable. What did this interruption mean to the client? Was college education a premium, or is it now after long years without it? The astrologer must know the significance of a college education at the time and within the societal structure of the client's early growth. The astrologer must learn if the client has done anything about the problems with parents or of missing education, if either of these concerns actually took place and had value within development.

If the horoscope shows the significator of the IInd House of self-worth under aspect tension, the astrologer can anticipate self-worth concerns. From what area of environmental interaction did they emerge? Is there self-worth tension *and* parental tension *and/or* education anxiety? How are they related? Is there a carry-over of any of these tensions to relationships suggested through the significator of the VIIth House?

Later in this book, we will discuss all of these things in greater detail and include careful study of defense mechanisms, but now in this careful discussion of environmental dynamics we must see how an individual lives through his or her reactions to environmental prescriptions. The astrologer starts to follow reliable keys to fill out the status of the anticipated environmental profile. The astrologer knows the dynamics of environmental interaction. The horoscope keys specific areas that have a high potential to show developmental tension within the environmental interaction process. Through the client's discussion of these developmental points, the astrologer learns *of their value to the client.*

We must know that no event has meaning unto itself. *It is an individual's reaction to events in the developmental process that gives them values.* These values determine an individual's degree of environmental reflection, vulnerability to environmental victimization, and success with environmental change. These values determine the level of the horoscope and the manifestation of the Law of Naturalness. They determine why the client has come to the astrologer. They determine the client's level of awareness within the complicated process of living.

As consultation progresses, the astrologer will be able to clarify with the client how much of the client's reigning need has been fulfilled. No jargon is ever necessary; the art of conversation is good enough. —Generally, the Moon in Aries will suggest a need to be ego-important, to be number one (were there conflicts with this need; was the need subdued by environmental press?); the Moon in Taurus will suggest a deep need to keep things secure, to resist change because of the threat to security (has this reinforced environmental reflection?); in Gemini, the need for diversification (has this need diluted pointed self-application?).

In Cancer, the Moon registers the need for emotional security (has this need demanded self-sacrifice for the reward of security?); in Leo, a monarchical need to be king, queen, prince, or princess (has this need helped change environment, or has it been squelched?); in Virgo, the need to be correct and gain respect through accuracy of views (did the mind gain independence, or did it reinforce the formative environment?).

With the Moon in Libra, there is the need to be popular, to be accepted (a special propensity for environmental usurpation of individual awareness); in Scorpio, the Moon symbolizes the reigning need to be understood, to be thought deeply significant (was there withdrawal or successful tenacity to grasp individuation?); in Sagittarius, the need to have one's opinions respected (did this need help to take the person out of environmental stereotype?).

With the Moon in Capricorn, the need is to be strategically effective (what kind of environment accepts this need?); in Aquarius, to be enjoyed for personal idiosynchracy (did fulfillment of this need afford mobility and change?); in Pisces, the need to be appreciated for sensitivity (has this need invited victimization?).

These abbreviated reigning need profiles must be filled out fully by the astrologer, of course. Each one of them suggests a wealth of behavioral anticipation and, as well, questions of ramification as degrees of fulfillment are assessed. They serve to key us to certain undeniable interaction dynamics between the client and his or her environment. How much of the Sun-Moon blend is manifested within the client's self-presentation to the astrologer? Within anticipation, within illumination through conversation, what degree of fulfillment has been achieved by the client? What kind of phraseology does the client respond to knowingly in corroboration? Is it phraseology of academic or philosophical structure; is it diluted to street talk? What terms of what values communicate best to the client and from the client to the astrologer? These awarenesses capture the social facts merged with the individual facts within the human being. In effect, the astrologer works with the client to recreate, to reestablish developmental environments.

Of course, all people are aware of needs of a materialistic nature. Everyone can articulate needs for money, a house, or a job. But not everyone can articulate or even be aware of needs for love or status or even the dimensions of a "good relationship", of the meanings of interaction. These needs might never have registered in manageable form because they may never have been talked about or evidenced in the particular environment that embraced the individual's early development. Perhaps going away from home, a definite learning dimension of the college experience, really never took place in terms of changing environment and enlarging perspective.

In cases where articulation of feelings and nuance is difficult or not practicable, the astrologer will learn to watch facial and body expressions to reveal further articulation of needs, frustration, and fulfillment. *Just as we have seen that the environment can speak where the identity is silent, so the body remembers and stores what the mind forgets or never learns.*

Reaction Patterns

A great deal of experience with holistic analysis in astrology, studying the environment carefully and bringing the horoscope to life through the individual developing within and through societal structure, reveals viable reaction patterns within individual behavior. These reaction patterns must be in the astrologer's ready awareness. They can be keyed easily by astrological measurements, and this will be done gradually throughout this book, but it is vitally important to see the patterns *in life first, before seeing them symbolized in the horoscope.* In this way, we appreciate the message of the environment all the more, and we learn to anticipate the level of every horoscope we study.

Everyone is aware of the normal steps of societal development in the United States: the first five years are spent at home, the next years are in school with adolescent socialization experiences and then college decision; then there is marriage, job, and children; then moves, professional advancement, children's problems, then freedom from the children as they leave the home, then retirement; finally, grandchildren, and the last years spent at home. We do not need to study these thoroughly here; the process is being lived all around us and, in its outline, is obviously familiar. But we do need to study some of the reaction patterns established within these steps of societal development, especially within the formative development period within the family years.

Recall our first example, the woman born in the Southwest in the 1920's. We recognized the societal structure in which she developed. Her individuation energies had to fit into this structure, to be rewarded by it. It was the only reward and support available to her. Her reactions became routinized as she unconsciously maintained the security of sameness as time and development progressed. Her's was a very real and common reaction pattern.

Regional stereotypes within development vary slightly geographically and in terms of decade. Alert perception, reading family magazines, watching television commercials with a marketing eye, absorbing the social settings and drama values shown in movies, studying opinion polls that are broken down by geography, profession, education, income, etc....all these media articulate sociological profile through the years and in many different segments of societal structure. Every astrologer should be conversantly aware of the texture of life shared by all the people he or she could ever serve.

Let us look at typical reaction patterns as they emerge from three kinds of family environment. These patterns are typical, common, though extreme in example here for the sake of clarity. Ingredients of each can sometimes be found in the others.

First, we have the person who says everything was just fine at home, everything was simply ideal. Second, we have the homelife that was simply terrible, with more problems and trauma than would be believed on a theatre stage. Third, we have the description that homelife had its ups and downs, that one parent in particular was a problem some of the time.

Now, the reaction pattern of the first idealized example would be never wanting to leave. There would be a low measure of motivation for self-development. The insulating dimensions would be extremely high; idealization would be reinforced to such a degree that resourcefulness for outside world encounter (within a different variegated environment) could be minimal. At best, this reaction pattern is bland. At normal, this reaction pattern is a lie.

What the reaction pattern is telling us through the client is that emotions were hidden, that the decision making process was never shared with the child, that the values of endeavor, hope, recovery, planning, change, and resourcefulness were never dramatized within the learning and living process. Often within this pattern, there is strong identification between the person and the parent of the same gender. The daughter is brought up by "mummy" just perfectly in order for her to learn to care for her eventual husband the same way that the mother cares for hers. It never dawns on the daughter that her parents have separate bedrooms or are rarely together. The "daddy" was "so busy".

This pattern suggests that there was a stultified peace in the household. Everything fit the Norman Rockwell family scene. It suggests that everyone worked overtime to reflect the perfect environment, similar to the environment of all their friends (environmental sameness prescribed by the status neighborhood, the clique of job-circle friends, income awareness), and that all family members ended up victimized by it, cheated out of real living. As a result, the daughter faces challenge and change with no resourcefulness. —(Gender can easily be reversed in this pattern, to read son for daughter).

Within this pattern—extreme for clarity, but common in essence since it does fit the American ideal touted in the public media—there is a limited spectrum of established values. The parental attention is not balanced, therefore one parent dominates. The daughter or son does not have a real view of societal interaction. The real possibility exists that the mother lived her life through the daughter and perhaps against the father; the real possibility exists that the father related to the son as an ally against the mother. A further possibility is that this imbalance builds up a stereotypical reaction within the daughter or son to people of the opposite gender. The mother's feelings toward the father are extended by the daughter to all men; and vice versa for the son. This is thought to be model preference because of such love and respect felt in the home environment, but it is residually a functional security measure to maintain sameness. What so often happens is that daughter or son marries into similar environments. Why not? The security of sameness is perpetuated.

When this picture or one similar to it is presented to the experienced astrologer, he or she must be aware that the value given to this environmental pattern by the client may be a lie. It is only natural for the client to want to protect the samenesses that were the sum total of early upbringing. Now, out in the world, in an environment with much more texture, the person feels the lacks from his or her earlier environment. The client hears that environment criticised; the client tries hard to cling to what was of value, yet realizes that much was missing. The client sees the astrologer because of stress; some decision or perception demand has touched the nerve of unresourcefulness inherited from the idealized early environment. Under stress, defenses go up; the organism works hard to protect structure and ward off insecurity. To lie about the values of the early home in such a pattern is only natural.

The greatest tact is required in discussing understanding of this situation. Confrontation or exposure is not in order. Rather, gentle conversation must bring about secure objectification of the early environmental structure in relation to the demands of the present environmental concern: "You certainly had many blessings; a very special upbringing; and with so much that was ideal, we certainly can understand that some of the preparation for problems like the ones you're having now was lacking. Shall we talk about this? About the catching up we need to do?"—In holistic astrology, we may modify a dream but never puncture it; the client should do this, or the environment will do it all too efficiently.

The second reaction pattern in these abbreviated generalizations is the opposite extreme. The homelife was simply terrible. As a result, the individual usually develops extremely high motivation to leave the environment, to get off on his or her own to a different environment. The awareness would be felt early, strongly, perhaps with real trauma. This early awareness can become a high motivation force, but it also becomes a great well of sadness since many years must go by before understanding can assimilate all the dimensions of homelife upset and before individual resourcefulness can mature to affect environmental change.

The reaction pattern usually discloses withdrawal. The most natural defense mechanism within human beings is the *mind*. The young person must assimilate trauma. We can expect withdrawal into a dream world as part of the pattern. But here there are choices that will be determined by the strengths and weaknesses of the individual horoscope: Mercury's configuration with Neptune will suggest the availability and rewards of the dream world (we will see later in this book how conveniently this fantasy defense mechanism almost invariably accompanies the occurrence of keen difficulties in life); if Venus is also involved, an idealization perhaps to unattainable dimensions may occur; if Uranus is also involved sharply, an intensification of anxiety and eventually the fight or flight syndrome; with Jupiter, perhaps a spiritual or religious rationalization; with Saturn, perhaps a depression but eventually a mature transcendence; with Mars, perhaps a plan of attack, of running away, of behavioral combat; with Pluto, perhaps supportive identification with sub-groups outside the family.

Private rationalization then becomes extremely sensitive and important in such a reaction pattern to the environment. From ages 10 to 12, a young girl was forced to receive her father into her bed regularly for sexual activity. For two years she suffered the secret and the fears. At age 12, her father suddenly died. Her sensitivities tell her (Mercury in Sagittarius square Neptune and sextile Jupiter) that God had taken the father away because he was bad. In this case, that was that; God took care of things, and the problem was isolated within one person, the father, and not generalized to men in general. This mental explanation gave constructive and *final* value to the trauma; the young girl was very fortunate.

Possibly the mind does not get involved at all. Perhaps the mind becomes numb to the constant pain, the alcoholic ranting, the whippings, the loneliness within neglect. The body may register psychosomatic illnesses during childhood: asthma (Mercury again in another manifestation), eczema (Saturn), bad stomach (Mars and Cancer focus), over-indulgence of sweets leading to complexion and bowel problems (Venus-Jupiter, Pluto; Virgo tensions), etc.

The high tension reaction pattern eventually teaches rugged resourcefulness if the horoscope shows keenly etched individuation potential and if the client has revealed admirable poise in understanding the scene. When this is so, the situations rarely need to be discussed in detail by the astrologer. The client has already done a fine job managing it all. This home environment pattern will not be a base concern within the reason why this person has come to see the astrologer. Recognition of the client's personal triumph suffices to cover that area of the consultation and establish the astrologer's full awareness of that pattern.

On the other hand, this pattern can indeed overwhelm a young person not geared to resourcefulness, and it can leave self-worth and relationship problems in the adult that require much careful work and therapeutic assistance to undo.

The third reaction pattern, an environment with its ups and downs, makes problematic concerns more *specific*. Motivation strength and weakness are mixed. The danger here is that the problems specifically identified are a long time in resolution, if ever. It is not necessarily that the problems are severe, but it is that *they can be lived with* since the balance of "ups and downs" is tolerable, and is actually perceived as normal by the person who learns about similar situations from his or her peer group. This recognition within the environmental structure that such a home situation is "normal" does a great deal to take the sting out of the personally perceived specific problems. In later life, "I've seen worse" or "I've had rougher times" or "I know I've got a lot of attributes" become descriptions of practical and effective poise. Usually, there is a low enthusiasm profile, the blahs and indecision under pressure.

Ordinarily, in this situation, the pattern reveals one parent, usually the father, who is somehow not quite in the picture as the family authority figure. He is dead, absent, passive, or tyrannical and thus avoided. The authority figure of the home does not or can not give enough loving leadership to the young person. The mother has more work to do than is reasonable (and she may create work to avoid other problems), or she may be ill frequently. Affection between the parents or out-and-out arguments are rarely seen. Brothers and sisters come and go.

More often than not, the person is left to his or her own defices. There is judicious withdrawal, and time alone is instinctively made valuabe: daydreaming, reading books about adventure, romance, writing poetry, body building. There is no real pain and loneliness; no real feelings of rejection. It is just dull and routine, until as adults they are aware of unresolved problems that they think stem from the earlier environmental structure.

The horoscope will signify the specific problem areas through which the developmental tensions from the early "normal" environment are taken into the personality. The problems of self-worth in both male and female are most prevalent; probably, neither has learned to receive or give compliments. The sex profile will have to be studied in relation to the ease of function and the reward of function within socialization and in the fulfillment of those "rescue" fantasies set up earlier. For both male and female, some problematic dimension usually undermines the socialization process; there is shyness, not feeling popular—or overbearing reaction formation of arrogance to compensate for the legacy of inferiority feelings. But all of this is "normal" too, since the peer group in the main will be having the same "normal" homelife. For both male and female, this usually undermines socialization success. Intimacy frightens, and love response is uncomfortable. The prospect of marrying someone with similar concerns is extremely high, and such mirror reflection often serves to illuminate harshly the extent of the "normal" problems in each.

These three abbreviated reaction patterns to early environmental structure plus the one reviewed earlier all show the process of reflection of the environment to the point of complacency, acquiescence and victimization, and normalcy. Within the growth pattern, consciously or unconsciously, resources are being accumulated, individuation is being leaned and evaluated, all to affect change through eventual independence (the contrast with the family environment). The young organism *must* absorb it all. Major Arcs, Progressions, and/or transits to important points in the individual horoscope, to the angles especially, will suggest times of important developmental tension, but for the young this development is also *absorbed through the parental structure, through the family environment.*

For example, a major move by the family may upset the peer group support built up by the young person against the difficulties within the home. Another difficulty is encountered since the reward and support of the sub-environment are taken away. A major change in the father's job may alter the family income and social status importantly, introducing new value pressures into the parents' environment and thus into the child's environment. A death of one of the parents can upset the role expectations within the function of the family unit, demanding more of the child's resources in formation and also isolating the values of the remaining parent as prime conditioner of the child's values.

Astrologically, this thought is easily supported: major projection techniques touching the angles of the horoscope during the early developmental years must be pursued through the person's parents, through the environmental structure. The person's Ascendant is the fourth cusp of the parent shown in the Xth House, the tenth cusp of the parent shown in the IVth House. This is reversed in reference to the person's VIIth House. The Xth and IVth Houses are obviously the respective Ascendants of the person's parents. There is much more here that will be covered in later chapters, but the point now is for us to understand that occurrences within time within the family environmental structure will almost invariably occur through the parents. The young person will react and give value to whatever occurs, all in relation to the reaction pattern vital to developmental progress.

The accumulation of values through experience, knowledge of the functions within environmental structure tell the young person who he or she is. The young person must reflect this environmentally patterned picture of selfhood in order to stay alive, to gain support and reward, to keep whatever security is possible. The need to belong is essentially dominant regardless of the conditions. In the process, personal resources are developed and stored. Astrology keys us dramatically to the age of 21—and society reflects this equally as dramatically—when transiting Saturn makes the closing square to its natal position, when transiting Uranus squares its natal position, with transiting Jupiter making the closing square to its natal position, and with transiting Mars opposing its natal position: it is the time for change, for break away, for contrast. Socially, it is the time of precipitous marriages, for rebellion, for frantic job choice; it is the time for mistakes as the person leaves one environment and enters another with different values, expectations, and rules. The accumulated resources are severely tested.

College education can be viewed as the transition between the home environment and the broader social environment introduced at 21. College times usually take a person out of the home, to a different geography; often this displacement is the prime motive for attending college, providing escape and recuperative insulation! When the college benefits are *not* to be had, the transition into the broader environment is difficult. The samenesses of the family environment tend to be preserved for security, and the developmental period of mistakes is initiated earlier, with far longer lasting problems therefrom.

Now, of the patterns discussed above, certain glimpses can be interchanged. The objective is not to memorize a concrete formula but to understand the flow, the currents within environmental development pressure at different societal levels, at different societal times, in different societal locations. There is no negativism here in these pattern descriptions; there is only realism. All of us have lived related patterns. If we do not see the pattern pieces within ourselves, we can not see them in others. Holistic astrology is based upon awareness and feeling. We must inspect the roles of fantasy, of rationalization, of relationship dynamics not only in ourselves but in all others around us, not for value judgement but *for value recognition through the individual.*

In further relation to the example patterns, we can be sure that the majority living in each feel that the personal environmental pattern has some "normalcy" about it. Each person would find parallels of the environmental samenesses from peer group others within the same environment. Youths grow together in cliques, street gangs; debutantes go to cotillions, they "come out" from one environment to go into another; rural youths hunt, join youth clubs like the Y.M.C.A., the Scouts; fraternities and sororities organize sameness of background even further; jobs are gotten through parental friends or college placement services offering stereotyped profiles to employers aware of them. The intermeshing of samenesses within all weaves of environmental fabric is constant. Young people constantly seek out and are put together with people just like them. Older people follow similar need pressures. Belonging is vital for security; in belonging, support and approval are gained; *a sense of personal normalcy enters personal value judgement.*

But it is possible to be normal and miserable at the same time. If happiness (a concept that is particularly American within the world view) and contentment are such prime needs of our life, it is amazing how rarely they are fulfilled. The fulfillment process for happiness and contentment does not receive enough special attention from the individual since the definitions of these states in terms of tangible goals are not clearly defined by our society. We will soon see that concerns for money, status, job, popularity, and many more are higher in the need hierarchy than happiness and contentment. The problem is with the ordering of values in relation to personal resources conditioned by the environment. The manifestation of ulcers, anxiety patterns, diet problems, aggression, compulsiveness, and frustration are much more often fulfilled than happiness and contentment. These unhealthy fulfillments receive most of our creative attention because of the phenomenon of environmental prescriptions!

In his fine book, *The Transparent Self*, Sidney M. Jourard sums up our discussion perfectly: "As a psychotherapist, I have often been called upon to do family counseling, and I have been struck by the incredible lack of artistry and creativity in the participants. Any one of them may be imaginative in ways to make money or ways to decorate the household, but when it comes to altering the design for their relationships, it is as if their imagination was burnt out. Day after day for years, family members go to sleep with their family drama patterned in one way, a way that perhaps satisfies none—too close, too distant, boring, suffocating— and on awakening next morning, they reinvent the same roles, the same relationships, the same plot, the same scenery, the same victims. The way the wife and her husband and her children interact, long after it has ceased to engender delight, zest, and growth, will persist for years unchallenged and unchanged."[2]

The Dilemma of Freedom

The weight of environmental conditioning upon the individual's urge to be free, to feel free is enormous. The dilemma is that the individual seeking freedom actually needs that which makes the quest difficult; he or she actually needs the weighty environmental conditioning in order to learn, formulate, and store the personal resources that are reinforced by environmental reward in order to achieve the sense of personal freedom. As we will see in our study of anxiety in Part II of this book, anxiety can not be avoided. The human being must grow *through* anxiety. So the human being, as a social entity, must gain individual freedom *through* the conformity pressures of the environmental structures.

The human being feels free only if he or she has the capacity to behave in ways that are rewarding, fulfilling to the *inner* environment. The human being must have certain powers, certain resources. Amassing this personal "capacity", these resources, through outer societal approval presumes a great measure of environmental dependency. It is a complex reciprocal interaction.

To affect change eventually, to achieve individuation, demands that the human being not confuse personal identity awareness with the definition of his or her identity provided by the environment. The functional *balance* between the two is what becomes personal freedom; in this balance, in Alan Watts' phrase, the human being becomes "at once universal and unique".[3]

The human being is free to the extent to which he or she can choose personally significant goals or course of behavior, the extent to which he or she can choose among alternatives. We can recall Magda Sorrel's frustrated statement in the Consul's office: "To this we've come, that man be born a stranger upon God's earth, that he be chosen without a chance for choice." The degree to which we can make a choice in life depends upon personal resources to make the choice and the environment's supportive permission to do it. We can yearn for the opportunity to make Presidential decisions and save the world, but our resources to do so are not recognized, we are not President, and society will not allow us to do so. We can dream of being rescued by a knight on a white stallion, but our personal resources to attract the knight are not adequate, and we are forced by environmental prescriptions to adjust our fantasy. Hopes for personal freedom are constantly adjusted by environmental reality.

Since freedom to choose to do something is an extraordinarily complex concept within environmental structure, we usually give another simpler definition to the concept of freedom. We speak of "freedoms from": freedom from want, from parents, from ill health, from segregation, from tension, from stereotype, from expectations, from responsibility, and—indeed—from freedom itself. We long for freedom from whatever keeps us from being able to choose independently; *we long for freedom from the machinations of environmental dependency.*

These longings for freedom can become extremely intense. They can become functionally autonomous from the environmental demand to do our parts in maintaining sameness. They can become behavioral goals in themselves: dreams or fantasies can become so intensely idealized that even partial fulfillment of them is practicaly impossible, and the futile drive to fulfill them further dominates our lives. Such longings for freedom can be seen as avoidance (defense) mechanisms: they keep us from coming to grips with the *real* tensions within our world to balance self-awareness with environmental demand.

The longing for freedom *from* freedom is best understood in the fear of freedom. The sameness of identity, maintained by reflection of the societal structure, fears the change, the insecurity, represented by the freedom to choose. "I can't take that responsibility" or "Don't ask me, no sir" really says "I am not the one who is supposed to do that in my order of things", "What would the Joneses think if I did answer that question the way I'd like to." Diverging even the slightest bit from personal function specified within societal structure alerts the real fear of societal disapproval and insecurity. The black shoeshine man, bent over and victimized in so many ways by his environment, has learned that it is safe only to reply in agreement to any conversational chit-chat, to follow agreement with a chuckle, to speak with no personal investment whatsoever. The businessman at a cocktail party parrots the opinions of his group and, when confronted with a particularly incisive statement, simply repeats the gist of the sentence he just listened to and waits desperately to be taken off the hook, taken out of the pressure to choose an individual stand, to make an individual comment.

We fear freedom because, in getting away from environmental insulation, we fear resurrection of repressed personal anxieties, re-animation of the repressed societal pains absorbed through a life-time of environmental reflection. We fear that all we have put away will now come back; our bodies hurt with the fear as they remember the pains of development. In the face of freedom and our fear of it, we are often lost, speechless, powerless. Our fear of freedom is also fear of the personal unknown, just as a child fears when, being invited out away from the family group by a clown during a circus performance, he or she hides behind mother's dress. How often we feel, "I can't do this alone; I want this freedom of choice, but it frightens me."

This dilemma again suggests the importance of education to strengthen personal resources. Education raises the level of knowl-edge and reinforces the capacity for choice. When it is combined with conspicuous change of environment (as often is the case in going off to college), the experience of knowledge is strongly aug-mented. But education involves much more than formalized peda-gogy: it involves the fundamental base of *learning in any way about other environments*, other points of view. This process starts with reading, gaining awareness of dimensions beyond entertain-ment, for example, when watching television or motion pictures; the process continues by exploring intuition and experiencing feel-ings, by diversifying interests and cultivating hobbies.

Learning about other environments, diversifying interests, and constructing an awareness of as many human and societal values as possible *gives the human being resources*. Having re-sources builds up the capacity to make choices, to feel freedom and mold identity. When we go to any social gathering, we feel in-security until we learn that there will be someone there whom we know. We actually experience physical relief when we know that someone whom we know will be there *to know us*. We will fit it; there will be reflection of the sameness that ordinarily gives us security. When we are at the party, we can listen to the conversa-tion and hear the bland samenesses of the environment that shield us from ourselves; and we can search the air for the spark of ten-sion that signals a display of individual freedom backed up by indi-viduated resources. When the spark flashes, we can have a moment of choice: we can ignore the light and avoid being burned, or we can broaden personal environment by rewarding someone else's bid for freedom, fanning the fire, and coming nearer to the possibility of personal freedom for ourselves.

Ordinarily, a client will not speak immediately of fear. Society, with all its defenses readily available to the momentarily insecure, does not condone the feeling of fear since such a feeling implies that the societal structure does not function well enough: "What are you afraid of, dear? Haven't I been good to you?" The client will usually talk more about *confinement*, and this is something the societal structure understands well. Recognizing confinement implies the desire for freedom. Astrologically, we know that the XIIth House contains symbolic reference to confinement. This is so, not because of any occult, demonic, or hidden force, but simply because the XIIth House represents the institutionalization of society, the cooperation (sixth House dynamic of the public VIIth) of the societal structure with our work to feel freedom within identity. In this light, we must never forget that the XIIth House is adjacent to, leads to, and supports the Ascendant.

Within the process of development, with varying degrees of environmental reflection, environmental victimization, and feelings of confinement through a loss of freedom, human beings can totally give up the struggle of growth, the hope for change. They can adopt the confinement of societal sameness totally. Learning is curtailed; routine dominates choice; fantasies and dreams become so private and remote as to fade from life. Understandably, personal adult hopes can be transferred then to their offspring: "our children will have what we never had", "we want to do as much for our children as we possibly can." The focus upon the children is an easy and common rationalization for being alive, for being normal; it is also an easy and common escape for the parents from their insecurity when focus is placed upon themselves. —So it goes; so it has always gone.

When we acknowledge the copious directory of things from which we want to be free, we must ask at the same time what we would do with the freedom if we had it. To be free *from* something is a negative freedom; to use freedom constructively to create change for continued personal growth is positive freedom. This means that positive freedom works to make new relationships within a new or expanded societal structure, not through escape but through an expanded point of view. Where negative freedom *isolates* the human being, positive freedom relates the human being to the dimensions of continued growth.

"We have a house and it's paid for; in two more years we retire; we're free from debt and our children. We're looking forward to retirement!" *Looking forward to what?*

Another example of negative freedom: "We both have wonderful jobs, a great apartment; we don't want any children; we take two vacations each year; we're free, man!" *What will make it last?*

In the first example, a lifetime was spent to be free *from* environmental debts of many kinds. That was probably the major goal. Retirement will come, and there will be no more negative freedoms to work out. What will ignite the sense of positive freedom to build new growth into life? In the second example, negative freedom is thought to have been conquered very early. But when will the demands of positive freedom speak and challenge personal values into further relationships within an expanded environment? These points are vital in remediation, as we shall see in Part III of this book. Divorce can represent negative freedom; but the change *within* a marriage can represent positive freedom, not escaping problems but solving them; not fleeing anxiety subjectively but confronting anxiety objectively.

The answer to the dilemma of freedom, of negative freedom's dominance over positive freedom, takes one of two directions. First, imagined freedom within the conquering of "freedoms from" *will be surrendered* in order to avoid isolation and anxiety; environmental prescriptions of the old way will rise again. The retiring couple will buy a boat or trailer they really don't need; take on a part-time business by a franchise purchase. Being back in debt and within environmental traffic will feel good. They will feel alive again within the old samenesses. The young couple will overextend themselves in purchases beyond their means, lose the mirage of contentment, or become so bored with each other that the union that conquered "freedom froms" will split. Each person will be refreshed by re-entering the environmental growth pattern once again. —The chances are high that in neither case were the *support and approval* rewards, provided by each other within the shared inner environments, as substantive or important as *the support and approval rewards offered by the external environmental structure.*

A second answer, the healthy answer, suggests that freedom from the tendency to seek "freedom froms" can encourage adventurous new relatedness within an expanded and variegated environmental structure, through an expanded point of view. Courage and vision can be based upon *awareness of triumph*, upon struggle shared, upon a love matured, upon the base of two individuals who continue to make themselves interesting to one another because of the exercise of individuated identities. Their frantic activity over the years to allay the anxiety of confinements during development could also have been consciously planned to increase knowledge and refine sensitivity to interpersonal support and approval rewards for individuated resources.

Hopes for positive freedom begin at birth: the human being, while learning within environmental relationships, differentiates individualized values for the inner environment. These hopes for the freedom of inner environmental expression are related dynamically to the controls specified within outer environmental prescriptions. The balance determines individual points of view, horoscope level, and individual freedom.

Conclusion

In holistic analysis, we must recognize as thoroughly as possible the formative environmental message contained within the dynamics of societal structure. We must contend with all those things that work societally to preserve and augment what we know about our astrological symbolisms. Our use of astrology must fit the realities of the present *and* the past. We must contend with all those things that work within a human being's inner environment to relate the same astrological symbolisms to individual needs and behavior function. We must appreciate how a person needs to think, relate, apply energy, hope for reward, internalize controls for strategy, intensify selfhood, visualize change, and realize perspective. We must clarify needs that may be unknown to the person. *The planets must speak of involved interaction between inner and outer environments.* We must remember the "novelty" of Maslow's incisive observation that human beings become miserable, underachieve, only because of the environment, and that the relative fulfillment of needs determines positive or negative attitude.

Our astrology must be based upon keen awareness of extraordinarily repetitious environmental behavioral patterns and value prescriptions, and then be given personalized relevance through the extraordinarily complex response patterns from each individual's inner environment. By bringing the horoscope to an individual's life, we must allow and guide the human being to tell the tale through experience and fantasy. Together with the client, we must gracefully ascertain levels of environmental reflection and victimization and the accumulated resources for change. We must seek the meaning of freedom within the development of time.

By appreciating with the client his or her manifestation of environmental interaction, by giving meanings of growth to experiences of the past, we can give perspective to the present and knowing welcome to the future. Holistic understanding ties us empathically to the problems of generational growth. We unravel the security anxieties of personal identity within the adjustments demanded by time and change. By understanding—and showing that we do—we relate deeply with the client; we establish a loving rapport; we support the human condition and approve an individual's effort to be free. In this way, we present to an individual a cherished reward. . . through ourselves and through our astrology.

Chapter Two
THE HOROSCOPIC
ENVIRONMENT

We see the horoscopic wheel of Houses as a circular wholeness of life experience. Each day as the world turns completely upon its axis, all the values and potentials of whole life experience are reviewed within the fact of our existence. These Houses exist symbolically at two levels: first, they are zones of activity, philosophically and empirically determined, that reflect *external environmental experience*. Second, they are areas of psychodynamic reactions from a human being's *internal environment*, articulated by the significator planets and their aspect patterns. The significances of the Houses fluctuate between outer and inner environmental references; they change *level* of manifestation throughout life development. In fact, the circle of Houses during the growth of the human being becomes a spiral around an axis of time.

As the human being begins life, the dynamic of focus and initiation is taken on through the angles of the horoscope. The inner environment is immediately (often traumatically) made aware of the outer environment. The soul gains self-aware form within the environment. The process of environmental reflection begins. Immediately, the human being is aware of inspiration, of breathing in, and the demand for expiration, to breathe out, to give back. The exchange of resources commences; the dynamic of take and give is established; the inside becomes aware of the outside; the

39

self becomes aware of others. This confrontation establishes the horizon line linking the identity hemisphere in the East with the identity hemisphere of others in the West. The zones of life experience linking the two, in preparation below the horizon and in exposure above the horizon, jostle into orderly development, anchored to the spine of identity formed by the Zenith and Nadir, the parents within the structure of the home. These zones of life experience and psychodynamic reaction await cognition and differentiation by the emergent individual.

With each day of life, as the world to which we belong revolves, each of the Houses, each of our zones of experience and areas of reaction, gains ascendancy. It is as if we are reminded daily, within the inexorable turning of time, that we are potentially whole, that all is available to us. It is as if our constantly accumulated experience and evaluations pass in review to emphasize our balance of resources and our identity structure within the environment. At any given moment, we can stop the turning within our awareness and concentrate upon a particular experience or a particular reaction syndrome. The holistic view of the horoscope is momentarily frozen, allowing us as astrologers to establish an ascendant focus within any zone of experience or area of psychodynamic reaction. From that new starting point, we can then continue to reach out through the holistic interrelatedness represented by the horoscope.

Using this technique of derivative House analysis, for example, we can see that the IInd House of self-worth (on the psychodynamic level) is the fifth House of the parent symbolized in the Xth. When our world turns to focus upon the parent symbolized by the Midheaven, giving it momentary ascendancy, our self-worth concerns are shown to be involved in terms of the fifth House dynamic, giving love, in relation to the parent as the source. In holistic analysis, this tells us that so much of our self-worth concern is linked, for gain or for loss, to the love given by and absorbed from that parent. Even further, we can learn that the parent's show of affection to us—or to the other parent—enters into our concern of self-worth when we are invited to give love from ourselves to others. The whole process is fundamentally oriented within the fact that our IInd House area squares the area of our Vth House: *self-worth evaluation and giving love to others are necessarily always in developmental tension.* A problem in either dimension may be causally linked to the giving of love by the parent. The network of significators under tension in the horoscope will show this and be supported by client corroboration.

In the same derivative way, when momentary ascendancy is given to the Vth House, we can see that the parent of the IVth House relates to the Vth in a twelfth House dynamic. This teaches us that, within the environmental structure, one parent in particular may confine somehow our giving of love. This confinement might judiciously support our efficiency in Vth House matters until we learn to rely on our own judgement, or this confinement might undermine personal value judgement and confidence totally.

Such evaluation of the dynamics within the horoscopic environment, as it captures external and internal environments, as it captures social facts and individual facts merged within the human being, clarifies the response profile of the human being as he or she gains varying degrees of need fulfillment. Holistic astrology, by definition, is constantly derivative in every way.

The zones of experience and areas of psychodynamic reaction interrelate in this way, each one deriving substance and nuance from all the others as inner and outer environments interact. The human being gives meaning, gives functional operation to these interrelationships through the process of *cognition.* Cognition organizes zones of experience and areas of psychodynamic reaction into conscious behavioral patterns.

Within development, the human being sets up cognitive classes of experience and reaction. This process of cognitive classification really organizes the cusps of the Houses, defines boundaries between zones of experience and reaction. The baby becomes aware of its body in a very early stage of self-worth cognition. Then, the baby learns to make sounds and communicate in early cognition of the IIIrd House. In cognition of the parental axis, the baby holds tightly to everything the parents represent.

Later in development, as the Houses spiral onward around the axis of time, the person's IInd House continues to take on more complicated self-worth considerations, as do the IIIrd House in terms of communication and mental awareness and the IVth in terms of parental support. The spiral of significances continues to change level as cognition classifies ever more sophisticatedly. A very real measure of social growth then is revealed in the amount of meaning, the amount of understanding, established by cognition anywhere within the horoscopic environment.

Cognition ascertains not only a set of experiences and personal psychodynamic reactions but, as well, the interrelatedly derived networks involved in the routined behavior. Within the challenge of life's complexities in balancing self against environment in the quest for support and approval, the cognitive process tries *to abbreviate its terms*, works to organize definitively to avoid the constant harassment of learning, sorting, and storing nuance. *The effort is to pattern reactions reliably so that they may be taken for granted*. The complexity of the environment is reduced to the minimum to reinforce security. This is the beginning of unthinking routinized behavior and stagnated value judgement.

For example, a person receives little love attention from the parent of authority in the home. The person suffers from this and gradually *adapts* to it. A need has not been fulfilled. The cognitive process has recognized this by adjusting behavior and reaction: "I guess I'm not good enough, just as they say" or "I guess I'm not pretty enough to be hugged—I'll just stay out of the way." That's that. The pattern is explained; the aggravation is minimized by resignation; acquiescence becomes routinized. The need for love is never fulfilled in any comforting measure; cognition of this puts the need to sleep self-protectingly while the behavior pattern of acquiescence to the environmental situation endures. In adult life, the persons finds that love can not be accepted when it *is* offered.

Cognition, then, not only classifies environmental awareness, organizes behavioral patterns, and explains causality, but also establishes value judgements. The cognitive process works for order and, as a result, achieves a status quo, a recognizable stereotype. This status quo of identity growth can grind to a halt when enough prescriptions of environmental expectations are met so that functional security is predictable, when the needs to learn more and to differentiate resources more sensitively cease to be motivated by environmental leadership or personal dream.

For example, American blacks had acquiesced to irrationally demeaning environmental prescriptions until the Civil Rights Move- and Martin Luther King, Jr.'s example and dream reorganized black cognitive structures. Jews regularly combat irrational enmities through family environmental emphasis upon the resources of education, mercantile expediency, cultural involvement, and historical pride. Middle Americans, geographically removed from the intensely competitive and variegated values of major urban societies, seek pride in their "bread basket" resources that set a full family table for the nation. Urban Americans, regularly combatting a tremendous number of pressured stimuli within complex environmental traffic, are forced to champion survival resources over the values of love exchange, since so many contact demands and impermanence work against efficacious love exchange.

Within any of these sociological groups (and the many more that can be described), values and resources are clear, but they are identified in terms of group environment. These prescriptions do not guarantee that the individual within them will be fulfilled in terms of his or her *internal* environment. The *individual* needs *personalized* knowledge, example, and dream to meet environmental group prescriptions and, additionally, to continue to grow through them. This is the necessary focus upon the inner environment, the need profile, the personalized resources. —How many human beings avoid working through the anxieties of growth and grind to a halt in the routinized prescriptions of outer societal structure? This is denial of the inner environment to gain the support and approval rewards of the outer environment.

So we must know that the inner environment and the outer environment work for balance. On the one hand, the outer environment prescribes samenesses that work for environmental support and approval rewards. On the other hand, the inner environment prescribes needs that hope for fulfillment. The Houses contain both: the zones of external environmental experience and the areas of internal environmental expression. *Astrologically, each dimension is articulated by the same symbols and patterns and is given definition by the individual's cognitive awareness.*

Within the horoscope, it is very simple to understand then how definitive grouping of the planets within the *eastern* hemisphere somehow protects the midpoint focus of the Ascendant. The balance is upset. The pattern keys cognitive structures that will show this predisposition to identity defense. We can infer that individual cognition is more difficult, more complex, slower perhaps, continuously filtering awareness through self-oriented stipulations. Perhaps too much material is hoarded, taxing cognition to fatigue.

A definitive grouping of the planets within the *western* hemisphere suggests just the opposite: the balance is upset to orientation around the focus at the Descendant, the externals registered within relationships. We can infer that some of the self is sacrificed in the urge to reflect others, to build cognitive structures through others. —These two opposite orientations are captured beautifully in the symbolisms of Aries and Libra: the ego force pioneering for itself, and the ego force found through societal reflection.

We can understand how a definitive planetary grouping below the horizon, focused upon the midpoint of the Nadir, suggests a delayed process of cognition, clinging to the values of early life preparation before exposure is dared through relationships above the horizon. Definitively above the horizon, we can sense the potential of societal victimization, since the cognitive structures may have lost supportive anchor within the early foundations below the horizon. —These two opposite orientations are captured in the symbolisms of Cancer and Capricorn: the ego force preoccupied with security, and the ego force expressed through self-application.

Holistically, naturally, each of these definitive patterns spills over into others; the hemispheres of orientation are interrelated by the aspect patterns among significators. The same process of spilling over occurs within differentiation of the cognitive structures, within the individual determination of personal resources grounded within House reference. For example, the identity focus set up at the Ascendant spills over into the IInd House of self-worth concerns, which in turn spills over into awareness of opinions, siblings, neighborhood, thought processes. The three areas of cognition have cuspal boundaries to be sure, but these boundaries have different degrees of *permeability* keyed by the modality (Cardinal, Fixed, Mutable) of their significators within behavioral reaction patterns (aspect patterns).

We can go further with this example and see the core self-worth concerns spilling over into the Ascendant, affecting identity awareness, and into the IIIrd, conditioning communication and thought. The cusps are boundaries for cognitive reference *but not for functional isolation*. This thought parallels the fact that psychological "compartments" within us are not rigid. A reaction stimulated within a particular compartment of awareness spills over into compartments that are "nearby", i.e., related, and to a diminishing extent into compartments that are "farther away".

The "spilling over" is accomplished by significator aspect networks.

For example, losing your job (Xth House) primarily affects the goals set for yourself and the endorsement hoped for from others (XIth House, income from the job, the love-and-accolade-given fifth of the VIIth), and your awareness of the public society's prescriptions for you to have that certain type of job (IXth House, the third of the VIIth). But the cognitive pattern may go much further through the psychological patterns reflected in significator aspect networks within the horoscope: your self-worth may be crippled (the XIth is square to the IInd) if appropriate significators are stressed in natal predisposition or event orientation (inner or outer environment); your marriage may be affected (the Xth is square to the VIIth, and the VIIth is the tenth of the Xth); you may face parental admonishment or guilt within parentally conditioned prescriptions (the Xth is opposite the IVth); your feeling unloved (the XIth House, in second House self-worth relationship to the job in the Xth) may make it difficult to feel free with love giving (since the XIth is opposite the Vth), and this concern can determine the identity completely because the worth given to job position necessarily supports our identity focus (the XIth is sextile to the Ascendant).

Going even further: cooperative support and approval from the job society (sixth dynamic of the Xth, which is the IIIrd) are withdrawn, and this can force you into reassessment of the thinking cognitive structure (IIIrd); your cooperation with others is momentarily upset (VIth; square the IIIrd) because you can not easily communicate in job terms with society's institutionalized prescriptions (the XIIth, opposite the VIth, is the third of the Xth and squares the IIIrd). The goals set up from the job base (eleventh of the Xth, which is the VIIIth) have to be cognitively reassessed, and this may, in the process, affect the self-worth concerns of your spouse (the VIIIth is the second of the VIIth). —The whole world turns around. Many concerns gain ascendancy. The network of concerns spills out pervasively from the core center of the particular cognitive concern and is routed throughout the entire identity by significator aspect patterns and the level of individual awareness. All the Houses have been touched. This is holistic awareness in analysis, for ourselves and our clients.

In the case of fixation, of obsession, the spill-over does *not* occur. The boundaries around a cognitive concern holding a psychodynamic reaction pattern may have low permeability, may be fixed toward the extreme upon repetitive patterns. In this situation, the human being's world *stops* turning. Fixation isolates the problem and deprives the identity of the mitigating resourcefulness stored in other cognitive structures and psychodynamic behavioral reactions. The isolation upon job failure, for example, may be fixated in consciousness to the extent that ordinarily secure self-worth awareness or money in the bank or a marvelously supportive marriage can not be employed to mitigate need frustration and establish new perspective.

Normally, human beings amass enough security and balance within societal structures to absorb transient frustration and upset without experiencing crucial disequilibrium, but there may be certain sensitive areas in which frustration and upset are intolerable and awareness of them, defense of them become fixated in personality expression and behavior. Folk advice seeks to open up the boundaries of such isolating fixation: it says, "Get off it, move on; count your blessings!"

All of this shows us the complexity of the inner environment as it meets the prescriptions of the outer environment. The human being swims within the prescriptions to maintain samenesses, reflect societal specifications and suffer victimization in order to gain support and approval. All the while, the human being tries to fulfill personal needs to a measure that will allow change and further development to freedom. The human being stores resources (behavioral capacities) within various differentiated cognitive structures. Activation of the particular resources immediately triggers holistic arousal. This process is the process of living in life and growing in individuation. It is the process that lives within the horoscope.

Exchanging Resources with Others

Who we are at any level of development works to maintain balance with who others are at their levels of development within the societal structure that all share. Living and interacting together demands the exchange of resources between and among human beings. Everyone within the same societal structure has the same basic needs personalized by individuated cognitive process and must cooperate for fulfillment of these needs and for keeping peace within the structure.

Earlier on pages 10 and 11, we appreciated the orientation of the Grand Crosses of Houses within the horoscope. This orientation is elaborated throughout this book. We refer to it again now to understand the accumulation of personal resources and the exchange of these resources with others with the very same concerns. The following behavioral patterns comprise real life situations lived in varying degrees by us all, astrologers and their clients. We must know these possible patterns, feel them, in order to enrich astrological symbolisms and bring horoscopic patterns to life.

Basically, our resources are accumulated through experience and are differentiated through routinized behavior patterns in three classifications related to the Grand Crosses. Each of the three classifications functions within the cognitive structures at *two* levels to reflect outer environment prescriptions and inner environment needs. The Angular resources, referring to the Ist, IVth, VIIth, and Xth Houses, classify Status (outer) and Identity (inner). The Succedent resources (IInd, Vth, VIIIth, and XIth Houses) classify Money (outer) and Love (inner). The Cadent resources (IIIrd, VIth, IXth, and XIIth) classify Information (outer) and Perspective (inner). Immediately, we can anticipate the spill over among these resource classifications: status/identity spills over to relate to money/love, and money/love spills over to relate to information/perspective. In turn, information/perspective spills over to relate to status/identity. Constantly, the world turns; constantly, we move over the lines established by our cognitive structures; constantly, established behavior patterns interrelate *all* our resources.

For example, a child will expect certain services to be performed in its behalf long after the child is able to perform these services independently for itself, because the child equates these services with love. In astrology, "services" is within the cooperation dynamic assigned to the VIth House which is part of the information/perspective Grand Cross. The VIth House is the second House of the Vth, the fifth of the IInd; the VIth House relates to the XIth (love received, hoped for, expected, assumed) in a cooperative sixth House dynamic. The "services" performed in cooperation with others are always closely tied to our classification of love resource exchange.

We rationalize that others will feel better about themselves by cooperating with us, by serving us, by acknowledging our needs for love: the VIth House is in supportive sextile to the VIIIth, others' self-worth resources, and this VIIIth is opposite our IInd. At the same time, it is rare that an expression of love does not include a conferrence of status in external reference, which reinforces identity in internal reference (the IInd House relationship with the Ascendant; the XIth House sextile to the Ascendant; the XIth and Vth in second House dynamic to the Xth and IVth respectively; the XIth and Vth in trine and sextile relationship to the VIIth). Imagine how problems in any one area can spill over to so many more!

By sharing information, human beings establish personal status. Sharing privileged information invites someone else to more privileged status. In exchange payment, we expect to receive appreciation, love, respect, more status, greater intimacy. Sharing a secret invites intimacy specifically and increases personal status through specialized relationship... "We're in the know". The Cadent resources of information/perspective lead to the Angular resources of status/identity. By learning of any kind, we gain resources to shift levels, to focus and initiate new levels of experience.

Sidney M. Jourard in his *The Transparent Self* makes the observation that every person is an "animated questionnaire".[4] He sees that all human beings embody a whole batch of questions that they address to everyone with whom they come into contact. We can see this process within our discussion of resource accumulation and exchange with others. Through communication and observation of behavior, we mentally tick off answers to our batch of questions on two levels: first, how many resource samenesses can we ascertain to relate the other person to our environmental structure; second, what specific, personally differentiated resources can we ascertain in the other person that will make exchange profitable in helping us fulfill *our* personalized needs?

We know that each of the Houses (resource areas) below the horizon relates in opposition to the same resource areas of someone else in relationship with us within societal structure, i.e., the same House dynamics issuing from the VIIth as the others' Ascendant. In relationship, our identity focus at the Ascendant is in full awareness of (opposition) the identity focus of any other person, and, indeed, the public at large. This awareness is a challenge of status/identity. The resource core within the Angular

Cross involves all the four angles, since the Ascendant is in developmental tension with the Zenith-Nadir axis, and the developmental tension is exactly the same for the other person established by the derivative Ascendant in our VIIth. When two people marry, the parents of one become the in-laws of the other.

Everything each person has internalized and chosen to reflect from the formative relationship within early environment is focused within identity awareness. The individual status/identity level of one person meets the individual status/identity level of another. Two "questionnaires" meet. The process of answering the "questions" determines social interaction. *The awareness sets up the necessity for comparison and the potential for exchange.*

The comparison process is instinctive and vital: we must ascertain where the other is "coming from". We must know the other's background samenesses or divergencies. We must see how similar the other is to us in terms of potentially gaining support through exchange. We must see how the distance between us may be closed or should be opened. Behavior patterns explore the security positions possible within new challenging awareness. These deductions are often made instantly initially and then are laboriously worked out in minute detail of resource comparison and exchange.

For security, we work much more often than not to meet people who have something we need and, as well, enough samenesses shared with us to make exchange possible. We gather in environmental groups and institutions that offer a secure sameness of environmental structure. Individual resource strengths and deficits then are normally not extremely disparate. For example, Betty knows a lot about astrology. I met her at a convention and realize I need her information to help me with my status as an astrologer and my identity as a growing individual. My sensitivities tell me that Betty needs to be accepted for her individual ways. What she can give to me in terms of information is worth enough to me so that I will accept her into my personal sphere or my group; I will be kind to her in return. The margins of what both have to give meet on a middle ground of what both need, tolerated by the environmental structure both share.

This is the normal process. The process of exchange is evaluated by each person within a relationship in terms of each person's need. One person with self-worth needs that are particularly pressing (low self-worth resources) and possibly high information resources will exchange the latter for fulfillment of the former.

But if two people meet and *both* are low in the *same* broad resource classification, they must exchange other resources and often suffer a lack of fulfillment in the particular resource area in which they are both weak. For example, two people both low in information resources may have nothing to talk about, but both may be terribly lonely and find that they fulfill each other in terms of sharing security through samenesses of environmental reflection (a kind of love), in terms of reinforcing each other's status within similarly problematical structures. Friends and lovers build relationship upon mutual self-disclosure and always proceed first with happy recognition of samenesses.

As such a relationship evolves, there can be subtle spill-over into the weak areas from the strengths shared in other areas, and some adjustment is possible between the same weak areas shared in the relationship. However, more commonly, interpersonal exchange evaluations become extremely "touchy" in the area of common weakness: a beauty queen with deep self-worth concerns may give her beauty status in exchange for a rich man's financial security. The rich man gains the social status of "beauty queen wife". If the rich man has deep self-worth concerns as well, the values of exchange in the relationship may only temporarily alleviate the shared insecurites. Such a marriage (relationship) may ignor fundamental need concerns for the reward of peripheral fulfillment.

A rich man will seek social status by donating money to the social environment that may be extremely important to him, because of a low resource level in the classification of identity or love. A man will give up money for love-services to a prostitute; the prostitute will give up love-services for money or information. We shall see that the most common exchanges may overlook primary fundamental needs and substitute one resource for another.

Researchers in social psychology find that love is the most valued and fundamental resource exchange classification within normal societal interaction. We astrologers know that love begins with the IInd House concerns oriented around self-worth. We know the Biblical injunction to "love thy neighbor as thyself" (IIIrd House, Ist House; IInd House midpoint), suggesting that self-love is *not* a consideration that diverges from societal prescription. However, on the individual level of interaction, we can observe that having a good opinion of one's self is very often frowned upon by others. This suggests that, on the level of the inner environment, many individuals can not accept easily someone else's high self-evaluation *because they themselves do not have such a secure self-worth image.* The acknowledgement of another's self-worth is too glaring a comparison within the awareness of relationship (opposition). Conversely, the research of Fromm, Horney, Rogers, Adler, Crandall and Bellugi, Omwake, and Stock all report a positive relationship between self-acceptance and acceptance of others. Astrologically, the vital IInd House concern of self-worth faces in opposition awareness the VIIIth, the second House of the VIIth, others' self-worth concerns. This axis is anchored within horoscopic awareness by the Fixed signs naturally assigned to the Succedent Grand Cross. We can see that the interchange of self-worth dimensions and love occupy the core of the entire horoscopic wheel and the torque center of how the world turns.

As relationships meld, we say there is an increase of intimacy. Intimacy presupposes mutual personal self-disclosure. The inner environments of two human beings relate in increasing degrees of intimacy. Needs are fulfilled in varying measures by exchanges. Resources spill over into holistic interaction. Appreciation, understanding, and love bloom. Self-worth and self-esteem are shared and reflected. Within the merging of inner environments, samenesses are reinforced, victimization is diminished, individual strengths are reinforced to make further growth and change possible. The individual gains an ally, and the person majority is confirmed.

Seeking relationships with others very similar to us, creating intimacy, protects us from being alone. Someone personally acknowledging homosexual tendencies or extreme political leanings or intense religious awareness or special nutritional regimen as vital to his or her identity (anything highly individuated within the personal cognitive structure, reinforced by clear behavioral patterns) must seek out others with those particular samenesses in order to get meaningful exchange going. Not finding others with those samenesses introduces the constant accumulation of frustration. Regular frustration promotes further behavioral patterns that anticipate failure, that promote chronic feelings of low self-worth to the point that exchanges toward intimacy are impossible. Aloneness is perpetuated. Status can not be accepted if offered; love can not be accepted if offered; information can not be appreciated if given.

We can observe in life and in so many consultations that many people with self-worth anxieties feel uncomfortable in giving a compliment. They feel that they themselves are diminished by doing so. Often these same people can not accept a compliment either; they feel that it is insincere, that they do not deserve it. Yet psychological researchers have found time and time again that love given in exchange does *not* deplete the resources of love within the giver. Quite the contrary: giving love increases the love resources within the giver. This is because people love giving love, when they have the self-worth security to do so, knowing that love exchange is such a vital exchange resource within our societal structure and that the love given will be returned. So, acknowledging the exchange, the compliment, is extremely difficult for those with low self-worth awareness; yet learning to make such simple acknowledgement gradually restores self-worth resources and brings the person back into the mainstream of social interaction.

Acknowledging the offer of status/identity, money/love, information/perspective is a fundamental first step, then, in the vital resource exchange process of social interaction. That acknowledgement must include the awareness that recognition and resources are being offered by others *because the self has something else the other needs*. Personal resources somewhere within one's identity may not be seen by someone else as depleted as one may imagine about oneself. —These outlined concerns are at the core of every person's development. They work toward fulfillment, and they articulate the continuous thrust of anxiety.

Problem Patterns

When significators within horoscope patterns suggest that any of the Grand Crosses of the Houses are *under stress* (the developmental tension essential to growth), we can *anticipate* certain behavior patterns that work to defend the lack of resource security or to trade off other more developed resources within exchanges. Holistic analysis must be aware of the problem areas and the behavioral networks that issue from them; this awareness gives enormous substance and texture to the guide symbolisms used within astrological measurements. *We can visualize the client's life drama.*

Holistic analysis must remember the fact that problems from one Grand Cross area (status/identity, money/love, or infomation/ perspective) will easily spill over into other areas and *eventually settle within self-worth concerns linked to the Succedent Grand Cross of money/love.* Rarely will a person in our society express a "bottom line" reward freedom in terms other than those of money or love fulfillment.

Status/identity problems (significators of Angular Cross areas under developmental tension) can be caused within development by environmental difficulties in relation to personal needs at many different levels: a homelife with very little environmental status and/or without rewarding relationship with the father figure; denial of education resources to fortify the learning that fortifies environmental change; disparity between job status in terms of environmental evaluation and personal inner evaluation; a marriage relationship that does little to develop status/identity in terms of broadening environmental exposure and allowing change. All of these concerns (and many more) focus upon the reality perceived by awareness of the outer environmental structure and that reality assessed in relation to inner environmental needs.

With status/identity problems, relationship balances are upset; reciprocity is ignored. With such problems spurring on development, a person has two major choices for action: assertion or withdrawal. With assertion, there is aggression to found one's own status/identity; with withdrawal, there is denial of status/ identity to others and/or to the self.

In self-assertion, we can see aggressive social position and pretense. Inner insecurity triggers a reaction formation, a defense measure that displaces a focus of anxiety with the *opposite* complex characterized by extravagance, showiness, or compulsiveness. Astrologically, a powerfully reinforced reaction pattern overworks within the horoscope to make up for the resource lack elsewhere. A T-Square is typically such a reserve of energy ready to be expressed in a defensive reaction formation.

In such aggressive self-assertion, persons may be extremely alert to titles of bureaucratic function and surround themselves with the accouterments of status and authority, self-advertize more than the prescriptions of the particular environment will allow, seek status by affiliation with others who have established status, constantly recall moments of the past when status was acknowledged, defend everything they represent to the death, hypercritically putting down status positions of others. These persons may equate formality with status and flatter those with clearly established status (hoping for the same status recognition in return) or, for private fulfillment of the status "game" being played, exploit formality insincerely.

In withdrawal, there is denial of status/identity to others. Actually, the withdrawal is created in the sense of not wanting to relate the self to others since they do not "deserve" that relationship. Making oneself inaccessible is thought to increase personal status, but in actuality it impoverishes personal growth potential because it curtails the opportunities for resource exchanges which are vital to maintaining and improving status. There is a tremendous self-awareness, ego emphasis, that in itself isolates the person from the mainstream. The person will not give status directly to anyone. In order to keep a superficial peace, the person will substitute credit acknowledgement in resources other than the one of self-focus: one author will say to another, "I have your latest book; the dust jacket is really extremely beautiful. Who was the artist?"

People with status/identity problems will alternatively exploit *both* aggression and withdrawal, assertion and denial, in varying measures. They will aggressively find others who will support their own status/identity over-compensations and band them around self-prescribed standards. A sub-environment clique is established. The clique will then withdraw itself from the main group. A status focus is established precariously; real individual identity is clouded.

Within the middle ground of reactions within status/identity concerns, the person may lean toward aggression through full resource display, hoping for status conformation through acceptance of all or part of what is offered. Here aggression becomes promotion of real substance, graced with altruism. In effect, the pattern says, "Here I am, offering all I have to you; please accept me." Information/perspective resources are being offered earnestly in an exchange for appreciation (love) and eventual confirmation of status. The exchange plan has a broad spill-over. Horoscope strengths will spill naturally into the assertive display, but the normal balance of interaction dynamics experienced by others can be upset as well. The sheer exercise of so much can be *too* much. There is a flood. The uniqueness of the person with status/identity concerns gains acknowledgement but tends to lose intimacy. The uniqueness departs too far from sameness. In the opposition awareness within this relationship to others, self-comparison by others with the person triggers *their* timidity and insecurity reactions; assertion even without aggression can create distance, and the problem is not solved. Our language tells eloquently this acknowledgement of uniqueness that, at the same time, is out of reach for exchange: "*Too* much, man; far out!"

Another middle ground of reactions leans toward withdrawal. The mode actually is acquiescence, acceptance. The person offers little for resource exchange because of status/identity anxiety; the person asks for little, for the same reason. Enthusiasm seems muted; direct eye contact is avoided; personal opinion is rarely offered. This person opts to hold the status quo, whatever it is. Routine promotions and raises suffice professionally; bringing up children is good enough. The routine insulates and gives birth to the rationale, "Not many others have it any better." Here is the comfort of sameness.

Although status/identity concerns are always present within any generation, they seem particularly critical in different ways in relation to those born before or after 1940. In his book *The Identity Society*, William Glasser refers to the generation born before 1940 as the "survival society" and to those born after 1940 as the "identity society".[5] The former was goal oriented; the latter is role oriented. We can appreciate in our discussion how *goal orientation* relates a person to the prescriptions of the external environment and how *role orientation* relates a person to the needs of the inner environment. That Glasser convincingly makes the break between generations at 1940 reinforces astrological awareness of Pluto leaving twenty-five years of transit within Cancer and securely entering Leo in 1940. Generational perspective shifted from the goal of putting a meal on the table, having a secure job, and protecting family security to understanding the meaning of individual role playing within the drama of life, of exploiting society to support the individual's right to freedom.

Parents from the survival society today see their children within the identity society and experience a confusion in their own identity. They feel out of place since their shift into new societal value prescriptions tends to demean the status they had worked for for so long. They have given their children as much security as possible, often much more than they themselves ever had. The children assume the security they have enjoyed and now exploit personal freedoms. They do not easily understand that the security they enjoy is due to their parents' work and goal fulfillment within the home environment, that it is temporary, and that the outer, broader environment still maintains the same rigorous prescriptions met by their parents. The role oriented society expects the secure family environment to continue through institutional support and recognition of them as individuals. There is eventually environmental shock and status/identity crisis.

When we ask a person from the survival generation, "Who are you?", the answer will be "I am a builder, a lawyer, a doctor, a housewife, a farmer, a mechanic"; the answer is in terms of goal function. A person from the identity generation will answer, "I am a Leo; I'm a person; I'm Trudy Smith"; the answer is in terms of individuated awareness. Both answers are biased or incomplete: the survival response tends to acknowledge only the outer environment, and the identity answer tends to acknowledge only the inner environment. *The imbalance does not allow fulfillment to relate to survival or responsibility to relate to identity.*

During the survival society's absorption of Pluto's transit through Cancer from 1914 to 1940, the outer planets constantly made demanding aspects among themselves to signal vital developmental tension within the entire period. The period began with Saturn and Pluto in conjunction in Cancer late in 1914 and late in 1915: societal prescriptions and personal perspective buckled for resolution.[6]

Wherever within the horoscope circle of Houses this conjunction occurred, the person had to work hard to accumulate, maintain, and defend personal resources within the societal struggle for survival. If either planet by rulership or the conjunction by House tenancy keyed an angle, status/identity concerns would probably be vividly important within growth, especially when transiting Saturn made quadrature aspects to its natal position at ages seven, fourteen, twenty-one, twenty-eight, thirty-five, etc., and/or when Uranus squared the natal conjunction in mid-1927 and all through 1928 and 1929. These would be times of intense awareness of forced environmental compliance and the inner drive to change.

In mid-1917 through mid-1918, the birth configuration would be Saturn conjunct Neptune, suggesting two worlds existing simultaneously: the outer environmental prescriptions and the internal visualization potential for change, or rationalization of the status quo. In development, through this disposition, if signifying angular reference by rulership or tenancy, status/identity concerns would be clearly suggested and focused strongly during transiting Saturn's quadrature aspects to the natal conjunction, and/or when transiting Uranus squared the conjunction in the latter half of 1935, all through 1936, and into 1937. These would be times of intense awareness of environmental circumstance and the inner hope for change.

In mid-1920, the opposition of Saturn and Uranus would be a powerful accentuation of generational change potential, the old giving way to the new, the struggle between two poles. If angles of the horoscope were significated, the status/identity concern would be clear within our understanding of generational concerns within the decades of development, within the geographic and environmental structures. Transiting Saturn's quadrature aspects would accentuate these concerns regularly, and the conjunction of Neptune with the natal Saturn pole in late 1929 and all through 1930 and 1931 would work toward rationalization, toward compliance with survival society prescriptions. Of course, this developmental transit would occur in the horoscope at age 10 or 11 and be absorbed primarily through the parental position within the times of 1930 and 1931.

All through 1922, Saturn squared Pluto, and those born then internalized a revolutionary spirit: the press to internalize environmental prescriptions was in keen developmental tension with personal perspective; something would have to be done eventually. This potential for revolutionary change would be reinforced early in life, during very hard times, when transiting Uranus opposed natal Saturn and squared natal Pluto in 1928 and 1929. The potential could have retreated when transiting Neptune conjoined natal Saturn and squared natal Pluto throughout 1944, 1945, 1946, and 1947, with much of the energies having been discharged in the War effort. The potential finally could have responded again late in 1951 and 1952 when Uranus conjoined natal Pluto and squared natal Saturn, exciting individuation potential within a new generation, or in 1974 and 1975 when transiting Pluto conjoined natal Saturn and squared its own natal position.

In late 1925 and almost all of 1926, the key outer planet configuration was Saturn square Neptune. Again this corresponds to the essence of rationalization of compliance with stringent environmental prescriptions. Ambition would easily lie dormant. Times were hard then. The external environment pressed through the parents upon the child. Saturn's quadrature transit aspects would focus this awareness regularly, and Uranus would square Neptune and oppose Saturn within this natal configuration in 1939 and 1940, alerting during adolescence the capacity for eventual individuation, for breakaway someday. Perhaps this breakaway would be realized in 1979 at ages 53 and 54 when transiting Uranus would make another square to natal Neptune while conjoining natal Saturn, the new finally taking over the old.

In 1930 and 1931, Saturn was square Uranus, a lifelong development struggle to reconcile the new with the old, perhaps the key signification of the generational change challenge. Significating the angles would clearly suggest status/identity concerns within the grasp of change from tradition to avant garde. This struggle would have been reinforced for some eight years from 1943 through 1951 by Neptune's transit opposed natal Uranus and square natal Saturn. These adolescent years would normally see vacillation in courage, start and stop in the desire to adopt new generational values. Perhaps the process of new status/identity resolution was finally realized from 1950 through 1953 with transiting Uranus squaring natal Uranus and opposing natal Saturn, or similarly from 1969 through 1971 when transiting Uranus opposed its natal position and squared natal Saturn, or finally when transiting Pluto joined the struggle 1971 through 1979. —This particular generational signature founded in 1930-31 seems prototypical of the survival generation, recovering from the Depression, equidistant between two World Wars, reaching adolescence just after World War II, growing into greater educational opportunities and amplified societal securities.

The people born throughout 1932, 1933, and 1934 have Uranus square Pluto. There is typically manifested throughout development a premature awareness of personal potential for individuated perspective. They absorbed post-War benefits supplied by a more secured environment. They responded in a bid for personal freedom within new generational values, reinforced in late 1945 and into 1946 by Saturn's transit square to natal Uranus and conjunct natal Pluto. This effort to achieve new status/identity fulfillment was then subdued in 1968 and early 1969 when Saturn in transit conjoined natal Uranus and squared natal Pluto, but it is then pushed into fulfillment by Pluto's transit of the last half of Libra, opposed natal Uranus and square to its own natal position 1977 through 1983.

From the middle of 1935 into the spring of 1937, a key birth signature was Saturn opposed Neptune. This axis will occur somewhere within any one of six pairs of House axes, keying by House tenancy and rulership certain resource areas under developmental concern. When the angles are significated, the status/identity concerns will be linked to the fact that this group of people was born at the time of transition from the survival society to the identity society. The material structure, ambition, and the process of internalizing environmental prescriptions may face confusion. Ordinarily, these people can see the new societal values vividly. They have part of them in one frame of reference and part of them in another. The practical leads one way, the imaginative leads another. Status and identity may be challenged across generational lines. Behavior codes undergo regular adjustment. Decisions for one security or the other were probably urged into cognition in late 1965 or early 1966 when transiting Uranus conjoined Neptune and opposed Saturn. Frustration with whatever decision was made or a new, further decision can be focused by the transit of Neptune square to the natal axis in 1978-1980, with the Saturn opposition to its natal place occurring simultaneously conjunct natal Neptune.

The entrance of Pluto into Leo in 1940 grounds the identity society. In retrospect, we see that societal perspective accelerates: Pluto spent thirty-one years in Taurus, from February 1853 to spring 1884, relating survival to Reconstruction and the building of American life; Pluto spent thirty years in Gemini, from spring 1884 to spring 1914, relating survival to resourcefulness, dexterity, and invention; Pluto spent twenty-five years in Cancer, from spring 1914 to late 1939, relating survival to a full stomach and home security. Pluto will spend only eighteen years in Leo, fifteen years in Virgo, twelve years in Libra, and eleven years in Scorpio, entering Sagittarius at the end of 1995. Change accumulates and accelerates. New values cover old values more swiftly. Life development races forward around the globe and through the heavens. Status/identity concerns continue.

Greater responsibilities for growth and development focus upon the human beings born during three successively accelerated times. Those born in mid-1940 have Saturn square Pluto, with Jupiter and Mars involved as well if birth occurred in the summer. This powerful configuration promises accelerated, expansive revolution. The ego is highly focused, undergoing tremendous pressure in 1956-58, in young adulthood, when transiting Neptune opposed natal Saturn and squared natal Pluto and when transiting Uranus squared natal Saturn and squared natal Pluto. This was the dawn of the revolution manifested in the 1960's, with vision clouded by drugs and individuation obscured in new environmental prescriptions for samenesses. The environmental shock within status/identity concerns occurred with the individual Saturn returns experienced in 1969 and 1970 and later; the individually timed reminders that grander environmental prescriptions prevail.

Those people born from the middle of 1951 through the middle of 1955 have Neptune in Libra square Uranus in Cancer; spirituality (or self-deception) leads development of identity security. Pluto entered Virgo in mid-1957, focusing identity within environmental awareness, nutritional correctness, principles of cooperation and spiritual dogma. Transiting Pluto signals role illumination for these identities most strongly in the period 1977 through 1983 as it conjoins natal Neptune. All dreams and illusions will necessarily be thoroughly tested, studied, and valuated in terms of environmental reality. Deep personal transformation in one role or another will be clarified.

This study of status/identity problems has been tied to the angles of the horoscope, keyed by significators of these angles under developmental tension. The core focus of the resources of status/identity naturally spills over to engage all other resources holistically. Necessarily, concerns of status/identity will include behavior patterns of the other cognitive structures involving the broad classifications of money/love and information/perspective.

We can see this spill over in behavior patterns within the external environment and in measurement patterns within the horoscopic environment. Holistic analysis can explore myriad relationships for significance: *a structural cognition pervades life to explain behavioral interrelationships; a structural wisdom pervades the horoscope to reflect reality.* For example, in astrology we have the quincunx aspect of one hundred fifty degrees. We give to the quincunx the sense of *adjustment.* With reference to status/identity concerns within the holistic network of behavior patterns that support cognition of resources, we can see the Ascendant related by quincunx to the VIth and VIIIth Houses: the status of identity must constantly adjust itself to the realities of others' self worth concepts (VIIIth House, second of the VIIth) and to the dynamic of our cooperation with others (VIth House) within resource exchange. The middle ground is the VIIth, opposite the Ascendant: full awareness of relationship.

The IVth House is quincunx to the IXth and to the XIth: the status of our origin, the anchor of our homelife, adjusts itself through education (IXth House; what others have to say, the third of the VIIth) and the value of our job in life (XIth, the second of the Xth) in order to receive public accolade (the XIth is the fifth of the VIIth) and a place in the sun (the Xth House midpoint).

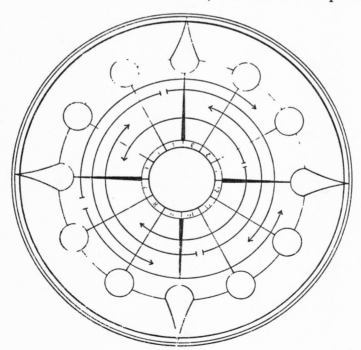

The VIIth House is quincunx to the IInd and to the XIIth: the status of relationships, wherein we see personal identity reflected, constantly must adjust in terms of personal self-worth valuation (IInd House) and the cooperation of society with our efforts (XIIth House, the sixth of the VIIth). The midpoint of this process clearly focuses reinforcement upon the Ascendant.

The Xth House is quincunx to the IIIrd and to the Vth: the status of our job, of our "place in life", adjusts always in terms of our thought processes and communication of them (IIIrd) and our creative self-presentation (Vth, including having children). In the process, we are aware of the anchor to our origin (IVth House midpoint), its support of our life efforts and our contrast to it as individuals.

So, in isolating, particular concerns and generalizing behavior patterns for clarity, we must not exclude the concerns and generalized patterns of other resource areas and we must not overlook their holistic interrelationships. *The horoscopic patterns of aspect networks, the significator keys, will call analytical attention to particular zones of experience and areas of behavioral resources.*

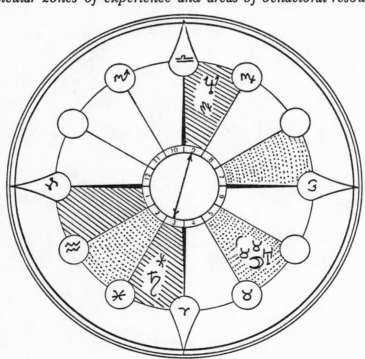

For example, the natal Saturn-Neptune opposition axis in a horoscope could be found in the IIIrd-IXth House axis. Saturn in Pisces would rule the Capricorn Ascendant, and Neptune in Virgo in the IXth would rule the IIIrd. By tenancy and rulership, the Ascendant, the IIIrd, and the IXth House would register developmental tension and draw the attention of holistic analysis. Status/identity concerns would undoubtedly involve information/perspective resources, ranging anywhere from education problems, frame of mind, conceptualization of reality, relationships with siblings, to cooperation with the parent in the Xth (the IIIrd is the sixth of the Xth; the IXth is the twelfth of the Xth, etc.).

If the Moon in this horoscope were in Taurus (a need to keep things as they are, to resist change for the value of whatever security exists within the status quo) conjunct Uranus in the Vth, relationships in the VIIth would be brought into analysis since the Moon rules Cancer on this example's VIIth, and so would the resources of giving love (the Vth), and as well the self-worth pressures, the Aquarian IInd, rules by Uranus. All these possible key interrelationships among these resources would be extremely clear within the potential behavior patterns being discussed and within the astrology that corresponds to the reality revealed by the client. *These deductions trigger the environmental awareness of the holistic astrologer; and the guide symbolisms of astrology come to life.*

Problems and behavior patterns involving the Succedent Grand Cross of Houses, the personal resources within the broad classification of money/love, are at the core of life and at the core of the horoscope. Material worth on the level of the external environment and self-worth concerns on the level of the psychodynamic inner environment are the primary references of "happiness" in our society. Material worth concerns are as perpetual as "Monopoly", our culture's most popular and endless game. Self-worth concerns are as pervasive as the hope for love that springs eternal from the human breast. These resources are constantly exchanged within relationships; there is constant assessment of our personal store of them; all of societal traffic is concerned with them, and the holistic astrologer must be aware of the traffic patterns.

Very often, the broad classification of "money" and the broad classification of "love" are interchanged. Psychodynamic awareness of self-worth is given security and even definition in terms of material assets, as when a person substantiates his or her capacity to give love or be loved in terms of material worth. Accepting the *lack* of material worth can trigger higher valuation of love dimensions within intimate relationships or world projection, as when lovers have love above all or when the riches of the world are forsaken for religious reward or humanitarian service.

Because of the thunderous prescriptions of the material external environment, needs relating to the broad classification of money are the easier to verbalize, to measure. Because of the vagueness of the inner environment within the onslaught of external prescriptions, needs relating to the broad classification of love are the more difficult to verbalize. The money needs are an accounting concern, and the love needs are a poetical concern. Within societal stereotypes, accountants and poets are not easily mixed; they supposedly do not have much to talk about in common(!). Yet, in the substitutive overlap of these two areas within relationships, the process of *earning* love is common, clear, and often problematic.

The dilemma is seen in the traditional meanings ascribed to astrology's IInd House orientation. For ages, the IInd House was given over to money concerns. Similarly, all the Houses were assigned essences in terms of the external environment, since through these ages of empirical astrological development the external environment was omnipotent. External prescriptions defined rigid codes of behavior and status. Precepts of social status were tied to personal worth, to taxation, to estate and lineage. With the awakening of the inner environment due greatly to the political freedoms within a maturing social structure, within a psychologically aware age, within the identity society, new dimensions had to be added to the essences of astrological House interpretations. Through my earlier works, *The Principles and Practice of Astrology*, I introduced the concepts of self-worth to recognize the inner environmental reference within the IInd House and the love-given and love-received references to the Vth and XIth Houses, respectively. Reference to either/both of the environments at work within the individual process of becoming helps holistic astrologers to seek dynamic significances within the money/love resource dilemma.

When significators within the horoscope key developmental tension in resource concerns of money/love, certain generalized behavior patterns can be anticipated. Similar to the generalized behavior patterns involved with status/identity concerns, there are two poles that help our organization: assertion or withdrawal, or, perhaps more specifically in relation to money/love concerns, overcompensation or sacrifice.

Within the broad classification of the money/love dilemma, our society frowns upon assertive overcompensation *in process* but admires assertive overcompensation *in fulfillment*. We sense that we may be individually victimized by the process, but we wish we could achieve the same goal through it. We are jealous often. We easily call overfinanciering sinful, but we admire the status achieved. This double standard gives birth to the societal expectation that the rich should contribute large donations back into the structure that may have been exploited or victimized by the process of amassing wealth. We then call the process of giving up riches, sacrificing part or all of the money goal, saintly; we call it an act of love. Our cognitive structures understand; we are all part of the process, and we endure it at various personal levels, for comfort or problem. Robert Louis Stevenson captured this insight perfectly when he wrote, "Saints are sinners who keep on going."

When a person has a concern about money in terms of social status and/or a concern about love in terms of interpersonal identity, he or she becomes aware of the particular resource insecurity through self-comparison with the societal image promulgated intensively by the public media or with the resources of others revealed through the complex dynamics of interpersonal relationships. A degree of lack is felt. Overcompensation is usually the first reaction pattern (especially if Mars is strengthened in the horoscope by sign and aspect network). Other resources are brought into the relationship to achieve balance or tip the scales in personal favor: children will brag about their parents' resources since their own are not yet clearly formulated; adults will hoard symbols of higher income status that belie reality and even deplete actual resource reserve further; people will try to increase their value through information, by hoarding gossip or becoming a "wealth of information", to become indispensible at different levels in different relationships.

On the interpersonal level, someone overcompensating for self-worth concerns may assertively give excessive compliments to others in hope of gaining compliments in return (especially true in show business, for example, where the pressures of performance for immediate evaluation intensify individual insecurities greatly); someone may give effusive love attention to overwhelm, to establish the giver's indispensible value to the receiver in terms of this precious resource; someone may reinforce self-worth through braggadocio about personal sexual prowess.

Overcompensation efforts cut to the core needs of others in ways that are hoped to be significant, to establish personal value by reflection in turn. Money gifts and excessive spending, excessive and lofty promises often are concomitant with insecurity within money/love cognitive structures. The down-and-out theatrical agent, for example, worried about paying office rent, still will need to say, "Sign with me, and I'll make you a star!" The promise hits the core need of the other person, is planned to elicit confidence and love in return, and alleviates concern. The dynamics here help life continue for both.

The resources of information/perspective can be tapped and fanned by the defense mechanisms of fantasy and dream to the point that projections of empires and Camelots and Nirvanas can come forth in overcompensation, to establish personal worth by affiliation with imagined states of high value to the target person. The insecure teacher or guru promises excessive accomplishment for the investment of money, loyalty, and love by students or followers.

As was seen in the aggression portion of our discussion of status/identity concerns, excessiveness creates distance by its quantitative uniqueness. Overcompensatory behavior demands capitulation but most often loses ground within the powerful demands for balance, for normalcy, for sameness set up by the external environment and maintained within the other person's individual development structure. Our society has taught us, in the main, to mistrust overselling. Yet, it is terribly difficult to do so if the sales pitch is for resources we need, if it promises status through money or love.

Progressing through middle grounds, people with concerns in the money/love resources classification may eventually become so intimidated by the observed personal lack in these resources that they *believe* their diminished status and acquiesce to the routinized behavior of withdrawal, of sacrifice. These people may find it difficult or impractical to give a compliment because they would feel further diminished if they did; they may hoard private supportive fantasies of glory and demean the money/love resourcefulness and standards of others; in essence, they will withhold their personal resources from any area and thereby curtail resources exchange within relationships. Through insecurity, they sacrifice growth potential and make insecurity worse.

When the tightness of loneliness exceeds endurance, there is often overt self-demeaning in order to attract supportive attention or pity. In essence, individual status is sacrificed to the status quo in external environmental terms, and individual identity needs are sacrificed to the values and needs of others. For so many, the difficulties with self-worth can lead to preoccupation with suicide, to masochism, to attract attention and loving leadership out of depression.

We can see the loss of self-awareness as a kind of identity death to avoid the tension of feeling unloveable, of feeling not particularly worthy of more than what is normal within any routinized setting. We can see self-aggrandizement as a kind of identity life at others' expense.

A most important point emerges in this general inspection of some behavior patterns stimulated by self-worth concerns: the core concern, the concept of the need for love that must be grounded upon self-worth, self-love, *is overlooked*. Other resources are easily and continuously substituted when actual love concerns are at issue. This occurs because *the dynamics of love are too difficult for our society to articulate*. We have only one word for "love"; we have little historical background material in our society from which to learn the meanings of love; we have no American knights, troubadours, art history; our psychologists have barely begun to study the concepts of identity, self-worth, love exchange, idealization, communication of aesthetic values, self-awareness in reference to the inner environment; we are barely adolescent in our development within world society.

The survival society romanticized stoic behavior, with love acknowledged or expressed only in special prescribed circumstances, or in trauma when the inner environment was brought into awareness, or just before death, as if to make life finally complete. The identity society now emerging into social leadership roles during the 1980's acknowledges and expresses concepts of love first and foremost, projected in terms of international brotherhood, societal collectivity, and spiritual awareness. This shift captures the historical truth that one generation's neuroses always become the freedoms of the next generation. But the middle ground of interpersonal love exchange founded upon acknowledged self-worth is still a communication problem, an evaluation problem, and a socialization challenge. And it all starts with appreciation of the self, the inner environment of personal needs in relationship with the outer environment of societal prescriptions. —These are all vital concerns for the holistic astrologer in order to anticipate the background and pattern possibilities within an individual's horoscopic environment.

One of most powerful diagnostic keys within astrology is found within the occurrence of *Saturn retrograde*, with particular significance within self-worth concerns. Saturn functions symbolically as the essence of time, what is learned for growth strategy within the passage of the time of life. Necessarily, this focus of learning is focused within societal authority figures, beginning with the authority figure within the home, usually the father, extending to teachers in school, leadership figures in job situations, community affairs, governmental laws, and religious precepts. In short, Saturn symbolizes environmental structure internalized throughout development time. I have suggested in past works, that Saturn symbolizes the concept of "necessary controls". The controls *must* be internalized for strategy of growth. Lessons are learned to allow the individual to create balance between inner environment and outer environment. The process of internalizing these controls, learning these lessons, may be subjectively burdensome, but eventually they serve subjective efficiency. Within the symbolism of Saturn much of the drama of socialization occurs.

We know that the process of growth is initially and most powerfully organized within the early home. Wherever Saturn is placed within the Houses of the horoscope, we can expect a developmental tension in terms of learning controls necessary to eventual efficiency within relationship dynamics and resources cognition. For example, placed in the XIth House, Saturn will focus the learning process within controls that affect the expectation of love. Behaviorally, an enormous need for love will register. If placed in the Vth House, a control concept is placed within the learning process relating to the capacity of giving love easily. Aspect patterns within signification dynamics will relate other areas to the concern as, holistically, the entire behavioral identity profile speaks.

When Saturn is retrograde, a counterpoint concern is emphasized. The controls are suggested by House placement, and the retrogradation factor suggests a delay in the internalization process. Holistically, we can look for this socialization phenomenon first and foremost within the early home development years within the authority figure in the early home, usually the father.

With Saturn retrograde, almost invariably, a legacy of inferiority feelings is suggested because of one or more of the following circumstances: the authority figure of the early home, usually the father, was somehow not in the picture clearly, in terms of loving guidance and support. The father was taken away by death, separation, or was passive (muted characterologically or alcoholically, or was subjugated by the mother); or he was away much of the time because of travel. There is also the possibility that the father was tyrannical to the end that loving guidance and support to the child never manifested. Any one or more of these circumstances are suggested by Saturn retrograde. The child loses the reinforcement of loving guidance in relation to its particular inner needs. A sense of insecurity grows. Almost invariably, self-worth awareness is threatened. Very strong Solar Arc projections to the horoscope angles (or similarly powerful transits to the angles) within the first fourteen years of life will usually date the critical times of this developmental focus within and through the family structure and also within the child's own awareness when around 10 or 12 years of age and later.

Within this occurrence, feelings of inferiority form *in relation to the emergent needs individualized within the child through the planetary profile.* For example, a strong Aries focus, especially within a female, demands much attention for learning strategic control of ego impulse. With Saturn retrograde, the Aries needs that are so intense may go more conspicuously unfulfilled than if the horoscopic planetary profile focuses on Taurus or Pisces. In Taurus, the needs can accept the situation and work within the environmental lack; in Pisces, the needs can accept the situation privately and seek reinforcement from an inner realm. In Gemini, Sagittarius, and Aquarius, personal resourcefulness can save the day superficially, but the inner core may never gain the stabilization that becomes essential for security in later life. The feelings of inferiority dig very deeply into the identity. Resources work externally to achieve some kind of manageable status; the concept of self-worth pain is covered over by other resources. Reaction formations are born. With the Sun in Aries and the Moon in Pisces, for example, the Saturn retrograde occurrence will emphasize that which is normally a life development condition within this Sun-Moon blend: an external show of force covering an inner timidity.

The reaction formations to make up for this uncomfortable lack of loving guidance and early self-worth reinforcement often take on a compensatory superiority complex. In effect, the child grows and learns to think, "You people out there in the world, you can do what you want, but down deep I know I'm better than you are!" In actuality, this concept of overcompensatory superiority feelings makes the person malleable to the leadership of others. Such a person is extremely vulnerable to flattery, to the loving reinforcement they need so much.

Extremely often, solitary rewards and self-worth confirmation are taken up within the loneliness that itself is the burden: young people will retreat, go off privately and dream. Especially if there is a Mercury configuration with Neptune, the daydreaming will support identity. Idealization will influence the early fantasy development, especially with the Mercury-Venus conjunction or Venus configurated strongly with Neptune and/or Jupiter, or Jupiter configurated with Neptune. The idealizations become protectors for identity and self-worth awareness; they become projections for development. Within such a complex, especially if the significator of the VIIth is under tension, the idealization process will be projected into relationships, making relationships very difficult since few others will be able to meet the idealized expectations.

These are the undeniable patterns triggered within the holistic awareness of self-worth anxiety. These patterns are practically invariable when they center around Saturn retrograde. Acknowledging them leads holistic analysis to immediately relevant observations.

These patterns can be present in a person's reality *without* Saturn retrograde indicated in the horoscope. Self-worth signification can be under developmental tension in many ways. What is more important than the measurement keys themselves is that the holistic astrologer must have always in mind a rich awareness of the reality of identity and self-worth anxiety during development, along with the basic behavior patterns that accompany the syndrome (whether shown by Saturn retrograde, other configurations more subtle, or simply revealed by the client).

For example, a horoscope has Virgo rising and Virgo on the IInd House cusp (because of interception). The interception may place Gemini within the Xth House. Saturn is not retrograde, but Mercury is in Pisces in the VIIth opposed Neptune in Virgo in the Ascendant. Mercury, the significator of the Ascendant, the IInd House of self-worth concerns, and the Gemini intercepted portion of the parental Xth is under developmental tension through opposition with Neptune. Additionally, the Ascendant is keyed further within the developmental tension by Neptune's position there, and the VIIth House of relationships is keyed further by Mercury's position there. The aspect configuration is classically suggestive of daydreaming. The signification network implies confusion about identity (Ascendant) and self-worth (IInd) that is related to one parent in particular (Gemini intercepted in the Xth); this confusion involves relationships (Mercury's position in the VIIth). A vagueness about self-worth security is definitely indicated. The daydreaming would be a perfect defense mechanism within the

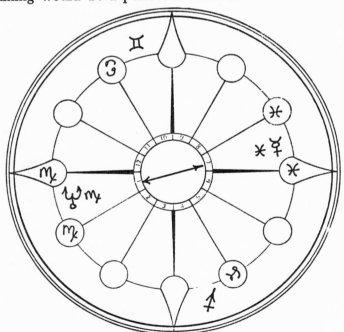

loneliness. *What* was daydreamed about will be important for analysis; *how idealized* relationship specifications became would be vitally important for the astrologer to ascertain. Remediation most certainly would work toward an efficient, practical balance among all these concerns.

In this example, if Saturn *were* retrograde, there simply would be no doubt about the self-worth anxiety syndrome. Saturn would rule the Capricorn Vth in this configuration. The difficulty in giving love would be automatically keyed in relation to the self-worth tensions suggested by the Mercury-Neptune opposition. In full awareness of the whole syndrome, the holistic astrologer is immediately ready, richly prepared to get into the developmental dynamics of the early home and relate them to the progress of identity development in the early home and relate them to the progress of identity development in the adult client.

There are situations where several children within the same family may show horoscopes wherein only one has specifically keyed self-worth concerns. Perhaps only one of the children has Saturn retrograde, and the other children do not. The phenomenon is still valid: the one with Saturn retrograde *will personally interpret family dynamics in personal terms, related to the personally individuated inner environment profile, in a way that will fit the behavioral syndrome.*

If parents have a young child who was born with Saturn retrograde, the syndrome *does not condemn that family's structure*. Rather, it illuminates the child's personal position of sensitivity in terms of its individual needs in relation to the family structure. It becomes a lesson learned by the parents to alert them to developmental needs in the child. That child, then, as an adult, will be able to respond to the sensitive astrologer's Saturn retrograde inquiry, "I know what you are saying: my parents seemed very aware of my needs; we talked about them often, and they were as loving and helpful as they could be. Sure, I thought things less than ideal many times, but I think we all did our best." This would be the healthiest cognitive structure under the circumstances. That awareness would have become a great strength for the human being.

Another very important point for us always to remember here within holistic analysis is that only a very, very small percentage of the population ever visits an astrologer, ever cares sensitively about improving self-awareness and understanding. A great majority of the population takes life as it is, finding support among others within societally structured samenesses. In astrological terms, the majority is undeveloped in introspection. Routines of living do not put a premium on self-study or do not allow time for that indulgence. So, an astrologer's deduction, no matter how penetrating, can be denied or invalidated easily because of the extreme strength of insulating routines and peer group reflection. Often, the approach to the concerns must shift subtly. The astrologer must know when to share deep analytical probes with the client or when to approach them from less incisive positions. The *client's* level of cognition provides the key: his or her awareness level, articulation facility, sensitivity, and hierarchy of values tell an astrologer how to communicate analytical insight effectively. Astute questions about causal connections within behavior patterns often are more manageable than direct analytical statement. Ordinarily, however, the astrologer serving a client enjoys a bias in the astrologer's favor: the client is ready to dig inside. The astrologer's grace in doing so determines the gain for the client.

Another extremely powerful key within the horoscope, within the early home environment in regard to self-worth awareness, is seen with the nodal axis of the Moon. My extensive research in client service has suggested undeniably that the close configuration of any planet, the Ascendant, or the Midheaven with the lunar nodal axis (either pole) suggests a *maternal influence* that is extremely important within life development. Tight orbs are essential (within one or two degrees, most reliably); the conjunction/opposition, i.e., sharing the nodal axis, or squares to it are most telling. With Mercury, the maternal influence on the person's need to think a certain way are obvious. A simple question about the maternal influence during development will reveal a great deal of relevant analytical material.

The keys of Saturn retrograde and a configuration with the lunar node axis suggest *imbalances*. The father's loving guidance was absent or the mother's influence was excessive. Often the two concepts go together. Either or both key rich analytical substance and guide knowingly secure analysis.

As the IInd House of self-worth concerns relates further within the Grand Cross of Succedent Houses, we come to another vital level of behavioral patterning symbolized within the Vth House, the giving of love. In our society, this dynamic is most obviously manifested within sexuality. The sexuality profile within interpersonal relationships is crucial. It is within the sexuality profile that individual psychology, the nervous system, and interrelationships all come together. It is through Vth House concerns that each person seeks to support meaningful relationships (the Vth House is sextile to the VIIth). The sexual dimension of the Vth House is grounded upon its procreative relationship by trine with the Ascendant: we create fascimilies of ourselves by conceiving children to keep life processes going. The Vth is the fifth of the Ist; the IXth is the fifth of the Vth; in turn, the Ist is the fifth of the IXth. This network holds the fire signs of astrology deeply within its symbolism: it is the inspirational glorification of the act of creation through projection of ourselves to others, to times to come through our children, through our children's children's children.

In our discussion of the Succedent Grand Cross values of money/love, the Vth House takes on the essences of speculation (hopeful, creative extension of self) with regard to the outer environment and sexuality with regard to the inner environment of psychodynamic need fulfillment. Again, within the exchange of resources vital to relationships and individual growth, we have a complicated worth concern: when we give out money speculatively to someone else, we need a return. At least, we hope to break even. We suffer a period of deficiency (depleted resource) to get the fulfillment of a gain in the future. In terms of love or sexuality, the balance of payments, so to speak, is not so clear: we know from conclusive psychological research that we do not lose love by giving it. The resources of love or sexuality do not deplete themselves.

Indeed, this is not to say that we do not withhold love and sexuality purposely in order to reinforce personal status and identity or fearfully guard these resources in insecurity, but we can fulfill ourselves by the actual act of giving love or sexuality. Returns are hoped for but are not essential.

Sexuality can easily be differentiated from love since love is so difficult for our society to articulate. Sexuality is a pressing natural resource linked powerfully to our nervous system. Only societal prescriptions cloud the naturalness of this function. Restrictions upon sexuality make sexuality all the more pressing; idealizations about love make love all the more nebulous and unattainable. Although problematic, then, *sexuality gains ascendancy over love concerns because it is more directly manageable than love.*

When the Vth House significator is under developmental tension within the horoscope or when the self-worth concerns from the IInd are under stress, the sexuality profile must be inspected. For the male, sexuality is mainly tied to status/identity reinforcement, fulfilling societal bias toward masculine prerogatives. For the female, sexuality is mainly tied to status/identity *complementation* to the male, fulfilling social bias to the feminine support function.

Within the identity generation, societal prescriptions are changing to allow women equal rights to status/identity individuation and to sexual fulfillment on individual terms. This represents a new freedom for many women, and the freedom easily clashes with deeply internalized societal prescriptions from the survival generation. Without any doubt, the complexity of social precepts, their change, the complexity of the sexual response within the female, all focus developmental tension in sexuality *upon the female more than upon the male.*[7]

When strong self-worth concerns are present within a woman's horoscope, especially if they relate by signification to the Vth House, there is every reason to anticipate sexual dysfunction, a lack of fulfillment through a difficulty to experience sexual orgasm (at all, or reliably) in sexual relationship. Under complementation pressures in an older generation, this difficulty was reinforced by repetition through time, was coldly exacerbated by a lack of information and non-communication between partners, and became known and accepted as a "sexual problem"; the woman was "frigid". The woman's self-worth profile became even more depleted; unfulfillment within sexuality worked to diminish frequency of intercourse; and spill over of the concern into relationship resources other than sexuality caused imbalances in other areas of life and resource exchange. In many, many instances, the whole life profile was affected by the supposed sexual problem.

The bothersome dysfunction still occurs among women in the younger generation, but they are more inclined to talk about it, to investigate solution. The orgasm is now highly touted in public media; every woman's magazine discusses this concern. The orgasm easily can be seen as a modern woman's badge of personal freedom. A shining "O" has replaced the scarlet letter "A". But just as easily, orgasmic dysfunction can become a heavy weight loaded with self-worth anxiety.

Holistic awareness that love-giving concerns (including sexuality) are always in developmental tension with self-worth concerns (the Vth is always square to the IInd; the Vth sextiles the VIIth; the IInd is quincunx to the VIIth) tells us clearly that so-called sexual problems are almost invariably not sexual problems at all; *they are relationship concerns*. We know someone with self-worth anxieties will work to free them most often through fantasy, through idealization, by clearly holding in mind that which will set free the feelings of anxiety. Through idealization, sexuality relates again to love; freedom will be gained through "the love of my life."

In relationships, so vital to growth and resource exchange, partners do not meet the idealized prescriptions of the inner environment. Relationships can not be trusting, complete, free. The psycho-neurological process holds back the sexual response. Dysfunction occurs. Reactions to unfulfillment and guilt in not fulfilling expectations spill over into communication resources and status/identity concerns. Repeat dysfunction is avoided; relationship dynamics and frequency break down. Freedoms failed become confinements gained. Blame is assigned, guilt is taken on, self-worth is worsened. Sexuality can be denied, sublimated. Nervous tensions increase and spill over into other resources. The whole personality can be affected. —Presenting this pattern to a client with such concerns is a powerful reflection of reality, identifying astrologer and client in productive rapport.

Since such dysfunction is almost invariably a relationship concern rather than a primary neuro-physical problem, we can expect that orgasm is reliable and natural in occurrence during masturbation, sexual gratification not dependent upon personal relationship. Again, almost invariably, we find that this is true. It is often revelatory to women with this problem that, because orgasm during masturbation is no problem, supposed sexual problem in relationship is not sexual at all but relational! Careful inspection of the general essence of masturbation fantasy will reveal clear dynamics that support self-worth idealization needs clearly. Adjustment of these fantasies to allow reality relationships to fit them more practicably is a key to the remediation of sexual anxiety linked with self-worth concerns. Sexuality therapists recommend and explore masturbation technique, fantasy, and success to build a base of self-appreciation (self-worth) that is then carried over into sexual relationships. The response in relationships becomes reliable when the response is sure alone. The Vth House in so many dimensions, emerges out of developmental tension with the IInd. Security in the Vth is based upon security in the IInd.

Houses within the Succedent Grand Cross that are above the horizon, the VIIIth and the XIth, dynamically symbolize the self-worth and love-giving resources of others with whom we are in relationship. The dynamism is truly monumental, as developed in this chapter and further throughout this book. The concerns of money/love drive our lives inexorably. They energize the structure and catalyze the chemistry of all interrelationships. They commandeer other resources into the battle for fulfillment. In the natural distribution of the signs, it is no wonder that the Houses of the Succedent Grand Cross hold the signs of fixed modality.

Self-worth anxieties can be at the root of gambling, prostituting any personal resource, promiscuous speculation in any level of life expression, overselling and underselling, the loss of opportunity through the delays or avoidances couched in impractical idealization. Self-worth anxieties *must* exist to make personality development possible. When they are keyed within the horoscopic environment, they are pronounced, they are linked to the individual's inner environmental need profile. Through our own individual growth energies we become aware not only of ourselves and our problems but also of *others with the same concerns.* Everyone shares the same complexities in order to help each other eventually toward fulfillment. In the words of Montaigne, "There is as much difference between us and ourselves as between us and others."

Problems and behavior patterns involving the Cadent Grand Cross of Houses, the personal resources within the broad classification of information/perspective, by their Cadent nature (mutable signs) spill over easily into other areas of resource concern. We have seen how information can be used to support status/identity; we can appreciate how perspective is related to money/love concerns. In the Angular Cross of Houses, status/identity concerns revealed a Mars dynamic of focus and initiation, related to Aries naturally on the cusp of the Ist House. In the Succedent Cross of

Houses, money/love concerns revealed a Venus dynamic of value organization related to Taurus naturally on the IInd House. Now, in the Cadent Cross of Houses, involving information concerns in relation to the outer environment and perspective evaluation in relation to the inner environment, we are discussing a Mercury dynamic related to Gemini naturally on the cusp of the IIIrd House.

We are now concerned with adaptability, flexibility, and adjustments, all primarily focused through thought and communication (III), cooperation with others (VIth), learning the thoughts of others (IX), and gaining the support of society's institutions (XII). Within this network, we accumulate awareness of status/ identity; we even mentally set personal prescriptions for what we need in those concerns; we accumulate comparative values of money/love resources. In short, we gather answers to our own personal questionnaires, compare them with answers we give to others' questionnaires, and determine our attitude toward where we are in developmental progress. As the spiral of Houses relating external environmental concerns and internal environmental needs develops around the axis of time, the Cadent Cross of Houses keys the torque that shifts our development into another angular point of focus and initiation.

All self-help studies and institutions work upon the mind. Norman Vincent Peale, says, "Change your thoughts and you change the world". Dale Carnegie says, "Remember, happiness doesn't depend upon who you are or what you have; it depends solely upon what you think." Haridas Chaudhuri says, "The ability to make decisions according to the purpose and potentiality of one's own being is the most essential factor in constructive and meaningful growth." Buddha said, "Be a light unto yourself." All emphasize the mind. The identity society has taken the Cartesian thesis, "I think therefore I am", and changed it to "I am the way I think." Altered states of consciousness, mind control, biofeedback, cybernetics all work to reinforce individual self-perception within the information/perspective resources of a new age.

The mind always races to make any moment or any situation worthwhile. This is the process of cognition. It works to adjust personal perspective within the awareness of change, to give significance to routine, and to rationalize victimization. Our way of life, our societal prescriptions, press us to be involved, to do things, to be busy. Idleness is supposedly the devil's workshop, suggesting that idleness occurs when values do not exist or are not clear, when we are confused, indecisive, fixated, or uninvolved. We are pressed to think for ourselves, but to think in the "best way", in full awareness always of what and how everyone else thinks. We are told to do unto others as they do unto us, suggesting the ideal balance of societal cooperation within resource exchange. We are told how much education we need to have for different kinds of jobs. We pray when perspective is threatened, and we curse when we feel abandoned. —It is no wonder that societal information and personal perspective are constantly under developmental tension. The mind works overtime to assimilate a rapid reality in support of all resource exchanges. In holistic analysis, the astrologer must be completely aware of these resource tensions. Imagine the life problems linked to these networks of conceptualization!

Within the horoscopic environment, the IIIrd House is the midpoint between the Ascendant and the Vth House, and is trine the VIIth and the XIth: information/perspective mediates between status/identity and money/love resources. The IIIrd House is quincunx to the Xth: the adjustment of information/perspective should be achieved in part through cooperative relationship (sixth House dynamic) with the parent signified by the Xth and, as well, in adjustment to professional status. At the same time, we can see that the IIIrd House is the twelfth of the IVth, suggesting the possibility that a person's information/perspective resources may be cooperative with one parent (Xth House) and limiting or confining to the other parent. In such a situation, that parent symbolized in the IVth can in turn, be a limitation (judiciously or selfishly) to the Vth House resources of the person, the child (the IVth is the twelfth of the Vth). Again, holistic analysis enriches the House meanings powerfully.

When developmental tension is pronounced within the Cadent Grand Cross of Houses (III, VI, IX, XII), keyed by the aspect networks of the significators of the relevant Houses, we can expect that the information/perspective resources are of important developmental concern. The spectrum of reaction patterns can again span two poles, assertion or withdrawal, which, more appropriately, within information/perspective resources, become *imposition* and *adaptation*.

In the extreme behavioral reaction pattern, a person overcompensating for an interrupted education (incompleted learning experience of any kind), for example when the significator of the IXth House is under clear developmental tension, will tend to impose personal opinions on others, will tend to be judgemental to the extreme. A deficiency is felt, and all the resources are commandeered to make up for the deficiency. The person's way of seeing things is practically the *only* way of seeing things. The opposite behavior pattern is possible in reaction to the very same lack; complete adaptation to the thoughts and opinions of others. The person easily falls into how others think about things. The difference in reaction patterns emerges throughout life development in relation to the individuated patterning of personal resources, temperament, energy, relationship dynamics, ambition, etc.

For the imposer, at its extreme, personal information/perspective *is* personal status/identity: a political stand, a value system, or a religious belief becomes the identity. Being a "true blue Republican", a Ku Klux Klan member, a "Moonie" takes over societal status and individual identity autonomy. A belief system becomes paramount as a personal resource that defines who the person is. The person is fixated upon a thought process, a societal

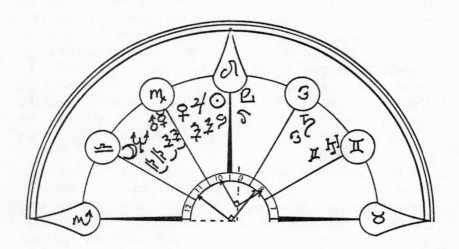

lable, an allegiance to group precepts at the expense of variegated personal needs fulfilled in balanced resource exchange with others. This extreme behavioral pattern is societal reflection and individual victimization at their most pronounced. Lacks in other resources usually have become unbearable, and the mind races to identify itself with something that has status in order for life to have meaning.

The same phenomenon can occur with an *inner* environmental reference: complete adaptation of individual awareness can be fastened to an idée fixé, a fear, a phobia, a set of suspicions, a compulsive thought process in order for the person to feel alive, to know who he or she is. For example, a man has all his planets clustered above the horizon between the VIIIth and XIth Houses (the potential to feel victimized by experience). Capricorn-Cancer hold the IIIrd-IXth House axis; one significator, Saturn in the VIIIth, squares Neptune and the Moon, the other significator. Venus rules the Libra XIIth and is square Uranus in the VIIIth; Mars rules the Aries VIth and is conjunct both Mercury and Neptune. The significators of the entire Cadent Grand Cross are under developmental tension, focusing upon Neptune. Finally, Pluto at the Midheaven, emphasizing strongly the awareness of self within/ against society, squares his Scorpio Ascendant. Recently in his life, a series of extreme measurements were corroborated by the death of both his parents within a week of each other, entirely without warning. The shock was enormous. Fear gripped his system. The mind raced in anxiety and, constantly since that traumatic time, has filled him with fears that he was next, that his brother or sister was next. The trauma worked itself into a natal predisposition to fear phantasmagorically. No other resources could be used to break this fixation; not rational discussion, not love, not diversion, not religion. In analysis, however, it was discovered that the fixation somehow made him feel terribly alive; the imagined threat emphasized his potential to live. A new perspective was awakening; trauma had dislodged a routined dullness that had been long in the making.

We have already discussed the dimension of self-disclosure as a means to build intimacy. Conversely, researchers have found that avoidance of self-disclosure is a major source of alienation from any group. The answering of personal "questionnaires" is essential to set the social scene for resource exchange and the clarification of status/identity, money/love, and information/perspective. Upon meeting, two people follow societal prescriptions and ask "How are you?". A question of generalized status is put forth. A perfunctory answer of "Fine, how are you?" is also prescribed. In other words, exchange conditions are set up on a basis that "things are fine all around", that there is *no imbalance to threaten resource exchange*. Actually the question in its formal entirety is, "How are things going for you?" It is clearer still how information/perception is required to get social interaction going. The fact that answers to this powerful inquiry are also prescribed *to be positive* points out the fact that neither party wants to get involved with an individual reality of personal dimension. *Meetings are for resource exchange more in terms of the outer environment than in terms of the inner environment*. This prescribed repression of the inner environment builds enormous tensions.

However, the question about personal information/perspective gives opportunity to people within the extremes of behavioral reaction pattern to do their thing: the imposer can spout off every dictum of his or her platform; the adapter can slip into victimization patterns of self-demeaning and chronic complaining. The imposer can easily put down the status of others, the adapter can seek commiseration. When we study the system of self-disclosure sensitively, we see that society makes it extraordinarily difficult to disclose one's self. As a result, intimacy is rare, routine is reinforced, social distances are balanced, and private conceptions rarely gain fulfillment.

Fantasy takes up its role to discharge private mental awareness: to protect self-worth weakness, to give support in the face of threatened status. The fantasy starts to live for itself. Idealization processes push the imposer into fanaticism and the adapter into self-isolation.

In the middle ground of information/perspective behavior problems when the significators of the Cadent Grand Cross of Houses are under strong developmental tension, we can anticipate indicision. Indecisiveness can often emerge from a lack of self-clarification in the early home environment. Parents necessarily must make decisions for their children, up to a point. As the children become clarified and differentiated as individuals, the actual decision to be made is less important than *the process of making it*.

In the horoscope, the three Grand Crosses of Houses (Angular, Succedent, and Cadent) of our parents and those with whom we make close relationships are congruent with the same Grand Crosses of Houses within our own horoscope. This reinforces the similarity and interaction of all concerns and behavioral patterns among those with whom we are in closest developmental contact. With regard to the information/perspective Grand Cross, we easily see that the third Houses of our parents fall into our VIth and XIIth Houses. Our parents put their thinking processes upon us necessarily, teaching us how to cooperate within relationships (VIth) and within society at large (XIIth). At the same time, we are aware (opposition) of how society thinks as we learn through societal education and the thoughts of those close to us (the IXth is the third of the VIIth). We are constantly pressured with judgemental dogma, and all too easily the routine of imposition upon us forces adaptation; we may never learn the process of evaluation, we may never learn our own mind.

As thought formations develop in tune with the prescriptions of early home environments and then extend to the societal structure immediately around the home center, societal reflection is highly reinforced. If further education through college experience (preferrably in a different environment) or hobbies or independent learning does not modify the personal reflection of societal structure, a person is anchored within environmental samenesses. Men's clubs, women's clubs, trade unions, and social activities all work to protect these samenesses and make them meaningful. The imposition dynamic can elevate the social organization into a vanguard position of a minority political position; the adaptation dynamic can merge the social organization into a majority support system. It is interesting to note that every clique or politically extreme movement, from the Ku Klux Klan to the Minutemen to Naziism, rationalizes its goals in terms of purifying society, protecting samenesses, for the good of the society itself. Patriotism abounds; identification with a "glorious" concept gives sharply defined identity to the massed individuals involved. Personal indecision is abandoned to a "meaningfully" decisive collective point of view that, in turn, patterns behavior within the sameness of a sub-environment. Specialized information confers status; clarified personal perspective establishes identity.

Religious teachings prescribe that we be good to our neighbors (IIIrd House), that we turn the other cheek, that we cooperate for the good of others. This tells us that we are to care what our neighbors think. So, we fear being ostracized, being socially exposed, being punished publicly through scandal. Conversely, *not* caring about our neighbors' opinions (withdrawing under information/perspective stress) suggests that going to jail in punishment, facing criticism, will not have any effect; we will not lose face. "Who cares?" and "What does it matter?" and "So what?" suggest that status/identity resources are clarified, stabilized, and stagnated in resignation; they suggest that information/perspective resources have no more potential. This attitude of helplessness can also be a reaction formation of superiority against constant unfulfillment: "I am what I am, and I don't care what others think." How often we discover this attitude during client consultation!

We spend most of our awake hours working with others. We must communicate constantly. In communication, we share our personal points of view with others. The developmental tension between our points of views and the points of view of others are pivotal (IIIrd-IXth axis) within the cooperative work situation (VIth House squares the IIIrd-IXth axis) since it operates to confirm or change status/identity (the Cadent complex leading to the Angular complex). If disagreement overbalances agreement within these view sharing activities, we say, "That person makes me sick!" (VIth House). We try to get out of the cooperative communication situation; we can not learn from it, we can not cooperate within it; it leads nowhere; we become ill. Illness can be dealt with objectively.[8]

The society we live in puts enormous importance upon our information/perspective resources. We *expect* aggressive imposition of information and perspective from political candidates. We call an assertive and sure information/perspective profile "charisma". John F. Kennedy had charisma: his IIIrd-IXth axis held the signs Sagittarius and Gemini. Mercury was trine the Moon in Virgo, conjunct Mars and Jupiter (the other significator), sextile Saturn and square Uranus, semisquare Pluto in the IXth. This is a tremendously powerful pattern of communication power, of strong information/perspective resources.

Adolf Hitler had charisma: his IIIrd-IXth axis also held the signs Sagittarius and Gemini. Jupiter trined the Sun in the VIIth, conjoined the Moon in the IIIrd, trined Venus and Mars. Mercury, the other significator conjoined the Sun, trined the Moon and opposed Uranus.

Edgar Cayce, the spiritualist healer and psychic, had charisma through his complete adaptation to the controls of another communication dimension: his IIIrd-IXth axis held Libra and Aries, with Venus sextile Moon, conjunct Mercury, sextile Mars, and conjunct Saturn. Mars, the other significator trined the Moon, sextiled Mercury and Saturn, and trined Neptune which was conjunct the Moon in the IXth.

The average person has charisma in terms of the sure strength of his or her communication power within his or her specific environmental prescriptions. Every astrologer, for example, practically every day within social traffic, is asked, "Do you believe in astrology?", "Do you believe in karma?" Such questions test the astrologer's belief system, his or her reservoir of information and position of personal perspective. Obviously, the questioner does *not* "believe", or the question would never be asked. The question, then, invites a proselytizing sermon from the imposer, charisma by sheer volume of answer, or a self-effacing "I'm just learning" response from the adapter, a kind of charisma routined never to alienate, never to lose status, but always to invite exchange.

Sensitive thought about the dynamics involved in such an exchange, a model that is repeated about various points of information and perspective constantly during socialization, can suggest that "belief" is not the fulcrum upon which information and perspective within astrology (or anything else) can be most practicably balanced. Astrology may not be something to believe in but something to know about. Such an answer shifts evaluation within potential resource exchange away from inner environmental perspective and toward outer environmental information. The information variable is easier to manage; the personal perspective variable based upon belief will always be threatening. This is a key understanding for sensitive remediation within holistic analysis.

The Cadent Cross of Houses defines resources that measure socialization through information and communication on the outer environmental scale and belief and perspective on the inner environmental scale. The former is much easier to manage within the self-comparative dynamics of social interchange. Therefore real self-disclosure is difficult and risky, and information/perspective resources, though constantly active in exchange, are fragile in registration.

So, in order to guard what status/identity resources we have, we often use our information/perspective resources defensively. We may hoard privileged information and gain the feeling of improved personal status perspective. We see people who will never ask a question since it would imply a weakness in personal information/perspective resources. We say everything is "fine, just fine" in order not to reveal a personal status/identity or money/love concern under developmental challenge. We may sacrifice world position for the sure embrace of religious information and reward perspective. We insulate ourselves with judgemental rationalizations, and we reward ourselves with fantasy.

All that we do comes *first* through the mutability of our information/perspective resources. On the one hand, these resources are the hardest to pin down within astrology, and on the other hand these resources are the key to remediation of personal concerns. Events occur constantly, and our minds race to give them value. What values we give to the events not only touch our patterns of information/perspective resources, but our self-worth concerns in terms of money/love and status/identity as well. Holistic analysis must be aware of the entire interrelated texture. Problems with appreciating the weave are reliably suggested by developmental tension within the aspect patterns formed by significators of the Cadent Grand Cross of Houses. Anticipating through knowing grounds the perception of the holistic astologer.

Conclusion

When the client comes to the astrologer, the client is finally asking "What do you know about me?" The client is asking for the astrologer's answers to the "questionnaire" about the client. It is a complicated questionnaire, and the astrologer must explore holistic awareness of environmental conditioning on two levels: the prescribed structure of the external environment and the pressing need structure of the internal environment. The astrologer must see how they work for balance and for imbalance within routinized behavior patterns. Significator networks key concerns of status/identity, money/love, and information/perspective. These concerns are then tested for cognitive structure and causal relationships within the client's own view of development.

The analytical process is simple, but the substance of it is not. The client's question is simple, but the answer is not. Yet, the astrologer's measurements always remain the same: the Houses tell the areas of concerns tied to external prescriptions, the planetary patterns within the Houses tell the areas of concerns tied to internal needs, and the planetary significators of the Houses tie both concerns together. The client must clarify level within his or her own Law of Naturalness. The pivotal focus of the entire process, then, is upon the astrologer. *What the astrologer knows about life holistically is what makes the measurements of astrology meaningful to the client.*

Knowing the patterns of the external environment and the horoscopic environment allows the astrologer to orient analysis easily to the client's inner environment. Knowing life through observation, experience, and empathy allows the astrologer to initiate meaningful conversation with the client. Being sure through all this that all people within our society are reliably like all others then allows the astrologer to be secure, wise, and helpful.

Chapter Three
APPLICATIONS IN
HOROSCOPE ANALYSIS

Within our society, astrology is very, very young. Its backbone was inherited from turn-of-the-century England, with vertebrae aligned in a structure of time, experience, values, and knowledge completely different from our own present. Superficial concerns of "things", of behavioral traffic, and events have too easily and for too long typified the mainstream of astrological practice. The psychodynamic essence of "things", the complex needs served by behavior, and the values given to events have been overlooked. Our spine has been slow to grow into flexibility and strength.

Times have changed, and so has our astrology: the acceleration of development within time and the complexity of external environment have finally revealed the integrity of the inner environment in its bid for personal fulfillment. Holistic analysis within holistic astrology must capture the modern dynamism that is within every individual's developmental process, that is shown within every individual's horoscope. Now, with full awareness of sociological background, generational profiles, external environmental prescriptions, and the struggle for individuation that occur within the exchange of resources within all interrelationships, the holistic astrologer must be prepared to direct analytical probes incisively to *developmental* concerns that are important, that *really matter* to the client.

Even further, it is not enough now simply to describe psycho-dynamic concerns; holistic analysis must be prepared *to explain* interconnected concerns within the client's reality, in terms of the client's individuated needs. The very word "analysis" comes from root words in Greek meaning *to break, to loosen.* Through analysis, we separate a whole into its component parts; we break up and loosen the personality structure in order to understand its developmental framework. But we must put the parts back to-gether again; we must holistically recognize *the function* among structural parts to give animated meaning to the whole. The holistic astrologer explains rather than describes; loosens rather than tightens; explores developmental function rather than static circumstance. The holistic astrologer's goal is to adjust awareness rather than to solve condition.

The following cases have not been specially selected. They are simply several of the cases in my practice within the past week. Within the scope of the first two chapters of this book, they are perfectly "regular" in that they become extremely and dramatical-ly individuated through holistic analysis. Any *ir*regularities within what is assumed to be normal horoscope readings simply suggest that normalcy is routinely shallow and that there is a difference between the sense of "reading" and the sense of "analysis".

CASE 1 (Chart on page 91)

Preparation Notes—Before the consultation appointment, the horoscope was fully prepared and certain preparation notes were made. The Sun-Moon blend, Sun in Aquarius and the Moon in Aries, suggested the following flow of personality energy that ideally would be at the core of the personality (Volume III, *The Principles and Practice of Astrology*): " . . . a quick and aggressive mind, a keen sense of intellectual powers . . . a sort of judicial attitude toward the rest of the world. This is one of the positions of a genuine superiority complex. The mind flames too brightly. The social balance must be considered in order for the mental powers and their expression to work efficiently." —This would be what normally could be expected: The Sun's Aquarian energy and the intense ego focus of the Arian Moon, social awareness energizing prominent ego needs to full display.

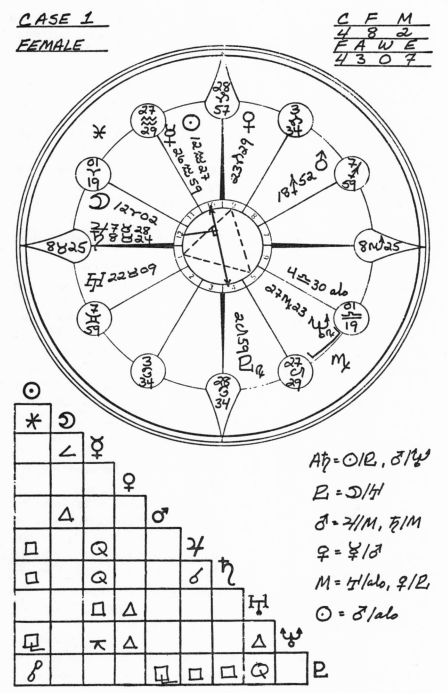

CASE 1
FEMALE

C	F	M
4	8	2
F	A	W	E
4	3	0	7

A♄ = ☉/♀, ♂/♅
♀ = ☽/♃
♂ = ♃/M, ♄/M
♀ = ☿/♂
M = ♃/Asc, ♀/♃
☉ = ♂/Asc

91

But the telephone call making the appointment revealed a woman whose words, reaction time, and diffidence suggested anything but what could be expected from the Sun-Moon blend. She was born at the bridge of generations and would take on the complexity of generational transition. Something was in the way of the normal Sun-Moon flow. She was born in a foreign country sociologically typified by strong sociological demarcation between the have's and have-not's, rationalized by a pervasive Catholic Church influence. Sociologically and generationally, I could begin to feel the woman's ego repressed by external circumstances.

Within the horoscope, the Arian Moon is in the XIIth, a clear indication of some veil muting its easy show of potential, probably in terms of sociology and perhaps her relationship or lack of it to the parent symbolized by the Xth House (XIIth is the sixth of the VIIth, the third of the Xth).

The planet Saturn, ruler of the Xth, is one minute of arc from precise conjunction with the Taurus Ascendant. This immediately keys the two angles, the Midheaven and the Ascendant by the significator Saturn; Saturn rules the Xth and is placed upon the Ascendant. Immediately further, we see that Saturn/Ascendant are square to the Sun-Pluto opposition axis within the parental axis. With the Sun-Pluto opposition placed within the Xth-IVth axis, the Moon ruling the IVth and placed in the XIIth, and Pluto ruling the VIIth, all the Houses of the Angular Grand Cross of Houses are involved within strong developmental tension. There is simply no doubt that the powerful Sun-Moon blend is muted by sociological circumstance and by early family environment, and that it forms a conspicuously important status/identity concern within relationships. There is simply no doubt about it.

We then check the self-worth profile, signified by the IInd House, here ruled by Mercury. Mercury is square to Uranus: the self-worth profile is under keen intensification, probably nervousness and anxiety, in terms of goals, being loved (Uranus rules the XIth), and this anxiety within the growing awareness of repression, seen in the analysis of the status/identity complex involving the angles, adjusts itself (naturally) through fantasy, through the quincunx between Mercury and Neptune.

The Vth House is ruled by the Sun and Mercury, because of interception. Neptune is retrograde and placed in the Vth. The tensions from status/identity concerns spill over into self-worth concerns and on to particular reference to security in giving of self. We immediately know that all of this preparatory analysis will affect the ease and fulfillment potential within interrelationships. We have seen that Pluto, ruling the VIIth, is retrograde and in the IVth, within a powerful fixed sign T-Square. The fixed signs within the T-Square and its angular orientation suggest *low permeability*, a resistance to change, to loosening. The status/identity problems with concomitant self-worth anxieties are rigid, deeply rooted within homelife, difficult within relationships, adjusted through fantasy, and are anxiously repressed.

The young organism within early development will need defense mechanisms to preserve identity under difficulty. Always this is so. Here, the fantasy component within the horoscope (Mercury quincunx Neptune) is not too strongly developed; there must be something more for defense.

We can immediately see the Earth Grand Trine involving Venus, ruler of the Ascendant, Uranus, and Neptune. This will register as a closed circuit of practical (Earth) self-sufficiency, a behavioral pattern eventually to take care of herself in the face of strong developmental pressures. In reality, such a self-contained defense mechanism will isolate her further from relationships while protecting her further from oppressive environmental pressures.

A special, unusual observation can be made within this Grand Trine: it does not involve the Sun or the Moon. The defense system will operate separately from the natural core energy of life flow. It will be independent, functioning *between* the deep self and the outer world. There is every indication then of further withdrawal from direct relationship with others.

The table of elements and modes reveals that there is a high fixity and an absence of water emphasis. The fixity emphasis relates to the T-Square with the Ascendant, suggesting low permeability and the enduring tightness of the status/identity concerns. The absence of water emphasis suggests that the parameters of emotional awareness and expression are weak on the personal level, corroborating the repression and the self-worth concerns spilling over from the IInd House to the Vth, as already discussed.

The preparation notes are conclusive. They direct holistic analysis eloquently into early homelife concerns and developmental patterns of personality protection and withdrawal from relationships.

Further nuance is similarly obvious: Pluto's position in the IVth suggests that defense of personal perspective will entail accumulation of awareness, maintaining poise, and defending substance all in terms of early upbringing.

Midpoint analysis shows that the Ascendant/Saturn conjunction is within tight orb of the Sun/Pluto midpoint, emphasizing even more the vital significance of the T-Square. This is a crisis of individual self-preservation under various kinds of restriction. The Ascendant is necessarily confined by the symbology of Saturn, and this drama occurs within early homelife development, finally placing life hope (Sun in the Xth) into full awareness (opposition) of value perspective (Pluto). This would entail *absorbing* homelife values and eventually *changing* them through broader environmental exchange within relationships (Pluto rules the VIIth). The fixity of the T-Square suggests this process will be difficult; the withdrawal profile emphasizes the difficulty further; and the self-worth concerns and undifferentiated emotional resources (no water emphasis) complicate matters thoroughly.

Other midpoint pictures are also telling: Mars squares the midpoint of Saturn/Midheaven (i.e., Mars = Saturn/Midheaven), showing applied energy (fleeting and possibly short-lived in Sagittarius) caught within the Saturn/Midheaven complex that keys the vital T-Square. We see that Pluto = Moon/Uranus, which Ebertin suggests as "building anew upon ruins". This midpoint picture corroborates our deduction from the defense profile of Pluto's occurrence in the IVth House.

Jupiter's conjunction with Saturn upon the Ascendant suggests that education and foreign travel would be vital for the woman to change environment, broaden horizons, and gain status/identity within new value perspectives. Saturn rules the IXth, suggesting that education would be interrupted, but the Jupiter conjunction with Saturn and square with the Sun and quintile with Mercury promise that the developmental tension would lead to reward eventually. If education were interrupted, it would surely be resumed. Venus and Saturn are in mutual reception, relating the slowness of emotional maturation (Venus in Capricorn) to the early homelife developmental concerns and also to the educational process and foreign relocation as outlets to fortify practical self-sufficiency (Venus in the IXth, ruling the Ascendant, and keying the Earth Grand Trine).

Finally, the planet Uranus, intensifying the nervous self-awareness within developmental tension (placed in the Ascendant, squared by Mercury, involved within the Grand Trine), relates loosely by sesquiquadrate to the lunar node. Along with the Moon's semisquare to Mercury and trine to Mars (Mars in the VIIIth, the fifth of the IVth, the love given by the mother, assuming the IVth to the mother because of the Cancer cusp and the Saturn dynamics so powerfully keying the Xth) we can expect a pervasive maternal influence.

The client's information/perspective resources reflected within the Cadent Grand Cross are obviously involved throughout this preparatory profile: Saturn rules the IXth, Venus rules the VIth, and the Moon in the XIIth rules the IIIrd: her perception of her abilities to communicate, cooperate, learn, and relate to societal institution are all deeply involved with the developmental tension structures already studied in these preparatory notes. The spill-over of status/identity concerns is holistically complete. The process is vividly clear through horoscopic guidelines. The astrologer is prepared for holistic analysis with the client, who will clarify deductions within her own level, within her Law of Naturalness.

Analysis and Client Response—The client arrived early (a responsible eagerness to share). She is trim, beautiful, well-dressed, carefully and quietly spoken. Her handshake is so weak as to be non-existant. Her eyes are bright, but her gaze is easily diverted by some inner self-consciousness. She has a nervous laugh that seems linked again to inner self-consciousness. She lives alone at present and has a secure, fine job in a world famous high-status international institution. Her job function is in the field of public relations!

Immediately, the preparatory notes for analysis begin to adjust themselves: a job in public relations (external environmental activity and status) takes the place of the fulfillment of personal interrelationships which are probably so difficult (internal environmental identity). Venus is oriental (rising just before the Sun) within her horoscope, suggesting that job evaluation will be important as a substitute for direct personal evaluation.

We can immediately expect that *external* status brightness emerges throughout developmental pressures in a secure light while *internal* identity concerns remain repressed in darkness.

The woman had just started astrological study. This suggested her eagerness to think personally, to get into her development on her own to learn about her growth and potential. During her short discussion of this, it was easy to glance at preparation measurements and note that this study began when the Secondary Progressed Moon had recently opposed her Mercury, a perfect corroboration not only of the event but of the significance of it within the anticipated analytical profile of her whole life development.

Using some simple astrological orientation at her beginner's level, I introduced the concerns of the T-Square. Quickly but gently, I was able to begin discussion of the early home environment, pointing out that her real ego strengths were somehow diverted through that environment within development. I asked particularly about the earliest concerns possible, those around her birth and shortly thereafter (since the Ascendant was so highly and tightly charged in the horoscopic pattern).

Without emotion, the client stated that she had never known her father, that he had died accidentally when she was two years old. A key deduction from the preparatory notes was confirmed. Quickly, it was easy to adjust measurement symbolism further within the horoscope: at two years of age (24+ months), the Secondary Progressed Moon would have been crossing the Ascendant and Saturn, transiting Pluto would have been squaring the sensitive Ascendant/Saturn complex, and the midpoint axis of the natal Sun/Pluto opposition at 7 Scorpio/Taurus would have been projected through the Ascendant/ Saturn focus. Additionally, projecting a two degree advance quickly to the natal position of Pluto, bringing Pluto to 5+ of Leo, would have created the picture Solar Arc Pluto = Sun/Midheaven (13½ degrees separate the Midheaven and the Sun; divided by 2 gives 6¾ degrees, which, added to the Midheaven, gives a Sun/Midheaven midpoint of between 5 and 6 degrees Aquarius/Leo).

The client's statement *is all that is necessary* to anchor the beginning of holistic analysis grounded in the preparatory notes. However, with experience and thorough horosocope measurement preparation, midpoint projections and Solar Arc approximations within development can be inspected while the client is actually speaking, in a flash, to ground measurement accuracy and client response solidly to the measurements. Finite measurements *after* the consultation revealed that the approximations were indeed accurate: SA Pluto came to the midpoint of Sun/Midheaven 8 months after her second birthday. Even further: SA Sun squared the midpoints of Saturn/Uranus and Uranus/Ascendant 9 months after her second birthday. It was a crucial time in her development.

The client's statement clarified the core of the preparatory notes: the father was taken away by death. Development followed without him. The mother never remarried. The client stated that life went on uneventfully, routinely. I suggested that life in the home environment continued "dully", and this was corroborated. I added, "Until, perhaps around the age of 13?" —This deduction simply projected the stressed Ascendant/Saturn point by Solar Arc to conjunction with natal Uranus, a distance of 13-14 degrees, 13-14 years with a winter birth. Experience and knowledge of transit rhythms suggested also that, in this span of time of 13-14 years, transiting Uranus would move two signs (7 years per sign; 7 x 12 = 84) and be close to her fourth cusp; that transiting Neptune would move one sign in that time period and be squaring the fourth cusp; that transiting Saturn would be opposed its natal position, crossing the seventh cusp. I could reliably expect another trauma within the developmental tension construct clarified in my preparatory notes.

The client corroborated that in November of her thirteenth year, her mother died. Her statement was calm and unemotional.

The client's statement was all that was necessary to guide holistic analysis further along. Experienced approximation of powerful measurement symbolisms reliably gave measurement corroboration to the reality of her life. Finite measurements after the consultation substantiated the deduction concretely: in the month of her mother's death, Secondary Progressed Moon was exactly opposed its natal position; SA Saturn was conjunct natal Uranus, and SA Ascendant was conjunct Uranus two months before her mother's death; SA Mars = Mercury/Saturn-Ascendant one month before her death; transiting Uranus was conjunct the fourth cusp and transiting Neptune was square the fourth cusp in the month of her death; and transiting Pluto was exactly opposed the client's natal Mercury at the mother's death. A complete shift of personal perspective was indicated.

The perparatory notes for this analysis were solidly grounded in the client's reality experience.

The developmental years between the father's death and the mother's death were thoroughly discussed within the behavior pattern that could be expected holistically (and was outlined in the preparation notes) and within the sociology of the client's birthplace. It was clear to both of us, that, after the father's death, the mother did not remarry but worked to preserve a comfortable, non-traumatic life. The young girl was left alone much of the time; there was no particular challenge placed upon her, no authoritative leadership to spur development, evaluate it, and guide it. Her fantasy started to support identity, "I dreamed about going away, marrying a prince; you know." The client thought this normal under the circumstance. She was correct; it is a very clear behavior pattern potential, as we have seen in the preceding chapters. She was insulated by routine, alone, needing encouragement and individual recognition (Aries Moon). She did not receive it; fantasy worked to project identity development idealistically elsewhere, within a different environment. The potentially powerful ego energies were being left dormant. Routine deprived her of developmental challenge.

Upon the mother's death, the client was alone. She had few developed resources. At thirteen, she was taken in by relatives. The defenses of her Earth Grand Trine were forced into operation: she slowly began to see that she would have to fend for herself in life, reinforce her aloneness, be careful and reserved in her expression, protect her sensibilities which had been seriously jarred by trauma, and try eventually to catch up with the developmental framework she lacked.

The client said, "For years I couldn't express myself at all. I felt that if I were to talk it would be stupid. It was a complex for sure. And I can remember since I was six or seven, that my mother and grandmother would tell me I was stubborn. I would be punished for something, and I would go right out and do the same thing again!" —The withdrawal was clearly corroborated; the reasons were clear, as the early life traumas fell into the status/identity vulnerabilities of her horoscope. The defense mechanisms began to isolate her; the emotional slowness in development reinforced the strategy of withdrawal. The fixity of the whole crisis began early as stubbornness and then endured for a long time as rigid behavioral routine. I suggested that her rebellious behavior moments as a child were really her effort to attract recognition, leadership, guidance, motivation. She agreed, and added, "Well, I didn't get it. I withdrew."

Her life took her through a few pristine relationships with young men, with Catholicism and social prescriptions placing the relationships into complicated networks of family approval, ethics, and support standards (as SA Venus conjoined the Sun). She left the home country and travelled to several countries, going in and out of schools and languages and sociological structures. Rarely did she ever have difficulty getting a good job, but always she had difficulty with interpersonal relationships: "I can't enter into relationships without fear. I protect myself. I always wonder how they will end before they even get started!"

Her pattern of behavior continued, with slight adjustments that corresponded to patterns set up by transiting Saturn, with an extremely responsive Zenith-Nadir axis. She has never had a deep, free, meaningful relationship, but she has always had fine job situations. Her work at present in public relations for a highly prestigeous international firm takes the place of unfulfillment in interpersonal relationships within the status/identity concerns that are so dramatically indicated within the horoscope.

Comments—The Sun-Moon blend of such high potential had been diverted from bloom by environmental circumstance and trauma. The client's defense mechanisms of withdrawal and self-sufficiency had gone into operation strongly. Fantasy had given her occasional contentment and fleeting hope. She had faced her options squarely: "I could have just stayed on, married someone and had children, and everything would have stayed the same. But I tried hard to get out and find a new life elsewhere." This was indeed a triumph for her, changing environments, but the routinized, defensive withdrawal patterns of behavior remained. They were deeply ingrained by her environment. She said, "I've always wondered why girls (from her country) don't seem to have a backbone."

The consultation accomplished full understanding of all the environmental pressures and the individual needs, and then turned to remediation. Remediation focused upon the potential symbolized within the horoscope by the opposition between the Sun and Pluto, the potential to break up early perspective to establish *new*

values. This was corroborated further in the horoscope by Pluto=
Moon/Uranus, "Building anew upon ruins." In other words, the
powerful environmental structure indicated within the horoscope
and manifested within the early developmental years was lifted to
another level through understanding, objectification, and changes
in environment, perspective, and time. The Venus factor was taken
out of the tightness of the Grand Trine and encouraged within its
midpoint picture Venus=Mercury/Mars, a quickness to love. The
Midheaven was reinforced through understanding of its position as
midpoint of Uranus/Node, sudden change through expanded relationships, and as square the midpoint of Venus/Pluto, a potential
for deep love awareness. Fear was removed through understanding;
energies were freed through acknowledgement of the security
finally enjoyed in the present; and the potentials for quicker, freer
growth into the future were encouraged through simple techniques
of self-assessment, which will be covered in detail in Part III of this
book, "Remediation". It was clear that the client had learned the
message of her environment, and her handshake was much stronger when the consultation ended.

CASE 2 (Chart on page 101)

Preparation Notes—This female client followed the woman of Case
1. Their horoscopes and their development concerns have obvious
similarities. Although client 2 is fourteen years younger than client
1, both share the fixed T-Square of Saturn square the Sun/Pluto
opposition axis. Both have Venus in Capricorn, with Venus ruling
the Ascendants in both cases. The fantasy dimension becomes the
primary defense in Case 2 since Neptune retrograde is conjunct the
Moon in the Ascendant. This fantasy dimension will work as
strongly for the woman of Case 2 as the Grand Trine works for the
woman of Case 1. In both cases, significators key a status/identity
concern linked in the horoscope to angular tensions and in reality
to family environment.

Although this young woman is in her mid-twenties, her
appointment was made by her mother. The mother tensely inquired if astrology could help her daughter, who did nothing but
"sit around the house all day". Inquiry about the length of time

CASE 2
FEMALE

C	F	M
9	5	0

E	A	W	E
2	7	4	1

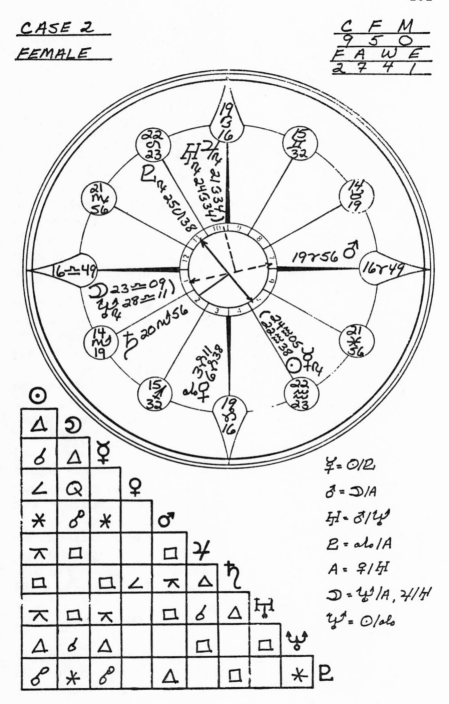

$\mathcal{Y} = \odot/\Box$

$\sigma = \mathcal{D}/A$

$\mathcal{H} = \sigma/\mathcal{Y}$

$\mathcal{P} = \sigma_0/A$

$A = \mathcal{Y}/\mathcal{H}$

$\mathcal{D} = \mathcal{Y}/A, \mathcal{Y}/\mathcal{H}$

$\mathcal{Y} = \odot/\sigma_0$

this situation had existed revealed that the daughter had been tested several times for learning disabilities, for psychological problems. Nothing conclusive had been determined. The daughter had graduated from highschool but had done nothing since. I asked to speak with the daughter, and we shared a halting, childish exchange of short, simple sentences. The appointment was made.

The horoscope revealed a pronounced degree of retrograda- tion, with only Venus (ruler of the Ascendant), Mars (in Aries upon the Descendant), and Saturn (involved in the fixed T-Square) in direct motion. The retrogradation pattern certainly reinforces the symbolism of the Sun-Mercury retrograde conjunction and the Moon-Neptune retrograde conjunction in the Ascendant: this young woman has a separate world of her own. The Venus in Capricorn suggests a slowness in maturation and is loosely con- junct the lunar node, bringing in the maternal influence in terms of the young woman's personal projection (Venus ruling the Ascendant).

Saturn rules the Capricorn IVth and squares the Sun-Pluto opposition; the Moon rules the opposite angle, the Cancer Xth, is conjunct Neptune and opposed Mars, ruler of the Aries VIIth. Venus, ruler of the Ascendant, has the nodal contact, suggesting the mother's influence, and is relatively weak by aspect, making only semisquares to the Sun and Saturn and a quintile to the Moon. In short, all the angles are involved in sharp developmental tension. The resources for status/identity confirmation are tense.

Additionally, the Jupiter-Uranus retrograde conjunction in the Xth, also keying that angular House, squares the angular and cardinal opposition of Moon-Neptune and Mars. This second T-Square is extremely strong, keying status/identity tension fur- ther. This T-Square, although angular and cardinal, will have more permeability than the succedent and fixed T-Square since the combination of angularity and cardinality suggests that something must be done to discharge the behavioral energy patterns con- tained within the cognitive structure. With the presence of Nep- tune retrograde, we can anticipate that the fantasy defense world will be the outlet for these tensions.

The succedent and fixed T-Square involving Saturn, Sun, and Pluto, will have much less permeability; it will be deeply en- trenched within personality development. The symbols within this T-Square key the XIth, Vth, and IInd Houses by tenancy, the XIth and IInd by rulership. The self-worth complex is extremely pressured; the self-worth concerns that relate to the capacity to give and expect love, recognition, etc. are strongly pressured in development. Additionally, Uranus, ruling the Vth, is squared by the Moon, Neptune, and Mars. The second T-Square within the status-identity complex relates to the first T-Square within self-worth concerns.

Every planet except Venus within the horoscope is involved within the two T-Squares. Venus also rules Taurus on the VIIIth, the second House of the VIIth, others' self-worth concerns, values, etc. In these preparatory observations, I felt keenly the young woman's status/identity, money/love concerns in all their ramifications. I saw the fantasy power as withdrawal into a private world. I felt that the energy resources had given up the struggle. The prominent Mars in Aries upon the Descendant had been muted by fantasy. This was all corroborated by the mother's phone call description of the young girl's laconic passivity and the daughter's halting conversation.

The Sun-Moon blend would be piped throughout all this complex "plumbing." With the Sun in Aquarius and the Moon in Libra, the expectation is for extremely easy flow in social and romantic traffic! This expectation is reasonable in generality, but the behavioral patterns here relating inner environment needs to outer environment structure suggest a short-circuit in this individual reality. At the same time, this Sun-Moon blend and its theoretical ease of expression usually carry with them a naiveté that easily dilutes persistence. Our young woman here, with tremendous developmental pressures, would probably easily give up the effort to do anything about them. She would acquiesce to the pressures, and she would enjoy her own private inner world.

The natal midpoint pictures corroborate much of the natal profile: Mercury is retrograde and is opposed Pluto (the inclination to avoid perception of the self's reality position when that position is under stress; a possible sense of futility); Mercury rules the IXth and XIIth, two of the Houses within the Cadent Cross of information/perspective resources; Mercury is at the midpoint of the Sun-Pluto opposition. This links Mercury even more strongly to the Sun-Pluto symbolism of a disappearance of values, an alteration of perspective.

Mars is opposed the Moon, but it is also at the midpoint of Moon/Ascendant, suggesting frequently changing moods. Since Neptune is strongly configured with the Moon and rules the

VIth House, another arm of the Cadent Cross of information/ perspective, we can expect moodiness and fantasy to be involved with gaining cooperation from others in terms of a job. The job status would be important to define identity values, especially with Venus oriental (as in Case 1). The reference for these value's is taken off the self and transferred to the job.

Uranus is at the midpoint of Mars/Neptune: changing energies and weakness. The Moon is at the midpoint of Neptune/ Ascendant: emotional unrest. Neptune squares the midpoint of Sun/node: a difficulty in adapting fantasy and identity to relationships (node).

Jupiter rules the IIIrd, the base House of information/perspective concerns. Jupiter is retrograde and conjunct the Midheaven. Its conjunction with Uranus, also retrograde, promises eventual fulfillment, but the retrogradation counterpoint is tied in with the angular and cardinal T-Square, reflects itself in terms of fantasy, and demands adjustment of life energy expression (Jupiter and Uranus are both quincunx to the Sun).

The entire horoscope is under extreme developmental tension. It is probably dormant, held down by acquiescence, tolerated within the rewards provided by fantasy, and projected to solution by job reference as a means to gain status/identity clarification. A major developmental change time would probably be around the age of 13 or 14 when the Solar Arc projection of Saturn, from within the succedent and fixed T-Square, ruling the IVth, would sesquiquadrate the Midheaven.

The young woman would probably not be able to articulate any of these concerns profitably. An immaturity informationally and emotionally is obvious. Values of self and for interaction with others have disappeared.

Analysis and Client Response—The young woman arrived for her appointment promptly. She was taller and stronger in appearance than I had expected. Her thick glasses obviously corroborated eye problems suggested by the highly stressed Sun and Moon in her horoscope. Her hair color was changed suggesting an aware sense of vanity. Her mood was much more cheerful and direct than it had been on the telephone, perhaps since she was on her own and not making a self-presentation through her mother.

We made friends through relaxed chit-chat. It became clear that conversation would not easily develop through theoretical exchange or introspective commentary. Careful questions had to seek out meaningful answers.

Gradually, I was able to inquire about her relationship with her mother in terms of her listless "sitting around the house". She revealed a very fair assessment of her mother's anxiety about her idleness. She was able to smile knowingly at her own situation. She was unable to get a job because "employers, interviewers see me as hesitant, tense, getting off the track." She would try to get a job when her mother's anxiety increased to a certain point. She would fail in getting a job, her mother would relax anxiety, and she would settle in to reading fun books and watching television.

The client revealed a good vocabulary. She said that she often looked things up in the dictionary. She functioned well in her own world. Her values were based upon her reading and her television enjoyment. She had few friends: "they all get married, move away, leave; you know."

Through all the descriptions, she was most pleasant. No deep hurt or emotion was revealed. Sentences were short, to the point, unembarrassed, and provided clear descriptions of the entire profile prepared in the horoscope analysis. Whatever was deeply significant in terms of astrological expectation was smoothed over and kept out of awareness.

I enquired about her father and learned that he had died four months after her thirteenth birthday, corresponding precisely with SA Saturn sesquiquadrate her Midheaven. There was little emotion in her explanation. She missed her father, and that was that. Of course, this was a crucial point in analysis, affecting not only the client but her mother, who never remarried. But there was no reason to dig deeply into the woman's life: its rigidity and closure were recognized and assimilated; there was no mutable sign emphasis to reveal reaction or resource for easy change. Emotion and introspection were underdeveloped. There was no specified hurt or problem manifested.

I next inquired into her fantasy life. The inquiry was greeted with a smile. "What is in your fantasy?" —"How I get along with people; how they react to me."

This was the Mars opposition with Moon-Neptune, the main axis of the angular and cardinal T-Square. I pressed further. The client revealed that she has fantasies of people fighting or "boxing with me. Sometimes I win". A big smile crossed her face.

Her tensions *were* discharged in her fantasies. Her anger, her energies were tied up with combatting the external environment within her daydreams. She knew that she was in a struggle for identity, and, again, that was that.

"What do you think holds you back?" I asked. — "Money. I want to go to Europe again."

"What holds you back from working to get money?" She replied, "Rejection keeps coming in."

I learned that she had travelled often with her mother during her mother's work vacations. The mother had to take the daughter along, and these trips were very important to the daughter. In fact, they were the only significant experiences she had had. Here was the Venus quintile with the Moon, the maternal influence somehow creatively establishing some base for the young girl's identity profile. The client revealed a tremendous interest in museums, in flowers and art works. She wanted a job in order to get money to go on more trips and enjoy museums and flowers and pretty clothes.

At no time in our conversation together were *emotional* values discussed. The conversation was dry because of their lack; the woman's life was lonely because these values were not developed (the Succedent Grand Cross). Self-worth was a meaningless concept. Money had been substituted for love values; job had been substituted for identity. I worked to test this further.

I commented to her that at no time in the conversation had she spoken of feelings, of relationship goals. She replied that she had always been able to get along with people (the easy Sun-Moon blend). I asked about a boyfriend, and she replied, "Not just yet."

Her reply "Not just yet" was dramatic. It showed an awareness of her own insecurity and emotional immaturity. This young woman with so many concerns had an uncanny wisdom in not revelling in self-pity and in having faith that development would come sooner or later. This was a key meeting of our minds that led us to explore what values would have to be developed within time and experiences to come.

I asked her to describe what she "thought of me?" She replied, "I think you have a great sense of humor; you're easygoing, and you're very tall." This description was certainly superficial, as expected, so I commented, "But what about my mind, my heart?" —The point was made. We explored how important these other, deeper dimensions were to successful and trusting relationships with others. We were off and running into a lively discussion of interpersonal dynamics. Relating observations of these to her magazines and television shows helped give her a vehicle to assess human values and remind herself of them regularly.

Finally, I pursued how she could learn to construct these values for herself, within herself. Guided by the power of her Neptune symbolism, I asked if she were interested in photography. She definitely was. This led us to a fascinating experiment that works to establish personal values without the presence of fear within interrelationships. The principle is to screen the self through the lens of a camera, and it will be discussed fully in Part III of this book, "Remediation".

Comments—The woman's horoscope rarely responded to transits and Solar Arc development. The father's death was the only major corroboration of strong astrological measurements. Transiting Uranus conjunct the Ascendant saw a time of vacation trips and no more. As transiting Uranus conjoined the Moon and Neptune, she was anxious about her grades in school. Her college try was interrupted when transiting Saturn was in Cancer squaring her Moon-Neptune conjunction. She revealed so much of the Cadent Grand Cross problems when she said simply and with a smile, "My professors weren't receptive to my ideas . . . and I was late with my papers."

I became intrigued with this woman's poise above all her problems. Rationalizations were working full time, but for every smiling rationalization there was a clear, self-aware wisdom. She realized her mother was a cushion that was too available to her. She knew that she was falling behind in development. The transit of Saturn opposed her Sun two years ago had corroborated a listless retreat from frustration. She saw herself the victim of her own routines. We agreed it was time to get "her act together"!

Fascinatingly, the consultation occurred with transiting Pluto precisely upon her Ascendant. She was fully prepared to change her life perspective, to build her self-worth resources (Pluto rules the IInd), to set new goals (Pluto in the XIth). She was totally ready to readjust her awareness of values and relationships. She had steps to take first, before relationships could be tried ("Not just yet"), but she was ready to get started.

The week before, transiting Saturn had semisquared her Moon as Mars had opposed her Saturn. She answered a job ad. The interview had gone well. A few days later, transiting Mars had squared her Pluto, and she had been accepted for job training. A triumph! That astrology measured these events exactly impressed her, so projections were immediately meaningful: transiting Jupiter would make strong supportive aspects with her Saturn, Sun, Mercury, and Pluto in the next three months. She had a good and knowing start indeed.

The rigidity of the horoscope pattern and the absence of mutability emphasis would not easily allow a change of structure or environment. Rather, the emphasis upon cardinality, triggered by the Pluto transit of her Ascendant, was awakened for her to *do* something *through* the structure, to catch up with development time.

CASE 3 (chart on page 109)

Preparation Notes—At first glance, it is obvious that the entire horoscope is focused upon the Sun-Saturn opposition in Cadent Houses. The Sun is in the XIIth House, ruling the IVth. Saturn is *retrograde* and in the VIth, ruling another zone of the Cadent Grand Cross of Houses, the IXth. Uranus is within the remaining zone of the Cadent Grand Cross, and it squares the opposition axis of Mercury-Neptune also in the XIIth and VIth, respectively. Although the orb is large between Mercury and Neptune, instinct and experience tell us that this nervously charged fantasy dimension will be validated in behavior patterns as a defense for the Saturn retrograde phenomenon.

This initial look at the horoscope ties the four Houses of the Cadent Grand Cross with the rulers of the parental axis, the Sun and Uranus. There is little doubt that the woman is under perceptual anxiety about herself and that this anxiety was taken on through the early home environment. We note further that Venus, ruler of the Ascendant, is square Pluto, ruler of the VIIth. The significators of the remaining two Houses of the Angular Grand Cross are in high developmental tension with each other. Pluto is retrograde in the IVth, reinforcing the parental base of the problems, and Venus is in the XIIth suggesting a private sense of what is ideal in self-fulfillment, probably locked into the fantasy protection against early environmental perceptions.

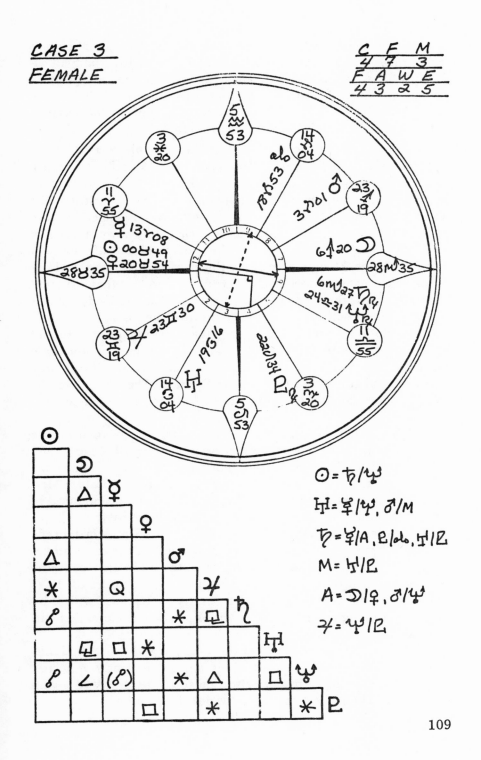

CASE 3
FEMALE

C	F	M
4	7	3

F	A	W	E
4	3	2	5

⊙ = ♄/♃

♅ = ☿/♃, ♂/M

♄ = ☿/A, ♇/☊, ♅/♇

M = ♄/♇

A = ☽/♀, ♂/♃

♃ = ♆/♇

109

Again, this horoscope shows eloquently a classic combination of normal developmental circumstances internalized individualistically. There are broad concerns within the information/perspective Grand Cross that affect status/identity concerns. The developmental tension is rooted to the home environment and extends into relationships with the outer environment.

The Sun-Moon blend must flow through this developmental "plumbing". With the Sun in Taurus and the Moon in Sagittarius, there is a deep need to create a well-articulated structure of morals, ethics, and perceptions upon which to build identity. The woman will need to know what is right and reliable, to have security in her perceptions, and apply what she knows in order to build her own identity. The plumbing of development shown in the horoscope blueprint suggests that a rigorous home environment has provided someone else's structure and that that structure is at odds with the woman's own structure. Here individual needs are threatened within development through the impress of parental prescriptions. Saturn retrograde, the Sun ruling the IVth and under great tension, Uranus ruling the Xth and in sesquiquadrate with the Moon, and Uranus conjunct the nodal axis all call clear attention to this early developmental profile. The father and the mother are anxiously pronounced within her self-conceptualization.

Self-worth is stressed since Mercury, ruler of Gemini on the IInd is squared by Uranus. Mercury is in Aries, linking strong mental needs and energies with important ego-orientation in terms of self-worth. Jupiter in the IInd sextiles the Sun, quintiles Mercury, and sextiles Pluto. The ego reward needs are pronounced in terms of finding clearly articulated self-worth security. But Jupiter is also sesquiquadrate to Saturn, linking these self-worth needs to the father figure, to the authority figure(s) in the early home. Jupiter is trine Neptune suggesting that the self-worth concerns will be softened or maintained by fantasy. Neptune rules the love-hoped-for, love-received XIth: the fantasy preoccupation will be linked to gaining acceptance in terms of personal achievement and intimate love received.

The strategic Mercury rules the Vth. The self-worth anxieties linked with ego tension, protected by fantasy, nervously projected in cerebral learning terms, are also tied to an insecurity of giving love easily. The mental process pervades the entire horoscope. We see a whole cognitive structure linked to finding out information/ perspective resources developed under a heavy home pressure that builds status/identity insecurity. Within the whole process, self-worth concerns abound in terms of giving and receiving love according to idealized mental prescriptions.

The expectation would be of a young woman feeling nervously confined, feeling inadequate. The intelligence would probably be extremely keen. Education would be threatened with interruption (Saturn ruling the IXth), but the mind's needs to learn, to figure out the identity's place in the world would fight through any obstacle to find a secure place for status, identity, information, perspective, and then have the security to give and receive love within relationships.

The midpoint pictures corroborate much of this preparatory analysis: Sun = Saturn/Neptune, a deep, possibly physical reaction to emotional stress; Uranus = Mars/Midheaven, the possibilities of rash anger within frustration; Saturn = Mercury/Ascendent, inhibitions and lonliness; Saturn = Pluto/node, the propensity to end relationships harshly; Saturn = Uranus/Pluto, rebellion against control from others; Midheaven = Uranus/Pluto, a thrust to grasp awareness of personal perspective.

We see the anxiety, the insecurities; we can anticipate the disruption in relationships because of the nervous fretting. But at the same time, we can appreciate a gentle poise within most of the identity search since the Ascendant squares the midpoint of Moon/Venus and Jupiter squares the midpoint of Neptune/Pluto. Mars in the VIIIth is in Capricorn, symbolizing a tremendous self-administration potential to get out of the feelings of inadequacy and confinement (Mars rules the XIIth). Mars trines the Sun, sextiles Saturn and sextiles Neptune. The Moon is in the VIIth House, reaching through learning and experience for acknowledgement and respect, and trines Mercury and semisquares Neptune.

The woman's written request for an appointment revealed a keen mind, an alert and unflagging introspective search, and a history of relationship break-up and vocational indecision. She had been in and out of several colleges. She was confused about what she wanted to do in life. She fleetingly touched upon difficulties of goal in relation to what she wanted and what her family urged. Her name was Lebanese.

It was clear that the entire preparatory analysis fit into a cultural tension in her family, perhaps focused upon the roles of women within a Lebanese cultural background and a modern American cultural expectation. With all her cerebral sensitivity, this young woman was caught between two worlds, between two parents. She could not find herself. Her Sun was in the XIIth, and her Moon was in the VIIth.

Analysis and Client Response—The young woman in her early twenties is slight of build, suggesting a Gemini Ascendant. Her birth certificate time was recorded to the minute and gave every indication of reliability. Solar Arc projections and major transits to the angles corroborated life events significantly; the birth time was indeed very close. The nervous Gemini characteristics could very well be the manifestation of all the nervous perceptual anxiety channeled through the Sagittarian Moon.

The client is very gently pretty and extremely intelligent. Her main interests have always been in languages. She has travelled widely. She has been through many different jobs including research, secretarial, and paralegal work. All of these stabs at finding a job role for herself related obviously to Jupiter, the Sagittarian Moon, and the IIIrd House.

Conversation was extremely easy. The woman's vocabulary and intellectualization skills were impressive. She wanted to understand herself better; she wanted to study "the undercurrent of unresolved tensions that have been stirred up by a relationship crisis two years ago." The crisis had been the break-up of a deep and profoundly important romantic situation. She had rashly broken off the relationship, and had suffered enormous remorse about it. After the crisis, an enormous depression followed and, as well, diagnosis that she had a mild case of multiple sclerosis, "which was definitely psychosomatic. That it affected my eyes was symbolic: I was refusing to see how I was responsible for much of the ennui I fell prey to, and my body responded in kind." (Sclerosis is the hardening of tissues, symbolized by Saturn.)

I avoided digging right into the dynamics of the relationship crisis and sought to corroborate the influence of the early home-life which surely was the base for her intellectual confusion and lingering emotional distress.

The client corroborated every deduction that had been pre-pared. There was a definite cultural gap within the family: the father is thirty-six years older than she and himself from a strict old-world upbringing. His authority in the home was dominant, but not oppressive. In this case, the Saturn retrograde phenom-enon registered a rare exception to the main substance of usual analytical expectation. The father was not out of the picture, was not passive, and was not tyrannical. She felt that she had been well-loved and provided for with maximum security.

I still pressed further to find the very individualized mani-festation of the undeniable symbolism. I asked how she actually *perceived* the love and attention from her father. The use of the world "perceived" was taking reality description away and replac-ing it with individual perception, the heart of her horoscope tension. She answered, "Well, I always thought his love and attention were narcissistic. He was proud to be my father. In other words, there, but for the grace of *him*, went I! I, my existence, was a credit *to him*."

It became clear that love and attention upon the client was perceived by her to be praise and reflection back upon the father. The client's perception adjusted circumstance to fit into her natal vulnerability to insecurity.

I pursued the fantasy content in her early life, her day-dreaming. She offered, "I would dream that I would get recogni-tion for something I would do, something really on a world scale, something enormously philanthropic, for example. I would dream about this as a way to attract my parents' pride in me." We discussed this thoroughly and saw how there was a short-circuit: the dreams were not for personal credit but for parental pride, which kept her anchored within the perception of her father's narcissism. She responded strongly in confirmation to my sugges-tion that this daydreaming, fantasy projection, into her parents' pride became cerebral overanalysis of deficiency within herself as she grew older: "I was continually afraid in anything I did that I would get a reprimanding look from my mother or an assumption of credit and pride from my father."

The analysis continued easily through all levels of perception. Basically, we were able to understand together that her own worth was left out of the picture repeatedly in the early home life. Her own perceptions were powerfully modified by her relationships with her parents. Nothing in the home life was confining or lonely or traumatically coercive, but the client's perception of it all worked to establish personal deficiencies, real or imagined. Relationships were overanalyzed; rejection was feared; relationships were broken; confusion about professional goals arose; a lack of confidence undermined energetic self-application and her capacity to give trustingly.

Comments—Intellectually, everything was understood by the client. I felt that *emotional* security within her intellectual understanding would take a longer time to form. Mercury, although extremely intense in Aries and squared by Uranus, was locked away in the opposition with Neptune and in XIIth House position. Cooperation from others (the XIIth is the sixth of the VIIth) would be terribly important as a proving ground for intellectual adjustment. Relationship challenges would be essential for the mind to test itself in adjusted realities.

We promised each other to stick with the understanding and try to relate it beneficially to her challenges in the near future. Knowing we would study the situation further as it began to work itself out in fresh experience, we concentrated upon a major job decision: to enter interpreter school in another city, in another environment. The client made the move and entered the program; a further adjustment was made to augment language studies with international affairs. All decisions and moves were planned and corroborated astrologically.

She wrote me a letter after that first visit. An excerpt from that letter reveals her perceptive tension *and* growing understanding: "I certainly walked away with a clearer vision of my reticence to give—not a pleasant view, but certainly worth working on. Interestingly enough, with a retrospective glance at times when I was more of a giver than is my habit, I gave more to those who were unreceptive or not visibly appreciative—another reflection perhaps of my own awkwardness and reinforcement of my own defensive behavior. My biggest fear now is that I will plunge ahead with the wrong perspective—that of recapturing lost time and then berating myself for not having done it from the very beginning in what I perceive to have been more auspicious times! The flip side to that is I may have greater and more confident resolve after having tripped all over myself and tested other areas."

There is a great cerebral bind in this fine, eager woman. Her mind works overtime, as it always has. She has many, many blessings which she must learn to trust through direct, reciprocal relationships. The bind has been reinforced through her fantasies. Usually, the fantasy life works to *free* a bind, even though the effort may be unrealistic. Here, the fantasies worked to create the bind and reinforce it in terms of personal perceptive vulnerabilities. She sees herself continually in terms of her father's pride; leaves herself behind. The anxiety still swirls within the intellect that works to understand it. Perception resources within the broad classification of the information/perspective cognitive structure are a source of great strength and dilemma at the same time.

Another session was planned. It was devoted to the source of the tension, which the client still ascribed to the big romance crisis several years earlier. She ascribed it to the Moon in the VIIth, so to speak. I knew it should be ascribed to her early homelife, the beginning of her life energy focus, the Sun in the XIIth. As opportunities started to fall in line for her, she began to become as anxious as before. New challenges were testing personal perspective crucially.

We met again, and together we got to the bottom of it all: the projection of personal pride to her father *and the counterbalancing projection of jealousy to her mother!* We can easily recall that her Sun was opposed by Saturn retrograde and her Uranus was only twenty-three minutes of arc away from precise conjunction with her nodal axis. Uranus rules her Midheaven. —The analytical technique that helped us and its results will be fully shared in Part III of this book, "Remediation".

CASE 4 (chart on page 116)

Preparation Notes—The next client in my schedule was also a woman. Her name prompted inquiry about her family: her parents were Slovakian, first generation American, and Catholic. She had been born in 1941 at the transition of the survival society to the identity society. Family background, religion, small town environment would all be important considerations within her development.

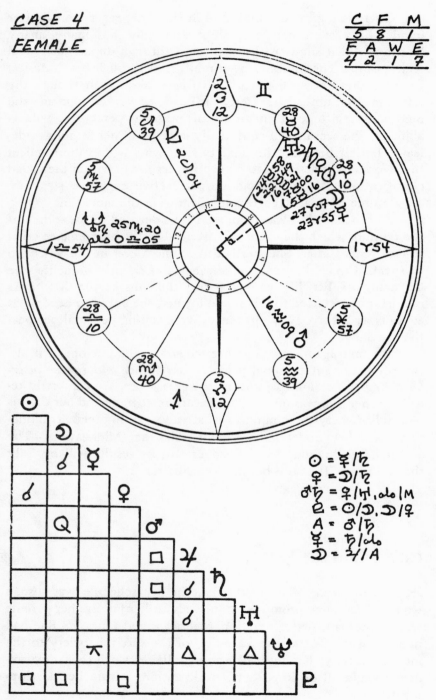

CASE 4
FEMALE

C	F	M
5	8	1
F	A	W	E
4	2	1	7

⊙ = ☿/♄
♀ = ☽/♄
♂♄ = ♀/♅, a/o|M
☋ = ⊙/☽, ☽/♀
A = ♂/♄
♀ = ♄/a/o
☽ = ♃/A

116

The environmental background gains immediate focus within development when we note the Aries Moon and its square across the signline to Pluto. The reigning need in this woman is to be number one. High ego emphasis would cross the generation line and be a developmental spur or frustration, or both.

Also within first glance at the horoscope, we see that the node is conjunct the Ascendant. The mother's influence upon the woman's personal projection would be very important within analysis. So quickly, we have been alerted to the angular Grand Cross: the Moon in the VIIth, the nodal axis upon the horizon, the Moon ruling the Xth. Saturn rules the IVth and is extremely closely squared by Mars, ruler of the VIIth. The cognitive structure of status/identity concerns is highly charged within a sociological stereotype of foreign background, Catholicism, and particular focus of it all is with the maternal influence as the client crosses generational values.

There is no opposition within the horoscope, suggesting that individual focus within development is not easily externalized. The client might not know "where to hang her hat". Her self-worth concerns would be strongly involved since Venus, the ruler of the Ascendant and the IInd House, squares Pluto. Venus and Pluto rule the IXth-IIIrd axis, involving information/perspective resources and suggesting that education and/or learning about other environments was interrupted somehow, that perhaps self-worth development was confined to the early home perspective (Pluto in the Xth). With only the Midheaven in the water element, we could expect that parameters for emotional expression would not be easily established. The square between Venus and Pluto would suggest that this vagueness in emotional orientation could trigger an excess of emotional expression to gain self-significance.

Very quickly, we see the reigning need for ego importance wanting to break out into a new generation of values on its own, yet it is confined to the maternally reinforced values in the early development. The Mars-Saturn square promises corroboration of this development dichotomy through frequent poor judgement, indecision, thrust and withdrawal, assertion and denial.

The aspect grid shows low aspect integration. The Mercury factor in Aries and in conjunction with the Moon, adjusting only perhaps to the mother's communication influence (Mercury quincunx to Neptune; Neptune in the XIIth, the communication third of the Xth), reinforces the ego needs of the Arian Moon within relationships. Mars ruling the VIIth and being square to Saturn suggests not only that these relationships to find ego recognition would be hot and cold, on and off, but also that a *lack* of resources would be felt from the parent symbolized by the IVth House, ruled by Saturn. With the Cancer-Capricorn polarity upon the parental axis and the lunar node conjunct the Ascendant, preparatory assignment of the mother to the Xth and the father to the IVth was reasonable.

The Sun-Moon blend, with the Sun in Taurus and the Moon in Aries, suggests flair and ego drive within a strong structure, the *expectation* of all that is needed for ego development. Especially with the Sun's position in the VIIIth House within such a powerful ego need complex, we can anticipate that others' needs are not easily or fully appreciated within relationships and that this oversight in development is also included within the Mars-Saturn square, linking the Vth (love-give), the VIIth (relationships), the VIII (other's resources and self-worth concerns), and the IVth (the tenth of the VIIth; the growth through fruitful relationships).

The stellium in the VIIIth focuses all the resources within the woman's cognitive structure of money/love resources: Uranus rules the Vth which holds Mars; the Sun rules the XIth; Venus rules the IInd; the stellium is in the VIIIth, centered around the Saturn which receives the powerful square from Mars. Through Mars and Saturn, the entire resource structure of self-worth dynamics is related to identity structures keyed by the angular Grand Cross. The information/perspective resources are keyed by Pluto and Venus in square, relating the IIIrd-IXth axis. The VIth-XIIth axis is not particularly under stress, but its influence is probably absorbed derivatively through the communication axis of the mother (placing her ascendant upon the client's Xth).

Midpoint pictures corroborate the overall preparation of analysis: the Sun is at the midpoint of Mercury/Saturn suggesting an early curtailment of learning and an eventual illumination of wisdom; Venus = Moon/Saturn, suggesting strong self-worth concerns within strategic ego ambitions, probably manifesting in inhibitions; Mars and Saturn relate to the midpoints of Venus/Uranus and node/Midheaven, suggesting excitability and withdrawal, the essence of the Mars-Saturn square, especially within romantic relationships and professional associations; Pluto squares the Sun/Moon midpoint, confirming the inner conflict of personal perspective symbolized within the parent of the Xth (probably the mother) and the generational background. All the preparatory analysis is probably summed up best by the Ascendant's position on the midpoint axis of Mars/Saturn, suggesting that advancement in life will procede with great difficulty because of conflicting pulls and pushes.

A timing key would be the Solar Arc projection of Neptune over the Ascendant, an early loss of identity consciousness at ages 7 to 8, with transiting Uranus one sign further on, close to transit of the Midheaven.

Analysis and Client Response—The woman now in her late thirties was quite late for her appointment. I had given her specific directions, but she had followed someone else's. She phoned, distraught and disoriented. Time adjustments for following appointments were made; the client arrived breathless. This little episode seemed to capture the essence of the Mars-Saturn square as it echoes throughout the horoscope and around the need fulfillment behaviors of the Moon in Aries.

The woman is lean and quite attractive, individualistically dressed and breezily charming (Moon = Jupiter/Ascendant). Yet, a sharp eye can feel pained loneliness held under the surface of cordiality. She has never married and lives alone.

It was very easy for me to explain the strong ego needs and how they are difficult for a woman in this society, especially as they press for fulfillment from a sociological, generational background like hers. The client gave full corroboration of this introductory presentation. I suggested that we had to talk about the development difficulties within the ego structure on several levels: relationships, self-worth awareness, and especially in relation to the influence of her mother.

With the mention of the word "mother", the client gave immediate, almost relieved confirmation: "Gosh, that's right! My mother doted on me, overprotected me for sure." I asked if there had been a major shift in the family structure when she was around 7 or 8 years old. "My parents separated then."

With the parents' separation, the client as a young girl was under the care of her mother and a sister thirteen years older than she. She was doted upon and over-protected to an extreme. Slovakian old-world concepts and Catholic regimen were put upon the young girl whose needs were fulfilled totally in terms of the mother's and sister's needs and prescriptions. "I was left to the strategies of women!"

The introduction of the sister into the analysis can be further corroboration of the prominent Pluto in the Xth and ruling the sibling IIIrd House. A close relationship with a brother came out later in the analysis, and perhaps this can be corroborated by the Jupiter interception rulership of the IIIrd, with Jupiter conjunct Uranus and Saturn and, as well, trine Neptune.

Checking the fantasy content explored by the woman in her childhood revealed a normal preoccupation with the adventure of travel, "for freedom and happiness of discovery on my own." The fantasies were not escapist, since the client's identity was doted upon and indulged, although within rigid structures not of her own making. The support rewards fanned the ego needs in the young organism; toeing the line to get the rewards was secure but suffocating to individual needs that would become articulated with age.

The fantasies revealed a hope for independent freedom.

Going further, the client revealed, "But I used to dream about a spider often; a spider attacking me." I asked who she thought the spider was, and the client replied, "My mother or my sister".

Through rich discussion, we agreed that the early environment completely fulfilled her needs on a superficial, non-individualistic level. She had not been recognized as an individual. She had not been challenged and guided to be herself as efficiently as possible. The father's absence from the home and the overpowering female domination made her feel important so long as she acquiesced to expectations. I suggested that that pattern was deeply entrenched within her and that now, still, *she expects that kind of attention from everyone she meets*. The client corroborated this deduction completely, adding "And I feel terribly torn." We agreed that the mother's excesses were for herself and not for the daughter; that the excesses were fulfilling on a superficial level but not at all fulfilling or helpful on an individualistic level. Individual freedom was longed for, but the developmental pattern had established that ego attention should be *expected* rather than earned in all relationships.

At age 18, the woman was still strongly under the female dominance of her home. College experience did little to break this influence. Part of her actually *enjoyed* the superficial security since the *other* part of her, wanting to fulfill individualistic needs for ego prominence, was unresourceful. The home environment had not built personal resourcefulness in terms of *individual* needs, so security of the mother's home still had value. The longer this situation endured, the harder it became for the woman to be free on her own and involved profitably and easily in relationships. At age 18, transiting Saturn crossed her fourth cusp as transiting Neptune opposed her Sun: "I didn't break away, but my dreams started to project me away from these household women."

Our discussion pursued the schooling years and the early professional experience as a teacher (which profession was abandoned because there was not enough personal recognition within it in terms of money).

A major time of development was suggested by a projection of the Ascendant by Solar Arc to opposition with the powerful but undeveloped Aries Moon, around the age of 26 or 27. At age 27, an extremely important romance ended. Her lover died; she left for a new environment. "My lover died. He had promised to help me figure things out. He understood my conflicts."

I asked if the lover had been like her father. (I was searching for the way the woman would work to balance the extreme maternal influence with the paternal guidance she never had in the home enviornment.) She replied, "Yes! He was very much like my father. He was 19 years older than I. I loved him so much; I told him that no one would ever be able to replace him. He died of a heart attack . . . just like my father."

A close relationship with a brother was introduced into our discussion. "When my brother went away to the service, I was robbed of another man."

The overbalance of the mother's and sister's influence had muted the woman's Arian Moon expression. The Libran Ascendant was particularly vulnerable to this superficial indulgence. The feminine imbalance of influence was exacerbated by the traumatic demise of her lover. Relationships became fearful, especially in the fleeting terms of love contacts within busy big cities, where she now lived and worked in various sales jobs (again the Pluto prominence as ruler of the IIIrd House and in the Xth, relating to others' values, the stellium in the VIIIth).

I suggested that there had to be an adjustment in her relationship expectancies. Insecurity and unresourcefulness had submitted her ego needs to vacillation, to bad judgement, to a waste of emotions, to a confused perspective (expansion of the Mars/Saturn analysis in the preparation notes). I submitted to her that one of the first principles to learn in making meaningful, balanced relationships would be to give others compliments, to respect the core concerns and value organizations in others (the obvious VIIIth House focus as well as the Sun-Moon blend potentials). She replied, "I have to try to remember that. I do think too much of myself." An instructive dramatization of this relationship process was shared with great effect; it will be presented in full in Part III of this book, "Remediation".

Comments—The client had to realize that at her age most hopes of motherhood were impractical (natal Pluto = Moon/Venus, "a deep desire for motherhood"). This was crucially important at the time of consultation which occurred one month after a miscarriage (SA Neptune square Pluto, transiting Mars conjunct Moon).

The client had to acknowledge that she was a professional woman (Mars sesquiquadrate Ascendant, Pluto sextile Ascendant, Sun sextile Midheaven, Mars sesquiquadrate Midheaven, Saturn semisquare Midheaven. The tremendous emphasis in the earth element, indices of sales, and the emphasis upon others' values all suggested real estate. With Solar Arc Pluto sesquiquadrate natal Mercury at the time of consultation, the client had just enrolled in a study course for her real estate license. At the conclusion of her study, Solar Arc Uranus would square her Ascendant and go on to conjoin her Midheaven four months later: her individuality would start anew and be fulfilled in ego terms through professional achievement. This professional status achievement would give security to identity concerns and allow secure self-worth exchange and balance within her relationships. Survival would finally give way to identity.

Conclusion—Within these four "regular" cases studied astrologically, it might by remarkable that there was no specific concern of getting married, of problems with children, of health concerns, of starting a business; there was no specific concern about selling a house or relocating, of so-called "secret enemies", of inheritance. This suggests that the stereotypical view of astrology as the "answer" to such specific concerns is invalid or that it is only occasional. Actually, such specific orientation of astrological analysis is rare as the point of primary focus in actual holistic analytical practice.

When a client comes to an astrologer for such specific help, the specific focus of the concern is only the tip of the iceberg. It is the focus of a concern that has emerged out of years of development and patterning of value judgement. Thorough inspection of status/identity, money/love, and information/perspective resources broadens the focus away from the specific decision or event and deeply into the whole-life development that supports personal judgement ability within the decision and the personal values given to any event. We know this easily from a moment's introspection about things that occur in everyday life: for example, a woman may be wrathful in her treatment of her children and feel there is a great problem with them, but that problem may be caused not by the children but by the woman's terrible insecurity in relation to her husband, to his own anxiety about his employment, etc. The children can become a scapegoat for other tensions. A man's dissatisfaction or underachievement on his job may not have anything to do with the job itself but be related to a legacy of dissonant parental prescriptions about what standard of life he should achieve for himself. This condition could be reinforced every time the families gather together at holiday season.

Every woman knows that overwork or emotional distress can affect her menstrual cycle. A menstrual difficulty does not necessarily suggest a gynecological problem. Every man knows that status tension of any kind can affect sexual need and alertness. Diminished sex drive and occasional impotency does not necessarily suggest a sexual problem, which all too easily can be erroneously transferred to dissatisfaction with the mate.

It is established fact that sicknesses can develop as more easily manageable areas for the focus of many, many other problems. It is established fact that our identities are covered over by vastly complex traffic patterns of behaviors taken on through developmental tension with vastly complex environmental prescriptions. At any given moment, it is extremely difficult for any of us to know who we really are. We confront this every day: we look at a television personality with whom we have logged many years of familiarity and we wonder, "what's he really like?"; we have a conversation of importance with someone, and we question, "what did she really say; what did he really mean by that?"

As all our environmental pressures work toward stereotypical personality development, the inner environment is progressively more and more ignored. The human being is all too easily left behind. A decision challenges or an event occurs, and we are all too easily all too often at a loss how really to respond in action or value judgement. The confusion stems from the clash between who we have become and who we really are.

Naturally, since astrologers are human beings so similar to their clients, this tension between the superficially more manageable and the profoundly more significant, between the stereotypically more comfortable and the individualistically more necessary, is within our astrology as well. What is our astrology really like? How real do we want our astrology to be? Should it leave the human being behind and completely espouse the messages of the environment? Should it ignore the environment and displace the human being to some transcendant spiritual plane? Or should it blend the structure of fate contained within environment and articulated through time with the press of free will organized by needs and expressed through living? —These questions define the differences in orientation between a "reading" and an "analysis".

In holisitc analysis, regardless of what the specific problem is in the client's reality, the full spectrum of developmental resources must be studied: the dynamics of relationship that issue from the Angular Grand Cross; the fortification of self-worth resources that issues from the Succedent Grand Cross; the clarification of perception that issues from the Cadent Grand Cross. All of this must serve to clarify the client's own reality in the individualistic terms that are all too easily obliterated by the accumulated environmental pressures within development. In holistic analysis, the astrologer illuminates and fortifies, guides and adjusts, aids evaluation and provides applause.

In these first case studies, we have only seen holistic analysis at work. The presentations do not yet include remediation measures. These will be developed in Part III of this book. Perhaps the several brief allusions to the ways of remediation in several of the cases appeared simplistic or superficial in relation to the textures of the various developmental problems. For example, in Case 4, the recommendation to the ego-stressed woman that giving others compliments would help balance relationship interaction. This remedial sharing was anything but simplistic or superficial. It was fully developed as we will see later in this book, dramatized very effectively. But its thrust was to balance the ego problems in terms of the relationship problems that were constantly problematic, to allow fulfilling resource exchange. This was the concern; *not* the job concern, the new profession, the loss of hope for a meaningful marriage, the fixation upon the lover who had died; *not* when a Prince Charming would arrive out of fantasy and into the real world. The concern was how to get along better and more fulfillingly with people *in terms of all the behavior routines and values she had gathered through environmental patterning*. If an astrologer had missed this point, analysis would have become a "reading", and the astrology would be worth as much as yesterday's newspaper or the isolated Nirvana goal soundlessly projected by an astrological measurement into the future.

The behavioral patterns developed in great specificity in chapter two were offered to the human awareness dimension of the astrologer rather than to the analytical dimension or client experience dimension. Rarely will a client exhibit natural behavior patterns directly to the astrologer; the client will usually be on his or her best behavior if the astrologer's dignity has earned it. But these behavior patterns linked to defensive attitudes, involving various degrees of aggression and withdrawal, exist individualistically in every human being in normal social interraction outside the astrologer's office. The astrologer has to be aware of the behavioral whole-form of life, infer the interconnection of behavioral resources, and seek them out in consultation discussion. In this way, the inner environment shared in the consultation is balanced with the outer environment shared in life.

Let us look at another case, the one that followed in sequence the cases presented earlier. A married couple in their 70's called for an appointment. The wife's birthtime was generally known; the husband's was not. They insisted on an appointment even though I suggested that analysis might not be astrologically complete because of the vague birth data. The consultation that took place relied almost entirely upon the message of the environment revealed by their births early in the first years of this century and by the general outline of their professional and social lives.

The wife had Sun-Saturn-Venus in close conjunction in Aries: tremendous ego drive and severity of purpose. This triple conjunction was opposed by a Moon definitely in Libra: the ego drive and purpose needed social reflection to establish itself. The Aries triple conjunction was squared by Neptune, which itself was opposed by Uranus. The entire profile was easily clarified: development of ego drive and purpose for a woman, who would have been going through puberty and early adolescence during the first World War, would have been very difficult. She would have sought out something of societal value in order to become individually important. She would have had to scramble to do so, since society then certainly did not devote itself to championing the individual female.

Our conversation together, with the wife alone, proceeded just this way, with these thoughts. She corroborated them completely. Her father had been a rigid Hungarian authority figure. She had indeed scrambled: she had become a nurse. "I was a very good nurse; I was given so much responsibility. It was at that hospital that I really was fulfilled."

The conjunction of Sun-Venus-Saturn in Aries fed into the Moon in Libra perfectly. The square with Neptune, which opposed Uranus, was also there and keyed my deductions further as she began to tell a little more of her life.

The warm, jolly, most attractive woman told how she married precipitously and was sorry for it, divorced, returned to nursing where again she was most fulfilled (environmental change, role change had not worked). While a nurse, she met her next husband, the one who waited in the next room for his consultation.

I asked, "Well, was that a good marriage; has it gone well all these years? What happened to nursing?" She hesitated to answer, but finally revealed that when they first met, her husband-to-be had told her flat out that he "could never satisfy a woman". She shared that their sex life over all the years had been poor. Her own needs were still alive, but there was nothing between them any more in this dimension. No children had been born of the union.

The woman had married him, with the curious warning ahead of time, thinking that she "could love him and care for him and bring him around." She transferred her nursing instincts into the socially necessary institution of marriage. Over the years, there had been much nursing of sick parents, in-laws, relations. In many ways, this couple's home was a nursing center with the wife fulfilling her ego needs in this way and relegating all other needs to fantasy (the Neptune square).

But, the amazing key to this oh-so-normal life drama was that her husband had had a significant military administrative career.

He had the Sun in Capricorn, the Moon in Leo, and Venus in
Scorpio. The wife corroborated all his bureaucratic strengths and
personal powers, which I began to see as overcompensatory defenses for some sexual problem. I inquired about his "swagger" or
arrogance, and she said how defined this was, how he embarrassed
her often in social gatherings and always shushed her up. Only
lately, she said, "has he been extremely attentive, caring. He's
trying to come around somehow, and that's the reason we're here
to see you!"

The husband's face had a frozen sternness, yet he spoke in
terms of grand understanding, eagerness for self-disclosure. I got
him to smile and laugh, and pointed out to him how much fun still
was inside him. Protecting the wife's confidences, I explored the
time he had met her, hoping for his willingness to volunteer the
sexual warning he had given her. He easily introduced the dimension, and we talked about it thoroughly. The so-called "problem"
was really endemic to the times of his early development: premature ejaculation under the fears of socio-sexual attitudes and an
enormous naiveté about sexual dynamics. His pride (Capricorn-
Leo) and his great sexual needs (Venus in Scorpio) buckled and
clashed within societal prescriptions. His early sex explorations
were always accompanied by fear, by sneak behavior, by speed, by
ignorance of sexual mechanics. Premature ejaculation emphasized
guilt. Guilt threatened to diminish status. The strong personality
took over and gained identity comfort *by taking status from the
self.* He warned his bride-to-be, therefore he couldn't be held at
fault! The problem simply was that he had warned her of a
problem when he did not really have one. He had a normal
concern. —And the years to follow were thus patterned. His
authority behaviors overcompensated for his presumed sexual
inadequacy. His wife adjusted, he endured, and the patterns
reigned supreme.

I pointed all this out to him as gracefully as I could, and
enormously to his credit he agreed with every point of the analysis. Moreover, he was eager to do something about it right then . . .
finally, in his mid 70's!

He had had two heart attacks, but his health at present was
fine with no residual damage from the attacks. He took medication that he stated had no side effects of any kind. He and his wife
walked for exercise and had a routine of reading and television
watching that was the same every day. They went on few trips
since he was "afraid to be away from the hospital". He had been

128

impotent for many years; they slept in twin beds and watched television in separate chairs. He knew his wife stilled longed for more, and he was deeply frustrated.

I asked his permission to improve his sexual information. He gladly agreed. By improving his information, we could adjust his perspective of the sexual concerns that had occupied his and his wife's lives. The benefits of improving these resources would spill over into their self-worth concerns; love would be freshly articulated. Then, status as husband and identity as a man, as a couple, would be illuminated. Life could mean much more to them.

The sexual information, supported by diagrams and humor, was based upon the distinction between intercourse (which was apparently impossible) and *intimacy* (which had never been understood).

Then, I spoke with the couple together, protecting the confidences of each. I worked the discussion to reinforce each person's resources in relation to the future life ahead for them. With humor and youthful glee, they resolved to push their twin beds together to encourage newly understood intimacy, to adjust the position of their television set so that they could sit together on a sofa, to share some wine and candlelight often, to touch each other more often. They resolved to explore the travel dreams they had had to tour Europe. We searched out guided tours especially designed for people of their age. The enthusiasm climaxed when we all realized that, if fear of dying from a heart attack were the question, experiencing it in Paris would be more fun than experiencing it in a small town in Virginia! The laughter was thrilling. And perhaps the greatest endorsements of our time of sharing together came when the husband, with a full smile, said, "My doctor would agree with you one-hundred percent", and then when he hugged his wife warmly and invited her out to lunch.

This couple appreciated themselves in that moment. They had penetrated the routines that had encased them for so many, many years. It was beautiful to see free will unlock the routinized structure of fate. They could satisfy eachother.

Personally, I was almost thankful that the horoscope support of their situation had been minimal. I had worked with human beings challenged by normal environmental circumstances, which had been exacerbated by individual vulnerabilities. Experience told me that an incredible number of developmental measurements in their lifetime astrological profile would have failed to manifest. The short-circuits had been many. If measurements alone had been applied to their lives, their lives would have been confined by the stereotypical essence established by the measurements. With minimal astrological frameworks, the human drama had become all the more dramatically clear. The message of the environment had been clearly anticipated, assessed, illuminated, and adjusted.

Part Two:
AWARENESS
OF ANXIETY

Chapter Four
OBSERVATIONS

Who among us. has not felt anxiety? We talk alarmingly easily about the atomic threat to the entire world, how the push of a button could wipe out an existence that has taken billions of years to develop. We are aware of dread and anxiety as potential concomitants of everything we do or think. Anxiety is inexorably linked to our concepts of survival, collectively and individually. At different levels in different eras, it has always been so.

Yet, throughout the massive eleven volumes of *The Story of Civilization* by Will and Ariel Durant, the subject of anxiety does not appear at all in the index. Throughout the eight volumes of the Collier Macmillan *Encyclopedia of Philosophy*, the subject of anxiety is only keyed to three short paragraphs and is treated, as it always had been, within the aegis of religion and ethics. Interestingly, it was not until Sigmund Freud's work reached the minds of the world that anxiety really captured the analytical attention of social theorists.

Rarely when we feel anxious do we understand why. Anxiety has always been basically irrational. Throughout history, anything that was not rational was not tenable: philosophers were condemned, religions were martyred, visionaries were burned at the stake. Human beings repressed anxiety, kept silent about it, or discharged it through religious faith. Rational thought continuously gained refinement as human beings sought to master the outer environment. The ages of discovery could not relate to the *irration-ality* of anxiety. It was not until the inner environment of human beings was acknowledged that anxiety was studied.

Just as psychology existed before the word was coined, so anxiety existed before it was formally appreciated. Anxiety was chiefly transmuted into emotions and fears. The rationalist philosophies of the seventeenth century, having developed during the Renaissance, stated that man could control emotions and manage fears through reason. Still today, when someone complains of feelings of anxiety, the cure-all is thought to be reasonable explanation, logical study, and practical control. We say, "Be reasonable; get control of yourself!"

But reason is the stuff of the external environment: it measures substantive alternatives, objective choice. Reason can support confidence to continue life in spite of anxiety, but it can not dispel anxiety altogether. For example, within the past hour, I received a telephone call from a client suffering strong anxiety. Her husband has accepted a tremendous job opportunity that will make their retirement plans golden in a few years. The couple must relocate. The wife resists relocation because she fears many readjustment problems, and she is using her knowledge of astrology to support her fears. She told me she now thinks continuously about suicide. In the face of marvelous opportunity and adventure, this fine woman is suffering acute anxiety. —Her husband, also my client, describes his wife as "paranoid".

No amount or technique of astrology or reason can dispel the anxiety groomed throughout the woman's lifetime. The help I offered to her was to clarify one essential point, the point of focus of this discussion of anxiety: *it is fighting the battle of life through anxiety that keeps human beings alive.* Reason builds confidence to endure; enduring leads personality to growth.

Anxiety is thought by many theorists to be innate. The newborn greets the world with apprehension about its survival. This apprehension is anxiety, and it becomes differentiated in myriad specific fears as life goes on. The specified fears are managed within the growth process, and anxiety moves on to define further fears. As a birth phenomenon, anxiety and its individual levels must be visible within the natal horoscope.

Anxiety exists within the inner environment to alert our behavioral faculties to service our needs. *It is the state of potential.*

I would submit that the heart is anxious between beats: at rest, there is potential and awareness of the body's needs. Will it beat again or will it not? *The anxiety demands performance.*

The brilliant psychoanalyst, Rollo May, in his *The Meaning of Anxiety*, says, "Anxiety is essential to the human condition ... The confrontation with anxiety can relieve us from boredom, sharpen our sensitivity, and assure the presence of the tension that is necessary to preserve human existence."[9]

May sees anxiety as the reaction to the "threat to any pattern which the individual has developed upon which he feels his safety to depend." Basically then, anxiety is how we handle stress. Here we see the clear awareness opposition between the inner environment and the outer environment: inner anxiety meets external stress; inner potentials meet external stimuli. The awareness of anxiety formulates within the mind. The mind triggers resources for survival and growth. The horoscope patterns of identity become defined.

Anxiety is the state of potential. It is registered and personalized within the mind. The Grand Cross of Cadent Houses will key the information/perspective resources in relation to outer

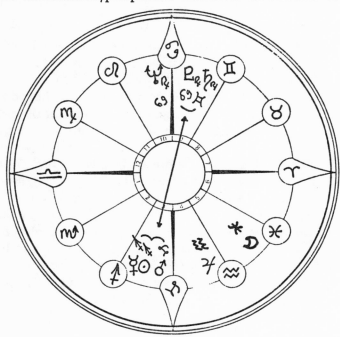

environmental stress, and the planetary symbols will suggest a profile of inner environmental needs and reaction to developmental tension.

In the partial horoscope (page 135), we see anxiety clearly indicated. The individual pattern of needs and behavioral faculties is clearly tied to developmental stress in terms of information/perspective resources. The triple conjunction of Mercury-Sun-Mars opposes the strong conjunction of Pluto and Saturn, both of which are retrograde. This mighty opposition clearly establishes the IIIrd-IXth axis as the dominant spine of the horoscope. Mercury rules the IXth and the XIIth, and Neptune retrograde rules the remaining area of the Cadent Grand Cross, the Piscean VIth. Neptune makes an almost precise quincunx to the Sun (enormous adjustment between the life energy core and the capacity for creative visualization). The Piscean Moon is weakly aspected, i.e., unanchored within its expansive needs to absorb and feel. Jupiter, ruler of the IIIrd, makes a sesquiquadrate to Pluto. Anxiety is extremely strong at all times. Perception and activation of information/perspective resources are always highly developmentally charged in the cognitive grounding within the early homelife, with the parent of the IVth in particular, since Saturn is retrograde, opposes the Sun-Mercury-Mars conjunction, and rules the Capricorn IVth. Naturally, IInd House concerns of self-worth are keyed by Pluto's signification of the IInd and the Sun's signification of the XIth. The analysis is immediately expanded holistically. —This horoscope fragment belongs to the woman who telephoned a short while ago, earnestly trying to enjoy the freedom of opportunity within the embrace of lifelong anxiety, as transiting Pluto challenges with new life perspective in its passage across her Ascendant.

We can refer back for a moment to Case 3 (page 109), the young woman of Lebanese background with perceptual anxiety about relationships with her parents. Again, we saw the Cadent Grand Cross of information/perspective resources dramatically keyed within horoscopic analysis, with Mercury highly charged. This young woman has so many blessings. Everything in her life is going well. She is on the threshold of grand professional opportunity. Her keen intelligence accepts reason superbly, but her anxiety developed throughout life constantly creates apprehension . . . and potential.

Ever so naturally, as we have seen in Part I of this book, developmental tension with the information/perspective resources can spill over into the other zones of money/love and status/identity. Anxiety races through the mind to relate itself meaningfully to some specific resource. Anxiety works to focus itself into something specifically more manageable. Anxiety searches to articulate apprehension in terms of a specific fear. This does not dispel anxiety; it is always there at different levels for different individuals. But it does stir the system to do something about the challenges of growth. *Anxiety is a fuel.*

When we are aware of anxiety, our body does things. Random movements occur that in themselves signal an inner state of apprehension. The body is eager to get moving, to become active, to express potential, to protect being. For example, a performer before an audition, a father in a maternity ward waiting room, anyone before an important job interview, making a speech, initiating contact for an important meeting—all will evidence some bodily function in relation to the anxiety that is highly keyed in relation to the challenge and/or opportunity at hand. The Self is "on the line", so to speak. Apprehension surfaces. We pace the floor, our bladders work overtime, we perspire. When we wring our hands— even to pray or applaud—we may be covering reflexology (accupressure) points in the hands to stimulate bodily resources into reliable equilibrium. We can call the bodily activity adrenaline, the stimulant of energy associated with Mars. Our bodies are highly alert to take action to protect the patterns of identity.

In our anxious readiness, we are continually caught in dilemma: we want desperately to preserve the security of the status quo, the samenesses we have worked for in our lifelong interaction with the external environment; and we want to create change in order to develop personality, to fulfill more of our needs. We fear a step backward to gain a step forward. With the Moon in Aries, for example, registering a reigning need to put the self forward at any opportunity, the person may take any step at all to fulfill identity needs, registering a high degree of self-motivation. Anxiety might have a hair trigger to meet stress swiftly. With the Moon in Taurus, registering a reigning need to preserve the status quo, the person may shy away from taking that step. Anxiety might be routinely held back in temperamental frustration. With the Moon

138

in Gemini, registering a reigning need to diversify, the person may take several steps at once, breaking down the focus of anxiety and scattering energy potentials.

The modality of the Moon sign, then, can suggest the mode through which we articulate awareness of anxiety. This registration can apply to the modalities of any planet in relation to the needs symbolized by the planet.

The element of the Moon sign can suggest the quality of approach within articulation of anxiety awareness. The Moon in Cancer can suggest that the reigning need for emotional security will be paramount in the person's awareness of anxiety management. The person will need to seek emotional security first and most swiftly within anxiety. With the Moon in Leo, the fixed assumption of personal importance will be sorely tested in its natural inflexibility when articulating anxiety. The Moon in Virgo will suggest a perceptive scattering of idealizations alerted within anxiety management, potentially registering even more anxiety.

In Case 1 (page 91), the Aries Moon was left behind in development. The needs were sorely muted. Repression within the Earth Grand Trine dominated. Anxiety was managed by practical self-sufficiency rather than ego assertion.

In Case 2 (page 101), the Libra Moon promised a headlong need to gain identity clarification through social reflection, but the repression of this energy within development registered clearly throughout the rigid T-Square patterns. The needs within anxiety were discharged through fantasy, through the Moon's conjunction with Neptune within the Ascendant.

The young woman in Case 3 (page 109) has a Sagittarius Moon, suggesting a need to have her own perceptions and opinions respected, to risk adventure to establish self. But here again, as is normal, developmental tensions work to refine personal resources. Eventually, anxiety *will* clarify identity, as is normal, and the VIIth House Moon will go on to further challenges, more reinforced and with anxiety fueling even further development.

In Case 4 (page 116), the Aries Moon must work to readjust ego values against a backdrop of developmental pressure within the early home. The anxiety registered here is to create alteration of value structures within relationships.

The anxiety concern for the woman facing relocation with her husband is emphasized not only by her tense pattern of information/perspective resources but, as well, by the needs of her Pisces Moon, to filter the truths of emotions through private suffering, to give form to feelings through experience.

With the Moon in Scorpio, the fixity of will and purpose, if it emerges through privacy, will be challenged dramatically by anxiety. The piping of the fuel may take potentials deeply underground before surfacing for growth.

In Capricorn, the reigning need to assume responsibility and administer resources may welcome anxiety, to give headlong impetus to strategic development.

In Aquarius, the reigning need to be humanitarian and innovative may assimilate anxiety into real personal power or into vacuous spirituality or diffused eccentricity.

The steps individuals take within life development are fueled by anxiety about survival and growth. The Sun-Moon blend registers the life energy core and reigning need of every human organism. The personality establishes its way of managing anxiety as it meets stress from the environment. The structures of interaction with the environment trigger personal resources in exchange with others, and personality develops. The accumulated development of all human beings defines an era: its religion, its science, its art, its politics, its history. Rollo May makes the same observation: "Culture is the product of man's conquest of anxiety in that culture represents man's progressive making of his environment adequate to himself, and himself adequate to his environment."[10]

We must remember that anxiety is not negative. Nor is it positive. Anxiety is literally the state of being, the means of development, the defense of identity. Awareness of anxiety arouses behavioral defenses within challenge and alerts suspicion within opportunity. Anxiety relieves complacency in order to create growth. Anxiety provides the tension for growth. When we raise our voices in command to someone—our child, colleague, or someone working for us—we project personal anxiety exasperatedly to that someone in order to get the same motivational drive alerted within the other person. We say, "Get with it! Get moving! Wake up!" Anxiety is catalyst for development, individually and in relationships.

The goal of course is personal development, *safe* personal development. Development represents the essence of personal freedom. The dilemma we face as we take each developmental step between sameness and change is the arena for anxiety awareness. The great Danish philosopher Søren Kierkegaard, frequently considered the first important existentialist thinker, phrased this concept perfectly: "Anxiety is the dizziness of freedom."

Anxiety and the Sense of Sacrifice

History records fully the terror with which our Old World ancestors experienced eclipse phenomena. The sun god was robbed of its light, or the sun god took its light away from the observers on earth below. Life and light were threatened, were sacrificed. Legends grew to explain the phenomena. The loss of light, literally and symbolically, has always been associated with anxiety.

Interestingly, to the Mesoamericans in the western hemisphere eclipses were not spectacles of terror. The Mesoamericans had amassed extremely sophisticated astronomical measurements of the world. They viewed eclipses as a way to check further on their measurements that dynamically interrelated the returns of all the planets to certain positions. The rational reason of their measurements supported their confidence and hope that life would continue. *Their* anxieties still existed but were handled differently: the Aztecs, for example, believed that the earth had been through four cataclysmic periods; they were the "Sons of the Sun", nourished directly and metaphysically by the sun; in turn, the sun needed the sacrifice of human blood for its nourishment. The hearts of victims by the thousands were ripped out to stave off cosmic disaster.

There are two thoughts here important to our discussion: first, the Sun represents the life force. Constant threat to it is manifested in the perpetuity of anxiety, and the threat/anxiety relationship manifests at different levels of awareness dependent upon external circumstance and individual proclivity. Second, to have confidence to grow, life behavior must be in touch with the Sun through patterns of interaction between inner needs and outer expectations. Within the horoscope, anxiety will be keenly alerted by developmentally tense aspects to the Sun most importantly and in varying degrees by aspects to all other planet/need symbolisms.

We can note easily that all the case study horoscopes in Chapter Three have sharply aspected Suns. The woman with acute anxiety in the face of relocation challenge has a Sun in strong tension as well.

In our contact with the Sun, in our involvement with life, we constantly meet three major experiences that trigger anxiety and the resources to reestablish security. First, there is the experience of *separation*: we feel that we have been taken off the path of the Sun in its development within our life; we feel that some life energy has been taken away. When our parents are prematurely taken from us, we are alone. We must fend for ourselves. Some resources are underdeveloped. We experience an anxiety that pushes us to transcend the lack we feel. When we lose a job identification, when we lose an opportunity, when we are denied what we need, we experience an anxiety that stimulates adjustment to a new security.

The psychologist Otto Rank viewed anxiety in terms of individuation through *necessary* separation. Each separation increases the opportunity for individual autonomy. In this light, we can say with validity that our needs for our parents are two-fold: for nurturance and eventually for contrast. We can understand that losing a job gives us the opportunity to do something different or better. We can appreciate that partners in a marriage can affect separation simply because they have outgrown each other, i.e., one's individuation has outdistanced the other's.

Rank's views were based greatly upon the separation experienced within the birth trauma. He termed the anxiety base of the newborn "the fear in the face of life." Rank established anxiety before the newborn meets the world.

Anxiety then is obviously contained within the threat of separation. We feel anxiety when we are off the track. Conversely, when we are "on the track", we feel anxious that we may be diverted. Anxiety about separations is perpetually within the self-preservation dynamics that build growth in life. In the heavens, we have instinctive anxiety about being separated from the sun. In our lives, we have instinctive anxiety about being separated from what we need for life fulfillment. In our horoscopes, patterns of anxiety are shown through the heavens and throughout our lives as the planetary symbols reflect the Sun's light and relate developmentally to each other.

The anxiety of separation implies that we feel something important to us will be sacrificed. We will have to give something up, something that is part of who we are. We have difficulty appreciating objectively that we can become more through adjustment to momentary lack. The Mesoamericans had faith in their objective measurements. They knew during an eclipse of the sun that *the sun would return*.

Fascinatingly, under the threat of separation, we instinctively bargain with life. The prayers of children—and adults—trade off values. Something will be sacrificed if something else will be assured. We feel more noble when we have sacrificed something; for a moment or a lifetime, we feel that freedom of some kind is due to us in return for the sacrifice we have made. *The sense of personal sacrifice works to preclude external denial.* The Mesoamericans had no anxiety about the sun's return since they had nourished the sun god with blood sacrifice.

A second major area of life experience that triggers anxiety and the resources to reestablish security is *disapproval*: when a light source in our life is extinguished, we feel the anxiety of disapproval; we no longer can reflect the light that has warmed or illuminated us. When a parent turns off the roomlight for a child to go to sleep, he or she must accompany the action with some statement to deter the rise of anxiety within the child. The threat of disapproval accompanying being left alone in the dark must be avoided. Similarly, as loved ones reflect each other's light, so criticisms one to the other can register as painful disapproval, arousing the most poignant anxiety. Disapproval triggers the anxiety of not being loved.

The psychologist Harry Stack Sullivan studied anxiety within interpersonal relationships. As Rank did, he too set the beginning of anxiety within the arena of the infant's earliest experience of the world. The infant apprehends the potential disapproval of the persons most significant to its growing interpersonal world of experience. Sullivan maintains that personality develops out of the need to distinguish which behaviors will gain support and reward and which behaviors will not. Security within the early homelife is the natural goal for the infant, and maintenance of the behavioral process for security is the goal of anxiety throughout life development. Here we see dramatically the prescriptions of the external environment forming the behavioral patterns issuing from the inner environment.

Sullivan's ideas are that "the self is formed to protect us from anxiety." Whatever tendencies in behavior attract *dis*approval are kept out of awareness as much as possible. This is the phenomenon of repression, a classic defense mechanism. Through repression to gain approval, much individuality is sacrificed.

Our Old World ancestors, experiencing an eclipse, projected upon the sun god disapproval of themselves. Punishment was symbolized by the withdrawal of light. Irrational anxiety dictated sacrifices to be made in terms of religious faith, overthrow of a monarch, heeding a prophet, surrendering to an invading horde. Adjustment had to be made to make permanent the return of light.

All of us constantly check behavior patterns in order to avoid the disapproval of others. Anxiety keeps the checking process alert. Criticism is most easily interpreted as a withdrawal of light, of love. Repression occurs, and the light of the individual Sun, the potentials within life-sustaining anxiety are muted in uneasiness, unnaturalness, or agony. *Individuated growth is sacrificed through repression as outer prescriptions are internalized.*

The third major area of life experience that triggers anxiety is a perceived threat to being. This threat is to personal safety, of course, but it is also the threat to psychodynamic awareness of identity.

The theologian Paul Tillich, in his *Courage to Be*, cites the anxieties of death, meaninglessness, and guilt as the great concerns of modern man. We must note that the anxieties we feel about death are not necessarily those of life termination. In the horoscope, the IVth House is abbreviated "the end of the matter", but it is also the House of new beginnings, successive points of new focus and initiation on the spiral of Houses along an axis of time. Constantly, we experience ends and new beginnings, and constantly we experience anxiety about every step of life involved with growth through these deaths and new beginnings. The reality situation may be dramatically emphasized by actual deaths as in Case 1 in Chapter Three, or in the parental separation and imbalance of attention as in Case 4, or in the relocation situation mentioned earlier in this chapter. The concept of death at any level of meaning presupposes separation. This area of anxiety is definitely contained within the Angular Grand Cross concerns of status/identity.

Anxieties about meaninglessness rest upon the concept of worth, in terms of money and/or love, the Succedent Grand Cross of Houses. Meaninglessness is closely related to the anxiety of disapproval. Support and reward are desperately needed always to give meaning to life. The apprehension of possible disapproval can force repression and uneasy maintenance of the status quo. Case 2 in Chapter Three, the young woman in inactive routine and immature fantasy, tired of environmental rejection, illustrates the anxiety of meaninglessness perfectly.

In my earlier works, I have suggested that the concept of guilt can be productively understood in terms of feeling that we have not done our best to help others fulfill *their* needs or their prescriptions upon us. Guilt can not exist without relationship to something, to some person, belief, or value. This premise recognizes not only the vital importance of relationships and resource exchange within life but also one's individual perception of those relationships' dynamics. The concept of guilt is tied tightly to perception, to awareness of personal perspective within relationships of many kinds. To alleviate guilt, we sacrifice self through reparation.

Apprehension of separations or deaths of many kinds in change of status and growth of identity; apprehension of disapproval or meaninglessness as a result of a loss of worth awareness; and apprehension of guilt within perception of relationships comprise all our considerations developed so far within the topography of the horoscope. Our concept of the holistic spill over of resource concerns in support of personality growth applies to the concept of anxiety as well: anxiety is omnipresent within life and within the horoscope and keys the dynamic behavioral patterns that sustain individual life. Anxiety is a defense against non-being, against non-fulfillment.

Christianity is a clear example of the entire process: the concept of separation by death to life in heaven promises status reward for identity conversion; the concept of sin and rewarding forgiveness clarifies love and worth relationship to the Godlight; the concept of guilt encourages perception of relationships within the model prescriptions established by the sacrificed Son of God.

Constantly within every life, anxiety is the state of being, the measure of potential, and the defense against extinction. It is the press and support of earth, the dizziness of the freely blowing winds, and the sacrifice of leaves to the seasons of time that encourage every flower to reach for the sun.

Anxiety Meets Environment

The inner state of all human beings is anxiety to defend the state of being. The anxiety becomes specified frequently in terms of manageable fears. The mind directs the application of resources to defend identity and create growth. Anxiety through the mind meets the stress of the outer environment. The inner environment rallies to meet outer demands. The horoscope shows dramatically the meeting between inner environmental needs and resources and our outer environmental prescriptions. This is the awareness of anxiety meeting the message of the environment.

The theologian Reinhold Niebuhr theorized that human beings have their personal anxieties alerted by criticising themselves and their world. Human beings recognize personal limitations (lack of resources) within the threat of a brief existence in a troubled world. In defense, they imagine a life infinitely better than what actually is. —Here we see keen awareness of personal perspective within the world, symbolized astrologically by Pluto. Here we see the idealization potentials of fantasy that we know is symbolized astrologically by Neptune.

Niebuhr theologically states that anxiety can lead to sin, but that this can be averted by trusting ourselves to God's forgiving love and ultimate power. This is the phenomenon of religious revival, of being "saved" and "born again". It is a dedication of personal perspective to God; it is a sacrifice of the self-realization theme born in the Renaissance for the salvation theme championed so rigorously in the Middle Ages. The opposite path away from "sin", from unrequited anxiety, is the pretense of having power, knowledge, or special compensation from God. Niebuhr's middle ground is our tendency to dull awareness of anxiety with charade, sensuality, alcohol, drugs. —Again, it is easy to see here the interplay of Pluto and Neptune, for a better or worse condition in the struggle between anxiety and environment. Perhaps it is emphasized now in the late seventies as Pluto has moved within the orbit of Neptune, perhaps to signal a new generational perspective, a *spiritual* society.

146

This basically similar view can be studied from an entirely different viewpoint through the work of Haridas Chaudhuri, a disciple of Sri Aurobindo, the renowned Indian spiritual teacher. Chaudhuri also sees the root cause of anxiety as the conflict between individual behavior and social norm. Some of us try to solve the conflict by unthinking conformity, others by open rebellion (acquiescence and change, respectively). His summation is an echo of our discussion to this point: "The more the person succeeds in engineering his life accordingly, the more anxiety is transmuted from a corrosive force into a stimulating factor. That which threatens mental equilibrium becomes an ingredient of mental growth."[11]

Astrologically the House position of Pluto in a horoscope can key us immediately to the dynamic of personal anxiety perspective in the face of environmental stress. It can alert us to the life engineering that must take place to gain fleeting moments of choice during life development.

Since its discovery on the night of 18 February 1930 in Flagstaff, Arizona,[12] Pluto has been given symbolic significance in terms of great force and reference to the masses. Although these symbolic dimensions work well in mundane astrology, they have been cumbersome in analytical application to individual horoscopes. In my earlier works, I have suggested that Pluto is the symbol of *personal perspective*. The concept of "force" is translated into the adverbial dimension of the amount of activity and the intensity of the application of personal resources that manifest to establish personal perspective within the prescriptions of the world, of the "masses" if you will. Specifically within the analysis frame of holistic astrology, Pluto symbolizes the personal efforts *to accumulate, maintain, and defend personal perspective*. These efforts are the inner anxiety responses to the outer stress demands. Wherever in the wheel of Houses within the horoscope Pluto is found, the person will necessarily have to work hard to accumulate, maintain, and defend personal resources. The concerns of the House tenanted by Pluto will be the referential dimensions of this work to establish personal perspective.

Pluto within the Ascendant establishes strong self-awareness. Anxiety about status and identity works to establish personal perspective firmly, powerfully projected to accumulate, maintain, and defend personality resources. The person is keenly aware of personal position within interpersonal relationships. The exchange of resources for personal status/identity is vitally important to accumulate dimensions of self-awareness. This status/identity profile must be maintained through all relationships and defended by all possible resources.

With Pluto positioned in the IInd House, the accentuation of personal perspective is obviously in terms of money/love, in terms of material worth and psychodynamic awareness of self-worth. Stress from the outer environment is rapidly assimilated mainly in these terms. Behavioral resources are pressed to accumulate, maintain, and defend symbols and substance of material or emotional security. The anxiety for development lives within the motivating question, "How valuable am I?"

In the IIIrd House, Pluto suggests that personal perspective is tied up with information exchange, with building self-awareness through matching personal opinions and information with others. "Where do I stand?" is the question, and the answer to it clarifies status/identity as the resources here spill over into the Angular Grand Cross. Depending upon the aspect configuration, of course, this conceptual orientation of personal perspective can range from acquiescent and conforming opinionation to progressive and courageous thrust.

As anxiety meets environmental stress, overall personal resources are challenged. As resources within interpersonal exchange reach a critical point, personal perspective—being—can be threatened. Often, then, the House position symbolism of Pluto manifests defensively in its most obvious form. The Ascendant Pluto can suggest that a threat will be absorbed and then that the person will attack the challenge, using all resources available; the IInd House Pluto person can face extreme anxiety about personal worth and become mired in painful self-pity for quite some time or project efforts into reconstruction schemes of significant material scope; the IIIrd House Pluto person will most often manifest confusion and nervousness before gathering new and objective views about personal perspective. Defensively, in any analysis of personal perspective tension, *we can always expect an implosion before an explosion,* a momentary withdrawal of varying lengths of time before an assertion. This is the process that "gets the act together", that organizes the needs of the inner environment before meeting the stressful prescriptions of the outer environment. This is the process that harnesses the potentials of anxiety.

With Pluto positioned in the IVth House, personal perspective is very likely to be tied to early home environment concerns. Status/identity perspective may need to catch up with unfulfilled dimensions of that early time. Under pressure, there may be a super-sensitive "chip on the shoulder" and, thus, a perpetuation of defensive patterns started very early in development, or an over-compensatory self-assertion of personal authority as if the present status is more important than the accumulated development. —Cases 1 and 3 (pages 91 and 109) in Chapter Three are very good examples of the IVth House Pluto's anchor of personal perspective to early home development concerns. The early position must be clarified as resources through life are accumulated and maintained. The process to do so is constantly defended in many ways.

Pluto within the Vth House can focus personal perspective within the arena of the emotions, within the many dimensions of giving love. The sharing of self-awareness can be covered over by complex insecurities or overextended through an experimental excess. Learning the parameters for giving love can become extremely important. How love is offered to the person can be a crucial assessment of personal perspective. Resources are accumulated, maintained, and defended to establish value of love received and to allow secure freedom in the love given.

In the VIth House, Pluto relates personal perspective to cooperation dynamics, usually in work-service situations. During cooperative ventures, personal opinions are tested and measured within interpersonal relationships. This will be important in establishing and maintaining personal self-awareness. The individual can ally himself or herself with the larger group, the Labor Union, the social clique, the proletariat. Under pressure, the person with Pluto in the VIth may feel self-awareness as "underdog" and then champion the underdog in order to reestablish strength within personal perspective broadened through the concerns of others who are similar. There may be the very real manifestation of illnesses to discharge anxiety through more manageable symptoms.

Throughout the horoscope, when keying upon the House position of Pluto, we must be aware also of the House Pluto rules. Holistically, we have seen dramatically how significator networks dynamically involve tenancy and rulership to relate inner needs and external concerns. From a key such as Pluto, we start to branch out awareness holistically into the complex horoscopic environment. Anxiety about personal perspective is grounded within a particular House concern and is immediately related to another House as well.

For example, in Case 1 (page 91), Pluto in the IVth keyed unfulfilled roots within early homelife environmental concerns. This was obvious and was concretely corroborated immediately in analysis. This Pluto in Leo in the IVth rules Scorpio on the VIIth. The early homelife concerns must be related to relationships in general. There is very little doubt about it, and it is just that simple to see. In Case 3 (page 109), Pluto again in the IVth again ruled the Scorpio VIIth, and again the homelife concerns were the base for anxiety projection within relationships.

If Pluto is in the Ascendant, in Cancer, for example, it will most often rule Scorpio on the Vth. The potentially powerful projection of self-awareness is enormously reinforced in terms of the dynamics of giving love, giving of the self, projecting the personal perspective speculatively for gain. If, because of interception, this Ascendant Pluto rules the IVth, projection of personal perspective will be linked in terms of resources and development within the early home environment. Of course, all of this is clarified by the aspect pattern revealed within the entire horoscopic environment.

We can generalize the anticipation that Pluto in Cancer will ordinarily relate by trine to Scorpio on the complementary House being considered. Pluto in Cancer has the essence of cardinality within its symbolism of personal perspective, identifying it strongly with the survival generation, as we have seen. The trine relationship to the Scorpio House will bring in supportive (trine) resources for that survival. The aspect network involving Pluto within the entire horoscopic environment will refine the interrelationship of these resource zones for accumulating, maintaining, and defending personal perspective.

We can generalize that, if an interception relates Pluto in Cancer to a Scorpio *House* of the same angular, succedent, or cadent mode, an extra dimension of developmental tension can be anticipated with regard to the growing holistic profile of personal perspective resources. With Pluto in Leo, signifying the identity society, we most often will have the tenancy and rulership of

Pluto relating two Houses of such same mode. The square relationship will establish the possibility and probability of keen developmental tension between the two Houses, as related resources working to develop personal perspective throughout life. If the two referent Houses relate by square, we are quickly alerted to the dynamics we have discussed within the Angular, Succedent, and Cadent Grand Crosses.

When Pluto was in Gemini from mid 1884 through 1913, symbolizing the resourceful society, the work and inventiveness of the industrial revolution, Pluto by House position usually related to Scorpio House resources by quincunx, by adjustment. The Ascendant Pluto in Gemini would relate to Scorpio on the VIth, allying personal power projection with work-service resources; money/love concerns of the IInd would relate to relationship resources in the VIIth; the IIIrd House concept of personal "salesmanship", if you will, would relate in quincunx adjustment dynamic to the VIIIth House, others' values. With the IIIrd House closely linked to the Gemini essence, we can feel that this position of Pluto typifies the era of expansion, growth, and the birth of ideas.

Similarly, with Pluto in the sign of Virgo 1957 to 1971, the House relationship with the Scorpio House will usually be a sextile, suggesting again a supportive link between resources. As an echo of a trine, the sextile would link the Ascendant and the IIIrd, the IInd and the IVth, the IIIrd and the Vth, the IVth and the VIth, the Vth and the VIIth, the VIth and the VIIIth, etc. We can feel the tensions of the identity society (Pluto in Leo) relaxing, the seed taking hold, as the next generation is born into a changing world.

The symbolic signal of Pluto is accelerating. (Please recall page 59.) Pluto in Libra suggests personal perspective of a generation that has a twelfth House dynamic to the Scorpio zone: perhaps a full awareness of social reform possibilities, especially through resurrection of ancient wisdoms, as Pluto reaches for its own sign. —Pluto, as symbol of personal perspective, very easily extends from the personal orientation of an individual within world society to a profile of that very society itself. And this is the focus of personal anxiety as the inner environment meets the outer environment.

With Pluto in the VIIth House, personal perspective relies upon social reflection. Relationships become the arena for clarifying personal perspective. Tremendous public enthusiasm and public projection are possible, or pervasive difficulties with making productive relationships. Under developmental pressures, the person with a VIIth House Pluto can acquiesce bitterly to the public projections of a mate, for example, or fight a struggle for personal independence that can lead to eccentricity and discord. Pluto in the VIIth in Cancer will relate by trine to Scorpio on the XIth, easing greatly the accumulation and maintenance of relationships to establish personal perspective. Pluto in the VIIth in Leo will most often be in square House relationship with Scorpio on the Midheaven, adding strong developmental tension to establishing identity within society through job position. Tensions can occur within the resources of personal status/identity as they relate to early homelife environment and recognition of the public establishment. Time and time again, we see this conflict among those born with Saturn conjunct Pluto with both positioned in the VIIth House.

Pluto in the VIIIth House links personal perspective with a deep preoccupation with the values of others. The self-worth axis IInd-VIIIth is highly charged. Introspection ordinarily is deep and provides access to the individual's real worth awareness. The question is "How valuable am I in relation to others?" From the Cancer Pluto, the related resources are usually Scorpio on the XIIth. From the Leo Pluto, the keen awareness of self-worth concerns is sharply related to the XIth, another arm of the money/love Succedent Grand Cross. The introspective demands of Pluto in the VIIIth uncannily often lead to the study of the occult, of astrology, the unconscious, and, under pressure, to the growth available through psychotherapy.

Pluto in the IXth accentuates the information Grand Cross once again. Personal opinion is allied with the communication of the society (the third of the VIIth). Personal perspective is tied to the precepts of the masses. Under keen pressure in development, the person with Pluto in the IXth can lose autonomy by merging with societal precepts or, under pressure, assert autonomy powerfully by proclaiming personal authority through all-knowing opinionation. Obviously, the relationship between the IXth House

Pluto and the XIIth House or Ascendant by rulership suggests reliably the degree of overt opinion expression, from held-in nervous preoccupation to driving personal projection, respectively. —The chart fragment on page 135, the woman facing relocation with deep anxiety, shows the kind of network that departs from what is generally normal, but our general principle of this discussion still applies: her IXth House Pluto rules the IInd House, *a quincunx relationship*. Her keen, lifelong conceptualization anxiety (the Cadent Grand Cross) constantly causes self-worth anxiety and requires not only behavioral adjustments but conceptual ones as well. The rigid constructs of the IIIrd-IXth axis keep the anxiety deep inside. She works constantly with her own analysis of personal circumstances, and her opinions of it all—very self-deprecating—are hard to shake.

Naturally, our growing awareness of Pluto keyed by House tenancy, then by relationship with the Scorpio House, must immediately include aspect dynamics as well. In our case studies so far, we have seen how aspect patterns relate House areas of concern. Anxiety lives throughout the aspect network in terms of quality and throughout the House resources in terms of substance.

With Pluto in the Xth, personal perspective needs accomplishment and reward recognition for clarification. It symbolizes a natural extension from the status/identity founded within the early homelife to the status/identity established within societal reward and recognition levels. Personal authority, power, or exhibitionistic outlet are required, especially under pressure. Of course, this occurs at many different levels. In Case 4, for example (page 116), the woman needs to understand the problems of her early homelife, recognize that she will not easily be a mother herself, and be proud of her status/identity as a professional woman. Her Leo Pluto, because of interception, relates by quincunx to her IIIrd: this is the adjustment concern of how she sees herself in her own information/perception resources. Pluto is square the Sun, Moon, and Venus (ruler of the IXth and the Ascendant). She had tried to be a teacher (Moon oriental) but had given up that profession to work in sales. Now she is in real estate as a salesperson, and she feels that she is on the right track. This is a perfect example of Pluto by House relating to other resources within the dynamics of developmental tension.

In the XIth, Pluto accentuates another arm of the Succedent Grand Cross of Houses. Personal perspective is usually dependent upon approval, love hoped for or expected, the supports of friendship. Further, there can be a naiveté about these concerns and a reliance upon job income to establish societal level of personal perspective. The young woman of Case 2 is a perfect example of this (page 101): Pluto's tension by aspect is critical, and its House position relates by square to her IInd. As we can recall from the analysis notes, she was "tired of rejection", her friends had "all gotten married and moved away". She withdrew. Her naiveté and withdrawal spare her awareness of deep hurt. Her job income would become the base of her personal perspective (the XIth is the second of the Xth). Its resources would be vital to accumulate, maintain, and defend personal perspective. Additionally, our analysis revealed a vagueness about personal values. Hopefully these resources will catch up in her development and amplify her personal perspective as she makes friends on ever-maturing levels.

Pluto in the XIIth establishes personal perspective within the area of accumulated experience, sensitively and privately assessed and ordered. As I have suggested in an earlier work, the IVth, VIIIth, and XIIth Houses ground the matrix of the unconscious.[13] Pluto in the XIIth links personal perspective not only to the accumulated confinements of prescriptive societal experience or to the revelations from them but also to the need to evaluate everything deeply. Under excessive pressure, resources that are accumulated are often too much for the analytical abilities and they are just filed away. The person adopts the resigned attitude, "The world just doesn't understand me!" Under pressure, the person may dwell deeply within the resources adjusted in lifelong accumulation and become lost in conceptual confusion. Pluto in the XIIth will relate by square to the IIIrd, accentuating the concerns of the information/perspective Cadent Grand Cross; by trine to the IVth, introducing early homelife prescriptions as the value base for life experience accumulation; or by quincunx to the Vth, requiring many adjustments between self-conceptualization through experience and the giving of love. Whatever perceptual profile is established carries with it the anxiety about change to a new level of security, as the XIIth House promises to lift the cycle of development into new ascendancy.

Pluto keys personal perspective undeniably. It affords quick access into holistic analysis based upon awareness of the personal position within the embrace of the outer environment. It keys the focal point of heightened anxiety under keen developmental tension. It immediately keys related concerns by rulership signification and aspect routing. Pluto clearly relates personal perspective to the world at large. When Pluto is *oriental*, i.e., rising just before the Sun, therefore, the next planet behind the Sun in longitude, the horoscope will suggest strongly that personal perspective will be achieved greatly by prestige affiliation. The person with Pluto oriental will tend to collect personal contacts that have established personal perspective securely within the public arena. Rising just before the Sun, Pluto is announcing personal perspective parameters before the identity is presented into full view.

Niebuhr's theory that personal anxiety is alerted in criticising the self's position within the personal view of the world is beautifully symbolized by Pluto. When we recognize personal limitations (lack of resources) we become aware of anxiety. Pluto's interrelationships within the horoscopic environment key this awareness reliably. In defense, we imagine a life infinitely better than what actually is. We set up a separate level in our fantasy life. We create specifically tailored idealizations to help us have hope; we adopt the idealization precepts of formalized religion; or we dull anxiety awareness through charade, sensuality, drugs, alcohol. This introduces the symbolization of Neptune.

We learn through experience how, uncannily often, the manifestation of high anxiety in a horoscope life also symbolically presents the escape valve or complications of fantasy, of Neptunian faculties. As inner anxiety meets environmental stress, the sense of sacrifice is felt or actual sacrifice is made. Somehow, we work for adjustment, for respite under siege, for avoidance. Neptune sharply configured with Saturn, for example, will suggest that under pressure the resources of ambition may sacrifice their drive, may go to sleep, may withdraw for varying periods of time to allow wounds to heal, and this process may become a habit pattern.

Within the Houses, Neptune's symbolism can key a vagueness, a potential sacrifice, some other level of concern that responds reliably under developmental pressure. In Case 2, for example (page 101), the young woman's fantasy life is clearly keyed by the Moon-Neptune conjunction within the Ascendant. In a real sense, her core status/identity concerns are sacrificed greatly to the rewards of fantasy. Her unawareness of her personal position is a naiveté that saves her from much pain indeed. But this unawareness also robs her of focused anxiety to do something about it. Her Neptune rules her VIth: her job hopes are the singular dream of her life.

In Case 1 (page 91), Neptune is in the Vth, ruling Pisces in the XIth, and is part of the defensive Earth Grand Trine. Unmarried, diffident about relationships, insecure on the shaky base of early homelife concerns, the woman fantasized ideal love situations but is terribly anxious about creating the circumstances that would make them possible. She fears that any love relationship will end before it actually gets started. Rather than to keep trying, the tendency is to give up trying, to sacrifice these resources and continue in defensive practical self-sufficiency.

In Case 3 (page 109), Neptune is in the VIth and sharply configurated with the Sun and Mercury in the XIIth. Neptune rules the XIth. We have studied how the perceptual framework of early homelife perspective (Pluto in the IVth) is a focus of her anxiety. Her constant focus of these concerns within reality are in terms of finding the right job for her very specialized talents. It would be entirely possible for her to sacrifice any job at all (unrealistically) if she could feel secure in a love exchange relationship (Mercury, opposed Neptune, rules the Vth; Pluto, ruling the VIIth, squares Venus in the XIIth). The VIth House is the third of the IVth (the communication of that parent) and the ninth of the Xth. This woman's own perceptual anxiety is keyed through Neptune to the information/perspective resources of her parents. We have seen that this is indeed the major core concern of her anxiety. Through understanding and time within new environments, she will surely have to sacrifice her perceptual framework involving her parents, and that sacrifice indeed will be a freedom for her.

In Case 4 (page 116), Neptune is in the XIIth, just above the Ascendant keyed so clearly by the nodal axis. This woman has a lifelong confusion about the experiences accumulated through her early home environment. It has been transfered to her confusion about being a mother and/or a professional woman (Neptune rules Pisces on the VIth). Neptune makes trines to her Jupiter (reward needs) and Uranus (individuation accentuation). The adjustment demands are clear through the Neptune quincunx with Mercury. She must sacrifice what she has accumulated by adjusting understanding of it all as it affects her interrelationships. The transition to freedom can bring dizziness and confusion, but that is the normal process of adjustment and growth.

In the horoscope fragment on page 135, with Neptune in the Xth, anxiety threatens always with sacrifice of personal status/ identity, especially through the husband's new starts in his growth (the Xth is the fourth of the VIIth). The adjustment demands within the confusion of anxiety are clearly defined by the almost precise quincunx between Neptune and the Sun. The capacity for creative visualization is constantly under stress through the keen perceptual anxiety indicated in the Cadent Grand Cross matrix. Neptune here rules the VIth: she is confused how to cooperate with the world stress around and upon her. Her cooperation is a very sensitive concern to her husband (the VIth is the twelfth of the VIIth). He himself told me that the only thing that could keep him from taking the golden opportunity he has been offered would be his wife's fear and reluctance to relocate.

With Neptune in the IInd or IIIrd, we can expect that something of the self-worth or the perceptual resources is sacrificed under pressure. A depletion may be felt or another stratum of awareness may be created as a comforting illusion, misrepresentation, or protective act. In the IVth or VIIth, usually something is sacrificed in terms of early homelife or relationships, respectively. Something is given away, never received, or not acknowledged. With the sense of vague or very specific incompleteness, appearances must be adjusted so that the outer world sees balance and contentment. Vulnerability is veiled; the real significances of these Houses become other than they seem. Difficulties in the homelife may be used to excess as excuses for some lack of new start motivation; a person may gain important status/identity reinforcement by being extremely supportive of or dedicated to (self-sacrifice) a mate whose own need problems fall perfectly in line with the service abilities of someone with Neptune in the VIIth.

Neptune in the VIIIth can key deep introspection, psychic or spiritual awareness, whereby much of the self's reality awareness of societal values is sacrificed. The process of rationalization may work overtime to alleviate the pangs of anxiety through idealization or transcendence. In the IXth, adventurous learning and dreaming can transport awareness away from reality conceptualization of anxiety states, as, in an extreme, astral projection takes one away from bodily environment. In the XIth, Neptune can suggest strong idealization of the love hoped for for personal fulfillment, possibly to the point that fulfillment is unattainable (sacrificed).

Neptune oriental, rising just before the Sun, as harbinger of the person's identity, seeks an idealized perfection, a harmony between what is expected and what can be.

Two brief examples conclude our discussion of Pluto and Neptune in terms of personal perspective awareness and the idealization that protects the sense of sacrifice. First, we can note that the great spiritual teacher Paramanhansa Yogananda was born on 5 January 1893 with Pluto and Neptune, both retrograde, forty-nine minutes of arc from exact conjunction in his Xth, widely opposed by Mercury and Venus in conjunction in Sagittarius. This teacher's concept of personal perspective was completely fused with the idealization process. In effect, this master preached that the individual is one with the world, that within this status/identity of oneness the individual creates his *own* reality.

Second, we can note that this century will not experience a square between Neptune and Pluto, but the sextile between them (idealization, illusion, the sense of sacrifice blending supportively with the needs to establish personal perspective) occurred on 11 January 1979. Days earlier, with only minutes of arc separating Neptune from the exact sextile to Pluto, the mass suicide took place in Jonestown, Guyana as hundreds left the anxiety perceived within this world to meet together in another.

Chapter Five
DEVELOPMENTAL
TENSION

"He's got connections!" —This phrase describes someone who can get things done. Being well-connected implies strategy, resourcefulness, and potential. It promises action, development, and results. "Connections" are essential within life. They frame all resource exchange, making possible the development of information, money, and status to clarify identity, worth, and perspective. Connections take life-energy, behavior, and need awareness from the inner environment to the outer environment and back for fulfillment. Connections make things happen.

Astrologically, connections are aspects. The planetary symbols relate to each other and define networks of behavioral faculties working to fulfill needs. The *entire* horoscopic network articulates the anxiety that makes life possible; specific aspect configurations of high focus within the horoscope life delineate anxiety in terms of particular developmental tension. These particular developmental tensions press the human being to make judgements, to establish worth, and to achieve status.

The keenest aspect of developmental tension we have in astrology is, of course, the square. This dimension of the fourth harmonic that squares the circle gives angularity to wholeness. It makes the circle manageable, rational, and dynamic. It provides starting points for active orientation. The semisquare, square, and sesquiquadrate define connections that focus anxiety into developmental tension.

When we are awake and active we stand at ninety degrees to the surface of the earth. This is the upright position of the human being and our point of view of the world. Anything divergent from this angle is less productive, is weak, is tipsy.

Other aspects defined through other harmonic divisions of the circle complement the square family derived from the fourth harmonic. The conjunction suggests a unison, a strong synthesized focus; the sextile suggests support; the trine, ease; the quintile, creativity; the quincunx, adjustment; and the opposition, an awareness of polarity. But as I have shown in my earlier works, *all aspects have the essence of the square* since they are all measured within the reference polarity of the semi-circle, and any angle inscribed in a semi-circle is a right angle, a square. In this sense, every aspect, every connection, within the horoscope is a symbol of developmental tension. The aspects emerging from this essence of developmental tension take on different qualities, but all work to focus anxiety within its function to sustain life and articulate being.[14]

In the horoscope *Example 1*, the Sun-Moon blend suggests that self-dramatization will alternate between two poles: reticent, unassuming peacefulness and aggressive, theatrical promotion. There can be extreme sureness covering a real diffidence. We feel a split, a division between external show and internal feeling. We see the Leo Moon in the VIIth, dramatic and strong; we see the Pisces Sun in the Ascendant opposed Neptune retrograde in the VIIth. The split between personal environment and outer environment is clear. Further, with Neptune in the VIIth, we know that something of the self may seem sacrificed in support of others. The Sun rules the VIIth and opposes Neptune. The inner dimension is sacrificed or hidden to favor the outer dimension (the Leo Moon) in full, bold view.

Immediately, we have made something out of the connection between the Sun and Neptune. Life-energy is connected in awareness to the capacity for creative visualization, for seeing the personal world as it can be within some compensatory idealization. Neptune rules the self-worth IInd. This key opposition is corroborated even further by the significator dynamics. The Ascendant

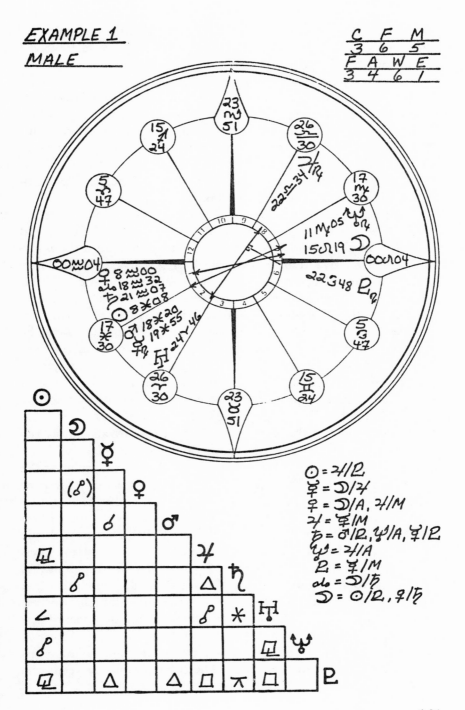

EXAMPLE 1
MALE

C	F	M
3	6	5

F	A	W	E
3	4	6	1

☉ = ♃/♇
☿ = ☽/♃
♀ = ☽/A, ♃/M
♃ = ♇/M
♄ = ♂/♇, ♅/A, ♀/♇
♅ = ♃/A
♇ = ♀/M
☊ = ☽/♄
☽ = ☉/♇, ♀/♄

161

holding the Sun, the VIIth House holding Neptune and ruled by the Sun, and the IInd House ruled by Neptune are all involved with a muting of personal identity.

At the same time, the powerful Moon is fortified strongly through the opposition with Saturn. Full awareness of necessary controls, of the strategies necessary for dramatic public presentation and establishment of status is connected to the Moon. This opposition aspect also crosses the angular Houses at the horizon. This is the powerful, purposeful driving status dimension of the self operating publicly while the sensitive, idealistic, perhaps withdrawn dimension of the inner self takes a back seat.

We see that Saturn rules the XIIth and the Moon rules the VIth. There is strong developmental tension within the drive and ambition of the Moon-Saturn opposition that includes the information/perspective resources of the VIth-XIIth axis. With Pluto placed in the VIth, we know immediately to suspect that this man's personal perspective will relate itself to work and service, perhaps to the underdog, which his withdrawn Piscean sensitivities may have created as a self-image as well (Neptune ruling the IInd). In summation, we have developed the portents of the Sun-Moon blend and have seen a dual organization of identity: the private sensitive self may be withdrawn, sacrificed, in a sense of strong purpose and projected severely and dramatically to the public. The public life is everything or is all that shows.

The Houses of the Succedent Grand Cross are all sharply significated: Neptune retrograde, ruling the IInd, is involved with the opposition with the Sun and is sesquiquadrate Uranus, ruler of the Ascendant (another vagueness in identity intensification); Mercury rules the Vth and the VIIIth and is retrograde and in conjunction with Mars in the IInd; Jupiter rules the XIth and is not only retrograde but also opposes Uranus from the VIIIth House. With the Succedent Grand Cross so sharply developed, we know that a question of values is the main focus of personality development and projection to the world at large. We can visualize analytically a man dedicating himself to the values of the underdog, the worker, the proletariat; fulfilling himself through a dramatic sense of service. The retrograde counterpoint that is so clear continues to show our analysis of the external image working along with a private inner stratum of awareness. The latter definitely feeds the former.

Another main aspect connection focus is the T-Square among Jupiter-Uranus and Pluto. Very simply, this man's hope for public reward (Jupiter in Libra echoing the Leo Moon in the VIIth) is in full awareness of his individually intensified identity (Uranus, ruler of the Ascendant, in Aries) and both are sharply energized by the Pluto symbolism. Everything then is tied together by the Pluto rulership of the Midheaven and its trine to it. The man will easily forget his personal concerns and dedicate himself dramatically to public service, transfering concerns about personal values to the concerns of values for others, possibly championing the underdog. —This is the horoscope of consumer advocate Ralph Nader.[15]

The aspect connections are extremely clear in terms of how they *create action* by relating behavioral potentials to fulfill needs and project the personal identity to the public for *their fulfillment.* Nadar is an extremely private man. We know only his Moon.

The midpoint pictures further corroborate this general analysis: the Sun is on the midpoint axis of Jupiter/Pluto Here is the connection that feeds the private anxieties of the inner environment into the energies of personal perspective achieved through the outer environment. This same theme is stated again by the Moon's square to the Sun-Pluto midpoint: there could be a supression of personal feelings in the name of public dedication. Saturn squares the midpoint of Mars-Pluto creating the image of hard work, strategy, seriousness, and enormous drive. Saturn is oriental, rising just before the Sun, symbolizing enormous patience and perseverance. —The suggestion of the Sun-Moon blend is corroborated easily by the aspect networks. Anxiety to live and grow has been channeled away from personal worth concerns and timidity in personal relationships. toward public values and bravura in public presentation. The inner environment's fulfillment has been sublimated to external environment dedication.

A final observation shows this same holistic insight again: Venus is very weakly aspected. It makes a wide opposition to the Moon and that is all. It is ostensibly peregrine, "wandering", although it is strongly placed at the Ascendant. In Aquarius, Venus symbolizes aesthetic and social needs of a humanitarian nature. Undoubtedly, these needs are fulfilled here by the public service projection, by the single-mindedness of the whole identity (the Moon's singular aspect is the opposition with Saturn); perhaps the personal reference point for these Venus needs has been sacrificed since there is no viable connection between them and the other behavioral faculty symbols.

In astrological analysis, we can ordinarily expect a peregrine planet's symbolism to run wild. Perhaps that *has* happened here: the essence of self-awareness has transcended the concerns of early unfulfillment in the early homelife (Venus rules the IVth) and projected all compensatory efforts into the resources of the law and public opinion that support all of Nader's public activities (Venus rules the IXth). Again, sublimation and overcompensation are vividly symbolized.

The aspect connections in Nader's horoscope are simple, few, and powerful. The key is Pluto. As ruler of the Midheaven, Pluto channels personal perspective strongly to career: it trines the Midheaven and directs there the energy of the T-Square involving Uranus, ruler of the Ascendant. A further connection between Ascendant and Midheaven is established very subtly by Pluto's involvement within the midpoint picture Ascendant = Venus/Pluto. This picture promises great emotional appeal (in Venus' Aquarian terms) but discharges it professionally in the main. We can note that Venus and Neptune (two keys to private emotional concerns) both make quintiles to the Midheaven, suggesting still again that the personal concerns are creatively funneled into the professional status profile. Nader has used education, enormous drive, and singularity of purpose to transcend personal environmental concerns and use their developmental tensions *to change* the values of the external environment. The prominence of the Leo Moon avoids societal reflection or acquiesence.

In *Example 2*, the Sun-Moon blend suggests that emotions and practicality will always fight for the center of the stage. This is strongly reinforced by the Sun's conjunction with Pluto in the Ascendant in Cancer and the Moon's conjunction with Jupiter in the VIIth House in Capricorn. This is a tremendous focus of personal power projected to the public. The power is reinforced by the collection of important other people with power as well (Pluto oriental). But the seesaw, polarized dimension within the profile is unmistakable. We begin to sense an imbalance through the retrogradation of Jupiter with the Moon in the VIIth. Capricorn on the VIIth is ruled by Saturn, which is retrograde and in the Vth, squaring Mercury, Venus, and Mars in the IInd. The self-worth tensions are obvious, keyed by Saturn retrograde and the heavy squares to

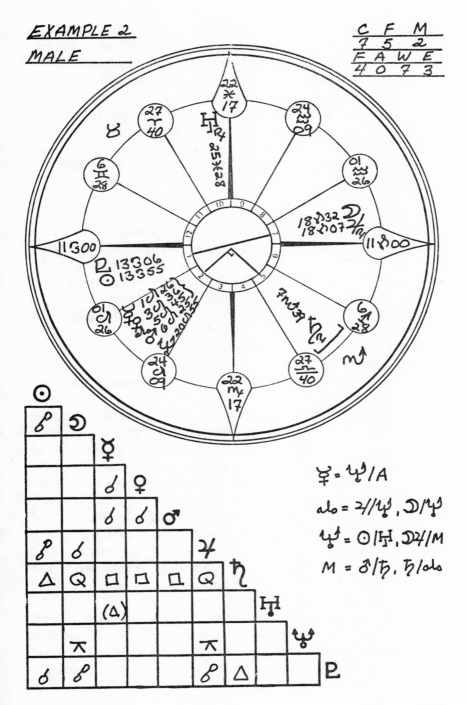

EXAMPLE 2
MALE

	C	F	M
	7	5	2
	F	A	W	E
	4	0	7	3

$\mathrm{\check{Q}} = \mathrm{\Psi}/A$

$alo = \mathrm{\mathcal{Z}}/\mathrm{\Psi}, \mathrm{D}/\mathrm{\Psi}$

$\mathrm{\Psi} = \mathrm{\odot}/\mathrm{H}, \mathrm{D}\mathrm{\mathcal{Z}}/M$

$M = \mathrm{\delta}/\mathrm{\hbar}, \mathrm{\hbar}/alo$

165

the IInd House. Personal emotional concerns may easily give way to administrative power and the collection of powerful contacts (Pluto oriental opposing the Moon). The emotional self can be separated from the public thrust, which is enormous. The resources of status/identity are under strong developmental tension (rulers of the angles in strong aspects). This developmental tension naturally *spurs* development (Mars sesquiquadrate the Midheaven, Saturn sesquiquadrate the Midheaven, Saturn trine the Ascendant, Moon-Jupiter sextile the Midheaven), especially through the profession. Additionally, the Sun-Pluto conjunction makes a wide trine to the Midheaven, and the powerful Moon makes a quintile with Saturn.

Again, we can easily see personal developmental concerns within the self-worth profile specifying the anxiety that spurs development. The developmental tension is channeled into the profession. The Pluto position in the Ascendant promises dramatic personal power in terms of personal projection and creativity (Pluto rules Scorpio in the Vth), in spite of or because of the early developmental difficulties symbolized within the Saturn retrograde profile. Personal relationships on intimate emotional levels may be difficult (Saturn ruling the VIIth; the self-worth concerns) but these difficulties, these anxieties, fuel professional ascendancy through administrative power.

Neptune's position within the IInd House further suggests that a sacrifice in self-worth fulfillment could be made under developmental stress and that the idealization process could be projected for fulfillment through the profession: Neptune makes adjustment contacts (quincunxes) to the Midheaven, Moon, and Jupiter. Neptune may run "loose", as it were, since it is not really securely grounded within the aspect network. It rules the Midheaven, and the Piscean duality there suggests several professional outlets and constant creative activity. Uranus at the Midheaven, barely aspected (easy trine to Mercury), could be dramatically overstated in the profession as well, in terms of inventiveness, communication, and self-aggrandizement. All of this, projected to the public administratively (Capricorn Moon) and creatively (Neptune assimilation), suggests a public performer of sorts, surrounded by important people sharing their personal perspective (Pluto oriental). —This is the horoscope of Merv Griffin, who not only hosts his own nationally popular daily talk show but also produces several other television shows under the aegis of Griffin Productions and other firms.[16]

Further inspection of the horoscope shows an absence of Air emphasis, which usually suggests a difficulty of seeing one's self as others do. This is a most sensitive point here: the public acclaim and the empire accumulated may be at odds with the deep insecure beginnings. The private emotional world of self-worth concerns may still nag for resolution even within the public glamour taken on from others and administrated externally. The dramatic midpoint picture of Midheaven = Mars/Saturn suggests similarly the enormous difficulties this very creative man has had to overcome, his endurance and powers of resistance. Here is the dilemma of personal emotional freedom within public image emphasis. The powerful Saturn in the Vth has focused the developmental tension throughout life to build a public tower. That tower now works full time chiefly to fulfill public expectations (the Vth is the eleventh of the VIIth).

In each of these examples, talented and complex individuals' lives have been analyzed developmentally, holistically. The Sun-Moon blend flowed through aspect connections that symbolize behavioral needs and personal resources interchanged with the environment. Coincidentally, both horoscope networks are similar in that both have built public careers through the anxiety specified within early life stress, especially in the broad area of self-worth concerns. It is a common pattern in life.

The wisdom learned within these analyses is that *that's the way these men were supposed to build their careers*! The astrology of analysis does not reveal problems that must be solved; rather, the astrology reveals the *natural* patterns of individuation that must be expressed. The *quality* of the individual's life is for the *individual* to assess, not for the astrologer. Understanding the specifications of life-sustaining anxiety allows objectification and adjustment if needed. But concerns will always endure as long as anxiety is present and life continues.

Example 3 reveals a horoscope of extreme power and, naturally, extreme anxiety. The Sun-Moon blend suggests that strong ambition is lifted into dynamic opinionation. The Capricorn strength drives the Sagittarian Moon into intellectual pride and restless acquisition. There is no doubt about it, especially with

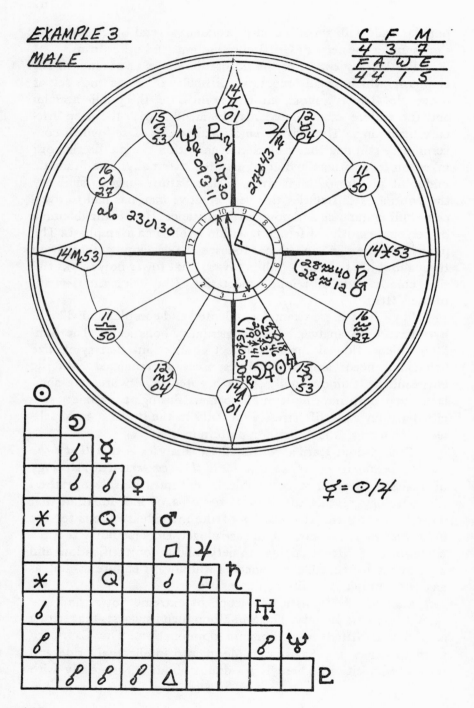

EXAMPLE 3
MALE

	C	F	M
	4	3	7
	E	A	W	E
	4	4	1	5

☿ = ☉/♃

168

Uranus conjunct the Sun, and the Moon opposed Pluto. The dynamic personal power takes on intense individual focus and full awareness of maximum perspective. The angular accentuation within the IVth-Xth axis dominates the horoscope.

Pluto in the Xth identifies personal perspective with exhibitionistic power, public acclaim. But Neptune is there as well, suggesting that for so much power part of the status/identity resources may have to be sacrificed. Pluto in Gemini rules Scorpio on the IIIrd, suggesting that personal perspective power position could be wisely built upon sales, travel, inventiveness. Neptune in Cancer rules the VIIth, suggesting that part of the status/identity sacrifice would be in terms of relationships or public acclaim. There is tremendous conflict brewing within the analysis.

Mercury rules the Midheaven and the Ascendant and is related to both by strong aspects. Mercury is retrograde and opposes Pluto: there are counterpoint concerns within the status/identity resources. Finally, we see that Neptune opposes the Sun-Uranus conjunction. Ambition will be veiled somehow, public acclaim achieved yet sacrificed. The mind (Mercury) will be at odds with itself, working always on two levels, internal and external. We can say that there is a conflict between the awarenesses of rational power and irrational motivation.

A further indication of the enormous anxiety building power is the almost exact conjunction of Mars and Saturn in the VIth, both square Jupiter retrograde in the IXth. Here is a holding back of enthusiams, another conflict with the needs of the Sagittarian Moon. In the VIth, the tensions of Mars and Saturn work hot and cold within the dynamic of cooperation. The VIth-XIIth axis is dramatically keyed not only by this Mars-Saturn conjunction but by the conjunction of Sun and Uranus, rulers of Leo and Aquarius.

Overall, the status/identity profile is under extreme developmental tension as signified by Mercury, Jupiter, and Neptune; the conceptualization dimensions of the information/perspective profile are also under high developmental tension as signified by the Sun, Pluto, Uranus, rulers of the XIIth, IIIrd, and VIth, and by Jupiter retrograde in the IXth, receiving the Mars-Saturn square. The key IInd House of money/love resources, the base of self-worth concerns, is ruled by Venus, in conjunction with the Moon and Mercury. Venus is in mutual reception with Jupiter but is only aspected by Pluto, and this opposition suggests a potential loss of value perspective. Noting that Saturn rules the Vth and is stressed within the pressured network of aspects suggests that giving of self, giving of love may be difficult. The sense of values, then, may be given over to money, and the overcompensatory acquisition of wealth may outdistance the perspective of personal emotional fulfillment.

This is the horoscope of Howard Hughes, the billionaire aviation, oil, and real estate tycoon who died as an irrational recluse, a hypochondriac for years.[1][7]

The singular sharp midpoint picture within Hughes' horoscope is Mercury = Sun/Jupiter, symbolizing great success with the mind, with communication, speaking, ideas. This conflicts greatly with Hughes' crisp, sarcastic, defiant communication style in his early years and his complete lack of communication during the last half of his life. Mercury is extremely prominent in the horoscope as ruler of both Midheaven and Ascendant and closely aspected to both. Through its retrogradation and opposition with Pluto, we can surmise that the mind and communication power could have been lost within the power perspective as well. With all the material rewards in hand, anxiety about emotional fulfillment still stirred. The mind perhaps became resourceless in the personal relationships dimension and turned inward. The charade of personal image (Neptune opposed Sun) could have been adopted to protect against the stress felt in giving emotionally (Saturn ruling the Vth). In this sense of avoidance of developmental tension, the mind was creatively successful (Mercury quintile Saturn) but contrapuntally detrimental to balanced fulfillment. Hughes "bought" the pleasures of many Hollywood starlets, as is well known, but rarely met them. Acquisition outdistanced sharing.

Finally, we can note that the only accentuation of the water element (emotions) is Neptune in Cancer, the sacrifice made in the quest for power. And beneath the entire struggle, we know the key: the early homelife and the father figure in particular from whom Hughes inherited the beginning of his fortune at a very early age.

As we develop holistic analyses throughout this book, we become increasingly aware of the ubiquity of the patterns thoroughly studied in Part I. We *always* see the interplay of status/identity, money/love, and information/perspective resources within the needs of the inner environment as its anxiety to grow meets the prescriptive stresses of the outer environment. Every human being faces these invariable challenges. The individualistic pattern that defines how these challenges are met is within the horoscopic connection pattern of every individual. Individual sociological circumstance provides a base for that individual's level of fulfillment, that individual's Law of Naturalness, as the patterns energize individual levels of fulfillment.

Overall conceptualization of holistic astrological analysis is extremely simple: we know about the significances of the three Grand Crosses of Houses and how they are interrelated by significator dynamics; we know about the needs of the inner environment and the prescriptions of the outer environment; we know about the necessity of anxiety and its expression in terms of developmental tension; and we can ascertain an individual's fulfillment at any given time through his or her job position and self-assessment. The overall conceptualization is the same for everyone; only the level changes. The integration of these concepts within holistic analysis depends not upon any magical astrological lexicon of keywords but *upon the astrologer's refined awareness of the ubiquitous patterns as they reflect natural societal growth.* The horoscope comes literally *to* life as its patterns and concepts of developmental tension are given meaning by, are connected to any individual's reality.

Fear and Hope

In his *The Meaning of Anxiety,* Rollo May summarizes that moving *through* rather than *away from* anxiety not only allows the individual to achieve self-development but also to enlarge the scope of his world. Astrologically, we see that omnipresent anxiety becomes developmental tension and is registered within the aspect patterns and significator dynamics in individual horoscopes. This developmental tension focuses itself within the individual's mind, as the individual specifies anxiety in terms of hear and hope.

The mind works because it is challenged. The registration of anxiety and the need to plan, to think through, to cope are normally inseparable. Mercury's sign suggests the subsidiary need of how we need to think in our management of anxiety. Aspects to Mercury reflect developmental connections of tension that affect how we need to think, and the significator dynamics of Mercury and any other planet involved within an aspect network involving Mercury relate environmental concerns (inner resources and outer experiences) to the mind's function.

For example, Ralph Nader's Mercury (page 161) is in Pisces and retrograde. We know that his need to think a certain way will be highly influenced by sense impressions, with an extreme receptivity. This is reinforced by the mutual reception between Mercury and Neptune in his horoscope. With Neptune in his VIIth, we can anticipate that the sensitive thinking process will relate importantly with public relationships (intimate or collective). Neptune rules the self-worth IInd where Mercury is placed. The mental sensitivities will relate self-worth and relationship concerns. This is reinforced by the Pisces Sun, ruling the VIIth and placed in the Ascendant, in opposition to Neptune in the VIIth. Mercury in turn rules the Vth and the VIIIth, two other areas within the Succedent Grand Cross of money/love concerns. Mercury's retrogradation suggests that these sensitive and personally oriented dimensions of the mental process work at one level, while another level is also present.

Mercury is conjunct Mars, indicating an invigoration of the mental process, but an invigoration in sensitivity concerns as well since Mars is also in Pisces. We can feel that the energized mental process still has difficulty with direct expression. This is reinforced by the Mars rulership of the communication IIIrd.

Both Mercury and Mars make only one other aspect, a trine with Pluto. The personal unrest within personal sensitivities will be eased (trine) through Pluto to the establishment of personal perspective. The Pluto is also retrograde, echoing the retrogradation of Mercury, and surely is the channel of the other level of expression. This other level is undoubtedly away from the personal and toward the professional, since Pluto rules the Midheaven, trines it, and is disposited by the Moon in Leo in the VIIth House with Neptune. The Moon in turn rules the VIth and is disposited by the Sun ruling the VIIth. The whole network issuing from Mercury places intimate self-worth pressures and sensitivity into developmental counterpoint with large-scale, dramatic public expression.

Nader's Mercury, the innermost planet, is related to energy focus (Mars) and the public perspective through Pluto, the outermost planet. This network is extremely clear.

Now, we know that anxiety generates growth through mental awareness and resourcefulness. We know the quality of the mental resourcefulness and the presence of two planes. We are oriented within our discussion throughout this book to the constant interplay between inner and outer environments. We can safely state that Nader's personal inner tensions about self-worth focused his anxiety into defensive overcompensation through his professional service in establishing fair value constructs for the public at large.

In the personal life, these tensions become manageably articulated in terms of fear. With Mercury in Pisces, the fear can easily be articulated as the fear of *being taken advantage of*. In Aries, the fear of *being ignored* can fuel the ego-awareness constructs of the horoscopes, usually involving the nervous system, to overstate personal position, to protect by attack. Passion and temper can be common modes of expression. The fear would be similar for Mercury in Leo and Sagittarius as well, with obvious slight ramifications. In the Water signs, adjustments to fear constructs would all be based upon emotional defensiveness. In the Air signs, the fears of *being unappreciated*; in the Earth signs, the fears of *losing values*.

These fears reflect how the mind needs to work, to develop through anxiety toward self-development. The mind energizes all the other behavioral faculties in their particular subsidiary need fulfillment networks.

Merv Griffin's Mercury is in a powerful aspect network in Leo, conjunct Venus, the node, and Mars, all square Saturn retrograde in Scorpio (page 165). Related resources within development are very clear: the parental profile (Saturn retrograde, Mercury ruling the IVth, the close nodal conjunction with Mars); the communication with the parent of the Xth (Mercury ruling the XIIth, the third of the Xth); the self-worth anxiety (the cluster in the IInd, the Sun's network as ruler of the IInd). In the extremely powerful configuration with Saturn retrograde in Scorpio, this Mercury fear of being ignored (Fire) is extremely strong, real, and important. With our awareness of life development patterns, we can appreciate the entire development drama here from this Mercury network alone. The fear, the developmental tensions, created compensatory behavior and bolstered personal identity through glamorous public status.

Howard Hughes' Mercury retrograde in Sagittarius is complex, as we have seen (page 168), but the developmental tensions are clear: status/identity concerns were under deep conflict in awareness of inheritance and resources and, as well, the diffidence within personal relationships. Mercury's two quintiles to the Mars-Saturn conjunction articulate clearly the essence of the whole horoscope: the fear of being ignored but, at the same time, the difficulty with accepting recognition.

In the open acknowledgement of fear or in the instinctive reactions to it, anxiety meets stress. Inner anxiety meets external demand that is embodied within various environmental constructs throughout life. The ultimate symbolism of this environmental fear is Saturn. Saturn represents the fear of deprivation through control. When Saturn is sharply configurated with other need symbols within the horoscope, a fear is established in terms of fulfillment deprivation related to the configurated needs. In Case 1 (page 91), Saturn upon the Ascendant, ruling the Xth, squared the Sun in Aquarius in the Xth: we saw vividly the environmental press upon the core identity needs, the needs to be importantly individual. The fears have a strong hold upon the woman in terms of giving love, since the Sun rules the Vth. In Case 2 (page 101), the manifestation is very similar, with the love given and love received axis dramatically keyed. Both women have Mercury in Aquarius: in Case 1, the great nervous tension about being unappreciated (Mercury in Air and square Uranus) is held in check and anchor through the rigid defensive construct of the Earth Grand Trine (keyed by Uranus); in Case 2, the depression (Mercury square Saturn) dulls the awareness of the unappreciation fear and is channeled through the fantasy (Mercury trine with the key Moon-Neptune conjunction).

In Case 3 (page 109), there is highly nervous reaction to the perceptual anxiety (Mercury in Aries square Uranus), a great fear of being rejected (ignored) in terms of giving love (Mercury rules the Vth), and a creative effort to achieve security within life development through advanced education (Mercury quintile Jupiter). These fears work in response to the deeper concerns set up by Saturn's opposition with the Sun. In Case 4, (page 116), the same fear of being ignored (Mercury in Aries conjunct the Moon in the VIIth) is not exacerbated by any clear aspect relationship; the fear is vague, pervasive, uncomfortable but not sharply focused. Of course, it is part of the problem of early homelife concerns, as we have seen, in relation to standards of personal relationships on her own (Mars ruling the VIIth, square Saturn ruling the IVth). Mer-

cury rules the IXth and the XIIth, communication and cooperation with and from others.

When Mercury is aspected sharply with Uranus, we can naturally expect an intensification of anxiety awareness. The mind
can be expected to involve the nervous system with fear registration intensely. When Mercury is sharply configurated with Neptune, the mind's awareness of anxiety can be vague, the articulation into specific fears more nebulous. Where Saturn symbolizes
the fear of deprivation through control and Uranus, fear through
urgency, Neptune suggests fear through imagination or delusion,
of dissolution through alienation or collusion. Pluto in sharp
aspect with Mercury can suggest fear in terms of futility.

The focus of fear symbolized by strong aspect patterns is
awareness that some condition exists to thwart customary, individualized fulfillment of specific needs. It is the state of alert to dis-
turb homeostasis and create change. As we shared in Part I of this
book, the environment continuously forces choice within the individual. Through awareness of anxiety within environmental prescriptions, the individual must choose in terms of inner environmental needs and outer environmental rewards whether to reflect
the environment at all costs (through varying degrees of self-development sacrifice), to be victimized by the environment (through
complete acquiescence), or to change the environment (through
personal development). The individual's awareness of anxiety specified in fears must be continuously weighed by the individual
within these alternatives. Reactions through the lifelong developmental process organize themselves into patterns, into stereotypes.
Behaviorally, aggression works to surmount fear and create change
and development; withdrawal works to avoid fear and gain security by reflection.

When we study horoscopes of the famous, we continuously
see patterns of high developmental tension. When we learn of the
lives of the famous, we learn about dramatic hardships, poignant
struggles, great tensions. These pains seem somehow to be in proportion to the fame. We say often, "He's a self-made man",
"Gosh, she went through a lot to get where she is", or "So-and-
so's really going places!" Developmental tension and fear spur
development and fulfillment. The famous become famous by
"overcoming" adversity, playing roles as identity develops, growing into those roles, sacrificing much to gain much. Many times,

the progress in development involves enormous changes in geographical environment, citizenship, and even name.

However, during the development process —the stress between socialization and individuation— our culture dictates that we should *avoid* tension, that we should seek peace and security. We are told "not to rock the boat", to "toe the mark". We are told by dictum and example to do as we are told and live the way our parents did, the way our neighbors do, the way our social status says we should. The dilemma between outer environmental prescription and inner environmental need is crucial, *but the crucial stress is what makes self-development possible.*

In contrast, we have the calm sea of people who have adapted, who have routinized behavior, who have learned the message of particular environments and have reflected societal prescriptions for security rewards, given in to victimization to avoid fear. These horoscopes show tension networks that have rarely manifested. Life is steady, molded, predictable. Inner needs have been repressed along with the behaviors to fulfill them individualistically. Introspection sleeps. The mind becomes dulled. Marriage, job, and time are endured. Self-development stops.

When developmental tension is avoided in order to gain outer environmental support and approval(!), personal perspective is diminished. The natural manifestation of anxiety is muted to a diminished scope. A little development can become mountainously disruptive since personal resources to manage the slight threat to security are lacking. Anxiety surfaces weakly, fears are vaguely specified if at all, and irrational pettiness emerges. As fear is avoided, so is hope abandoned. —How many clients manifest this syndrome precisely!

Fear is anxiety specified, is anxiety with a specific focus. Fear is anxiety made rational. It is the recognition of challenge to be met by behavioral faculties led by reason. My suggestion that Saturn, as a general symbol for fear (the developmental challenges that structure development in life time), symbolizes *necessary* controls captures the essential nature of anxiety and the rational role of fear.

When we fear that something of us will be taken away (separation, disapproval, or non-being), we simultaneously have hope that something rewarding will come to pass. Fear and hope are unfailingly reciprocal. We see this bond through Jupiter, the symbol of hope (need) for reward, the symbol of Saturn inverted.

Jupiter in Fire signs suggests ramifications of a hope (need) for reward in terms of gaining recognition, obviously in ego terms. In Water signs, this hope is in terms of gaining emotional security; in Air signs, the reward of appreciation; in Earth signs, the reward of establishing personal values. Ralph Nader's Jupiter is in Libra in the VIIIth House, symbolizing his hope for social appreciation in terms of public values. His Jupiter rules the XIth, another area of the value resources of the Succedent Grand Cross. His Jupiter is retrograde, echoing the counterpoint between personal life and public arena, as was clearly established through the analysis of his horoscope.

Merv Griffin's Jupiter is conjunct his Moon in Capricorn in the VIIth. What could be clearer than his hope for reward in terms of establishing personal values through public projection? His Jupiter rules his VIth: he must perform a service, an information service, to earn this position. His Jupiter is retrograde, again echoing the counterpoint between personal life developmental tension and public life overcompensation.

Howard Hughes' Jupiter was also in an Earth sign, symbolizing the hope/reward need in terms of value structure (Taurus). His Jupiter makes the only squares within the horoscope, to Mars and Saturn. Jupiter is retrograde, ruling the IVth, calling attention clearly to the counterpoint issuing from the early home environment, the father, the inheritance.

In Hughes' case, Jupiter was closely squared to Saturn; hope was in developmental tension with fear; judgement of values was in developmental tension with the rationale for choice. This square aspect always suggests strong confusion within self-awareness. Self-deprecation must always be dealt with. Because of the clash between hope and fear, between judgement and reason, the enthusiasms can be held back. Anxiety loses specific fear focus, yet its driving energy abounds. The person must fight a dynamic battle of self-esteem and enterprise. In Hughes' life and horoscope, the psychological battle was enormous.

When Jupiter opposes Saturn, hope is in full awareness of fear. The personally oriented hope network seems to go against societal prescriptions. Insecurity in the face of others' values can

178

dominate as anxiety tries to find its path to specify a fear and thus motivate developmental behavior. Here in the opposition, choices are still muddled, judgement vacillates, but all work for concensus and growth.

When Jupiter and Saturn are in conjunction, hope and fear are highly focused. There seems to be a sense of just balance within the psychological manifestation. In Cases 1 and 4 (pages 91 and 116), this conjunction symbolism helped each woman to justify her personal circumstances and fit in with society. Hope for growth balances fear of challenge; this conjunction in Taurus emphasizes assessment of values, which for each woman is extremely importantly (personally for Case 1 and empathetically for Case 2).

Finally, this sense of justice, of balance between hope and fear, within the conjunction of Jupiter and Saturn captures the natural human awareness that success and fulfillment *do* emerge out of hardship. Somehow, we instinctively know that hardships are justified if growth is achieved. It is a sense of natural law and order.

However, our culture works to upset this natural balance. Our culture tells us to avoid fear and tension at all costs; our culture tells us energetically to have hope, to make a better life for ourselves. This message of hope is embodied in the awesomely powerful marketing thrust of our economy. We are told to use open-ended charge accounts for ever-inflating luxuries. Improved status is supposedly established through giving up work, by utilizing labor-saving devices, by espousing indolent luxury. The powerful message of hope for success along the lines of media prescriptions calls attention to our personal "hardships". We deprecate ourselves for not being "with it". We tend to expect windfall rewards for our silent struggles. We slowly begin to devalue our spouses, our jobs, our life times. Fears, tensions, and developmental concerns are pushed out of sight, and hopes, value judgements, and development rewards are pushed into view. We become flabby and resourceless; we do not have the tension to make decisions for values; anxiety reigns irrational and vague. We doubt the products of our developmental experience; we depreciate the rewards we have gained by taking them for granted; we become dissatisfied with who we are. Progress personally becomes our most important problem.

How often in clients' lives I have seen acute anxiety within confusion made productive through explanation of the process of development and the just balancing and personalization of necessary fears and realistic hopes! Pride then emerges and becomes a most powerful stabilizing focus of self-awareness; the pride of fulfillment during growth, our vital connection with ourselves.

Defense Mechanisms

Someone who has connections gets things done. At the same time that connections facilitate development, they defend the personality resources of status/identity, money/love, and information/perspective. As further development is planned, preservation of the status quo is essential. Chimpanzees band together and post lookouts, chameleons change color to blend with their immediate environment, porcupines stiffen their spines to protect themselves, and human beings do all these things and more to defend their flanks within the process of development. Human beings use many different behavioral faculties to butt like rams, hold ground bullishly, adopt resourceful twin argumentative positions, sink their claws into emotional security, roar defiantly, protect value judgements meticulously, balance engineered social acceptance, sting back at environmental intrusion, escape rootedness, manufacture solitary austerity, innovate eccentric exemptions, and exploit self-sacrifice.

As anxiety naturally gives rise to growth efforts, it also gives rise necessarily to defenses of those efforts. Within the horoscope, connective patterns define not only developmental tension and fear specifications for personal need fulfillment within environmental press but also the organization of defenses to protect status and insulate identity.

Defense constructs are not necessarily negative. For example, in our society, defensiveness is often regarded as symptomatic of problems on a personal level but as a posture of strength on the national level. When we say to someone, "Don't be so defensive", we are actually signalling a willingness to share resources, i.e.,

"Don't be afraid of me; let's share." On the national level, we say, "Let it be known how strong we are; be afraid of us!"

Then, there are shifts in these positions: as soon as resources are accumulated on the personal level —starting a business, buying a house, gaining an honor— we rush to defend them as best we can. We hire lawyers to protect us, we install burglar alarms, we work overtime to preserve the honor position after we receive it. Shifting on the national level is clear when we say, "We're already strong enough; let's cut back on the defense budget and use it for improving our lot here at home."

Although these insights uncover a fascinatingly complex discussion area, we can safely generalize that defensive behavior implies, on the one hand, a protection of vulnerabilities and, on the other hand, a protection of strengths. The point of view changes, but defensiveness does not. *Just as anxiety is essential for life itself, so defensiveness is essential for security during that life development.*

When we encounter defensive behavior in others, we instinctively suspect that vulnerabilities are being protected. We can identify with this position since we ourselves are defensively fortified as well. We say, "Don't be so defensive" when we want to assure others that their vulnerabilities will not be taken advantage of if they relax defenses somewhat. The adverb "so" describes degree. On the other hand, when we assess that others have a great deal of resources and yet are defensive, we say, "You don't *need* to be defensive." We are comparing our observation of others' resources to how secure we feel when we have such levels of resources. In both situations and in all nuance positions, defenses are related to inner awareness and outer assessment of personal resources. Again, the traffic of development and the structuring of position between inner environment and outer environment comprise the base for degrees of tension and degrees of defense.

So, it is definitely positive to have well articulated defense mechanisms within life development. But it is the *degree* of defensiveness that is important, that must be studied in holistic astrology. The degree of defensiveness usually varies in relation to real or imagined appraisal of resources within life development. For example, defensiveness can become so strong and isolating that insecurities rarely can gain opportunities for remediation through relationship and resource exchange. This is the profile of *defensive withdrawal.*

Defensiveness can become patterned into habit and represent a waste of energies, energies diverted from development. This is especially typical in adult years when early life problems no longer exist or have been put into proper perspective. The patterns may still endure in this profile of *defensive habit.*

Defensiveness can be weakened by needs dependent upon non-defensive relationship. Emotional security through a bond with someone else can be so powerful that other resources of identity, undefended, are totally neglected and are wiped out. This is the profile of *defensive self-sacrifice.*

Already within this book, we have touched upon classical defense mechanisms. We saw Harry Stack Sullivan's view of *repression* (page 143) whereby we keep out of awareness behavioral tendencies that may attract disapproval. Of course, repression takes behavioral potentials out of circulation and forces other behaviors to work overtime. For example, a young boy with great sensitivities that are not understood or appreciated or rewarded by his family may learn to repress them and adopt more masculine behaviors. Overcompensation may push him into materialism and pronounced machismo in his adult years, while the sensitivities languish within imbalance. The sensitivities unfulfilled cause great anxiety.

Repression of early developmental anxieties about self-worth bring about overcompensation in external environmental values as we suspect from the horoscopes of Ralph Nader and Merv Griffin. Repression does not eliminate specific anxieties; it delays their press for fulfillment through substitution.

We have discussed the classic defense mechanism of *projection* which occurs when the source of internal anxiety is identified with an external challenge in terms of fear. This process of projection can become extremely complicated and profound through symbolic substitution. For example, we will see in Part III of this book how the young woman of Case 3 (page 109) fears her ability to succeed in love relationships and postgraduate education as a projected substitution of her perceived conflict with her mother: the young woman fears the personal success that might intensify her mother's jealousy of her.

Reaction formations were discussed (page 53) in relation to displacement of an anxiety focus with an opposite complex, usually aggressive external overcompensations for vulnerable internal resources. President Richard Nixon, with Saturn retrograde square his Moon, ruler of the XIth, and square his Venus, ruler of the IInd, with Neptune retrograde in opposition to his Sun, has very real deep inferiority concerns. His horoscope is a perfect example of both projection and reaction formation: as a patriotic politician, the "enemy" to be feared is the other party or the foreign powers that threaten to undermine the national system. As a young congressman in 1948, Nixon's ambition was arch and earned him the reputation for ruthless political strategies even then. Nixon made his mark by leading that era's over-reaction against communists, specifically against Alger Hiss. We can see this as a projection by Nixon, with the substitution of Hiss for his own insecurity tension as a congressman and lawyer. Overzealous patriotic achievement (political "overkill") was the reaction formation against inner insecurity, but the beginning and end of his career.

Sublimation is another classic defense mechanism within psychology. Through sublimation certain behaviors or needs are renounced for a supposedly more noble self-dedication. This process is extraordinarily dangerous and extremely simple at the same time: renunciation is extremely easy since it is praised by society and religion (external rewards) but it avoids full growth responsibilities in relation to the developmental hazards of life (the inner needs in relation to others). Usually sublimation takes place with sexual energies, to avoid relationship anxiety. A problem area of resource exchange and behaviors to fulfill needs, when it is sublimated without being solved, ravages the system continuously. If the problem area is solved first, before being sublimated, it refines the system. This tells us the enormous amount of self-knowledge, circumspection, and maturity required within sublimation.

The horoscope can speak eloquently about other defensive structures as well. Chief among the defensive aspect connections is the Grand Trine. The Grand Trine links planetary symbols of needs and behavioral faculties into smoothly flowing closed circuits of self-sufficiency. The sense of self-sufficiency immediately registers the essence of defense. The self is protected unto itself. Naturally, such a defense measure works against relationship and the resource exchanges with others that are absolutely vital to growth and development. We can anticipate degrees of withdrawal, habit, and self-sacrifice.

The Earth Grand Trine describes a closed circuit of practical self-sufficiency. We have the sense of "I don't need your help" which can become patterned out of the practical resourcefulness necessary to establish a sense of worth in the early home environment. When built upon powerful resources, the Earth Grand Trine can register as "I'm going to over-do all of this to prove a point". When resources are solely depleted, the vain sense of "I don't need your help" is prevalent. The self-sufficiency defines and protects self-awareness of values. It defines individuation, but it works against relationship. The closed circuit can become patterned into habit, but it must be relaxed to free energies and encourage resource exchange within relationships.

The Water Grand Trine describes a closed circuit of emotional self-sufficiency. The defense is against being taken advantage of in the sense, "I've been hurt too many times, so I'll keep to myself." In the extreme, this can become, "I don't need your feelings, and you don't need mine", working self-isolatingly against relationships and resource exchange, or the structure can be totally given over in external dependency.

The Air Grand Trine suggests a closed circuit of intellectual or social self-sufficiency, defending against the fear of not being appreciated. It is a perfect defense for the problems symbolized by Saturn retrograde (pages 68-72) and remarkably often appears along with Saturn retrograde. There is the sense of "Sticks and stones can break my bones, but names will never hurt me!" The person has a deep reaction formation of superiority feelings that swirls within the resources of the Air Grand Trine, strengthening the inner environment against the outer environment: "Down deep, I know I'm good, even better than all you others." In the extreme, the Air Grand Trine symbolizes tremendous self-isolation, whereby no need is felt for relationships.

The Fire Grand Trine defends against the fear of being ignored. It symbolizes a closed circuit of motivational self-sufficiency: "You can't tell me anything I don't know". Naturally, this is an aggressive conferment of status upon the self, often part of a clear reaction formation defending inner insecurity. There is the essence often of, "I know exactly where I'm going, and I don't need your energy to get there!"

These generalities must speak within holistic appreciation of the whole horoscope drama within the human being's whole life experience. Each of these generalities requires adjustment to each individual case, so what is important for the holistic astrologer is the *principle* symbolized by the Grand Trine: there is too much of a good thing. The potentially good offense is lost in defensive preoccupation. At least three behavioral need faculties are confined to a specific element and related too easily to one another. There is a stifled balance. There is not enough developmental tension to distribute these faculties throughout the life. They become routined in a cluster and are very easily detected within life behavior.[18]

Most often, the Sun and/or the Moon is involved within the Grand Trine construct. This allies the Grand Trine behavioral defense construct with the Sun-Moon blend of life energy and reigning need. However, when neither the Sun nor the Moon is involved within the Grand Trine, the self-sufficiency patterning of behavioral defenses tends to exist dramatically *separate* from the Sun-Moon thrust of life development.

In Case 1 (page 91), the woman has a clear Earth Grand Trine that does not involve the Sun or the Moon. Within the analysis, it was easily clarified how the defense system of practical self-sufficiency evolved in reaction to the death of both her parents. She has dedicated all her life to building a fine *employment* record. Her jobs helped her *change environments* many times. She works in public relations, which is the very area of her personal concerns. Practical self-sufficiency has worked admirably to give her status, but practical self-sufficiency has kept her from easily making fulfilling personal relationships. The defenses that emerged within early life trauma have become later life strengths, but they are directed to public status more than to private identity. Her Venus, within the Grand Trine, rules her Ascendant, but it makes *no other aspect* connection outside the Grand Trine. The pattern exists in extreme autonomy, emphasizing private loneliness. Remediation must work to have her count her blessings, believe in her resourcefulness, and appreciate that the defenses of self-sufficiency do not need to be so rigid anymore.

CASE 5 appears on page 185. In the first glance at the horoscope, we become aware of the Scorpio concentration (Mercury, Ascendant, Mars, and Sun). Its ruler, Pluto is in the VIIIth. We know immediately to expect intense emotional focus, perhaps an

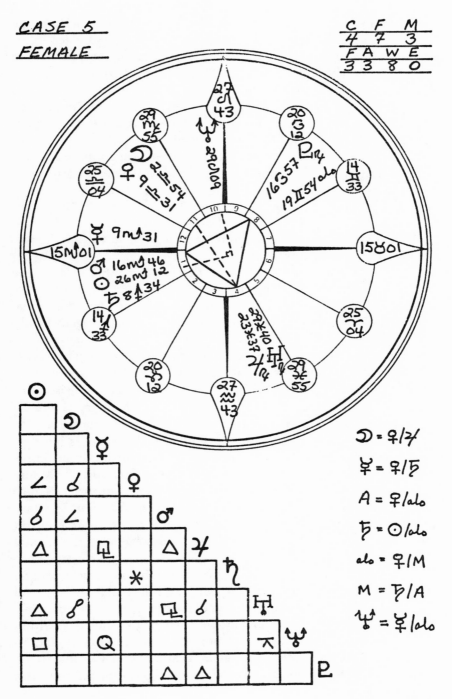

CASE 5
FEMALE

C	F	M
4	7	3
F	A	W	E
3	3	8	0

☽ = ♀/♃
☿ = ♀/♄
A = ♀/☊
♄ = ☉/☊
☊ = ♀/M
M = ♄/A
♇ = ☿/☊

185

anxiety about being taken advantage of (Mercury in Scorpio in the XIIth), and a sense of personal perspective linked with deep intro-spection that could lead to psychotherapy if the emotional stresses were strong within devleopment (Pluto in the VIIIth). We see Nep-tune prominent at the Midheaven, and we know to sense the po-tential of self-sacrifice in terms of ego awareness (the Xth House). In this first glance, we are aware of the potential for extreme man-ifestation of anxiety in terms of personal awareness.

The aspect grid tells us that there is only one square and one opposition within the horoscope. The developmental tension is concentrated in the main upon the Neptune square to the Sun and the Uranus opposition with the Moon. The Sun rules the Xth, hold-ing Neptune, and Uranus rules the IVth where it is placed. Obvi-iously, there is extreme parental tension present within the wo-man's core development.

Going further, we see the Water Grand Trine that involves the Mars-Sun conjunction, the Jupiter-Uranus conjunction, both retro-grade, and Pluto. We see a powerful closed circuit of emotional self-sufficiency, probably used as a defense mechanism against early developmental problems in the home in relation to the parents.

The absence of behavioral faculties symbolized by planets in Earth is conspicuous, suggesting an impracticality within the devel-opmental tension network. Neptune is assimilated into the isolating Grand Trine through its square with the Sun; Mercury is also in-cluded by its XIIth House dynamic and its sesquiquadrate with Jupiter within the configuration. Similarly, the Moon is incorpo-rated through its opposition with Uranus within the Grand Trine, and Venus is allied as well through conjunction with the Moon. Only Saturn is not integrated into the emotional construct. Saturn is weakly aspected (only the sextile with Venus) and, in Sagittari-us, we can expect its higher mind ethical profile to be rampant within the personality, especially since Saturn rules the mental IIIrd.

With the Midheaven-Nadir axis under obvious developmental tension through tenancy and aspects, we know that the parental environment will be important within status/identity concerns. With the rulers of the Ascendant-Descendant axis involved within the Grand Trine, we know that personal projection and relation-ships will be vital development areas. Status/identity problems are sure and strong, and it is clear that they trigger ego defensiveness emotionally.

The fifty-one year old woman arrived for her consultation, laconic and slightly disheveled. Her speech was slurred. I asked if she were on some kind of medication. She said that she was not. As we chatted a bit, I became aware of how intelligent and precise she was with her thoughts and words. Her constrasting appearance and lethargy suggested to me that she had been through a great deal for a long time, that she was dulled somehow. Later in the consultation, she corroborated my suspicion voluntarily: she said, "I feel dullness from all the stress."

Asking about her early homelife, I learned quite a story: her family had made a major move when she was about two years old (SA Ascendant conjunct Mars). She had had a formal Dutch upbringing. Everything in the home had been conducted rigidly. I suggested that the rigidity had worked against the recognition of her as a person, and she replied simply, "Very much." She told of three older brothers who got all the attention (Saturn, ruler of the IIIrd, almost peregrine?; generational sociology).

As she talked, I started to adjust the measurements and initial deductions *to* her life. I inquired about her father. She said, "My father really loved me, but he would say that we should all be like 'mother'. She was perfection in home organization." I felt that the mother had to be symbolized by this woman's Xth, the Neptune conjunct the Midheaven. It was reasonable to see the mother's intrusion upon my client's life through the Neptune square with her Sun. I remarked, "And your mother's ideal became *your* ideal? Hard to live up to?" The woman simply said, "Oh God!" in corroboration. The Grand Trine would be dedicated to that ideal.

The woman revealed that she had been in psychotherapy for three years and was ready to leave (transiting Pluto exactly square natal Pluto at the time of consultation, with transiting Saturn square Saturn). I shared with her how sound her story was (a compliment to her therapist and to her as well) as she told harrowing tales of personal victimization by the mother's ideal.

I began to inspect the pattern I knew would be there in her life: the young girl with deep emotional needs (Scorpio and Grand Trine construction) and strong social needs (Moon-Venus conjunction in Libra in the XIth, Venus ruling the VIIth) dedicating herself to her father's loving suggestion to be like her mother, working day and night to be as perfect as she within the rigid "churchy" and ethical home environment (Saturn in Sagittarius running wild); feeling alone on the personal level, exploring fantasies to establish identity. She easily corroborated all this and as well "enormous fantasy dimensions" to the point that she eventually "couldn't grasp reality."

I suggested that she had to work all the harder then to fulfill all the ideals anchored to the mother's model. This was so. I began to see the Grand Trine working against her, taken over by emulation of her mother: Neptune square the Sun from the Midheaven, quintile Mercury in the XIIth and quincunx Uranus, ruler of the IVth, that opposed the Moon. The whole horoscope circuitry flooded into this mother focal point. Knowing the maternal symbolism of the nodal axis made the midpoints node=Venus/Midheaven and Neptune=Mercury/node all the more meaningful.

As soon as I said, "You had to defend at all costs who you thought you were *in terms of your mother's image*?", she interrupted with an apparent non sequitur, "You know? I'm scared of water to this day. My brothers threw water on me when I had tantrums. I can't stand to this day to have *water* on my head, even washing my hair, which I do a special way."

The symbolism was so clear. Her own emotional balance was completely wiped out by the mother model. Self-confidence was never formed in any way. Frustration came out in tantrums. Emotions were punitively washed away with a flood of "water". She defended herself in and through the ideal of her mother.

Later, in her marriage, the identity problems continued: sex virtually stopped after three years, twenty-eight years ago! She took the blame upon herself, saw it as rejection (Neptune ruling the Vth). I suggested that she had then probably tried to be again as perfect as her mother, and the woman corroborated this in detail: "I had a fixation that I kept a dirty house and that that's why things were bad. . . ." She tried obsessively to reattract her husband, failed, had a nervous breakdown, and became suicidal.

Trying to detect somewhere within all her tension if her Mars in Scorpio, conjunct the Ascendant and oriental, was ever activated defensively beyond the tantrums, I asked why she had never divorced her husband. She said that her husband would say, "You'll never divorce me; your *mother* would never bear it!" —A painful scenario unfolded here, with the woman calmly setting everything in clear perspective: a life of victimization to an external ideal, emotional resources fixed upon the mother, and the pain of it all apparently exploited by the husband for particular aggression needs within his own development.

Sharing her deep, analytically distilled insights gave me further instructive understanding of the manifestation of her Grand Trine. Note carefully how the Grand Trine really should only formally include Mars, Pluto, and Jupiter. The base from which orb measurement should begin is really established by Mars and Pluto in sixteen degrees of Scorpio and Cancer, respectively. This Grand Trine would then operate *without* the Sun and Moon, the blend of which promises self-confidence, poise, and pride finally learned within worldly social ease—just the opposite from the state of affairs in her life. Her life behavior did begin that way, probably, but with time and development, with the father's loving urging within a rigid environment to "be like mother", the Sun and Uranus were nudged into the emotionally idealized closed circuit. We can interpret the Moon's opposition over the sign-line with Uranus similarly, the Moon nudged into echo of the Grand Trine through the opposition. Uranus (the intensification of individuation) is almost exactly quincunx (adjustment) the powerful Neptune. We can see the planetary need-behavior symbols being sucked into the Grand Trine dominance, rigidly kept there by the configuration and the Fixed angles of the horoscope, as the self was left behind.

The woman never existed for herself. She feared disapproval. The whole horoscope can be read through the mother-Xth as the Ascendant: my client's Moon would be in her mother's second; her Mars, Sun, and Saturn would be in her mother's fourth; my client's Pluto would be in the her mother's eleventh with the dynamic of the mother's expectations transfered to my client's personal perspective. The adjustment between my client's parents, i.e., her father pushing her toward the mother's perfection, is outlined by the Uranus quincunx with Neptune from the IVth to the Xth, from the mother's seventh to her derived Ascendant.

The energy of this woman's emotions worked *to defend her idealized concept* rather than to express herself. This was a defensive withdrawal profile, with projection upon the mother, that became a habit and culminated in self-sacrifice, through fixation upon the ideal and attempted elimination of the self (and its anxiety) through suicide. Her marriage repeated and extended the pattern and exploited her vulnerabilities painfully.

The woman is now aware, sound, and finally proud today (Ascendant potential). She is working to regain her strength and interest in her own personal perspective, to get a job, to come out from under years of dulled identity awareness, as transiting

Saturn and Pluto square their natal positions and as the Progressed Moon conjoins her Midheaven. —Her psychiatrist and she had done a fine job to take the Sun and Moon out of the Grand Trine and vitalize the sesquiquadrate between Uranus and Ascendant-Mars. She has a new start for sure, with no more self-criticism.

This case was extremely complex, to be sure. I did little to help except confirm the analytical perspective distilled from her three years of intensive psychotherapy. The woman and I got along well. She was amazed how astrology could delineate the developmental tensions she actually experienced. She was able to gain further security for the new starts that were symbolized by natural projection of measurements from the past into the near future.

CASE 6 (page 191) is much less complex. The Sun-Moon blend promises a terrific thrust of opinions and higher mind emphasis that should find keen administrative outlet. But we know that this would require strong energy application and drive. There is only one square within the horoscope: Jupiter square Neptune, hope and visualization within developmental tension, "vision in philosophy and religion. A stratum of mysticism underlies the thinking. Reality is where the feet too rarely are."[19] Neptune is retrograde and rising in the Ascendant. It rules the IXth House and further corroborates the position of philosophy and religion deeply at the core of personality formation. —The Sun-Moon blend, with its administrated thrust, is definitely weakened or diverted.

Mars (the need to apply energy in a specific way to fulfill needs) is weakened as well in relation to the Sun-Moon blend. Mars is in *Pisces*, conjunct Uranus, in the VIIIth. Mars rules the Midheaven, but it is captured within the tight Water Grand Trine involving Mars-Uranus, Pluto, and Jupiter. Neptune is included through the square with Jupiter within the configuration. The Sun and Moon are excluded from the Grand Trine network and are very weakly aspected. The Sun has only the ease of relationship with Neptune (trine) and the creative connection (quintile) with Uranus within the Grand Trine.

It is obvious at first glance that the Sun-Moon blend is simply not supported behaviorally. Its administrative thrust is diluted. What dominates is an emotionally self-sufficient network loaded with philosophical, religious, higher mind, perhaps occult orientations. The Grand Trine occupies the Houses of the matrix of the unconscious.[20]

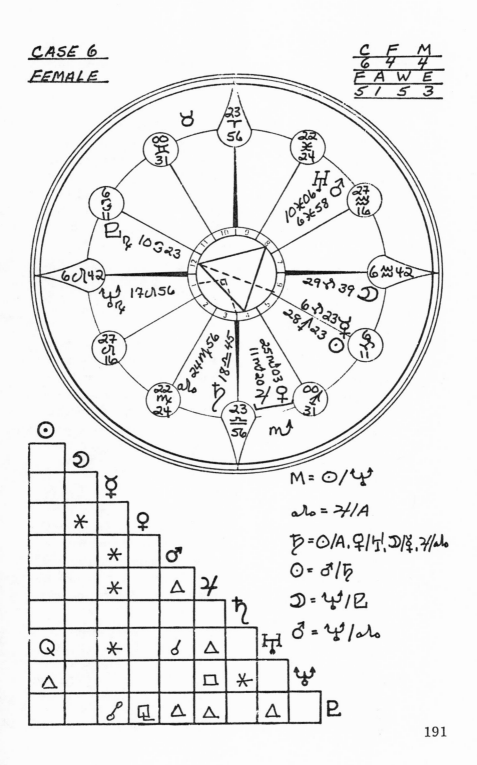

CASE 6
FEMALE

C	F	M
6	4	4
F	A	W	E
5	1	5	3

M = ⊙/♆

♑ = ♃/A

♄ = ⊙/A, ♀/♆, ☽/♅, ♃/♑

⊙ = ♂/♄

☽ = ♆/♇

♂ = ♆/♑

191

The only opposition within the horoscope is between Mercury and Pluto. Mercury is fully aware of this philosophical, spiritual perspective. Through this opposition, the mind could easily wander from the practical needs symbolized by Capricorn, since personal perspective is determined through the Grand Trine and undoubtedly adopts the defense of "the world doesn't understand me" (Pluto in the XIIth). Neptune in the Ascendant, involved within the Grand Trine indirectly through the singular square with Jupiter, suggests a potential sacrifice of status-identity awareness.

The Mercury-Pluto opposition, the spine of the Grand Trine, keys two areas of the Cadent Grand Cross resources of information/perspective. Mercury additionally rules the IIIrd; Neptune rules the IXth. The information/perspective resources are under clear developmental tension.

In holistic analysis, we must reach for the root developmental cause. Jupiter in the IVth makes the powerful square with Neptune in the Ascendant. Venus, ruling the IVth has only one aspect, the sesquiquadrate with Pluto. Venus also rules Taurus intercepted in the Xth, and Pluto rules Scorpio intercepted in the IVth. Uranus, ruler of the VIIth, the fourth area of the status/identity Angular Grand Cross, is conjoined with Mars, ruler of the Xth, and is involved within the Grand Trine. Again, it is clear: there is keen developmental tension within status/identity concerns, formatively within the early home environment. These developmental concerns spill over into information/perspective resources, and the whole developmental process is defended by the Grand Trine in Water, by a closed circuit of emotional self-sufficiency.

Similarly, the Succedent Grand Cross is under tension: Jupiter rules the Vth, Uranus rules the VIIth, and Mercury rules the XIth. The value resources are tied in with some kind of emotional, spiritual rationale. The Sun rules the self-worth concerns of the IInd House but is weakly aspected. The developmental tension here is not crucial, nor is it reinforced. Self-worth concerns will be tied to the spirit of the Grand trine through the Sun's trine with Neptune and quintile with Uranus.

The midpoint pictures corroborate these initial deductions taken from my preparatory notes before the consultation: Midheaven=Sun/Neptune, impressionable, possible loss of ego awareness; Saturn=Sun/Ascendant, inhibition or restriction on personal development; Sun=Mars/Saturn, development torn into two directions; Moon=Neptune/Pluto, moodiness and perhaps "peculiar" perspectives.

The middle-aged woman arrived punctually. She was tidy, bright, attractive, and had an air of knowing wisdom revealed in a subtle smile during our opening conversation. I had difficulty getting started because of her bearing. I was feeling the Capricorn Moon, the Capricorn Mercury, and the Leo Ascendant, but I was reaching for the conceptual tensions deep within, the criticisms of herself and her life position (pages 145, 154). I felt as if I were being controlled to keep astrological analysis on a superficial level.

I decided to puncture the defenses, so I said firmly, "Look, this horoscope tells me a lot, and I want to share it with you in depth. I don't just want to sit here and talk about how you protect all your emotions deep inside and meet the world with defensive, petulant temperament; let's face it, the queen complex isn't really you!" This was a forceful onslaught indeed, working with the obvious belligerent defensive posture her Capricorn Moon would express through the Mars-Uranus conjunction (Uranus ruling the VIIth), framed within the Leo Ascendant and fueled by the anxiety within the enormous Grand Trine network held deep inside.— The woman smiled, relaxed, and made a motion with her hand in the air to "chalk one up for the astrologer!" We could begin.

I discussed all that I suspected (of course, without any astrological jargon) and, with each step of our discussion, watched and listened carefully for corroboration. The exchange was clarifying her personal Level of Naturalness, and I was fitting her horoscope to that level, to her life. The clear status/identity concerns were corroborated through her strict religious upbringing, "very strict and very turned to God." She never knew her father, and she remembered her step-father as authoritarian and unfair. I suggested that these developmental difficulties that we were discussing within the early home environment had caused "conceptualization problems about why she was alive". I phrased this observation purposely to lift the level of conversation to the philosophical, spiritual level I thought dominated her. She replied immediately, "That's the biggest point. I almost died at birth and again last September. Many times I've asked the [spirits], 'what the hell do you want with me? Give me something constructive to do in life'."

Our discussion blew wide open. The woman corroborated every deduction I had made in preparation for the consultation. In short, she felt "cheated by reincarnation. I'm living life sloppily until I get another chance. I'm really into metaphysics. That's where I'm happiest. There's more than one of me isn't there? I feel it's my mother's fault. I love her so. I haven't wanted to find out that she caused the trauma; it would ruin her image in my eyes."

She acknowledged that she is angry with the world at times, that she has a "sadistic streak" (Mars conjunct Uranus), but "I like me alright." The rigidity of her homelife was linked to her mother's guilt complex about having given birth to my client out of wedlock. This tension can easily be filled out within the guilt picture in a strict religious environment, a further analytical adjustment to her developmental level. The client's sensitivities as a young girl were ignored. She became personally vulnerable to the mother's and step-father's overcompensatory rigidities. She adopted a too easy set of defenses in loneliness: emotional self-sufficiency supercharged by fantasy and unreal sensitivities.

I inquired about a traumatic focus of all of this when she was about 5 years old (SA Saturn conjunct the fourth cusp and related measurements). She replied, "I know there was one, a nervous seizure about that time, but it is totally blanked out." Whatever this was, it probably was the time that she adopted withdrawal to protect herself.

Noting that SA Uranus squared the Sun at the same time as SA Pluto opposed the Moon at about age 18, I asked if she had wanted to run away, to change her environment, possibly get married. She corroborated that she had indeed gotten married at the first opportunity, totally naive and unexposed because of the environmental confinement. "I got married to get away from the domination by my parents; my husband was almost illiterate, but so decent. But my parents disowned me."

The pressures of confinement within the early home had been so great, that the woman was completely unexposed at the time of her marriage. She even took her most prized "doll" with her into the marriage —at age 18! She volunteered that she had not been allowed to date and that she had a twelve year old mind in a mature body.

Further measurements paralleled her slow development, from one routine of authority into another routine of ignorance. Emotional self-containment became a powerful defensive pattern. I looked for a break and suggested age 27-28 when SA Pluto would have come to her Ascendant. She said, "That was the time I realized I was a woman. Sex started to bloom, and I went berserk!"

Sex became her favorite "hobby" for years. She broke out of loneliness. The marriage continued in spite of her self-oriented hobbying. The defense mechanisms of emotional self-containment adopted a new level of self-containment: from protection to growth, from fantasy to sexuality. The next step would be to the spiritual.

After a divorce at age 36 and her mother's death, just after transiting Uranus crossed her Ascendant and transiting Saturn conjoined her Sun, she remarried, slowed down her "hobby" and then divorced again fifteen years later as transiting Uranus crossed her fourth cusp.

As the patterns of self-isolating emotionalism were all clarified, this sensitive woman's eyes filled with tears, and she was momentarily embarrassed. She said, with a fascinating slip of the tounge, "No one ever sees me with *water*." I asked why. "It's private." I pointed out that productive relationships require private sharing. "I never have." I asked if she realized that not sharing makes relationships difficult, that it perpetuates her loneliness. She answered, "But I like it that way."

The Grand Trine in Water was extremely powerful in her life. Conditioned by a rigid homelife, intensified by an empty first marriage, privately reinforced by fantasy and sexual adventure (the Neptune square with Jupiter, ruler of the Vth, the Sun within the Vth, the Pluto emphasis within the Grand Trine, etc.). Relationships became increasingly difficult, since the emotions could not get out of the self-protecting and self-indulgent habit pattern (Uranus, ruler of the VIIth, within the Grand Trine, keying the marriages and their break-ups). Her outer world did not understand her. She sacrificed herself to her inner world.

The inner world, the next step in the perceptual growth concerns, began to manifest when transiting Neptune conjoined natal Jupiter in 1962 and as SA Neptune began to square the natal Sun. After five years, the pursuit of "anything and everything metaphysical" dominated her life, as transiting Uranus squared her Sun in 1967 and as the Solar Arc accumulation of forty-five degrees placed the semisquare developmental tension throughout her entire life. This new level of growth led to her second divorce as transiting Uranus crossed the fourth cusp.

The Grand Trine was now operating to defend self-awareness with metaphysical and spiritual rationale. Her early words about her adult perspective really took form, "There's more than one of me isn't there?"

Out of her marriage, she gave up sex. She sublimated these energies and became an ascetic. She calmed down her temper, calmed down the occult, and eliminated sex precisely with the Uranus transit of her fourth cusp. The whole Grand Trine of self-sufficiency established a new individual and lonely level. SA Saturn squared Uranus and quincunxed Pluto as SA Ascendant squared the Sun.

The woman had accumulated much, much wisdom through her private forays from the inner, defensive environment into the outer, misunderstanding environment. Saturn in Libra, almost pere-grine natally, finally developed the controlling parameters of social awareness in philosophical and religious terms. Characteristically from this symbolic sign position, the woman learned tact for her minimal relationship contact with the outer environment and she learned dignity through self-sacrifice within her inner environment. Her hopes were lifted to the higher Scorpionic levels (Jupiter in Scorpio maturing through the Neptune contact). She works to support herself as an *accountant*, the antithesis of her spiritual orientation (the Mercury-Pluto opposition with the Moon in the Capricorn VIth).

She now faces a major readjustment in her life. She has covered the spectrum of emotional awareness from confined ignorance to poetical wisdom. Relationships with the world have been sacrificed for this growth process. Now, with SA Ascendant squaring the midpoint of Sun/Pluto, she is feeling the need to reestablish personal perspective in a balanced way (still the demand need of Saturn in Libra). Transiting Saturn at the same time is building its second return, and transiting Pluto is conjoining her natal Saturn.

These examples of the Grand Trine (Cases 1,5, and 6) are atypical. They function without clear inclusion of the Sun and/or the Moon. Therefore, the defense systems operate quite independently from the Sun-Moon blend and are more difficult for personality assimilation. The anxiety is dissociated somehow and is vulnerable to diversion into other aspect structures (reality formations) keyed within the networks involving portions of the Grand Trine. The valid descriptive epithets, "I've been hurt too many times, so I'll keep to myself," "I don't need your help", etc. (page 183), do not easily serve understanding of the complexities of the Grand Trine formations that exclude the Sun and Moon. The "I" has been abandoned usually, and the self-sufficient circuit searches to be taken over, to be connected and guided somehow to relevance. Then, that position is defended at all costs.

Within defenses we always see very clearly special functions linked symbolically to the planets. With Mercury, we have a most sensitive key, involving perception, the registration of awareness. This perception may articulate fears in accord with the element of the sign holding Mercury (page 173) and then be articulated further by aspects (page 175). With Venus, it is similar, but the registration of fear, for example, is in terms of aesthetic and socialization needs. In Case 5 (page 185), the women's Venus in Libra registered the fear of not being appreciated (Air) unless she were like her mother. This was transferred to her marriage as well (Venus ruling her VIIth). In Case 6 (page 191), the woman's Venus in Scorpio registered a fear of being taken advantage of, of her sensitivities not being recognized in the authoritarian homelife. In Scorpionic depth, she was alerted to her confinement, but the break out could only wait for time to pass and bring courage. Her Venus was similarly weakly "connected" as in Case 5. —When Mercury and Venus are closely configurated by conjunction or sextile, there can be the manifestation of idealization to transcend difficulties. The idealization creates further anxiety since it is not easily attainable in reality. Almost invariably, the defense of idealization is comprised of Mercury, Venus, Neptune and the signs these planets rule, frequently involving Jupiter and Sagittarius as well.

With Mars, we have the potential of aggression, of hostility. Under confinement, we feel anger toward that which suppresses us. Mars in its sign suggests the nature of this aggression. In Case 5, the Mars in Scorpio, which would react strongly to the fear of being taken advantage of emotionally, was turned inward against the woman herself. The position of Mars within the awesome Grand Trine configuration kept it from working to extricate the woman from the oppressive environment that always took advantage of her emotionally. In Case 6, Mars in Pisces was weaker. There was belligerance against the world (Mars conjunct Uranus, ruler of the

198

VIIth; Pluto in the XIIth), but this Mars energy was all caught up within the Grand Trine defense configuration and muted by the Piscean coloration.

Saturn of course symbolizes within defensiveness the concepts of rigidity, convention, abstinence. In neither Case 5 nor Case 6 was Saturn significantly connected. If it were, there would have been a "handle" on the complexes, something to focus upon in concrete terms. With Uranus within defensiveness, we can expect nervous intensification, sexuality (since it is within sex that psychology and neurology combine for naked individuation), and escapist eccentricity. In Case 5, we saw how the individuation potential was sucked into the status/identity problems through the mother's ideal (Uranus opposed the Moon). In Case 6, we saw Uranus keying the Grand Trine itself, ruling the VIIth, and being discharged only sexually at one level of the woman's growth voyage.

With Neptune, there has been much evidence of its symbolic supression, dissolution of ego-consciousness, and fantasy. The pronounced degree of these dimensions were amply shown in both Case 5 and Case 6. We saw this effect also earlier in Case 2 (page 101) where fantasy gives comfort and Case 3 (109) where fantasy still channels anxiety into perceptual ambiguity.

With Pluto within defensiveness, we have the problem of personal perspective, of our awareness of personal anxiety face to face with the world (page 146). In Case 5, Pluto was deeply involved within the Grand Trine and ruled the Ascendant. Its position within the VIIIth House promised the deep introspection that could and did lead to developmental pain and to remedial psychotherapy. In Case 6, Pluto opposed Mercury suggesting that the mind could easily, in defense, shift from seeing accurately the reality position. It manifested just that way: giving the woman a professional hold upon the real world which didn't understand her (Pluto in the XIIth) but establishing a more important deep metaphysical perspective by its position within the Grand Trine.

In *CASE* 7, the man's Sun-Moon blend suggests a polarized potential, an outer bravado that protects a sensitive core. With both the Sun and the Moon in the VIIIth, we sense the protection of this polarization. Mercury retrograde in between the Sun and Moon echoes this further. There is this polarity, and it is carefully protected. The Aries bravura must protect the Pisces sensitivity.

CASE 7

MALE

C	F	M
4	6	4

F	A	W	E
6	0	3	5

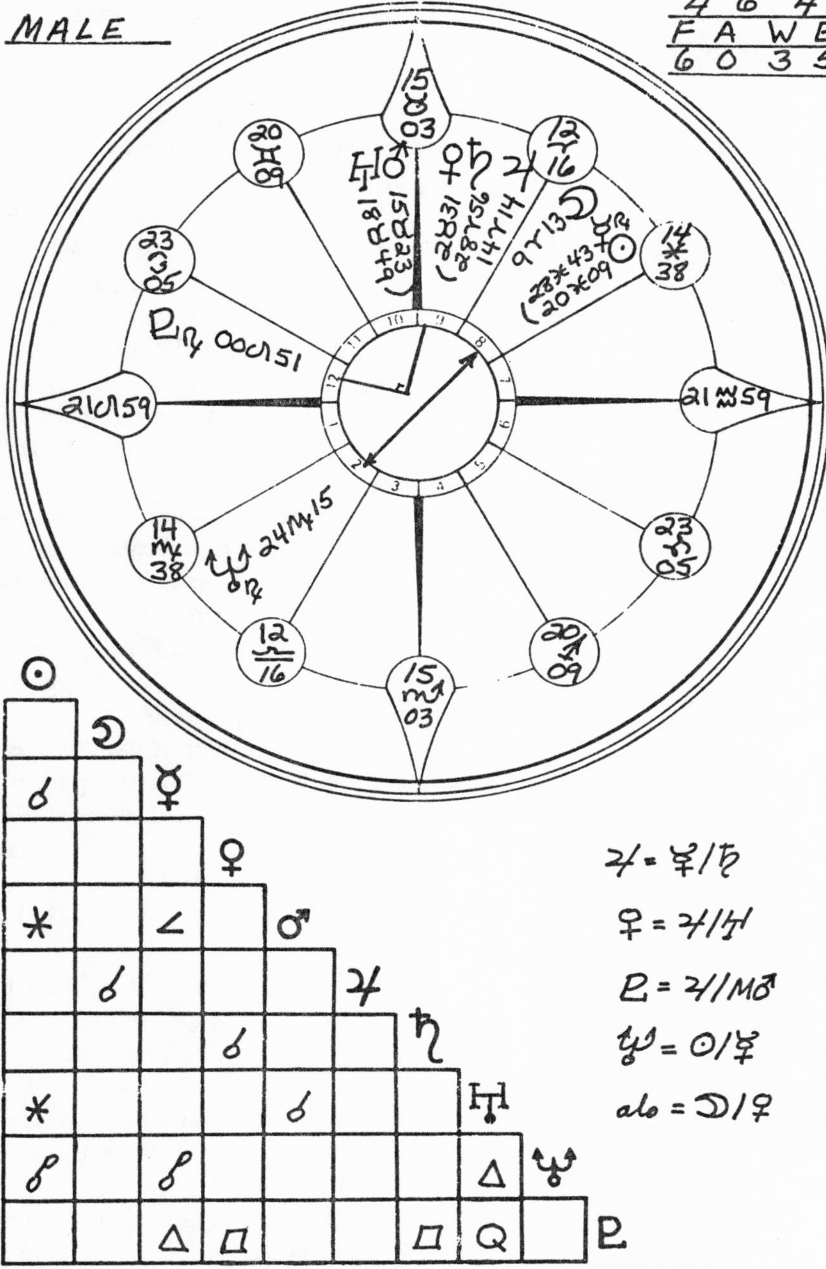

	☉	☽	☿	♀	♂	♃	♄	♅	♆
☽									
☿	☌								
♀									
♂	⚹		∠						
♃		☌							
♄				☌					
♅	⚹				☌				
♆	☍		☍					△	
♇			△	□			□	Q	

♃ = ☿/♄

♀ = ♃/♅

♇ = ♃/M♂

♆ = ☉/☿

ab = ☽/♀

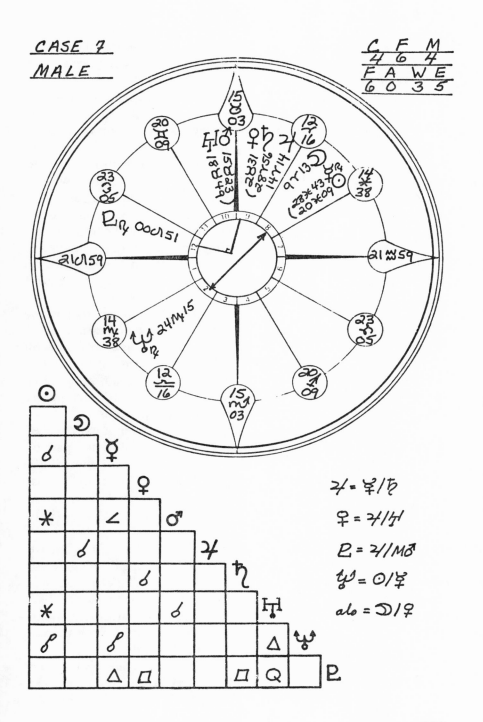

This swift deduction is immediately corroborated by Neptune's opposition to the Sun and Mercury. Immediately we see the self-worth axis keyed within value concerns. Money/love resources are under stress. There is conspicuous self-worth tension (Neptune in the IInd, ruled by Mercury, the opposition, and the mutual reception between Neptune and Mercury). Mercury rules the XIth, love hoped for, values received. Jupiter rules the Vth and conjoins the Moon, the only aspect for either body. This man hopes to be recognized (Aries) and given ego reward. He hopes to give love and receive it in return. The polarized split in the Sun-Moon blend suggests a split in environmental orientation within resources as well: he may build a tower with money and languish for the foundations of sensitive love fulfillment. With the node also symbolizing "associations", we see the corroboration clearly, almost poignantly, in the midpoint picture node=Moon/Venus, the longing for tenderness in associations, within the bravura of the Aries Moon.

Pluto in the XIIth keys us to expect the defenses of this polarized situation in terms of "the world doesn't understand me". Pluto rules the IVth and involves the early home environment within this defensive perception. Pluto is squared by Venus and Saturn, suggesting on the one hand an excess of emotions and, on the other, a dynamic ego-oriented ambition (Saturn in Aries). Again, we see a split between external drive and internal needs.

The man is deeply entrenched in environmental experiences (the southern hemisphere emphasis) while the emotional part of him is dissolved below the horizon in his earlier environmental life preparation. Mars conjoins the Midheaven and Uranus in Taurus, symbolising the constructed tower for sure. And here again, we see the polorization: Mars is conjunct the Midheaven and Uranus (individuation) squares the Ascendant.

Our view of the polarization is completed subtly when we see that the rulers of every House are under strong developmental tension except for the XIIth (the Moon) and the Vth (Jupiter). These two rulers are conjunct each other and make no other aspect. Giving love (Vth) has to make enormous adjustments (quincunx) to the personal perspective within the world, with the co-operation of others (the XIIth is quincunx the Vth).

The resources of the status/identity matrix are under keen developmental tension: Pluto, ruling the IVth, squares Venus and Saturn, with Venus ruling the Xth. In the Xth, Mars conjoins

201

Uranus, ruler of the VIIth. And, of course, the Sun opposes Neptune. In fact, the pattern of significator dynamics relates all resources within developmental tension, thrown into experience, yet isolates the Vth House within the sensitive personal core.

It was no surprise to meet the handsome, strong client, who is the head of several *construction* corporations. My first words to him at the beginning of the consultation were, "Well, your life and this horoscope picture here suggest that you indeed have built a tower for yourself. But it all protects an extremely sensitive core that we have to talk about." A flicker of surprise came through his eyes as he simply nodded corroboration . . . and permission for me to continue.

Following the guidelines of holistic analysis, I continued, "When we see such extreme development as you have accomplished in your profession, we have to look at it as something overcompensatory. You have this tower in terms of money and success, in terms of ego recognition . . . bravura . . . but these have all overcompensated for a self-worth anxiety in terms of sensitivity, love. I guess we could say there is a tremendous longing for tenderness. The picture also suggests that the roots of this split, of this separation of ego strength from sensitive love needs occurred in the early homelife, in relation to your parents."

Again, my client nodded confirmation. He said simply, "Sure." I prodded him to discuss it with me. He replied freely then, "I really can't remember. I can't remember sitting down to dinner with my parents! I can't remember anything!" Indeed, he could not. He vaguely recalled a grade school teacher's last name, but he could not remember anything. I remarked that this was amnesic, and he confirmed that his psychotherapist thought so too. He had just begun psychotherapy to get some answers, as transiting Neptune squared his Sun and as SA Sun conjoined his Saturn.

In discussing the dichotomization of money/love resources (along the lines being studied in this book), my client confirmed his awareness of the difficulty by saying, "I'm very money inclined. I want to change it to love."

I tried again to pursue some memory of the early years. My client's parents still live, and he could corroborate as "reasonable" my description of them from his horoscope: an iron, rigid, macho father, temperamental and blustering (the Xth House) and a

202

mother silent, repressed, tolerant, unassuming (the IVth keyed by Pluto and its square with Saturn). I projected the pattern *typical of such a situation*: the young man growing up with his sensitivities ignored, not understood, not guided. These were repressed in order to champion reward producing behaviors along the macho ideal. My client said, "Sounds right." Then, trying to prod even deeper awareness of the split, I phrased my summation a special way: "I guess it is safe to say that no one ever said, 'let me help you with your tears'?"

This inquiry got a significant response from the client. He said, "Right. I cried once when my father went off to war in 1942 and never again until I was 18, at a break up with a girl, and then never again until 1978 when my marriage was breaking up." This is all he could remember about his sensitivities. He summarized, "I build up a shield. I can't project my sensitivities to anyone else. I just broke up with a wonderful girl because she *saw* my sensitivities, and this frightened me."

With Uranus ruling his VIIth and conjoined with Mars in the Midheaven, I suggested, "Do you have a history of fast break-ups?" He replied, "Yes! Two this week!" —There was some humor here, but the major serious point was that the split between corporation executive and sensitive romantic was enormous; the tower gave no joy because its foundations were weak. Privately, this man collects roses to acknowledge his sensitivities and appreciate them, yet he flies from every interpersonal relationship that could seed his garden.

He became an alcoholic (the powerful Neptune structure defending self-criticism). Now a non-drinking alcoholic, he agreed with my suggestion that his alcoholism was not an escape but, rather, an effort to plunge inside and come to grips with the sensitivity and the fears of expressing it that were locked in his amnesia of early developmental circumstances.

The man could easily defend himself against fears of being ignored (Aries emphasis) through his enormous professional drive. But through this heavy overcompensation, he had not been able to grow through the anxiety contained within his sensitive emotional needs (Pisces emphasis). The isolation constructd by his outer defenses focused his anxiety into inner pain and a fear of intimate relationships.

He told how he had had an "anxiety attack" in January, 1979, *precisely as SA Neptune opposed his natal Venus and SA Pluto quincunxed his Moon.* He adjusted his life perspective. He quit drinking, lost fifty pounds, and ended his marriage. He said, "All my defenses were dropped. I couldn't rebuild them." I suggested that that was good, and he replied, "Right. I now enjoy the hell out of it! I allow myself to be in a position to be hurt. I don't mind it now."

His words were words of great strength and wisdom.

As anxiety flows through us, articulated in developmental tension and specified in fears, life develops with hurts and blessings. We must allow anxiety to live, balanced with defenses; we must appreciate the causal connections that stimulate compensatory efforts. We must constantly gain equilibrium at every point in change as we live the dizziness of our freedoms, as our suns return to shine.

The celebrated television reporter Mike Wallace, when asked how he chooses whom to interview, replied, "I like the concept of difficulty. Nobody is worth talking to who hasn't had the experience."[21]

Chapter Six
THE SEXUAL PROFILE

"Perhaps the most lavish source of insight into human nature lies in sexual personality. Sexual attitudes, activities, and fantasies constitute the most graphic measure we have of character. In our sexual lives, we express our basic relations to others. We show whether we fundamentally prefer to go it alone or to act in concert. We display our tastes for submission, domination, dependence, conquest, or cooperation. In sex, a person's generosity or selfishness, sense of responsibility or carelessness, may be so easily defined that it is small wonder so many people prefer to have sex either in anonymity or as a profound commitment of trust. We are chary with information about our bedroom lives, even to best friends, but not because genitals are private parts by virtue of being covered most of the time. We simply don't enjoy being psychologically naked. —What we do, think, and feel sexually represents the entire spectrum of our personality traits."[2 2]

These are the powerful and brave introductory words of Dr. Avodah K. Offit, a psychiatrist and Coordinator of The Sexual Therapy and Consultation Center of Lenox Hill Hospital in New York City, in her book *The Sexual Self*. They are powerful because they are dramatically insightful; they are brave because they pierce into any reader's inner privacy.

Indeed Offit's view may reflect the seasoned bias of a specialist, but we may think so as a protection of the private parts of our own lives. In no way, though, can holistic astrology —any kind of serious astrology—ignore the sexual needs, the sexual fantasies, and the sexual anxiety that swirl within every human being's life for expression or repression, for supportive joy in resources exchange or for pain in relationship avoidance. Inadequacies within astrology's purvue for so, so long have been a manifestation of avoiding *substance*, symptomized in part by neglecting sexuality. The inadequacies have naturally reflected uninformed and repressed human beings (astrologers) living in uninformed and repressed times.

Just as psychology existed before the word was coined and just as anxiety existed before it was formally studied, so sexuality has created life and reflected personality expression before it was appreciated as individual, psychodynamic, and developmentally urgent. In our times now, with ever-growing appreciation for the inner environment as it meets the outer environment, the lights and shadows of sexuality are more freed to add holistic dimension to individuation and relationship.

But there are still analytical problems with sexuality. The subject is so personally sensitive and so holistically dynamic that proper survey of sexuality is relatively impossible within one or two visits to a psychotherapist or an astrologer; and proper management of this vast dimension requires specialized education, training, and experience. In one sense, astrology is spared a great amount of these operational problems since it is rare that a person will come to an astrologer for a specific sexual problem, unless the astrologer is indeed well trained in the subject and has established expertise with it. —But this does not mean that sexuality should be neglected in astrological analysis by an astrologer who is not so specifically trained. Since the concerns of sexuality brought out in normal astrological practice are rarely crucial, they *can* be assimilated for analytical substance and, often, beginning remediation.

The sexual profiles normally revealed to astrologers who seek out their holistically vital dimensions reflect *the degree* to which sexual anxiety affects and reflects status/identity, money/love, and information/perspective resources within the exchange patterns within relationships. The most common concerns are linked to societal generation gaps, routined unfulfillment, and communication difficulties. These concerns reflect personality profiles of

207

identity dependency, self-worth insecurity, and defensive conceptualization. And these concerns are inexorably tied to the developmental tensions between the inner environment and the outer environment, between individual needs and outer prescriptions. We see easily how the entire horoscope pattern of personal resources defined by the three Grand Crosses of Houses is activated within the sexual profile. Within sexuality, psychology and sociology and neurology combine in naked personality revelation.

Many have been the times that clients and I have spent half or more of the consultation discussing analytical significances, practical technique, and emotional adjustments within their sexual profile. Other life concerns were not ignored, rather, *they were dramatically included* since the sex profile reflects the holistic personality: parental relationships, idealization fantasies, defense mechanisms, education, societal identification, and interpersonal resource exchange. These concerns reflect generational patterns, religious orientation, love articulation, guilt, and health. There is little doubt that more people go for self-awareness assistance (camouflaged) to doctors, ministers, and astrologers than to psychologists or psychiatrists. Analytical awareness of the sexual profile need not be the private domain of the latter group. It *must not be* if holistic appreciation of a human being is to be served sensitively.

Within the discussion thesis of this book, appreciating individual development within the environmental embrace, we can recall the philosophical dilemma of reducing social facts to individual facts (page 7). We know that the human being is the focus of both within the assimilation of anxiety. During the process of becoming, we continually establish moments of individual majority, protecting our stand in order to define status and identity. Within sexuality, we must reduce societal information and prescriptions about sexuality to levels of individual significance and comfort. This involves distilling personal needs through the filters of parental inculcation, religious prescription, and social propaganda. But then, the individual majority position is established only to be put into developmental tension with another individual majority, another person, in order for sexuality to be fulfilled most adequately.

There is a developmental conflict between individuation and relationship. This is an extremely keen focus of anxiety as everything about the identity is at stake in the naked aloneness with sexual connection. One person's needs and defenses and another person's needs and defenses meet. Anxiety and the potential of guilt, union and separation, approval and disapproval, being and non-being are subtly but dynamically intertwined. Growth change to new positions of individual majority is possible through the benefits of resource exchange; routinized reflection of a repressed status quo is possible through silent homeostasis; or victimization of personal awareness is possible through identity sacrifice.

One of the main complications within analytical awareness of sexuality is that sex is the focus of different needs, prescriptions, fulfillments, and responses in woman and in men. All throughout history, women have been regarded, trained, and treated as sub-servient to and dependent upon men. Sexually, their function was to submit, endure, and keep silent. Procreation was their responsibility, chore, and glory. All throughout history, men were regarded, trained, and treated as dominant. Sexually, their function was to relieve tension and affirm masculine power and prerogative, to pursue, conquer, and proclaim success. Procreation was incidental for men, reward enough for women.

As a result of this primitive and polarized evolution, women sought fulfillment through idealization, through fantasy, through romance, and the male sought further conquests. Societies sanctioned this polarization through religious rationale and political organization, but, to keep social order, prescribed monogamy upon humans, the animal species for which monogamy has never been shown to be intrinsically needed. Women were always victimized; men were always worshipped; society placed the Moon in a dependent position upon the Sun to reflect its light.

This polarization continues into our times now. Religious teachings, social institutionalization, legacies of parental instruction and example still stratify women as inferior, selfless, and negative and men as superior, self-aware, and positive. Women are receptive to men's initiation. Women's emotional expression is thought hysterical, and men's is thought to be virile. Sensitive introspection is woman's bailiwick; men do not need it, unless "something's wrong with them!" Aggressive drive is man's prerogative; women don't express it, unless "something's wrong with them!"

But times now are changing. The identity society has called for recognition of individuated roles. Gender equality is being championed politically, religiously, socially, and sexually. Older people are caught in the anxiety of self-evaluation with respect to past prescriptions and new freedoms; younger people are caught in the anxiety of dramatically pioneered new values that "go against" all they have learned from institutionalized learning and older parents. New problems arise. Sensitive introspection is now demanded of men, and aggressive drive is now expected from women. Both are now entitled to sexual fulfillment, since sex focuses so completely all the dimensions of identity. Both must contend with the anxious dizziness of new freedoms.

Roots of Problems

There is no need that can be fulfilled without relationship, without contact, without connection with someone, something, some fantasy, some ideal, some value construct. Fulfillment of any need is fulfillment through relationship. Anxiety is fulfilled through developmental tension related to growth, to fears, to more growth. To fulfill needs means to be in touch with something. *Without* relationship connections, life cannot endure, life is hopeless.

In its earliest form, sexuality is primal awareness of the anxiety necessary to live. The child emerges from the womb, in relationship to a new world. It emerges into prescriptions already established months or years before with regard to name and behavior pattern specified by gender. The child's role is preordained. The environmental shock of independent breathing is complicated immediately by parental and societal prescriptions. The child's needs are urgent. They reach out for fulfillment through contact and relationship with the parents, through the touch of someone who cares.

We can agree easily with Offit that "touching is the basis for all sexual relations." It begins at birth and extends through death. Touching is the basis for all need fulfillment and interrelationship, but it is dramatically specified with sexuality. "Touching" is relationship and resource exchange.

We say "that was touching" or "you touched me" when we feel emotionally moved. We ask friends to "stay in touch". We express security in "touching down", improvement by "touching up". In the presence of beauty in a museum or in social intercourse, we are warned of the fragility of relationship by "Look but don't touch". Touching is sensitive; it promises the rewards *and* the responsibilities of relationship.

In a highly uncertain situation, we say that it is "touch and go", that relationship is insecure. When temperament threatens relationship stability, we are aware of "touchiness". When we cause disruption, we "touch off" explosion.

From the first touch of our mother's arms, we begin to issue forth our needs toward fulfillment. We soon learn to touch ourselves in order to know who we are. We eventually must learn to touch others in order to become more.

We are touched and we touch in return in many different ways, of course: tactilely, emotionally, informationally. In touch with our environment, we learn how to behave, how to feel, and how to think. From earliest times, how we are touched determines how we touch back. There may be tremendous gaps in certain areas of personal resources where we were not touched at all, and those same areas will be lacking in our resources to touch others. There may be areas where touching was rough and where we children had no choice but to identify parental rough-touching with parental love.

The need to love and obey the parents is fundamental to dependent survival. The dynamics of that interaction are carried forward naturally as the individual separates from parental dependency and strives for individual autonomy. Within sexuality, the development sprectrum of touching originates in those earliest times and extends throughout a lifetime.

Upon this basis, preservation of samenesses and the hope for individuation struggle within developmental growth. We have seen how parental influence relates dynamically to individual needs within the early stress situations of a human being's life. With specific reference to sexuality, we must be aware that sexuality, touching, begins before romance is associated with it or before biological and anatomical capacities mature. The rocking cradle, the suckling at mother's breast, and genital stimulation are all early life pacifying functions. Anxiety is rested as basic needs are sated. With development, individual needs become ever more differentiated. Information and experience constantly grow. Autonomous thinking emerges and the body changes. The whole process plunges into developmental conflict: the dependency upon the parents and, at the same time, the urge to individuate, to establish personal autonomy away from the parents. "First love" is the focus of this urge to autonomy, the awakening of ideals, and the first critical focus upon sexual resources within outside relationship. It is part of the adolescent crisis.

We know vividly how parental influence is crucial to the organization of a young human being's resources. We know that parental relationships shape our development, and we know that we must struggle on our own to shape our own development further, entrenched always within the formative development times in the home environment. Sexually, gentle touching and loving care may very well have started a child's life, but, as the parents develop *themselves* within stressful patterns, their relationship with the child can change. The child's trust and love of parents can modulate gradually into distrust and fear as the parents displace gentle touching and love with punitive aggression and apathy. The child's self-worth profile becomes confused. Withdrawal into fantasy idealization of how love and fulfillment should be evolves to help with the confused self-concept. Projections of the ideal unconsciously reflect how ideal it used to be. These fantasy projections are fueled by fairy tales, story books, and public media massage.

For girls, these fantasies usually reflect being rescued by a shining knight, by marrying and having six children in a little white house behind a little white picket fence. For boys, these fantasies usually reflect conquering an army, the world, gaining strength and honor. For both, the fantasies prepare for escape.

First love is the first experiment of fantasy actualization. Fantasies are adjusted. Dependency upon the parents is momentarily shifted to someone else. Each of us searches out a kind of touching dynamic that represents security, that fulfills a need. Within emergent autonomy, needs are sharply differentiated, and the young person begins to grow away from the parents.

But patterns are already deeply established. Fantasies of expectation are reinforced sexually often by masturbation. Masturbation defines sexual individuation potential. Guilt feelings established by parental inculcation and/or religious rationale have been routinized. Ideals are jarred into reality tests. The nerves are on edge; the skin erupts; sexuality's powerful force pervades individuation.

At this point of this study, we can be helped by the Jungian postulation of the *animus* and *anima*, the masculine component within the female and the female component within the male, respectively. These components help each gender understand, appreciate, and complement the other. It is a concept of balance between things feminine and things masculine. This sense of balance applies to parental relationship as well: we need to be in touch with *both* mother and father. We see all too axiomatically the phenomenon of Saturn retrograde as it suggests an imbalance through the lack, absence, or tyranny of the father that intrudes upon secure self-worth conceptualization. We see all too easily how self-worth confusion relates developmentally to the capacity to give love (IInd House square to the Vth) and to expecting it (the XIth House).

In Case 5 (page 185), the woman was urged lovingly by her father to emulate the mother's ideal. We saw the woman's enormous vulnerability to such a suggestion (the Water Grand Trine that sucked in the Sun and the Moon). We saw the ideal taking hold deeply within her (Neptune square the Sun from the Midheaven), and we saw the dependency complex transferred into the marriage (Venus ruling the VIIth). The marital sexlife was practically nil (her powerful Neptune ruling the Vth) as the woman's complex pattern of needs and their usurpation by the maternal ideal met her husband's apparent aggression needs. Victim met conqueror.

In Case 6 (page 191), the woman was completely confined by her homelife and her mother's own sexual guilt. Undoubtedly she became a scapegoat for her mother's problems. She entered marriage totally naive and immature. Her life perspective changed when she realized she was a woman (Solar Arc Pluto upon her Ascendant) and she experimented with sex voraciously in hope of finding some emotional reward (Jupiter ruling the Vth, in the singular powerful square with Neptune).

The man in Case 7 (page 199) remembers crying three times: his father going off to war, the break up of his important first love, and the break up of his marriage. Sex had always been ego conquest since he defended himself against intimate sharing. He is amnesic about his entire childhood. The imbalance of parental models can only be conjectured: the strong father, reinforcing my client's Aries profile; and the stoic mother, not reinforcing my client's sensitivities.

None of these three people has a specifically sexual problem, but the sexuality of each reflects early home environment circumstances. The woman obsessed with her ideal mother could live for a quarter century without sexuality because of the implosion of the Water Grand Trine; the woman on her way to finding spiritual fulfillment could give up sex totally after so much experimentation because of her emotional self-sufficiency. The corporation president could finally realize that intimacy now must catch up with an austere childhood he can not remember. All three of these people have characterological need concerns that appear on many levels of environmental interaction, including that of sexuality.

There are few people who can show love by touching if they can not remember being touched at home or seeing love expressed between their parents.

As we grow, realizing the importance of relationship, we seek to depend on others. We fear being too alone with ourselves. We reach out in resource exchange at many different levels. Sexually, we can become dependent as well. At one pole, two people can grow to depend on each other with complete trust, exchange of strength, and fulfillment. At another pole, two people can grow to depend on each other as a matter of routine, in the fear of being alone. Sex for the former is free and enriching; sex for the latter is mechanical and boring.

Within routinization, sexuality ceases to be an expression of individuation. Its excitement in "first love" break away from parental protection (or that of previous marriages) into individual autonomy may be quickly lost. In place of this excitement of independence, dependency mires personalities upon a battleground of quicksand. Competitiveness and punishments are exchanged in other areas of life and slowly take their toll in sexuality. The woman loses interest and/or capacity to respond or she attempts retributive measures or demands upon the husband. Hidden angers emerge further into other areas of life. Communication breaks down. The man suffers gradual impotence and self-doubt and/or places blame for dullness upon the wife. Hidden angers emerge further into other areas of life.

The women will fantasize about romance and/or develop "crushes" upon idealized men who are unattainable but fulfill the need to be in touch somehow with what she needs or imagines she needs. The man will fantasize about sexual conquest and flirt with other women to bolster his sagging ego. The women he flirts with probably will have the same problems as his own wife, and so each supports the other's illusion. The woman will dream and the man will boast or withdraw. Together they stagnate. Neither can face the aloneness of change.

It is easy to appreciate this general profile of the sexually disappointing marriage since each of us knows so many, many couples who fit the mechanical dependency pattern. They are at all age levels from all walks of life. They are beings in distress.

But what has caused the problem? —I feel that we can be guided to understanding by four considerations: idealized expectations, reward needs, resource exchange, and communication.

Idealized Expectations—During development, there are always slights to self-worth concepts. These come and go normally as we alter status and expand identity, as we traffic in money and arrange love resources, as we absorb information and adjust perspective. Self-worth concerns come more than they go for some people (and the horoscope shows this definitively, as we know.)All of us construct ideals to help us visualize a target for our management of self-worth anxiety during growth. Some of us rely much, much more on fantasized reinforcement of these ideals than others do.

Every time we say or think or dream a "wish", we are projecting an ideal. It is the construction of hope; it is the hope for reward. The ideals that comprise children's storybooks and now television become the grammar of the children's own fantasies. Gradually, these fantasized ideals become expectations. It is extremely instructive to realize that the XIth House of love hoped for, received, earned is also the House of expectations; that the expectations of the parent in the IVth is congruent with our IInd. In short, the process of idealization is personally taken on swiftly and easily from our parents and our environment, as reflection or defense. It energizes our earliest information/perspective resources, and it begins our life pattern of fulfillment and frustration. Personal needs, only beginning their differentiation, are ignored.

Very, very easily we can make lightening quick adjustments to these fantasized idealizations in order to gain momentary fulfillment. In the excitement of "first love" (even the fourth or fifth time!), we overlook dimensions that disappoint our ideals and em-

phasize dimensions that fulfill our ideals. Our ideals are fresh, un-
seasoned, deeply entrenched. Through their formation, they are
direct extensions of our parents and our early home environment,
whether we consciously try to rebel against that fact or not. The
ideals fulfilled our earliest needs, and these parental touches upon
us endure in essence though they may change form.

Within adjustments, sexual bond is made. Sexual dysfunction
may occur as a clue that some dimension of the relationship is
under tension, but this may be overlooked in ignorance, dependency, and excitement. After the new level of autonomy is established within the new relationship, the mate's shortcomings in relation to the ideals emerge.

This horoscope fragment shows a dramatic configuration involving sexuality importantly. Pluto and the Mars-Saturn conjunction within the IInd House square the triple conjunction of Mercury
retrograde, the Moon, and the Sun. There is a constant developmental tension polarized (hot and cold) within this delightful,
breezy, highly intelligent single woman of 30. She is appealing in
every way, but beneath the strong "ideal", all-happy-smiles self-
presentation is a tremendous tension that must be linked to her
early home environment (Mars rules the Aries Midheaven), her relationship resources (Saturn rules the VIIth), and her giving of love
(Pluto rules the Vth, etc.). The beautiful self-projection that she
exudes is a manifestation of her idealism (Venus-Jupiter conjunc-

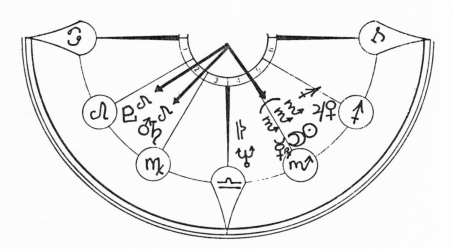

tion in Sagittarius, sextile Neptune in the IVth), transcending her gnawing self-worth concerns (the Sun ruling the IInd, square and in mutual reception with Pluto).

The configuration, although dynamic, is extremely simple to analyze. Without doubt, there were severe problems in the early homelife that tore it apart. The young woman developed idealizations about her damaged self-worth concept that were very principled on the one hand (Saturn) and very avant garde on the other (Mars). These idealizations would have to involve one parent strongly, probably the father.

My client shared all details in corroboration of my deductions: her father was an extremely beautiful, artistic, man of genius. His womanizing and alcoholism were grievous immaturities which ruptured the home when she was 8 years. She has idealized him incessantly since early childhood, and continues to apply exacting standards in his image upon whomever she "falls in love with". There is no sexual dysfunction or concern, only continual emotional hurt since her idealized prescriptions can never be met. With recently ruptured marriage plans, with transiting Uranus conjoining her Sun, she finally has realized all this and can now work to adjust her idealization pattern to make life more enjoyable as she becomes who she really is.

For this young woman, fantasy was a powerful defense mechanism against early home upheaval and her great need for her father (Neptune=Venus/Pluto; Saturn ruling the VIIth square the Sun). Her private sexual fantasies have always been of rape and bondage, symbolizing in her words "searching for a man stronger than I." She then agreed with my addition, "One who could hold you tight, touch you strongly, never let you go, to prove his love and your trust, as you father should have."

The pressure to marry has always been very strong in her, to fulfill a home bond and the home security needs of her Cancer Ascendant. Imagine this woman if she had married several years ago. Imagine the frustrations as she would realize that her fantasized ideals had not been met. In that case, would she have had the courage to end the marriage, learn a lesson, and grow further? Or would she have adjusted in mechanical dependency upon the marriage union, returned to the depths of her fantasy, and grown away from her mate?

In the horoscope fragment above, Venus rules not only the IVth but also the XIth. The ideal conceptualized (Mercury retrograde, ruling the IIIrd and the XIIth) out of the broken family life was reinforced by fantasy, particularly through sexual symbolism in this case. Mercury is unaspected except for the conjunction with the reigning need symbol of the Moon in Scorpio (the need for personal profundity to be fulfilled, a deep sense of purpose). Her emotions and sexuality were anchored to a purpose that was idealized powerfully, that became her expectation of love deserved and hoped for. Jupiter's conjunction with Venus, ruler of the XIth, with Neptune at the midpoint of Venus/Pluto, merged hope with ideal powerfully. Here is accentuated what is so common within idealization: hope becomes reality upside down. Jupiter's only aspect is the conjunction with Venus.

Reward Needs—How often in discussions about relationship values we hear the complaints, "My husband (or wife) doesn't give me what I need" or "He (or she) doesn't understand me". This is a direct reference to personal reward needs, to personal needs that are unfulfilled within the relationship. Of course, these needs may be individualistically articulated through years of accumulated compensatory fantasy idealization, and this is all complicated by the fact that *at one time* the reward needs were about to be fulfilled or the bond would not have been established in the first place.

But initiation of the bond is subject to many pressures and adjustments as we have seen. For example, when the ruler of the VIIth (or planets in the VIIth) is in high developmental tension with the nodal axis or a parental ruler, the expectations are extremely high that the mother or the parent significated by the parental ruler influenced the person powerfully with regard to relationship choice. Almost invariably in such a pattern, there is an extension of the parental idealization process into the daughter or son to adjust personal needs to please parental expectations. How many, many people are pushed into marriages by subtle, forceful, loving, or punitive parental pressure? The marriage represents an escape from the parents while at the same time pleasing them. The self is forgotten until it is reawakened shortly thereafter, after the excitement of break away and newness.

Personal needs are constantly undergoing differentiation and refinement within fantasy adjustment. The whole personality speaks. The reward needs symbolized by the planets are linked with the elements of their signs: Fire, the need to be recognized; Air, the need to be appreciated; Water, the need to be secure; Earth, the need to be valued. Of course, these needs become refined by the particular cardinal, fixed, or mutable mode of any particular element family; by the intrinsic resources symbolized by the planet; and by the aspect pattern and significator dynamics involved. But the needs become progressively more refined and individualized as time and anxiety develop through life.

Sexuality must begin with reference to the Vth House. Sexuality is complexly personal. It is one of the many forms of personal projection within our lives. The Vth House in the natural distribution of the signs is linked with the Ascendant and the IXth House within the Fire family, the need to be recognized, through our speculation of the self's position in adjustment with the job (Vth House quincunx to the Midheaven), through our assimilation of teaching and the laws of the land (the IXth), and through our children's children's children. Sexuality is another personality base for being recognized through the sharing of profound resources.

The VIIIth House is not the base of sexuality delineation, simply because the sign of Scorpio is there in the natural distribution of signs. Indeed, the VIIIth House—like all the other Houses—is involved within sexuality, but it is involved within dimensions of others' self-worth values as they relate with personal self-worth values (the VIIIth is opposite the IInd). Indeed, this powerful axis of self-worth concerns is dynamically involved with sexuality, but the base for personal sexuality must begin with the Vth House as *personal* self-extension, developmentally tied to self-worth concerns and then projected within relationship to those concerns in others. Throughout this book, we have appreciated time and time again these values of the Succedent Grand Cross of Houses.

The XIIth House, as a further example, is not the base of sexuality delineation, even if sexuality is problematic. The XIIth House plays a role within sexuality as personal sexual awareness adjusts to the institutional prescriptions of society, the cooperation of others, and parental communcation, for example (the XIIth House is quincunx the Vth and is the sixth of the VIIth and the third of the Xth). The entire horoscope, *all* personal resources and needs are focused within the sexual profile, the base of which is the Vth House.

In the horoscope fragment just studied, the Vth House is obviously powerfully accentuated (page 215). It is ruled by Pluto which is placed in the IInd. The Water sign Scorpio suggests the fear of being taken advantage of, deeply entrenched within the personality, and the need to be emotionally secure in depth. The extreme focus upon this is obvious within this fragment. Pluto in the IInd, ruling the Vth suggests, as we have seen throughout this section of the book, that the sense of personal perspective within self-worth concerns is in vital developmental tension with the capacity to give love, under idealized conditions (Jupiter-Venus conjunction within the Vth, etc.). Sex here is one thing; love fulfillment is another. The sense of sacrifice underneath the need motivations for compensatory fulfillment is symbolized by Neptune in the IVth. The whole conceptualization of holistic analysis is then corroborated by aspects and significator networks, filled out by client corroboration.

Within aesthetics, emotions, and love—within the idealized components of sexuality, Venus tells us much. In Earth signs, signifying the needs to be valued (and the fears of not being valued), emotional maturation in the differentiation of these needs may be delayed in Capricorn, organized materialistically or idealistically around faithfulness in Taurus, or judgementally assessed within critical principles in Virgo. In Water signs, signifying the needs to be emotionally secure (and the fears of being taken advantage of), emotional dependency can manifest through dreamy voluptuousness in Cancer, protectively controlled or reactionarily overindulged in Scorpio, or martyred in fantasized values in Pisces. In Air signs, signifying the needs to be appreciated (and the fears of not being appreciated), social dimensions can transcend the emotional and neurophysical when Venus is in Libra, respect for kindness and enjoyment of innovation are emphasized in Aquarius, and the mental prerequisites of idealized possibilities dominate in Gemini. Finally, in Fire signs, signifying needs to be recognized (and the fears of being ignored), Venus in Aries can require teasing flirtatiousness for fulfillment of recognition and regular reinforcement of attractiveness; Venus in Leo can define needs of emotional power and self-aggrandizement; and Venus in Sagittarius can differentiate needs into variety and fickleness or enthusiasm for adventurous sharing.

These Venus needs are logically extremely important within relationship dynamics. They are highly accentuated within sexuality, as all other personality dimensions are. In the natural distribution of signs, we know that Venus rules Taurus on the self-worth IInd and Libra on the relationship VIIth. Jupiter, as our need for reward, our hope for fulfillment, similarly carries with it overtones established by element, mode, aspect pattern, and House placement. Again, the conjunction of these two within the varietist dimensions of Sagittarius, rationalized by idealism, was perfectly obvious within the sexual profile of the horoscope fragment delineated above.

Within sexuality, needs press for fulfillment, for reward. All personality needs do, led by Venus/Jupiter idealizations that may be keyed to Mercury, energies keyed to Mars, the defense situations keyed to Saturn, Neptune, and Pluto, wrapped within the intensification that may be symbolized by Uranus. The individual presents his or her sexuality through these complex networks and meets another individual doing the same. In relation to their power, the potential for needs being *un*rewarded is enormous.

Similarly, House placements of planets are often powerful keys within sexual concerns. For example, when Venus is in the XIIth, there is a tremendous incidence of what I call "a private sense of beauty". The aesthetic and emotional needs are privately protected within the accumulation of all societal prescriptions. The privacy makes them difficult to fulfill. We can see this symptom vividly in the metaphor of a music critic listening for five years to a symphony through the finest stereo-headphones at home and then being totally disappointed when hearing a live performance of the same symphony in the concert hall! This Venus is very hard to please. An enormous amount of graceful introspection is required to distill just what the parameters of these needs are.

I have a client with Venus in Capricorn in the XIIth House. His maturation within emotional needs was delayed for sure. They imploded into fantasy resources (Venus square Neptune). Uranus retrograde, Mars, and *Saturn retrograde* are in the Vth House, ruled by Venus. Venus also rules the IVth. —From this fragment

alone, we know about home tensions, delayed emotional maturation, fantasized ideals, undoubtedly discharged in energy laden
sexual fantasies. The man has very strong sado-masochistic fantasies as do many, many, many others. His emotional needs have
been strongly affected by homelife and rarely can be fulfilled outside private fantasy.

With Saturn in the XIth, we have an immediate awareness
of a tremendous need for love. Somehow within the life, there is
the absorption of some curtailment, some control necessary for
growth, within the zone registering love hoped for.

With Saturn in the Vth, we have an immediate awareness of
a curtailment of the ease in giving love. For example, a female
client of mine has Saturn retrograde in the Vth and ruling it. Her
Sun, Mercury, and Venus are in triple conjunction in Gemini in
the IXth, square Neptune in the XIIth. She performs sexually very
well in her marriage, but the marriage is cold and aloof to the
point that the sharing of resources sexually is infrequent, becoming less and less. There have been estrangements. Sexually, she can
not respond fulfillingly to other men outside her marriage. Her
fantasized idealism is powerful within her cerebral needs (the
Gemini emphasis), put there in the name of "virgin marriage"
many years ago by her mother (nodal axis conjoining Neptune and
also squaring the Sun).

Another woman has Venus in Gemini in the XIIth, ruling the
Vth. Saturn is retrograde, ruling the VIIth, and conjunct Pluto
retrograde, both in the IInd. From this tiny fragment alone we can
be sure of parental imbalance, paternal neglect, cerebrated emotional needs difficult to fulfill out of deep privacy. The self-worth
stress is clear; giving love easily is difficult. There must be orgasmic
dysfunction when sex relationships are attempted. My client corroborated all of this entirely. For her, "Camelot was better dreamed
than visited"; her Moon is in Pisces square the XIIth House Venus.
She has no problem with orgasm in masturbation. She has a poor
sexual relationship with a man her father's age. The analytical outline is extremely clear from the horoscope fragment.

Human beings present specialized needs for fulfillment within
sexual relations. Fantasized ideals are parental extensions. Escape
from the parental environment rarely dispenses with ideals. Personal needs become differentiated through the filter of idealized

expectations. Degrees of dependency for fulfillment emerge within relationship. Hope is fulfilled or hope is stifled. Defenses rise. Routine protects sensibility. Self expression is lost. "My husband (wife) doesn't give me what I need"; "He (or she) doesn't understand me."

Resource Exchange—In money matters, within speculation in the proferring of financial resources, we hope at least to break even. We never hope for less. Astrologically and socio-psychologically, we know that money/love resources are deeply intertwined with each other. Within this broad, vital area of resources, sexuality also carries with it the minimal hope for fair exchange, for breaking even. Throughout life development, sexual disclosure en route to sexual sharing demands step-by-step parity. Children at play in sex games of exploration say, "You show me yours and I'll show you mine." Teenagers keep a sharp ear to what levels of petting and sexual sharing are prescribed by their social group and balance these levels against the familial and religious prescriptions established within the home. Adults play hide-and-seek gambits among more complicatedly articulated standards through cosmetic and sartorial allurement, veiled conversation cues, and all sorts of fantasized analyses of social exchanges. Self-disclosure sexually is omnipresent, sensitive, and essential. Throughout the entire process, seeking parity, searching for sameness, is present. We compare ourselves with others for security, and sexuality is not excluded.

In any relationship, resource exchange must take place. One person has something the other person needs. The exchange is set up, and each hopes at least for equal fulfillment. Resources within status/identity, money/love, information/perspective constantly interact as we have seen. One resource is traded off to gain reinforcement of resource in an area felt lacking. Sexually, the process is loaded with fantasy as defense, rationale, and idealized hope.

In today's freedoms, men and women are barraged with media disclosure of sexual adventure. Their minds boggle at the openness of the talk, and their sexual awarenesses constantly compare public media disclosure with private life reality. Women learn of orgasmic fulfillment if they have personal orgasmic dysfunction in intercourse. Women learn of their capacity for multiple orgasm if they have always been routined to one. They begin to feel personally deprived or deficient, or they blame their mates for insensitivity or ineptitude. Men learn of exaggerated penis dimensions and sexual endurance if they are not so endowed, and they begin to feel personally deficient and embarrassed. Both men and women learn of the intimacy of oral sex, if they do not experience it in their lives, and both feel deprived. —Or all the feelings of inadequacy are rigorously repressed in defense of the status quo. However, in such repression, it is rare that the feelings and images do not continue to lurk in the fantasy structure.

Under these pressures forced upon us by environmental media prescriptions, we are jarred sexually. Our needs develop new nuance. Masturbation fantasies take on new heat. Behavioral interchange within relationship develops new tensions in other areas. The client says, "Something's wrong in my marriage, but I can't quite put my finger on it."

Again, we see personal resources fighting prescriptions of outer environment. Fascinatingly, as the man or woman travels away from the home environment, away from the routine, he or she is likely to experiment in sexual fulfillment of newly differentiated needs. Even a couple moving out of the house and into a motel for a relaxed weekend or a vacation or a business trip together find themselves sexually more awakened *because they are out of the home environment that is built upon routinized resource exchange*. Certain prescriptions are left behind. Singly with relative strangers, a man or woman can isolate the sexual needs away from status/identity concerns and seek fulfillment.

Slowly, individual needs change and a different position is adopted with regard to the omnipresent environmental prescriptions. The mind must work overtime to adjust ethics, morals, guilt. We see environmental awareness within the thought, "No one must ever know about this", and we see identity awareness within the thought, "I've only got one life to live, it's now or never."

When a person does feel "cheated" (a money term easily used in reference to love and sex resources), dissatisfaction manifests in many areas other than sex. The person becomes more and more involved with self. Narcissistic dimensions will become emphasized. Women may demand clothing, jewelry; men may buy special clothes, cars. Both may reinforce or pretend status in any way they can. The competition may easily involve the idea of fitting external specifications of success and appeal, attracting attention and sexual interest elsewhere, and in effect bribing the mate to take different notice, to adjust ministrations, to exchange resources on a different level. But routine is stolid. The accoutrements of status are put aside within naked sexuality. Identity is on the bed, and status is in the mind.

We have seen in Part I of this book, how people with status/ identity concerns can exploit aggressively the building of external status through acquisition, affiliation, and assumption. We have seen how people with money/love concerns can substitute material resources for emotional ones since the former are more easily managed. We have seen how information and perspective resources are keenly involved with the developmental process, spilling over into other resource areas naturally. So it is in sexuality: as we learn more, our perspective is challenged; as we earn more, we feel more attractive, more loveable; as we build status, we hope for identity development. In relationship with others, we seek for samenesses to open up disclosure, create intimacy, and arrange exchange. We gain transient freedoms when out of the routine environment. Yet, always, we take ourselves with us: our fantasized ideals, our need profiles, and our exchange potentials, and we constantly have the enormous challenge *to grow with others as they grow too.*

A recent client of mine, has Jupiter in Aries ruling her IInd House. This Jupiter makes no aspect to any planet within her horoscope. It does trine her Midheaven almost precisely from her VIth House. The significator of her VIIth is strongly tied to her parental profile. This tiny fragment is enough to explain so much within holistically acknowledged life patterns: she was indeed pushed lovingly into a marriage. Her mother's expectations for her (mother in the women's IVth; the eleventh House of the IVth is my client's IInd, ruled by the peregrine Jupiter trine the Midheaven) were for her "to be somebody", to be "well taken care of". My client remembers early fantasies of window-shopping and wishing for the time when she could buy anything she wanted. Upon her marriage she was able to do so, but enormous idealized moodiness still prevailed for many, many years. These fantasies were undefined, until she made some sexual discoveries through reading. These sexual discoveries were not realizable in her marriage. She developed new needs which she incorporated into her meditative fantasizing, still not knowing the answer in terms of her own personal needs.

With powerful Uranus development within her horoscope, she broke out to discover the "love of her life". Divorce and remarriage opened up her fantasies into individual terms. She began to work in a publishing job, did extremely well, gained strengths for her earlier self-worth fantasies, and her mood world practically stopped. Her Jupiter had been fulfilled. Jupiter in Aries in the VIth trine her Midheaven *earned* her being "somebody" and sexuality and love were earned as well. Her second husband supports and champions the ego hopes she has always had.

Another client has his Mars signifying his XIth. His wife's Saturn, signifying her IIIrd, *opposes his Mars*. His high energy constantly meets her opinionated controls. There is no greater polarity possible within relationship. When his enormous energies press out, she easily presses them back. He tends to feel unloved in the process (XIth). The tension has caused each to study the dynamics with me carefully.

Interestingly, the man's Mars also signifies his Vth. Under the controlling opinions of his wife, his sexuality would become cold. In sexuality, she rarely would exercise any control at all, giving up her Saturn dimension within the relationship almost entirely. Together we worked to understand how her controls feared change and how his energies misinterpreted caring concern. Together they loosened the arrangement and made the bond strategically productive, each respecting the other's strengths, gracefully appreciating the other's needs, and maintaining the fulfilling inversion of these resources within sexuality where energy control was totally given over to the man. Their developmental balance together is potentially awesome.

Within the exchange of resources, psychodynamic roles become sensitively defined in the search for parity. Within sexuality, these roles often have disguises. Rational honesty is terribly difficult because of the intense subjectivity of sexual points of view. The objectivity of the astrologer becomes extemely important in the remediation of sexual concerns linked with the parity of resource exchanges. Guilt, as we have discussed (page 144) can similarly be alleviated through objective appreciation of need networks within exchange.

When self-worth anxieties go unresolved through fantasy or reality adjustment, the defensive inclination to Narcissism can become excessive. Women can adopt promiscuity under the rationale

226

of gaining status by "doing men a favor", by exchanging sexual attention for material gifts, or by teasing men unfeelingly to establish potential for female self-aggrandizement. Men can adopt promiscuity to achieve status through conquest and to bolster private ego awareness, may feel free sexually only when they have "paid" for it somehow, or become selfishly penis-fixated to emphasize the great gift they have for womankind. —All of these potential stereotypes symptomize keen psychodynamic problems that have linked up with sex expression within resource exchange. *Exchange* has broken down within the ideal of parity, and loneliness emerges.

The whole concept of resource exchange captures the dynamic essences of astrology's elements. Fire needs Air to flame, yet Air can extinguish Fire. The Earth needs Water to be fertile, yet the Water can dissipate the Earth. Fire can scorch the Earth, but the Earth can snuff out the Fire. Water can lose itself to the Air. As these elements contain the behavioral symbols of needs pressing for fulfillment, the question becomes how much of what resources are involved? How are these resources individuated within contact networks of life development? What are the deeper meanings when we idly say, "Capricorn victimizes Pisces"? Is it that one person's needs to be valued usurp the emotional resources of another person bound to the process by dependency needs to feel secure? —These and many more nuances are the teachings of astrology and the articulation of life, focused within individual need profiles and illuminated holistically by the knowing astrologer.

Communication—Perhaps the biggest barrier human beings face within social interaction is between their thoughts. They can rarely be put into simple words, but even then the meaning is rarely as fully textured in objective understanding as it is in subjective conceptualization. Thoughts are conceived in patterns of extreme complexity. Everything we are to any point in time is reflected within the substance and interrelated patterns of thought. Everything we wish to be is echoed as well. It is these thoughts that spill over into behavioral motivation to make things happen. Some thoughts are fleeting, some are tenacious throughout a lifetime. Within sexuality, thoughts are protected by private fantasy and social taboos. They are formed in symbolic code, and they are not easily communicated.

Modern sexual freedoms promoted in the public media responsibly and irresponsibly, by authority and marketeer, often say, "Share your fantasies; tell your partner what you want." This advice is responsible in that it works to break down individual barriers, but it is dangerous because of the misinterpretation of symbolisms possible by both parties as soon as private thoughts are exposed.

For example, a woman fantasizes sexually that she is involved with several faceless people. She is passive. The men and women administer to her sexually and others watch. (How common this fantasy is!) To share this fantasy with her mate would be embarrassing perhaps, and probably shattering to his ego. The man could take it personally instead of lovingly sharing exploration of the symbolisms. In actuality, the woman would rarely allow herself to act out such a fantasy. What the fantasy may be saying in code is her need to be adored, to be catered to voluptuously, to have attention. *In these terms*, the husband and wife *could* creatively arrange such symbolic enactment: together they could set a scene with flowers, candlelight, incense; special clothing and music; they could pretend others were with them; they could let their imaginations run wild in "pretend" drama. Just as children play out mother and father fantasies, nurse and doctor, so sexually two people can play out vamp and stud fantasies. The fantasies are freed, both share fulfillment, communication creates deeper and freer bond.

A man fantasizes that two gorgeous women toy with him. If he shares this fantasy without examining symbolic content, his mate may feel inadequate. In actuality, the man may need to feel that he is attractive, a symbol of power. He may be a sultan in his fantasy. Together with his mate, they *could* act out such a scene. He could close his eyes and pretend more than one woman is present, guided by the woman's communicating participation within the fantasy outlines they have shared. There is fun present, freedom enjoyed, self-respect protected. Routine is broken, secrets are shared, no one is hurt.

If there are fantasies of rape or bondage or sado-masochism, the symbolizations require greater care in management. Deep parental anxieties are surfacing usually, as we have seen, and these must be carefully inspected first in non-sexual terms with a tactful and knowing counselor. The needs in such fantasies are basically needs for love and security to be expressed through possession, wherein strength and trust relate to define love and touching vigorously and convincingly.

Communication at any level in any area of human interchange is risky business since communication reveals where we stand, what we need, how we relate, and what we feel about ourselves and others. Sexual communication requires personal courage and mutual trust, and, as we will see in Part III of this book, the maturity of humor about one's self.

Sexual fantasies may not be as simple as those outlined above. They may be exaggerated not so much in atmosphere and symbolic setting as in specific, personalized attributes. The woman may fantasize particular complexes of attributes about men that, in reality, are absolutely unfulfillable. The man may fantasize extraordinary female attributes totally unrealistically, yet specified in actual human form. Understandably, these complex symbolisms are more difficult to analyze. Fantasy about an enormous penis, for example, may not be the woman's actual desire for such a penis but it may symbolize something as simple as misinformation about the mechanics of sexual fulfillment (a larger penis is never the answer to sexual anxiety) or as complex as her actual *fear of any penis*, exaggerated, symbolized, and inverted in enflaming fantasy. There may be psychodynamic fear of masculine authority, exacerbated by childhood tales about how men are so domineering, so crude and selfish. Fantasy about enormous breasts may be complex projections of a man's need for mothering. Men fantasizing about enormous penises, women fantasizing about enormous breasts may call attention to problems of inadequacy that have their roots in role awareness more than in actual sexual desire or anatomical contrast. Communication without full understanding is difficult and threatening.

Fantasies of a homosexual nature within heterosexual lives often are projections of self-idealization, again highlighting thoughts of personal role inadequacies, real or imagined.[23]

Perhaps the most difficult fantasy content within the normal range is when specific idealized prescriptions of character, behavior, technique, atmosphere are couched in reality terms and actively pursued within reality relationships.

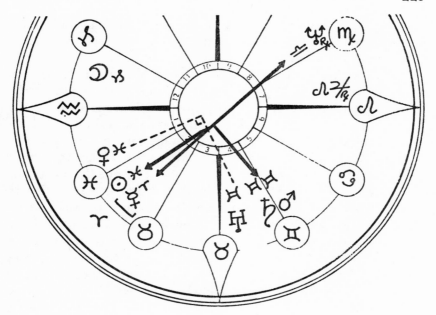

For example, the horoscope fragment shown here is of a woman of extreme idealized prescriptions. Her keen intelligence
makes those around her aware of every syllable they speak. Her
extreme attractiveness makes everyone want to try. Sexually, she
has developed enormous standards for relationships (Sun rules the
VIIth, opposes Neptune, and that axis is squared by the conjunction of Mars and Saturn in Gemini on the cusp of her Vth). Note
also that Mercury in *Aries* opposes Neptune as well and is in mutual reception with Mars. Mercury rules Virgo on the VIIIth, others'
self-worth. Her idealization about others' self-worth resources is
enormous, and it is centered upon relationship and sexual concerns.

Note further that Venus in Pisces is in mutual reception with
Neptune and is squared by Uranus, her Ascendant ruler, in the
IVth. There is no doubt that her early parental tensions within an
Italian family caused great fantasy protection of self-worth concerns, and that this protection was transferred to relationship prescriptions that are extremely hard for anyone to fulfill. Her anxiety about relationships is extreme. She can handle relationships
perfectly in every area but sex. She has an orgasmic dysfunction in
relationship. Her masturbation fantasies have the scenario of being

ideally adored, passively attended to in a *specifically* idealized situation, wherein the men have specifically defined social characteristics and qualifications.

The double mutual reception between Mercury and Mars and between Venus and Neptune links flirtatiousness to prove self-worth with romantic fantasy to protect it. There is a clear split. The young woman is in a terrific bind. Uranus intensifies the whole picture and as well indicates the early family source of the process. Even Jupiter retrograde in the VIIth, ruling the XIth, very weakly aspected within the horoscope, suggests that no one she meets can come up to snuff and return to her what she expects for giving of herself. Most recently, she had been able to communicate and relate for some passive fulfillment through an attachment with an impotent male (his Sun in the XIIth squared by Neptune in the IXth; his Moon, Mercury, and Pluto are related to his nodal axis; his Mars, ruling his Vth, is powerful in Capricorn, in the Ascendant, but all too easily trine Neptune) whose maternally conditioned fantasies have taken his strong sexual energy and imploded it upon his self image. Together, these sexually troubled people somehow fulfill each other's problematic fantasies.

The woman's Moon in the XIIth makes only two minor aspects: an adjustment quincunx to Jupiter and a sesquiquadrate to Uranus. Upon the recent death of her father, the woman has decided to see a psychiatrist. She must study and create deeper connections with herself.

This is an example of two people communicating at problem levels. Each needed the other for intensely complex personal need fulfillments. But their sharing did little to free either of them to greater understanding or enjoyment of their lives. She was able to care for someone totally out of her unrealistic specifications (since the specifications had proved so frustrating), and he was able to fulfill her passive requirements.

Offit makes an important point that underscores this discussion of communication and fantasy: "Just as it is one of the functions of a therapist to tame unmanageable fantasy, so it is also a goal to release severely constricted fantasy in the service of sexual pleasure. Such limitations are most common in women. Again, the key to fantasy release, as well as to relieving guilt of deviant fantasy, is not simple permissiveness. It is the therapist's ability to connect the mental production, however confined and tentative, to the best of early experience."[24]

For those who are repressed, symbolisms can be explored, inhibitions can be illuminated, and communication grace can be learned. For the idealistically isolated, reality prescriptions can be investigated for developmental symbolisms and reality can be explained to help the person appreciate that human perfection does not yet exist. Within the area of sexuality, astrology's planetary symbols symbolize *psychodynamic* symbols constructed by human beings throughout life development. Communication of them must first be to self and then to others within intimate disclosure. The astrologer can be a guide toward this freedom.

Communication is definitely a form of touching. In most cultures—certainly in all western cultures—communication begins with touching: two people meet and shake hands, they kiss each other in many different formalized ways, they embrace, they touch knees under a table. Cultures have enormous prescriptions established for showing respect and intimacy through a degree and style of touching that accompany communication. We instinctively touch inanimate articles to "get their feel".

Within these cultural prescriptions, there are contradictions that make the whole process terribly confusing for individual sensitivities. For example, males are taught to "be a man" and not let things touch them, not to cry as a child, not to kiss and hug their fathers as young boys become adolescents. Females are urged to touch continuously by parental example and expectation. Little girls are hugged and kissed by mothers *and* fathers, and this normally does not cease throughout life, except when one of the parents, usually the father, has not learned to touch easily. Adult females normally need touching to a high degree, and adult males normally do not touch enough, yet each supposedly relates to the other in great intimacy.

We see once again how the formative parental environment easily sets up sexual tensions within early development. Problems with touching can as easily set up great difficulties in intimate communication during adult life. Women with strong identity/status, self-worth, and conceptualization concerns can particularize anxieties within sexual fears and allow themselves to experience sexuality *just for the touching dimension alone*. Sexual dysfunction is accepted, idealizations in defense are fantasized, and sexual activity is allowed for the touching rewards alone. Men with strong personal resource concerns can explore sexuality for its neurophysical release rewards and technical conquest with no regard for the rewards of touching. In either or both cases, technical sexual activity takes place without the harmony of true communication.

Sex therapy for both male and female is based upon two levels of consideration: the illumination and communication of symbolic fantasy and the exploration of the awareness of sharing through touching.

Even with communication problems that may be specified within sexuality, even within the complicated environmental prescriptions for intimate communication, people with strong concerns continue to communicate sexually, sometimes to excess. The drive to do so is natural, instinctive, animal. For example, anthropologists have pointed out how, by wearing lipstick, women advertise symbolically the flushed redness of an excited vulva; how brassieres sculpt breastlines for maximum stylized attractiveness specified by the cultural specifications of any period; the provocative exposure of cleavage between breasts; tight fitting slacks, sweaters, blouses, dresses; perfume to recreate animal odors; shining jewelry and jangling bracelets to announce female presence and attract attention; how beauty marks echo more primitive tattoos; how changing hair color fulfills what is supposed to be more attractive within female and male fantasies. All women explore almost all of these forms (and others) of sexual communication, and yet many of them have specific problematic concerns within sexuality. Very often, these symbolic communications overcompensate for deeper, private lacks.

Anthropologists have pointed out how men also support sexual communication in many symbolic ways: fast cars have displaced the charging stallion; "sports cars" are associated with leisure, the relaxation of anxiety and the best temperament for sexuality, and there is the phallic symbolism of "stick shift" gear control; even neckties have been studied as phallic advertisement, the bright colors of neckware substituting for the bright plumage given in nature to the males of many species; tight slacks now reveal the male figure and genitals, just as tights and codpieces did in past times; indulgence in clothes, jewelry, status houses and automobiles advertise money resources and conquests won, in order to attract the female; macho symbols abound to establish virility. Very often, these symbolic communications overcompensate for deeper, private lacks.

These externalized symbolizations can easily take over *the bulk* of inter-personal communication! Symbolisms—sexual and otherwise—become entrenched within routine, and whole lives are lived through their communication. The human being sleeps behind symbolic masks. The human being works to avoid touching, to avoid contact. Gazes are averted in order not to meet another's eyes; one does not say what one means, but what one thinks needs to be heard; insincerity takes over and intimate disclosure is stifled.

We can observe so easily in any restaurant the stultified silence of communication between couples. So rarely is anything actually communicated. Conversations follow dull rhythms and perfunctory themes. We can think how deep and complicated the barriers have become, how much of intimate disclosure has been sacrificed. The couple has just spent a night together in bed. The couple has just spent a quarter century together in life. Routine dominates communication, yet symbolisms abound to attract intimacy, to preserve identity and augment vanity. Each works alone to preserve routine and avoid touching disclosure. Each releases anxiety through private fantasy. Neither remembers the togetherness of "first love," of intimate disclosure and individual spontaneity.

Astrologically, we know that communication is within the information/perspective resources of the Cadent Grand Cross of Houses. Communication is based within the IIIrd House. Topographically within the horoscope, communication (the IIIrd House) should function to ease relationships (the IIIrd House is trine to the VIIth). Communication supports personal projection and personal appearance (IIIrd House sextile to the Ascendant). Communication takes on adjustment from the job or social status position (the IIIrd House is quincunx to the Xth). Communication is the clarification of self-worth awareness (the IIIrd is the second of the IInd); in so many ways we communicate how we feel about ourselves. Communication is supportive of how we give love, how we seek to be sexual (the IIIrd is sextile to the Vth). Communication is in constant developmental tension with the cooperative dynamic of those with whom we work and share opinions at all times (IIIrd House square to the VIth). The resources of information/perspective, refined through communication, spill over to establish new levels of status/identity as the IIIrd House crosses the barrier of the Midheaven-Nadir axis into the angular House network.

Anxiety to seek fulfillment in life—to avoid disapproval, alienation, and non-being—courses throughout our nervous systems and communication resources: we are anxious about our appearance, our job or social status position, our self-worth awareness and loveability, our tensions in cooperation with others. We feel anxiety about changing from routinized status quo, and we feel anxiety about our partner changing status quo. We acknowledge growth through the anxiety, but progressively throughout development we experience continually increasing anxiety about growing further at the expense of status quo. We fear communicating anything disruptive. We form defenses, we ignore the energies of individuation, we suffer in silence and fantasy as we "settle down". We settle down and give up. We lose touch with life.

Indeed, the sexual profile of any horoscope life is a source of lavish insight into human nature and personality definition. The sexual profile is a reservoir of symbolisms created by fantasy, ingrained by development, and defended by behavior. As such a vital mirror of psychodynamic personality make-up, sexuality is a "touchy" subject. Yet, the informed and graceful astrologer can appreciate idealized expectations, reward needs, resource exchange, and communication dimensions within each client and discuss their manifestation within individuated sexuality. The message of the environment and the awareness of anxiety are extraordinarily juxtaposed within sexuality. In that juxtaposition, there is much understanding to be learned and much freedom to be enjoyed.

Conclusion

Anxiety is indomitable and essential. It sustains life. Metaphorically, we can see anxiety as light reflected upon challenges presented in relationships with the outer environment. The light is bright and nurturing or dull and disapproving, depending upon an individual's perspective of personal resources. Just as the Sun's light is reflected by the planets, so behavioral faculties and needs vary in their illumination by anxiety. Behavioral patterns form to meet challenges.

Human beings convert irrational anxiety to manageable fears. Their minds work with the speed of light to adjust constantly to new challenges. Within development, sacrifices are made and perspectives are established. Momentary rewards establish status and identity which are defended as much as possible. Then new anxiety pressure is felt for new levels of fears; hope springs eternal; and new status and identity positions are tried for.

Existence is complicated between self-centered survival and relationship cooperation. Needs meet needs; resources meet resources. Choice constantly presses for decision. The human being is free and not free at the same time. Being is dizzying.

So easily, within a momentarily adequate status quo, human beings give up development. Social routine protects status and identity. Money/love resources and information/perspective resources stay constant. Anxiety loses outward illumination and implodes. Dis-ease and discontent signal the frustrated personality. Defenses become rigid. Fears rise and remain irrational since the developmental tension to discharge them sleeps in underachieving security. Fantasy works to assimilate disgruntlement. Sexuality is one area of particularly sensitive importance where anxiety and fantasy may dwell privately and painfully.

By understanding that anxiety is essential, we must give up fear of anxiety itself. We must neither hope for miracles to rescue us, to waken us, nor allow ourselves to see planets attacking us, putting us out of life's picture. We must appreciate the holistic natural drama we live toward fulfillment. We must use our minds to assimilate necessary controls and administer energy through understanding of our personal needs and those needs of all who have touched us. We must study our clients' personal profiles of fulfillment, as inner environment works to live through outer environment. We must be honest with ourselves and we must be proud of ourselves. We must be developmentally informative to our clients and reinforce their pride in themselves.

The mind, the body, and the spirit have enormous stamina, subtlety, and flexibility. They can conquer disease, frustration, and misinterpretation. They need *time*: the edge given to the body's immune system by medicines; the development given to the personality's needs by aging; the clarification given to the mind's conceptualization by learning. Time strategizes our offense and fortifies our defense. Time is the patterning of anxiety to live to potential.

Part Three:
THE PROCESS OF
REMEDIATION

Chapter Seven
OBSERVATIONS

What does an astrologer *do*?" —This is an extremely important question, not only for the general public but for astrologers themselves. The answer in the minds of the lay public is most often erroneous; the answer on the business cards and in the practice of astrologers is very often presumptuous.

The word "astrologer" was born long ago when privileged wisemen read symbols in the heavens, at a time when the overwhelming majority of human beings could read nothing at all. In any epoch, meanings are given to symbols in terms of the substance of life at that time. Symbols always reflect reality as it is focused within the interpreter. Times were harsh then for all human beings; lives were short, and the perils of battle, coercion, and disease were constant. The symbols became portents of these harsh realities. Astrologers interpreted both, and history has identified astrologers and their work with such realities.

Long ago, the abject resourcelessness of human beings supported the imperious prescriptions of fate. Fate was in the hands of the astral gods, and astrology was most often in the hands of sacrosanct leaders. Fate was to be accepted; human beings rarely could get out of the way of what was happening *to* them. Astrologers were the focus of this tremendous drama. They had power as

240

a result of their position, but they also literally had to stake their lives on their interpretations.

Now, after millennia of evolution, learning, and experience, hundreds of millions of human beings are incredibly resourceful. Fate still exists in human beings' consciousness and is still part of religious dogma (God's will), but is enormously more secularized for practical management within life that now offers options of individual choice, change of environment, education, free enterprise, protection against battle, coercion, and disease. The astrologer has lost personal power and position within life drama. Indeed, within the pride of individual resourcefulness, many people denigrate astrology and astrologers as archaic, unnecessary, or fraudulent.

The change has been gradual but not complete. Individual resourcefulness is in great measure supported by socio-economics: the outer environment becomes affluent enough to prescribe, support, and protect the life of the individual; within this rewarding security, the individual's inner environment has the freedom and opportunity to learn growth and refinement. But the majority of the world is still socio-economically confined: impoverished outer environments still prescribe in terms of singularly privileged leaders just as in times long ago, and the human being's inner environment is turned over to religious and spiritual rationalization of the status quo. In turn, each society supports its own astrology within its own culture. The symbols for each reflect the anxiety to live that is embodied by each. Socio-economics determine political and personal freedoms which naturally are reflected within astrological interpretation of natural symbolisms.

Astrologers still reflect their epoch, society, and culture, but they are no longer priests or royal advisors. We have little recognized power as we live with the rest of the world. But, as life has become more humanized, more resourcefully personalized and individuated, we astrologers have become challenged in our interpretive position between the outer environmentally conditioned symbolisms of past societies and the inner environmentally enriched symbolisms of the present society. Astrology and astrologers are pressed demandingly to become human and individual.

Our interpretations now not only bring the astral gods of old down to earth but actually place them inside human beings. We acknowledge now what the great doctor, astrologer, seer

Paracelsus submitted almost 500 years ago, that *the planets are within*. The ancients balanced what is above with what is below. We now balance what is without with what is within.[25] Although we now work upon an empirical base of enormous scope in astrological theorization, we are innovators. With recognition of the inner environment, we have established a holistic axis that is brand new in astrological thought and practice.

But as innovators, we must remember that "what used to be" is not too far back in time, nor too far out of the structure of our thought. Astrologers still can ignore the richness of psychodynamic awareness and stress the dehumanized principles of anthropomorphized fate. *Their* lives are no longer at stake; their *clients'* lives are. And enough of this still occurs so that the historical record linking astrology with inexorable fate and tragedy is maintained.

The argument is not that there is no hardship in the present world generally and in the individual sphere personally. There most certainly is. But life and the people living now are different: they live longer, have more protections and resources and freedoms (within the western world that concerns us most), and they are aware as never before of the integrity of their personal *inner* awareness. The argument, then, most definitely is that we astrologers, reflecting the epoch, society, and culture in which we live, must enrich our work with holistic awareness. How much we know about life—about outer environments and inner environments, about outer stress and inner needs, about anxiety to live— should be more important to us as interpreters than what we know about formalized astrological techniques. Techniques clarify symbols, but we astrologers interpret them, and we must do so in terms of enriched life awareness.

So what do astrologers really *do*? There is confusion since astrologers who are not in pace with the times and the innovation of modern astrology still place upon their clients inexorable predictions with no respect for the integrity of the inner environment and the resourcefulness of modern life. These astrologers "read" symbols; they perform; they gain status through pronouncement; they attract attention and dependency by creating fears. They predict rather than project. They glamorize their prophetic role with stabs at celebrities through the public media, and, accepting sensationalism as entertainment, no one ever records the *incredible* failure rate of these predictions. What is remembered only is the power poise of the pronouncement. These astrologers do read the "stars", but they leave the human being behind in the dark.

Sensitive astrologers know this embarrassment. They know the inclination within all human beings to expect the worst, and they suffer the astrologers who fulfill that expectation. And so we seek to explain what we do. Many of us select the word "counselor".

I can not think of the word "counselor" without hearing the resounding D-major sweeps from the chorus, "For unto us a child is born" in Handel's *Messiah*, with the words "and the government shall be upon His shoulder; and His Name shall be called Wonderful, Counsellor, The mighty God, The everlasting Father, The Prince of Peace." A tough act to follow! This very personal feeling about the word "counselor" expresses my respect for the responsibility it implies.

To be a counselor implies expertise. It is a status label that should be supported by reputation, and not simply assumed in relation to intent. One goes to a counselor for professional guidance in a particular skill. *But that skill is important and is sought only in terms of how it relates to life in general and to an individual's life in particular.* When we seek a lawyer's counsel, we seek the lawyer's professional guidance in terms of how the law fits our personal life circumstances, our needs, hopes, fears, and status. When we seek an astrologer's counsel, it should be for the same reasons: to learn how our personal astrology fits our personal life circumstances, our needs, hopes, fears, and status. There must be a *connection* between client and counselor, and that connection must be the governing of life, shared upon shoulders, for the peace of understanding in awareness of life purpose.

To counsel is to know about life. —There is just so much law to learn, just so much astrology to absorb. But life changes at every moment, is different for every human being. The laws of the land or the laws of astrology represent outer prescriptions that must develop meaning in relation to the behavior and needs of individual human beings. Counseling without deep understanding and appreciation for the human being's inner environment is irresponsible.

What do astrologers do? Many give advice. Harry S. Truman once said, "I have found the best way to give advice to your children is to find out what they want and then advise them to do it." This aphorism is all too humanly valid: it captures what we know in life, that people ask advice to learn from someone else what they already know for themselves. Advisors don't have to work very hard to be effective: they can negate the complexities of individuation in the hope to be persuasive (and gain status without responsibility) by saying, "If I were you . . . !"

Many "solve problems." And here again we must ask ourselves, "Do we attempt to solve clients' problems from our personal viewpoint or *do we help clients solve their problems themselves*?" King Solomon was known for his wisdom, which he fulfilled by solving others' problems through the others themselves. The connection with others that is essential in solving problems is suggested in the words of Francis Bacon, *"A prudent question is one-half of wisdom."*

Astrologers can do many things. When we transcend the status lures of power and control over someone else, when we escape the echoes of fate divination and pronouncement, when we make intimate contact with clients, learn their needs and share objective awareness with them, when we reflect their problems and their solutions, and when we reinforce their pride and purpose of being alive, we awaken *their* wisdom, meaning, and resourcefulness. What astrologers do best is to guide others to appreciate themselves. There is no one word for this, except "astrologer" and *what our performance makes it mean at this time in history.*

There are many, many, many techniques that help any analyst guide others to self-appreciation (inner environment) and strategy (outer environment), but it has been shown clearly that the analyst's *attitude* is a strength greater than any technique or combination of techniques: George Mora has reported in the *American Handbook of Psychiatry*, "We find increasing acknowledgement of the fact that psychotherapeutic results are strikingly similar regardless of the theoretical framework followed by each therapist, that the personality of the therapist is more important than his adherence to a particular school of thought."[26]

This is eminently understandable. We astrologers are living together in this world with the clients we serve. We have no privileged status, not enough special education to gain special social recognition, yet we can be extremely helpful. We are helpful by identifying closely with the human condition. We creatively explore the samenesses of the human condition we share with our clients. Being part of the same developmental patterns, being

244

analytically aware of the manifestation of anxiety, we have access to empathy, objectivity, and helpful skill. *Our personalities and professional skill take on the learning of every life we serve.* As in any productive relationship, client and astrologer *share resources*: the client shares an individuated life pattern, which the astrologer needs in order to be helpful, and the astrologer shares an illuminated reflection, which the client needs in order to see himself more clearly. The theoretical framework of the sensitive and helpful astrologer must be based upon creative connection with the client, individualized application of astrological measurements, and a rich knowledge of life. Not only does this framework help us astrologers do what is helpful to others, but it helps us grow ourselves. It is our service to the outer environment and our reward for our inner environment.

In practically every appointment call to my office, I am asked what I do, what will take place during the appointment, during the consultation. This is a very powerful moment in establishing rapport connection with the potential client. The answer must remove fear and suggest potential. I emphasize togetherness in discussion to remove the fear of fatalistic pronouncement; I emphasize potential for reward in terms of that same togetherness. I say always, "We will have a thorough discussion of whatever we feel is important in your life, and it is usually very rewarding." So simple. And so often the caller will say, "That sounds fine!" —What do you say? What do you do?

Communication

Communication is indispensible to the astrologer's art. Without communication, symbols remain measurements and the astrologer remains out of contact with the world. Strong communication skills bring astrological measurements to life and relate astrologer to client. Weak communication skills tie the astrologer and his measurements to what codebooks communicate, to parroting what astrologers say about other lives in other times.

Communication reveals personal information/perspective resources. Through communication, a human being's own personal conceptualizations, value judgements, sense of worth and status are focused for identity and shared with the world for relationship.

The information/perspective resources of every astrologer are under the same developmental tensions as the information/perspective resources of every client he or she meets. Each human being works to establish the sense of individual majority. He or she can project personal views to the majority for authority or to one's personal group for support. In this way, samenesses are collected and position is justified and anchored.

How natural this is in life: "Jessica agrees with me that. . ." or "My interpretation of this aspect is just the same as what's-his-name's." Then, we flatter ourselves by projecting our personal support to others in terms of our own values, "If I were you, I'd look at it this way." How dangerous this is in astrological service, when the focus, entirely upon the astrologer in preliminary analysis, should shift totally upon the client in final communication. How easy it is to forget to make the shift from self to other, to take the easy route to self-fulfillment by spouting inscrutable jargon and personal value judgements.

If we are unaware of the human condition or if we are unable to adapt the symbolisms of astrology found within a particular horoscope *to* the life lived by a particular human being, we hide our lack of skill behind technical astrological jargon; there is no mutual discussion, there is no communication. If the astrologer takes the jargon completely out of client communication, there is an extraordinary amount of time and space within which to develop meaningful substance, meaningful communication. Jargon and symbolisms are the same thing: they are abbreviations only. To be meaningful, they must be amplified and communicated in terms of the client's life and information/perspective level.

Corroboration is the essence of resource exchange between any two people. One corroborates the other's opinion, worth, identity. Sharing information together, they establish perspective for both. The prudent question gains the other half of wisdom, *the revealing answer*. The astrological measurement, phrased by the astrologer in general human terms within anticipated behavioral patterns, is corroborated by the client in the client's terms and values. Through corroboration, astrologer and client understand each other. The process of corroboration is impossible without the process of communication.

One exchange of communication invites another. One exchange of communication builds upon the substance of previous exchanges. Communication creates intimate disclosure and empathy, which in turn allow objectification. The entire consultation between astrologer and client builds upon themes of importance, framed within the patterns of developmental time and given accumulated values by the client.

Creative communication is an art. It is developed through self-control and the faculties of listening and analyzing, through the economical use of observation, and through the rewards of experience. Communication is the vehicle for wisdom, for counsel. Half of the process is in the prudent question, and the other half is in listening to the revealing answer. The two halves are linked together by creative connections made through knowledge, experiment, and experience.

With the conceptual keys presented so far in this book, the intelligent astrologer is able to organize a core-beginning for meaningful horoscope analysis. That core, when holistically derived, encompasses the general developmental position of the human being within his or her environments (inner and outer). Certain specifics of the core analysis (Saturn retrograde for example) can be sharply incisive immediately. The process of communicating horoscope analysis is always intrusive. It is always an invasion of privacy. This is necessarily so, but it must be managed gracefully so that client response will be free, natural, and helpful through corroboration, adjustment, or amplification, and as introspective as possible.

On the other hand, statements of astrological recipes assail the client with fatalistic prescriptions. The client's defenses rise up instantly, or the client submits to victimization by the astrologer's "facts", "descriptions", jargon, and self-possessed personality.

Statements of inquiry—prudent questions—share exploration, invite discussion, and leave room for personal adjustment. Will is recognized; togetherness offers support; the client is no longer alone. The astrologer can do nothing without the client.

For example, in the case studies presented formally in this book, especially in Chapter Three, we began with an awareness of the Sun-Moon blend.[27] This core of life energy and personality need focus is obvious and undeniably essential. We presume that its "light" must flow through the development process of the human being and be conditioned (emphasized, modified, etc.) through behavioral patterns contained within the interdevelopment of inner environment and outer environment. We extend the "light" through the broad resource classifications of status/identity, money/love, and information/perspective. We note the developmental tension points of prominence within these resources, keyed by the behavioral need faculties symbolized by the planets and their aspects to one another. We put all this together within an awareness of generational and sociological background and focus it even more through our individual perception of the individual client. *In turn, this orientation adjusts the original generalization of the Sun-Moon blend.*

Our communication can begin very casually and simply, telling in just a few words what the astrologer does. I find it very helpful to present the client with a neat drawing of his or her horoscope, pointing out that, "the astrologer establishes the horizon line at the moment of your birth from the vantage point of your place of birth. Then the astrologer places the planets throughout the heavens. See how they start to form patterns? Well, these patterns tell us a lot, hopefully! Now, I've got a copy of the horoscope here, with much more detail worked out, as you can see. Please put your drawing aside. Take it with you with my compliments. We won't need it for our discussion. —Thank you very much. —Good. Now, Paul, the general overall pattern suggests that . . ."

Through this short introduction, I am able to explain the background of what supports the analysis to come, show a bit of the technical preparation, give a personal gift to the client, and establish that the first personal statements are general (therefore open to adjustment). There is not one word of jargon used. Through the sense of "patterns", client and astrologer are already prepared to talk about symbolic meanings individualized in personal behavior patterns. No specific bombardment is in the offing. —So far so good! The general orientation is leading up to the first prudent question, which will begin involvement of the client.

Please recall Case 1 (page 91). We saw that the strong, forthright Sun-Moon blend in Aquarius and Aries, respectively, was not obviously manifested. This could be felt within the telephone call to make the appointment, within the client's demeanor when she arrived for the consultation, within her handshake. To begin conversation with her, I openly discussed the Sun-Moon blend generality in its expected form—quickness, aggressiveness, innovative ego drive—and as I spoke I could easily see her inability to identify with this orientation. I simply added the thought, "Now, this is what we would *expect*. But the rest of the horoscope patterns suggest extenuating circumstances within development. You can feel the potential of what I'm saying, but we know that some experiences have gotten in the way of this easy flow. We have to talk about your early homelife, don't we?" Then, to soften the intrusion into what I anticipated would be a demanding parental situation, I used the client's beginning astrological knowledge to point out the T-Square. Here, a rare touch of jargon did not get in the way, but helped objectify her situation, for just a moment, away from her memories and heart and onto measurements and deduction.

For Case 2 (page 101), my notes for the Sun-Moon blend, Aquarius and Libra, respectively, read: "The social and the romantic become extreme in their importance. The duplicity of others is dumbfounding since the self values highly its own loyalty and stolidity. Tolerance and sympathy are learned. The ease within society is so easy as to dilute persistence." This is valid, indeed. But preparatory study of the young woman's horoscope had revealed extreme modification of this potential (the powerful T-Square involving the Sun; the Moon-Neptune conjunction in the Ascendant). Her mother's telephone call and the obvious laconic naiveté of the client corroborated the modifications completely. "The ease within society . . . to dilute persistence" naturally refers to the Moon in Libra and an assumed ease from the trine with the Aquarian Sun, but the modification here is clearly that the Aquarian support is under heavy tension and the social thrust is absorbed through fantasy, a private dream world. Her dulled temperament created for her a lonely "society" of television programs and magazines. Her fantasies and dreams discharged her Mars in Aries. Her whole matrix of resources focused upon a particular underachievement level that gave routinized comfort. The awareness of the "duplicity of others" triggered her tolerance and channeled itself into withdrawal and fantasy.

In Case 7 (page 199), the businessman exhibited Aries drive and Taurus organization obviously in several pre-consultation contacts: his secretary called to make his appointment; I insisted on talking with him personally; he called me, and his language, resourcefulness of juggling his business times to meet my schedule all showed breezy self-importance. The birth-time he gave was unreliably documented. I urged that he get his birth certificate. There was a delay. He went personally to get his certificate and called to report that my suspicions had been correct. He was still precisely officious but intrigued as well. He revealed the extent of his business holdings and practice. All clarified a mighty material tower, which was corroborated in the consultation, as we have seen. —But the Sun-Moon blend (Sun in Pisces and the Moon in Aries) suggested in my notes was incomplete: "The self is more reserved than it appears; more self-sufficient than it shows. Temperament nourishes and defends expression. Occasional bravado protects a sensitive core." I had heard and felt the bravado, the suggestion of professional self-sufficiency. I know that all this was protecting a sensitive core (VIIIth House Sun-Moon, retrograde Mercury and Sun opposition with Neptune retrograde, etc.). When we began our discussion, I amplified the Sun-Moon blend with an observation that always prevails *when any one major behavior pattern obviously dominates the life*: "When we see such extreme development as you have accomplished in your profession, we have to look at it as something healthfully *overcompensatory* (see page 201)."

So, the Sun-Moon blend is always valid, but it will always be tempered by individual circumstance. We must remember the thrust of this book: a horoscope works through an individual to express potentials and fulfill needs naturally, so far as the environment allows, supports, or rewards. The Sun-Moon blend can be blocked within development, stimulating resourceful defenses; it can be overwhelmed by environmental circumstances (see especially Case 5, page 185); it can split or be balanced by overcompensation. These modifications represent anxiety at work, manifested within developmental tension, registered in cognition, organized through personal resources, focused in fears, and compounded within relationships.

In Case 8, page 250, the horoscope represents a tall, strapping, sensitive, young man of 29. His call for an appointment revealed his sensitivity through the questions he asked, his word choice, his voice tone. His presence established strength and poise. He works in radio and television.

CASE 8
MALE

C	F	M
5	6	3
E	A	W	E
1	6	4	3

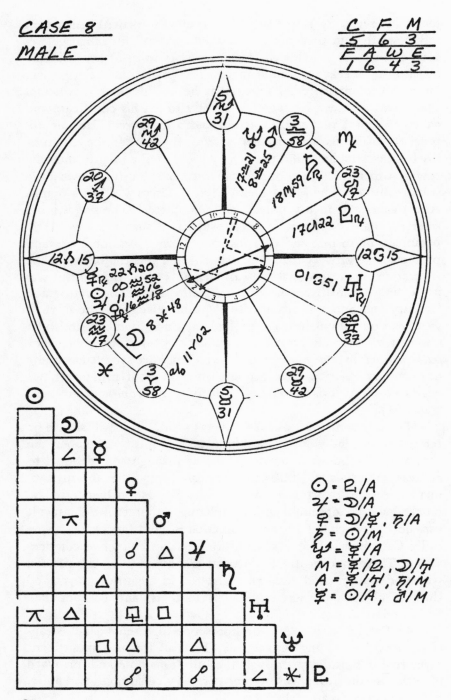

⊙ = ♃/A
♃ = ☽/A
♀ = ☽/☿, ♄/A
♄ = ⊙/M
♅ = ☿/A
M = ☿/♃, ☽/♅
A = ☿/♄, ♄/M
☿ = ⊙/A, ♄/M

250

Preparatory notes on the horoscope began as usual with the Sun-Moon blend: "The unusual, innovative qualities of Aquarius are reinforced by the receptivity of Pisces. Intuition and influences from the occult, the mystical, and the religious blend the real and the unreal, the practical and the theoretical, the scientific and the poetic. Without strong structure from the rest of the horoscope, these positions can bring self-delusion." Obviously, this strong reservoir of Piscean potential can be reinforced by Aquarian innovation. The Sun-Moon blend is valid. Now, the objective is to find what the balance will be within this human being as he has lived the blend potential throughout his environmental experience.

So obviously, we see the key of Saturn retrograde. This immediately leads us to check the parental axis. We see that the parental rulers (Venus and Pluto) are opposed. Venus and Pluto are both retrograde, keying the IVth, Vth, IXth, Xth, and XIth by rulership and the Ist and VIIth by tenancy. Saturn retrograde rules the Ascendant. Immediately we know that the Angular Grand Cross of status/identity concerns is highly charged developmentally, that undoubtedly the father will be keyed within this developmental tension, and that the young man's anxiety factors may explore the "occult, mystical, religious . . . the unreal, poetic, and theoretical" for defense, for eventually finding identity focus, or in discomfort.

Mercury in Capricorn suggests the great need "to hear the grass grow" (Grant Lewi's marvelous image), to be perceptive, to be real. But this young man's Mercury is retrograde as well and is in mutual reception with the telling Saturn retrograde. Again, we feel a split of awareness as suggested by the Sun-Moon blend. Mercury is square Neptune. The anticipation is complete.

Mercury and Neptune significate the Ist, VIIIth, IInd, and VIth. Uranus, ruler of the self-worth IInd, is squared by Mars, ruler of the IIIrd, and brings in signification of the IInd, IIIrd, and VIth, and IXth within the developmental tension construct.

The Sun is weakly aspected, with only the close quincunx with Uranus, the *adjustment* he will need to make in life energy expression (in individual terms) in relation to his balanced, cooperative awareness of self-worth and others' self-worth (Uranus rules the IInd and Sun rules the VIIIth, the second of the VIIth).

Jupiter, the symbol of his hope for reward, here in Aquarius, yearns for innovated individuation (placed within the Ascendant).

But Jupiter is also opposed Pluto: his hope and enthusiasms may be so aware of their personal perspective potential in the public arena and its prescriptions that they have little chance of fulfilling themselves. Jupiter rules the young man's XIIth.

The entire horoscope network, born within the Sun-Moon blend and developed through the key of Saturn retrograde and the patterns of early development, is highly charged within constant personal adjustments made through occult, mystical, religious, theoretical introspection. There is total spill over among his zones of experience and focal points of behavioral resources. Anywhere we look we see this repeated: Neptune in square with Mercury makes trines with (supports) Venus and Jupiter. Jupiter opposes Pluto but trines Mars, ruler of the base conceptualization House, the IIIrd. The Moon, weakly aspected, tries to support individuation through its Piscean potential (Moon trine Uranus) but must always adjust its sensitive needs to the other side of the coin (Moon quincunx Mars in Libra), others' views and, probably, religion and philosophy since Neptune and Mars are in the IXth, ruled by Venus retrograde. Even the Moon-Mercury semisquare, with Mercury rising and retrograde, square Neptune, suggests a mental tension within the network.

By constantly following the Sun-Moon blend potential within environmental patterns of development significated within the horoscope, we see an emergent image reinforced time and time again. Even two powerful midpoint pictures show the same tendencies further: Sun=Pluto/Ascendant, possible ruthless self-projection; Saturn=Sun/Midheaven, moody withdrawal.

It was so very easy to begin talking with this young man. I generalized the Sun-Moon blend and concluded with presentation of the Saturn retrograde key: "And this great sensitivity, and perhaps your confusion about who you really are, is almost surely linked to a very special consideration. Ordinarily we can expect a legacy of inferiority feelings —for the lack of a better expression— that usually stems from the father figure in the early home, usually the father. (I watched for the slightest reaction of corroboration. I felt his attention adjust, a smile begin; I saw the slightest shift in his body.) And, usually, the father is out of the picture somehow in early life: he dies, is absent or extremely passive, OR so tyrannical —any one or more of these— as to never give the authoritative support and love a young person needs. John, might this be the case? Did your father ever hug you and say, 'John, baby, I love you so much. Let me help you grow?"

John's response was immediate. He laughed warmly and said, "Amazing! True. Right. My Father was hostile from the cradle on. And you know? It's funny you say that, because I recently discovered this for myself."

I continued, "Now, usually, what happens is that the young person suffers quietly, all alone. Fantasy comes in 'to the rescue'! You probably dreamed of adventure, independence, conquest. Did you?"

John replied, "True again. I had fantasies of conquest, control, breaking out of my home and being on my own."

"How else, besides fantasy, did you rescue yourself?" I was looking for this big fellow's energy and poise that were so clear as he sat across from me.

"Sports came in. I was young and . . . mellow. A passive person. It, my sensitivity, as you point out, was misinterpreted as being a sissy. I discovered sports and became a football star. Defensive tackle."

It was easy to note reference to "defensive tackle" as over-compensation for intrinsic sensitivities within the macho male image prescriptions of the late 1960's when John was an adolescent. His overview of the "father scene" was clear and well sorted out. He had just "discovered" this for himself, and I did not need to add more. My objective was toward the self-worth construct *now*, within relationships, within the ability to give and expect love (the singular opposition matrix within the horoscope, linking Venus retrograde and Pluto retrograde, rulers of the V-XI axis, all within the idealization potential promised within his Sun-Moon blend, the Mercury-Neptune contact, and Jupiter's involvement within the Venus-Pluto opposition).

"John, your mother surely gave you lots of love, didn't she?" This question was prompted by the reasonable closeness of Mars and the nodal axis and the reasonable counterpoint expression within the retrogradation of both parental rulers. I was exploring the patterns of self-worth in his early homelife.

"Yes, I got love from my mother, but I loved myself."

Here was the adjustment of Sun quincunx Uranus flowing into the Moon trine Uranus; the Uranus sesquiquadrate with Venus retrograde; Uranus ruling the IInd House of self-worth holding the Moon in Pisces.

"John, as a football star in high school, did you date much? You probably were very popular?" Here I was testing the balance of the personal side within the athletic overcompensation, the relationship problems within the status/identity concerns.

"Football was like therapy to me. I like to demolish obstacles. (The Sun=Pluto/Ascendant picture.) But I wasn't interested in dating."

Before John had arrived for the consultation, I believed he was struggling with (homo)sexuality. This suggestion was grounded within my awareness of life pattern in relation to personal needs, not necessarily planetary signatures. The patterns of sensitive introspection, hostile father, fantasy defenses, loving self, indulgent mother, defenses against being "mellow", sensitive, "sissified", and the counterpoints within the love axis all suggested a consideration, perhaps a struggle with sexuality.

"John, if you don't mind, we should talk about sexuality at this point. How would you describe your sexual profile?" —Again, I did not presume to tell John anything. I was easing connections along. Only fifteen minutes of the consultation had gone by. I asked permission; I asked a question of self-evaluation.

John replied warmly, "You don't have to be afraid to say anything you want. I'm here to be wide open."

"Thank you for your trust." I reinforced our rapport gratefully, while John put his thoughts together.

"I'm not comfortable with my sexuality. I've had homosexual tendencies since I was ten years old. I just got along better with males."

I interrupted with an observation based upon experience of this pattern of behavior, "But there was no out-and-out homosexual activity for a long time, right?" A high school football star would suppress these inclinations almost definitely, especially with John's capacity for fantasy fulfillment.

"Right. I would just think about it, especially with someone I would meet fleetingly; someone who didn't know me and who I never would see again."

"Was your first homosexual experience in the summer when you were 22?" I was projecting the focal Venus by Solar Arc to conjunction with his natal Moon; the ruler of his Vth upon the significator of his extreme sensitivity: twenty-two and one-half degrees, six months after his twenty-second birthday in January, when transiting Saturn would be making its closing square to its natal position and when transiting Uranus would be just past its opening square and approaching natal Neptune.

John replied immediately, "That's RIGHT!"

Together we explored his feelings about his discomfort with sexuality. I asked him if I could explore sexuality in more detail, and he again gave free permission.

"John, what is the compliment that turns you on in a sexual situation?" Here I was trying to elicit artfully a response that would clarify the lack of resources in self-worth, inherited from the imbalanced home environment, needed so strongly by his sensitive needs, and suggested in the tensions related to the Succedent Grand Cross of Houses.

"Well, I soak up compliments like a sponge!" He offered no specifics.

"Why do you think that is so?" Another careful question to get his response.

"Probably to strengthen my insecurities."

"And, John, why do you think you have those insecurities?"

"My long relationship with my father."

Our conversation was precisely that simple. Its effectiveness was grounded upon the creative economy of our exchanges, the organization of the discussion along the deductions gleaned from the horoscope, and the trusting rapport we had easily established together. John was discovering who he was.

I asked one more probing question. "I have many, many homosexual clients, and for practically all of them, homosexuality is no longer a problem. Society has opened up so much to it, as you know. But you say you are not comfortable with your sexuality. Why do you feel uncomfortable with it?"

John's reply completed all that I had anticipated from the preparatory analysis, the blends between the real and the unreal, the religious dimensions, and more: *"I want to go to heaven rather than have sex and be wrong."*

This depth of analysis resulted from a combined effort between astrologer and client. Graceful questioning invited free response; communication was reciprocal; deep insights emerged smoothly; intrusion was eased through permission and trust.

Certain key phrases help with such resourceful communication. For example, the astrologer can precede investigation of a highly stressed parental situation revealed within the horoscope with a phrase as simple as, "I think it would be important if we discussed your parents, don't you?" If the client is not talkative at first, a careful command to talk freely must be given. This can be accomplished often this way, with a firm tone of voice: "Please, *tell* me about your father. I think you'll agree with me that it can be important." The client will usually respond with, "Well, what do you want to know?" Then, the astrologer has an opening: "What was your relationship with him (your mother, etc.)? Was there much love exchanged, was there distance? Please share this with me."

The astrologer should also explore the protective power of the word "probably". In moving the analysis along *within the anticipated patterns* known through experience, observation, and study, the astrologer can add on to client statements extra details: "And probably, you felt very alone. Unknowingly, your parents and their attention to their own problems ignored certain of your needs. Especially in those areas where you were most vulnerable. . . .?" The "probably" protects the focus of the discussion: it will not be right or wrong; it will have gradations that the client will make through corroboration. The analysis will have individuated meaning.

Along with creative communication technique of questioning, we have the creative communication technique of listening. Listening creatively presumes good organization, based upon careful preliminary horoscope preparation. The astrologer must have a clearly organized consultation format. The astrologer is listening for the connections that make things happen; the connections in life that corroborate the connections shown in the horoscope.

The importance of organization can be seen in every student astrologer's and, often, seasoned astrologer's dilemma: where in a client's reality does horoscope analysis begin? This book is dedicated to the principle of beginning with awareness of natural life patterns within the developmental pressures that occur throughout lifetime as inner environment meets outer environment. The organizational outlines presented in this book explore that awareness so that the horoscope symbols reflect real behavior potential. Overall, in the frame of holistic astrology, we can say that all clients, all human beings, will experience problematic concerns as anxiety emerges to maintain life and growth and that these concerns will always be residually within the concerns of status/identity, money/love, and information/perspective. The broad frame of this tri-partite analytical orientation is the base of humanized analytical organization.

Admittedly, the client will not necessarily phrase specific anxiety concern neatly into one of these three sectors. The client will almost always be concerned *with a symptom rather than a cause*. Marital misery or relationship difficulty may be the symptom of deep self-worth concerns; vocational dissatisfaction may be a symptom of parental expectations, dissatisfaction, pressure; relationship difficulties may be symptoms of job insecurities. The client may fix his or her focus of present problems upon those resources that are more easily manageable. Sensitive organization before the consultation prepares the astrologer for anticipation of deep causes. Listening creatively allows the astrologer to clarify anticipation, or learn of whole new dimensions concomitant with individuation.

For example, a young man came to see me during the writing of these pages. He cited his insomnia as a reason for the consultation. He has a horoscope without a square, and the VIIIth House Moon makes only one aspect, a quincux to the Sun. Developmental tension is extremely low. He is listless, passive, uninvolved. In response to a few questions, he told freely that he had been seeing a psychiatrist for many years; that he had once attempted suicide.

His horoscope is extremely difficult as far as a clear-cut starting place is concerned. The Sun-Moon blend promises a keen moral sense, an expressive lift, social receptivity, all within a strong personal interest reinforced further by the Aries Ascendant. But this would work through very weak connections, the weak aspects involving the Sun and Moon.

Along with the absence of clear developmental tension, there is also an absence of Water emphasis, a vagueness about the parameters of emotional resources. There is a weak defensive organization in the *inclination* to a Fire Grand Trine through Mars (the Ascendant ruler), Jupiter, and the Ascendant. He would probably isolate himself, withdraw defensively in an attempt to be motivationally self-sufficient.

He has a triple conjunction of Mars-Saturn-Pluto in the IVth House. This obviously was the starting place for analysis: a fixated focus of the root causes underneath external behavioral manifestations. The early home environment was filled with problems of neglect. Immediately, the study of deep developmental tensions was awakened, and the symptom of insomnia was put to sleep.

Another young man just telephoned me "for some advice". He has been a client of mine for two years. He has gone through nine months of turmoil in a relationship with a married woman. At the outset of the relationship, we had discussed its complications, but he was determined to try to work things out and "learn something." At the same time, his professional positions were equally insecure. Astrologically, there was no clear index of all the complicated unsettledness.

"Jack" called to report that he had finally broken off the relationship. He knows some astrology, and now was placing his anxiety upon measurements that threatened more relationship upset. For so long, relationships were his "symptom". Mercury rules his Midheaven and his Ascendant and is placed in his VIth, opposed his Moon and Saturn retrograde in the XIIth. Neptune rules his VIIth and is sesquiquadrate his Mercury and trine his Midheaven. His thinking process and nervous system were almost completely directed to relationship concerns. His very strong Mercury *was taken away from its Midheaven rulership* (it trines Uranus in the Xth) and was diverted by the tension aspect with Neptune, ruler of the VIIth. The Sun and Mars are in conjunction in the VIIth, square Uranus in the Midheaven. These measurements show the constant battle between profession and relationships for prime reference of status/identity resources.

When I asked about his job position, Jack said, "If I could only get some sort of relationship security worked out, I could put my mind to job security." I listened carefully. Jack was expressing the tense orientations of a major part of his horoscope.

To help him, I simply turned his statement around, i.e., I routed his Mercury back to the Midheaven; my "advice" would be an adjustment of material he already had in mind. "But Jack, what if you turned that around? What if you applied yourself totally to setting up job security? I'll bet you that that would make you feel better about yourself, and then your relationships would take care of themselves."

"But I always think it should be the other way around."

"I know. Why not change that?"

"Gosh! That gives me something to think about."

Jack had called in tension. Why had he called? He felt I could help. How could I help? By helping him help himself. How did I know how to help? By listening to him try to help himself.

When we listen in our astrological work, we also listen for clients' value judgements. We know that developmental tensions within the concerns of status/identity, money/love, information/ perspective will adjust every person's value judgements. Value judgements frame every individual's status quo. *Since no event has any value until a human being gives that event a value*, we know that the values in a human being's life are personally conceived. We listen for these value judgements as they accumulate within behavioral patterns within development time.

Time and time again, I have felt the trap that faces every astrologer in every consultation. Listening to the accumulation of value judgements that establish a client's individuality, I feel my personal value judgements awaken in comparison. This is perfectly normal within intimate disclosure and resource exchange, but it is absolutely essential that personal value judgements be put aside by the astrologer. For example, the astrologer may prize parental relationship highly and hear a client disclose hate for his or her parents. In such a case, creative listening must cut off personal value judgement comparison in order to allow appreciation of the client's personal perspective. Hate obviously is dysfunctional; it uses up energy through preoccupation and expression; it can easliy undermine self-application in other resource areas. But the astrologer does not work to remove hate, but to adjust the client's perspective through objectification of the development concern. *By adjusting perspective, the astrologer helps the client establish a different base for different value judgements.* Energies can be freed of fixation.

In the process of objectification, the astrologer takes what is learned by listening, formulates a further question, and works to create some distance between the focus of concern and the routined subjective point of view. The process of objectification —of removing subjectivity— allows the client *to confront anxiety and specific fears creatively*. Confrontation allows understanding and stimulates resourceful reaction.

First, the astrologer must *acknowledge* the client's value judgements and feelings. If the value judgements and feelings are ignored or attacked, astrologer and client are pushed into competition; the astrologer seeks vindication, and the client feels demeaned. Acknowledgement is so simple: "Lois, I appreciate what you are saying. I really do. But, please let me ask you something: your parents had lots and lots of problems of their own, didn't they?" The client's acknowledgement of this fact of life allows a change of focus in the discussion. The question opens up new territory without ignoring the old. "Do you think it's possible that you just got caught in their traffic patterns?" With a touch of calm logic and human warmth, the astrologer is able to achieve some distance between the client and his or her habitual conceptualization and the focus of a deep problem. Compassion through understanding can begin to displace hate.

Let us recall John's case (page 250). When asked why he felt uncomfortable with his sexuality, he replied, "I want to go to heaven rather than have sex and be wrong." The sensitive dichotomizations of his Sun-Moon blend emerged clearly.

Although, in my own personal life experience, I have experienced and thought through the problems of heaven and hell related through guilt to sexual concerns, there was no right or possibility for me to place my value judgements upon John. I had to bring his own circumspect value judgements out of *him*; work to adjust *his* perspective for his greater fulfillment.

In listening carefully to his powerful statement, I felt that it was too concrete to have been formulated on the spot. He had been through this logic many times. Almost definitely, he had talked the issue over with other "counselors". To be sure, I asked him simply, "Have you talked this over with many people?"

John said that he had shared his dilemma with only a few others.

I asked, "Have you ever talked this over with a priest?" This was a logical question, led by the religious suggestions within the Sun-Moon blend and from the obvious religious formality of his statement.

John laughed: "Yes I have! One priest said I'd burn in hell; another propositions you; and another says it's Okay." —It seems that many priests make the same value judgement mistakes that astrologers do.

Where was I to fit in? There was no astrology to take care of this dilemma, no planetary movement that would alleviate concern, bring the light, help free the anxiety.

Listening carefully to what John said as he elaborated upon his experiences with priestly counsel, I realized that John really had *not* made up his mind that sex was wrong and would keep him from going to heaven. His strong statement to that effect was a "trial balloon". He was bewildered, and he was asking me to help him further with his orientation. Several times in the discussion, he had said, "Don't hold anything back; I want to know what you think." —This is a pitfall for the astrologer, since giving advice is rarely productive, unless the advice is a formulation of what the recipient already has in mind. But this is also an opportunity for the astrologer since a new thought pattern can help the client find his or her own answer through fresh perspective. I wanted to help him confront his dilemma from another point of view.

John talked at length about feeling "controlled by guilt". Finally, the conversation stopped. John had said all he had to say. I had waited for the empty moment into which to place carefully and strongly an objective thought for his evaluation: "John, let me submit a thought to you. We all need all kinds of controls to help us live efficiently within freedom. Can you identify with that?" (Note the word "identify".) John agreed, and I continued, "Well, how about this: *no control is truly efficient if it curtails freedom*."

My statement had strong impact upon John. It had touched upon the wisdom of Saturn, a powerful focus in John's horoscope, and a powerful focus in his process of self-discovery as he was two months away from his Saturn return.

John showed relief. He smiled and said, "I had thought karma was punishing me! That's very interesting. I guess I've been scaring myself with too much thinking . . .."

"Important thinking, John, getting you ready to think further. You can work this out, just don't let all the thinking take energies away from the rest of your life."

The next day, I received a call from the local astrology bookstore. In the course of the conversation, I learned of a tall young man who had come into the store with great enthusiasm and interest. It was John. He had gone to the bookstore right after his appointment with me and was seeking out new books to broaden his knowledge about life. The theoretical was leading him to the practical; the unreality of his fantasies was dissolving to the real.

In all these case fragments, the preparatory astrological analysis has suggested core concerns connected to anxiety symptoms. The astrologer makes the symbolic connections within knowledge of life patterns, prompts intimate disclosure through artful communication, and listens creatively to client value judgements. In the process of communication, client perspective is established and horoscopic connections are corroborated and adjusted. The astrologer studies the client's own awareness of connections. Perhaps these connections are based upon a lack of information, incorrect information, or defensive subjective postures as a result of misinterpreted connections (often blown out of proportion by fantasy). The astrologer can give information, correct misconceptions, and objectively suggest alternative points of view. When this type of remedial adjustment takes place through creative communication, the client almost invariably says, "I never thought of that" or "I see!" The first statement shows displacement of one thought process by another, and the second suggests that vision improves through informative adjustment of objective perspective.

Making Connections

Connections makes things happen. We relate an action to a cause, a behavior to a need. The astrologer makes connections between horoscopic significators and behavior patterns anticipated logically and empirically. The astrologer refines the analytical connections as the client reveals the actual connections made within his or her life. Refined connections make analysis productive.

In artful communication, I have suggested that connections must never be made through jargon (except perhaps when the client is an astrologer and would benefit from the astrological signature of a particular insightful connection). Jargon immediately defies individual volition within the client and resurrects the austerity of fate. Connections are most dramatically made through the language of life translated into the client's perspective of values. For example, a young —and, indeed, very bright— woman corroborated periods of deep depression. My inquiry about her depressions was certainly prompted by the powerful midpoint picture Neptune=Moon/Saturn and its fit into her whole horoscope pattern, by part of a Mars-Saturn retrograde conjunction profile, especially with Saturn retrograde ruling her Ascendant; but explaining the jargon to her would have been a grotesque assault on her sensibilities and a waste of time. Such a response would certainly indicate that I knew nothing better to say. Instead, I replied, "and these depressions, we certainly can appreciate them within your isolation, within your loneliness, as we've discussed. We can't get relationships going because the ideals are in the way, those ideals that overcompensate for your father's vague relationship with you. Now, we know that relationships are essential for anything to happen; we need those connections. Let's try an experiment." —I acknowledged the depressions, recapitulated the major points of our sharing together to that point, always showed identification with her by using the word "we", and then shifted the focus of the conversation to the goal of contact with others. I introduced an experiment.

"Put your right hand in front of you like this (forearm vertical, in line with the spine, hand open) and put your left arm behind your back. Now, do as I say. Ready? *Clap with one hand.*" I was in the same position as she, one arm back and one arm poised in front of me. Each of us flexed fingers, patted a shoulder, etc., trying to "clap with one hand". Suddenly, she reached out to clap *my* hand. That was what I was hoping for! I repeated the clap upon hers with a sharp slap. We both laughed, and I explained warmly, holding both her hands, that we had just made contact, that the energy of contact was meaningful only through relationship, to another person, to a thing, to a memory, to a dream, to a goal. —The point was made: depression occurs; outer contact is lost; self is isolated; contact must be remade externally. This was especially important to my client since her beautiful hands had become lugubriously sensitive for her. She commented, with a knowing smile, "Since I slashed my wrists, I have not been able to touch anyone . . . I've given up touching." (Please recall Chapter Six.)

I continued to hold her hands as she paralleled our experiment with a story she knew about hell being starving people with plenty of food but with spoons of such length that feeding themselves was impossible, about heaven being people with the same plentiful food supply and similar long spoons but figuring out *how to feed each other* (resource exchange). The experiment had taken depression and self-isolation and connected it with relationship potentials. She was able to touch me with her hands. She was able to give a hug as she left the consultation later.

Shortly thereafter, I received a telehone call from a middle-aged client of mine. She was deeply depressed. Again, I had to say something beyond a promise that transiting Saturn would soon leave its sesquiquadrate connection with her Moon in Capricorn (how shallow and irresponsible such jargon begins to sound within holistic astrological awareness). I replied instead, "Doris, what you're feeling now is a frightened reaction to some opportunity on your job, wouldn't you say?"

Doris agreed. There were tensions in her job; she lives alone and has no one with whom to share her day. The tensions were all pointing to an improvement within her job position. (Her Moon is in her VIth, and Saturn rules her VIth.) Employee relationships were involved, and Doris was making a bid for more responsibility.

"Doris, I really know how your depression feels. I've been there many times myself (thorough identification with the client in acknowledgement of her depression). I always feel, when I'm depressed, like a big heavy spring pressed down so that the coils press together in a grating bunch."

Doris agreed with my imagery completely.

"Well, I ask myself when that happens —and I'm asking *you* now— what happens when we take the pressure off?"

Of course! The spring springs back up. This easily got our discussion out of depression and into the objective assessment of the reality situation, freeing energies for action. I became a job strategist in inter-office politics *as part of my role as astrologer*. I suggested that the whole situation would come to a focal point in four weeks (when transiting Pluto made a conjunction with her Saturn) and that the odds were really in her favor that she would improve her position at work (supportive Jupiter transits simultaneously).

Doris said, "Oh! I understand now. That's good to hear. *That's how I see it too!*" —Doris needed someone to talk to. We made a connection together that refined further the connections in her horoscope, in her life, and in her mind.

Depression can be normal or pathological. The former we all share and can easily be integrated within astrological consultation. The latter requires deep diagnosis and long-term remediation by a psychiatrist or spiritual teacher. Normal depression is sporadic; personal resources instinctively work to overcome it. Pathological depression is chronic; personal resources and the very spirit of life are suppressed. Normal depression is the ebb phase within the natural flow of life. It is subjective contact with anxiety before or after objective contact with the outer environment.

In astrological remediation, we can help clients to open up depression, to spoon their resources back to others, to uncoil their heavily weighted springs. We can dramatize that failures are integral to the flow of life. In fact, much more can be learned from failure than from success; after the initial subjective shock, objective perspective is clarified and strengthened. Normally, we can always look back upon depressed times and see the wisdom that was gained, what we "came up with" out of depression. Retrospection is always easier than awareness since the distance supporting perspective is greater when looking back than when experiencing now. Objectivity is a base for understanding, and objectivity can be explored as well within the present.

If setback is experienced within the job situation, subjective feelings of depression can spill over into many different related life zones of experience and behavioral patterns of expression. (Please recall pages 44 and 45.) These spill overs are very important connections that the astrologer can detect through creative communication with the client. Spill over tensions can be loosened in analysis; the dam holding anxiety can be buttressed; the potential power to live on contained within anxiety can be economically directed, productively channeled. Strategy brings reactive resources into action. The process is framed within time.

Analysis of several such setbacks throughout the past, reveals client resourcefulness under anxiety pressure, articulates client value judgement, and refines planetary symbolizations. The accumulated understanding through retrospective analysis —"What happened then? How did you work that out? What did you learn from that situation?— can illuminate objective assessment and resourceful strategy within present or future difficulty. The messages of the environment are learned as the human being becomes ever more aware of anxiety.

If setback is experienced in love relationship and deep depression is felt, we can check the degree of dependency that was invested within the relationship. Excessive dependency can easily inhibit personal growth, self-awareness, and freedom. The self-image can be lost, and, when the focus of status/identity dependency is taken away, resourcelessness is felt crucially. The process of dependency can be extravagantly inflated by idealized fantasies, as we have seen. Such excessive dependency suggests a connection with certain resource *values* established within the focus of dependency that are not established within the dependent person.

For example, the fantasies of a client for many, many years were projected out of the homelife, which was empty of any personal recognition, and onto Elvis Presley. The woman said, "By the time I was thirteen, I lived in a totally imaginary world. I would be discovered somehow, rescued." This was an opposition spreaking eloquently within her conceptualization resources of information/perspective, relating by rulership relationship concerns (VIIth), self-worth (IInd), and love and acclaim hoped for (XIth), all within the sense of an emphasized Jupiter. Her hopes and wishes could easily lose reference to reality. Her values hoped for, her needs, were not recognized within the family environment: ego importance (Aries Ascendant, Mars in Leo); the need to have her opinions respected far and wide (Moon in Sagittarius). Elvis Presley represented these values.

The woman outgrew Elvis, and he was taken away. Her legacy of inferiority feelings and dependency inherited from the early homelife imploded deeply. She "stayed stoned all the time" in her depressed withdrawal. I suggested that dependency upon someone outside herself had been too easy. She could not depend upon her parents. She had been lost. I submitted that getting *"stoned"* was an effort to *find* her personal center of gravity, rather than to fly high away from it! We then worked together in discussion to realize the importance of relationships with the outside world, and she was able to take a job for the first time in many months shortly thereafter.

With extravagant expectations or hopes, especially within the broad classification of money/love resources, we can begin to feel the efforts of overcompensation. Self-worth anxieties almost invariably are rescued by idealized fantasy. Prescriptions for relationship are exacting. Fulfillment is infrequent or impossible. Disappointment arises. Depression emerges within loneliness. Anxiety implodes. The fantasies are taxed to exhaustion, and they then implode in self-deprecation. Objective distance is lost. Subjective position is heavily depressed. —Explanation of this process through the client's retrospective objectivity, connected to the root concerns of early development, helps enormously to gain objectivity and resourceful strategy (strengthened self-awareness) within present and future echoes of similar concerns.

Diversification of interests can work to remedy emotional fixation. This is the concept of spill over in reverse: when there is a fixation within the state of depression, other resources are shadowed, are locked out. Folk wisdom reflects this insight in the adage, "Count your blessings!" The astrologer can help refocus a client's blessings, reinforce specifics of self-worth, distill the profile of status/identity resources, and help idealizations make adjustments to practicality.

Often, depression can be self-punishment encouraged within guilt formations. John thought karma was punishing him. He was incorrect in his knowledge of the philosophy of karma—karma is *not* punitive; it is equalizing—and this wrong view combined with the intrusion of religious guilt to depress his joy of living. His sensitivities had never been acknowledged and lovingly guided by an authority figure in his early development. In such cases, the astrologer and *what the astrologer knows about life and can communicate effectively* become a vital focus of, and a connection for such loving, guiding authority. The astrologer reflects an appreciating objective view of self back to the client, just as parents are supposed to do.

Many clients can not make any connections at all within their life. They are dulled within routine. Their lives meet environmental prescriptions. They live in "Blahsville". There is no developmental tension, since everything is taken care of. There is no hope for anything but continued sameness. They come to an astrologer for a miracle.

These are the most difficult cases for any astrologer, and these cases are presented most often to astrologers living very close to the same routine, within the same environmental prescriptions. Often, the only dimension that separates such clients from their astrologer/friends is that the friends have a special, exciting hobby. These astrologers must practice their craft in order to learn. They meet these most difficult cases representing routinized insulation against developmental energies. They are forced into routined descriptions of the status quo and, unfortunately, into miracle predictions. So easily, the concerns of pleasing the client/friend press the astrologer into empathic subjectivity. Objectivity is lost. Client, astrologer, and astrology all lose.

Even seasoned astrologers face this pressure. A routinized life is like dried clay: it has no flexibility, no stretch, no response. The life will not mold itself around the framework of any opportunity, including a miracle. It will not stick, will not make a connection. Humanly, we want to be of dramatic service and, all too easily, we can be involved subjectively within the clients' dreams that are not grounded upon activated resources.

The key in managing these cases helpfully is to direct analysis *away from* what is expected, i.e., a miracle from the outside environment, something "interesting and exciting". Analysis should work to awaken the *inner* environment, to encourage instrospection. For a man, the astrologer can study the values of job satisfaction, the potential for mobility, the hobbies that might really capture his sense of self-fulfillment. For a housewife, the astrologer can inspect her boredom, her community activities, her reading habits, her recreational interests, the values she has gotten for herself through her children. Creative communication about these spheres of status/identity reference should awaken the faculties of self-objectification and self-assessment. Then, the same inquiries can be applied in reference to the husband or wife of the client to determine one's awareness of the other's needs and resources.

Gradually, after communication has revealed that "nothing has happened" in life and after the astrologer has awakened potential interests and mobility potentials socially, professionally, or geographically, astrologer and client can begin to rekindle hopes in relation to resources, to pride within self-awareness and relationship. First remedial steps often can be within sexuality, where routinization and dullness so easily come to rest. Innovation within sexuality—revealing private fantasies, changing rooms, varying techniques—almost always recharges energy batteries, brings partners closer together at any age. With more energy, and more togetherness, more can happen. Husband and wife will feel better about themselves individually and as a unit.

For the man, key questions can spark his pride and strategies on the job: "What do you think you could do to improve your job performance? What would please you realistically on your job? What are your chances for relocation, for starting over somewhere else, for a promotion?" Naturally, such questions are keyed to transits and projection measurements (Solar Arcs, Secondary Progressions) of energy, resourcefulness, change (Mars relationships,

angular cusp connections, Jupiter contacts with Pluto, Saturn connections with its own position or the Sun or the Moon, Uranus
contacts, etc.). For the housewife or woman alone, if unemployed,
questions to arouse curiosity about the world larger than her own
immediate environment are helpful in stimulating activity: "What
do you do for exercise? Have you ever thought of going to a Yoga
class? What about those lectures at your local college or library?
You and your husband could plan a vacation in Mexico, see the
pyramids, read up on them before you go! What are some of your
private dreams, those you and your husband used to share?" These
questions could be related to measurements of socialization and
visualization and to study (Mercury, Venus, Jupiter, Neptune in
addition to the heavier measurements of energy and change). The
objective is to bring out clarified potentials from the client, help
with practical adjustment, and *then encourage activity to fulfill
them*. The inner environment is awakened, and things start to
happen as it is reconnected with the outer environment.

Two years ago, a man in his mid-thirties, good natured and
successful, but alone and unmarried, came to me for a consultation. He earned a tremendous salary as number two man in his
father's big firm, yet he dressed obviously carelessly. In many
ways, he showed low self-esteem and status incongruence: he was
where he was, but everything about him suggested that he felt he
did not belong there. He still lived with his parents. (Imagine how
other executives in the firm regarded him!) Absolutely nothing
had happened to this man, even in correspondence with the
strongest astrological measurements. His life was routined in tremendous insulation by his family at home and by his father on the
job. He was too comfortable and too routined in not being his
own man.

He was consulting me to test out some of his curiosities
about astrology and to find out about his potential for romantic
relationships. This was the "symptom". In talking with him, I dug
into the inner environment, and together we acknowledged the
core concern: the routine life in the shadow of his father. I listened carefully as he revealed that his father was quite old; still
active on the job, but very ill.

I asked a key question, "Why did your father work on so
long past retirement age?" I asked the question in such a way as to
demand a very careful, introspective answer.

The young man replied carefully, quietly, "I guess he doesn't have faith in me to run the company." This was the answer I had anticipated: the personal center of his clearly stressed status/identity concerns.

The young man's horoscope clearly showed definite parental restrictions, indeed, and his answer at this point in the consultation revealed how thorough these restrictions had been. His rejection of his objective status through almost adolescent dress and behavior suggested his subjective *acceptance* of lower status.

"You gave up a long time ago any effort to change his opinion, right?" My statement was corroborated. The man had settled into the routine of living and working in his father's shadow. He had a superb salary but no other meaningful values within his life. This position of restricted development and then the *dependency upon* that restrictive situation affected his personal interrelationships. I suggested that he was probably staying on at home hoping eventually to gain his father's love and respect. He agreed.

I felt that I had to rekindle his confidence and determination. His horoscope showed important changes within the next year, changes that could realistically include his father's death and the son's ascendancy into leadership of the business. I felt that the father had routinized *his* own reactions to his son as well, but that, old and ailing, he would be thinking about the change in company leadership, hoping finally to be proud of his son.

I asked the young man a deep question, "Think this through carefully please: please tell me, what you would like to have your father say to you from his deathbed?"

This question had quite an impact. The question had to be dramatic in order to give urgency to remediation. The man's answer was a formulation of his own image objectively through his father's eyes. It was a profile of what was really expected of him ideally, to please his father. Basically, the son was hoped *to be strong and independent*! These were the very attributes the father could never encourage in his son, for problems of his own; so the son stopped trying to achieve them. We discussed this thoroughly, and the young man resolved to get back to work to achieve those things. We came up with quite a list of specific projects to change his image, to buy his own home, to have Christmas for his parents at *his* home, to change his dress style, his business profile, and much more. We both knew his father would recognize his new image soon; he finally needed to; time was pressing.

In every way, then, what an astrologer does is alert a creative *balance* between the inner environment and the outer environment within every client's life. In the process, the astrologer helps the client with adjustments of that balance. Together, they work to avoid victimization for individual survival, measure just enough environmental reflection for security, and exploit the potential of change through application of personal resources. Astrologers help clients make connections within fears so that the anxiety to live toward fulfillment is causally understood. Objectification then helps to remove the fear of anxiety itself. Problems are analyzed for understanding, through meaningful connections, and then strategies are directed toward practical solutions. Together, astrologer and client explore growth, in the knowledge that changing life in any way is more important than ending it one way or another.

The Dynamics of Choice

Choice is a central fact of human nature. It is the focus of anxiety as the inner environment meets the outer environment. Choice creates growth and defines individuation.

We have seen constantly throughout this book how the prescriptions of the outer environment condition individual growth development. Choices of behavioral patterns are constantly made as a result of that developmental tension. We choose the behaviors that will bring support and reward from the outer environment, and we repress those behaviors that will not. Choices accumulate and are reflected within patterned behavior. Growth becomes a dynamic circle: choices condition choices as development continues through time. Behavior patterns define individuality. The horoscope image speaks as choices bring individual humanness into being.

In the process of making choices, we **make** value judgements in terms of our personal needs, our **inner** environment. When choices are made for us, when external events occur within our outer environment, we must make value judgements to assimilate circumstance. The circle is completed when we make those value judgements of circumstance in terms of our individuality built upon choices accumulated throughout development.

For example, when needs within status/identity concerns are under tension, choices will be made to ease that tension and fulfill those needs. In discharging anxiety, life develops. Behavioral patterns will be built upon choices that reflect aggression (if energy resources are high or supported) or withdrawal (if control assimilations are great). Please recall the general study of these problem behavior patterns covered in Chapter Two.

All celebrities, for example, must necessarily adopt aggressive commitment to energize the acquisition of celebrity status. That status may overcompensate for weakened personal identity resources and, indeed, status can *become* identity. In Ralph Nader's horoscope (page 161), we saw the clear split between inner and outer environments, the fulfillment of status publicly through the value structures of others while fulfillment of identity is hidden privately in the background. The Leo Moon in the VIIth, given tremendous spine and humanitarian ambition by the opposition of Saturn in Aquarius, certainly suggests aggressive confirmation of public purpose, but the Mars dimension is weakened in Pisces, as we have seen. The aggression to make a public mark professionally involves Pluto, ruler of the Midheaven, and here we see the tremendous strength to overcompensate for status/identity concerns: Pluto squares Uranus, ruler of the Ascendant, squares Jupiter, ruler of the XIth, and trines Mars and Mercury. In fact, we can begin to see the *inclination* to a Water Grand Trine among Mars-Pluto-Midheaven, a closed circuit of emotional self-sufficiency fulfilled through the profession.

Additionally, we must regard Pluto as one of the parental significators. In addition to its other aspects, Pluto makes a quincunx with Saturn: professional perspective would be fed into ambition awareness by one parent in particular. One parent would adjust his focus of status/identity fulfillment through the profession. In consultation, this would have to be explored. The client would respond with a parental assessment in terms of status support through the profession. In my opinion, in this case, it was Mr. Nader's mother. We gain some corroboration of this possibility through the midpoint picture node=Moon/Saturn.

In Merv Griffin's horoscope (page 165), we see a similar public projection of aggression for status confirmation (Moon-Jupiter conjunction in Capricorn in the VIIth, opposing Sun-Pluto conjunction in the Ascendant). We have studied the possible outlines of complexities within his status/identity and self-worth concerns. Here, with Mars in Leo we have the dramatic power potential as well as rearticulation of the problems spurring on development, since Mars squares Saturn retrograde. Mars is conjunct the nodal axis and, within awareness of the Saturn retrograde phenomenon, we can easily anticipate that Mr. Griffin's aggressive thrust was significantly supported by his mother.

In Howard Hughes' horoscope (page 168), we have the similar problem of intense status/identity concerns, exacerbated by the problems of Mars conjunct Saturn. Within his life development, aggression was attempted, but the identity controls inherited psychodynamically from the early home structure (taking over his father's empire at a very early age) won, and withdrawal was adopted. The opposition of Sun-Uranus with Neptune retrograde in the Xth, ruler of the VIIth, corroborates this deduction very cearly.

An extremely important point must be made again: these celebrities became famous and important within their spheres of life *because of* the developmental tensions within them. Every choice they made, supported by mothers, fathers, advisors, their own visualization potential, was conceived in terms of improving balance between inner environment and outer environment. Patterns, by definition, easily continue into overcompensation. Perhaps in Hughes' case, overcompensation was so vast that its values for inner reward were lost, and he chose to withdraw.

When a lack is felt consciously or unconsciously, the organism races to fulfill that lack. This is the purpose of anxiety, as we have seen, to keep life going to one point of balance after another. Choices articulate the route in terms of the lacks that are registered as motivation. Social interaction takes place, and behaviors that are rewarded are reinforced for patterned repetition. B. F. Skinner, one of the most celebrated psychologists of our time, writes, "The outer man whose behavior is to be explained could be very much like the inner man whose behavior is said to explain it. The inner man has been created in the image of the outer."[2][8]

Skinner reminds us that we do not *feel* the actual forces working upon us in development. For example, the introvert does not literally *feel* his introversion. The intelligent person does not literally *feel* his intelligence. No human being actually *feels* an astrological symbolism or the "connections" that make things happen. These intangibles are inner manifestations to outer definitions. Skinner says, "The environment acts in an inconspicuous way: it does not push or pull, it *selects*."

All of Nature operates upon the principles of natural selection. Our immediate societal environment operates through its prescriptions to select from us the behaviors it requires. The external environment rewards us for acquiesence to those prescriptions. The prescribed forces of selection challenge the choices of human beings. From earliest communication with parents to communion with God, we are told what is a "no-no", and we are told what to do "in remembrance of Me." The entire spectrum of life is embraced by the demands of selective prescriptions and the responsibilities of free choice.

Think of all the problems that exist within the process of choice. They involve us all—us astrologers and our clients! Constantly we are caught between the poles of aggression and withdrawal in status/identity terms, overcompensation and sacrifice in money/love terms, and imposition and adaptation in information/perspective terms. Constantly, all that we are is at stake as one choice confirms the pattern for the next choice, as individual resources pattern themselves within reality. The balances can easily be upset with value judgements derived from only the outer environment or only the inner environment, and choices made accordingly. More than any service, the astrologer offers objective help in achieving balance.

Anxiety is in high focus during the process of choice. Fear and hope are present simultaneously; despair and confidence; habit and chance. All behavioral faculties are commandeered to make a decision, to affect a choice. Holistically, the process of choice depends upon the individual's *life point of view*.

We have seen earlier in this book how very often a client will discuss a symptom rather than a cause at the beginning of consultation. Subjectivity has overpowered objectivity, and the decision making process loses its broad point of view to a tightly focused view of a specific point. For example, John had come to me with anxiety about his security in his television work. He thought he was going to lose his job because of intricate union minority prescriptions, seniority specifications, etc. Transiting Jupiter had opposed his Sun and then squared his Midheaven within 45 days two months before his consultation with me. He corroborated these transit dates precisely as dates of a raise and a promotion on his job. Everything was going extremely well. Our discussion turned to deeper considerations very quickly, and a broader point of view was clearly established, as we have seen. It was very, very clear that his anxiety about his sexuality, his thoughts of guilt and karmic punishment were spilling over into his attitude about job security. When this was opened up, the plans for job decisions within the near future were objective, strategic, and comforting.

How often a man or woman will state consideration of divorce plans when actually job security or self-worth anxieties are the real concern. By clarifying this, a broader point of view is established. The marriage partner is not used as a scapegoat. *Objectivity must always restore balance and clarify choice.*

CASE 9 (page 276) presents a synthesis of everything we have shared in this volume with particular focus upon the dynamics of choice.

My preparatory notes began, of course, with the Sun-Moon blend: "Intuitive intellectualism. The spectrum of feelings and the exploration needs are refined by sensitive receptivity. Infinite discrimination guides personal strength among concepts, people, feelings, and ideals. The inner side pleases and can offer comfort when reality becomes momentarily unyielding. There is an instinct for the 'right' thing." This is a valid awareness of Scorpio depth and Piscean sensitivity, especially with the Libran Ascendant. But the very powerful aspect patterns promise much modification: Saturn is retrograde and in conjunction with Mars retrograde, and the two square the Moon opposition with Venus-Neptune. Venus rules the Ascendant and Mars rules the VIIth. Two zones of status/identity concerns are highly pressured and probably withdrawn within the pattern we can anticipate from Saturn retrograde.

The Sun-Mercury conjunction is square Pluto from the Ascendant to the Xth House. The Sun and Pluto are in mutual reception, strengthening this powerful developmental tension. The Sun rules the Midheaven holding Pluto. Pluto rules Scorpio on the IInd. There is absolutely no doubt that, within the pattern of Saturn retrograde, this woman's status/identity concerns are powerfully stressed. With the node in contact with Pluto, and surmise of the father's condition through Saturn retrograde, we

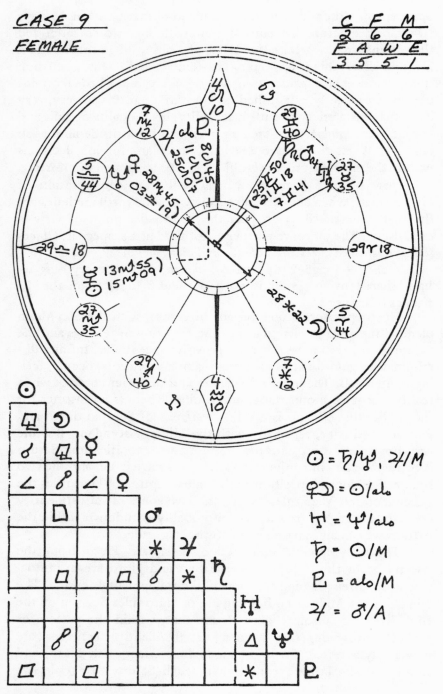

CASE 9
FEMALE

	C	F	M
	2	6	6
	F	A	W	E
	3	5	5	1

☉ = ♄/♆, ♃/M

♀☽ = ☉/♑

♅ = ♆/♑

♄ = ☉/M

♇ = ♑/M

♃ = ♂/A

276

can anticipate the ascendancy of the mother in influence over this woman's personal perspective. Somehow the pressures have made the woman cover over her personal powers. We remember that Venus is conjunct Neptune and square Mars and Saturn. Her sensitivities about self-worth can easily be deduced in our awareness of holistic patterns of behavior, and we can feel the quiet suffering within the Piscean Moon.

The conceptualization of self is broken down for sure. Her information/perspective resources are clearly under tension: Mercury squares Pluto and rules the IXth; the Moon rules Cancer in the IXth and squares Mars and Saturn; Saturn rules Capricorn in the IIIrd; Venus rules the XIIth and is conjunct Neptune and square Mars and Saturn; Mars rules the VIth and is retrograde and conjunct Saturn.

The self-worth complex is obviously stressed, keying from the Saturn retrograde pattern, Venus rulership of the VIIIth, Mercury's rulership of the XIth, Neptune's rulership of the Vth, and Pluto's rulership of the IInd, as we have seen.

Pluto in her Midheaven suggests that, under developmental tension, she would strive for professional ascendancy. Indeed, she would be professionally recognized *because of* all the other tensions, which surely included anxiety about relationships (Mars rulership of the VIIth). Neptune would be involved with idealisms about love given and received (Neptune rules the Vth and is in the XIth), and perhaps their sacrifice, especially through its conjunction with Venus and their square with Saturn.

I had noted further that Saturn retrograde was sharply semi-square her node, reinforcing my anticipation of the mother's influence and the father's lack.

The midpoint pictures of Saturn=Sun/Midheaven (Saturn square the midpoint of Sun-Midheaven) and Sun=Saturn/Neptune suggested a negative outlook on life, emotional suffering and, again, the parental pressures upon her. The inner environment was in turmoil, out of balance with the outer environment.

From her telephone conversation to make the appointment, I learned that she was a professional woman working with small children therapeutically in the mid-West. I learned that she was a black woman. Her place of birth in the early 1940's set up the sociological framework that would operate upon the parents and through them upon my client. She needed so much to be recognized and appreciated for her emotional sensitivity and depth; she would fear rejection and hope for supportive recognition and appreciation (Jupiter in the fire sign Leo in the Xth *sextile* Mars and Saturn; the Libra Ascendant; the midpoint picture Jupiter= Mars/Ascendant).

To me, in the scope of this book's holistic analytical presentation, the case, in its astrological guidelines, was routine. In its fit into my client's reality of individuated development, it would come to life dramatically and rewardingly for me and for her. She wanted to see me because of her marriage; she wanted to divorce her husband.

"Ann" arrived promptly; a truly beautiful, strong, poised black woman. We got along easily, with much humor and warmth. I presented her with her horoscope, with the very short explanation of what it represented. I began with the generalized restatement of the Sun-Moon blend, *with the modifications* that had been suggested in my preparation notes.

"Ann, let me discuss some general concepts with you; some of the suggestions of these patterns in the horoscope. We'll refine these general statements soon. The horoscope suggests that there is a deep intuitive, dreamy, maybe even intellectual sensitivity here. Perhaps you have refined it with great discrimination to guide you in working with people, their feelings, your feelings, ideals, etc."

I watched Ann very carefully. Her face was blank. She stared at me. I felt that she was hearing but not listening, or that she could not identify with what I was saying. I slowed down my speech, used some hand motions to get her gaze free from hypnotic focus.

"You know this is in you, Ann. It's that inner voice you listen to when things get rough. Right?" She tentatively agreed. She couldn't *feel* her actual inner environmental processes.

"Wouldn't you say that you have the instinct for the right thing?"

Ann responded strongly in confirmation. This told me that Ann's sensitivities were probably quite polarized between what was right and wrong, what was and what *was* not what should be. This is typical with dominant idealization or fantasy fixation.

"You have all of this sensitivity, *but no one has ever really appreciated it*, I'll bet!" This was a thrust to relate the inner environment to the outer, within all the tension I knew was there working against the reward needs of Jupiter in Leo.

Ann started to relax. She shifted position (an important sign, as we shall see in the next chapter), and corroborated that she *was* unappreciated for her sensitivities.

"All this is leading to the probable existence of a legacy of inferiority feelings, Ann, usually taken on from the father figure in the early home. Was this so? Was your father taken away or passive? Did he ever hug you, hold you, and help you with those sensitivities?"

Ann opened up and explained, almost with relief, that her father worked so hard, was always busy, and had never paid her any attention, given her any recognition.

"Did your mother run the show?"

Here, Ann practically took over the conversation with energetic corroboration: "There not only was no love shown at all, there always were put-downs. I never meant anything to my mother. She preferred an older sister to me. I tried so hard to get her attention . . . . and I don't want to care about it any more. I . . . I just want to get on with it." Ann had tears in her eyes.

I continued with the pattern expected from the measurements and from experience, trying to move the consultation along past over-description of past problems: "Did you go into your room alone many times and dream, fantasize?"

Ann replied, "Always. I would reach the state of Limbo . . . alone, peaceful. It was a place with God."

"Was God saying, 'I love you'?"

"No. It was only a warm place; yes, a loving place. No conversation. *But I can't seem to get there now.*"

Ann's needs for love and attention, for sensual touching and holding came out in detailed recall of put-downs and of reverie in her "loving place". Her statement about not being able to get back to that fantasy comfort anymore was very important: it corroborated present tensions and her weakened defense resources, those she had used for so long, long ago.

"Ann, do you think that the difficulty in getting back to old time comforts might mean that you should be going into the *opposite* direction, getting on with life and facing up to problems?"

"I suppose so, Mr. Tyl, but I'm afraid of *everyone*, of everyone but children and older people."

The entire horoscope pattern was corroborated for sure. Ten minutes had passed and we were well into the root concerns under

278
280

the symptom she had expressed at the outset: "I think I want to divorce my husband." Naturally, her fear of relationships was an extension of her deep self-worth anxiety, signalled so clearly by the retrograde Mars and its aspect configuration with the key Saturn. I anticipated that, now, as an adult, these accumulated problems of status/identity, self-worth, and information/perspective resources were being projected onto her husband specifically (Mars rules her VIIth).

Her younger years were so routinely lonely, but I did inquire about school success at ages 14 and 15 (projecting the Ascendant by Solar Arc to conjunction with Mercury and Sun).

"I did very well in school; I loved it, but that was also the start of my decline because I was pregnant then." Ann's smile turned into an anxious gaze.

At that same time, I saw that Solar Arc Uranus was conjunct Mars as well. I checked quickly in an abbreviated booklet of transit positions and saw that transiting Neptune was then approaching square to her Midheaven (diminishing ego consciousness) and transiting Uranus was crossing the Midheaven (intensifying individual choice). It was a time of enormous conflict about individual worth and identity.

"Ann, did you have this precocious affair because you needed love and attention so much?"

This was a key question. Ann had indeed loved the young man, but he had threatened to leave her for another girl if she didn't have sex with him. She needed his love and attention so much that she complied, and a baby was born out of wedlock.

I shifted the conversation to the adult present, knowing the patterns that would have issued from that early trauma and the self-worth weaknesses that had accumulated so much tension focus within her. I inquired about her sex-life as an adult.

"With this pattern of parental tension that we can see in so many ways, especially with your young boyfriend, I want to inspect with you how you feel about sex now. We know your fears about relationship; well, in sexuality neurology and psychology come together. It's suggested here in the horoscope (this was a touch of objectification so as not to accuse her or focus on her too strongly during such a delicate question) that there is a sexual dysfunction. Is there?"

"I'd rather not have sex."

"I appreciate that, Ann. I understand. But when you do, is there an orgasmic dysfunction?"

Any replied easily, "Yes. There is no orgasm ever. I feel I am about to lose my mind, He has his orgasm, and often I've just cried and screamed. I even hid under the bed once."

I listened to the great tension within her words, but pressed on to make a point that would be important later in remediation. "I understand what you are saying, but, when you masturbate, there *is no* problem?"

Ann corroborated this. She seemed relieved. We shared some humor about the fact that THAT was in the horoscope! I asked a further question about the essence of her erotic fantasies, and she revealed that no person was ever involved, only being hugged, held, loved. I assured her that this was perfectly "normal". I was calming her tensions.

"Ann you do *not* have a sexual problem. I want that to be perfectly clear to you. What you have is a relationship concern."

This was a very important clarification of very tense anxiety concerns (it always is). The "problem"—this "problem"—is so easily substituted for real, more fundamental concerns.

Ann continued: "I feel totally repelled by my husband."

"*Why did you marry him, then*?" This was a powerful thrust to her base of value judgements.

"My mother." Ann was enormously relieved. Only thirty-two minutes had gone by in the consultation.

This was the answer I had anticipated. The maternal pressure, suggested within the preparatory measurements, was completely corroborated; the self-worth concerns and the problems she had with understanding love and loveability; the confusion of being ignored and yet being so very, very beautiful and attracting; the child born of an early bid for love; the tainted profile of sexuality after that trauma; the continuation of the routined problems through the mother's enormous pressure to marry a well-educated and secure man; and now, precisely under the projected measurements of SA Sun opposed Mars, ruler of her VIIth, SA Ascendant=Sun/Saturn, and SA Uranus=Moon/Ascendant, all combined, she was feeling that she was 'losing her mind." She wanted *freedom from* her husband. She wanted to withdraw to the inner warm place, the aloneness that pleased her.

Noting that SA Moon would have crossed her seventh cusp at age 29, with transiting Saturn making its return, I asked Ann if there had possibly been a split in her marriage at 28 or 30 years of age. She corroborated that she had indeed left then, but that the mother had brought her back to the husband.

Our discussion went into some details about the intervening years. The established pattern was played out completely. Ann was in turmoil for sure, and the husband was stoically putting up with a lot and getting deeper and deeper into his own problems, having emerged from a family background very similar to Ann's. It was reasonable that Ann and her husband intensified each other's problem concerns unconsciously, instinctively; each could find the other's vulnerabilities so easily; their points of view were similar from a shared background. Ann summed it all up by saying, "My husband makes me feel so dirty."

The problem was rich in nuance, but it was singularly clear that Ann had bartered sex for love attention a long time ago. That son born of that trauma still was with her and her husband (not his father). Tension involved this son too. He endured as a symbolic reminder of Ann's earlier times of upset. Sexuality was traumatized.

We began to talk about what she could do. In my mind, I could hear some "star-reading" astrologer saying, "Well, she's got the ruler of the VIIth in a double-bodied sign. She's gonna be married more than once. So, Ann had better get a divorce while she's still got some good years ahead of her!" *How easy is the trap of confining someone's life to what we know about astrology.*

Ann's whole life had been tremendous vigor rejected by heavy controls. Indecision had become an anathema to her. The energy always detoured inward. Now, she was finally convinced. Finally, she was determined to leave her husband. To establish her conviction, she tried the rationale that her leaving would be a relief for her husband. She tried the rationale that her leaving would give her an opportunity to meet other men and try relationships with different people. Ann had always worked *within* problems, short-circuiting her own energies to adapt herself to problematic oppressions. *Ann had tried everything but solving her problems*; she had never felt fortified enough to do so. The inner environment was crucially out of balance in relation to the outer environment.

I began the remediation section of the consultation: "Ann, do you and your husband exchange Christmas presents at Christmas time?"

Ann was startled by the apparent absurdity of my question. I urged her to reply, and she corroborated that she and her husband exchanged gifts, but she had to add, "but I never like what he gives me." As soon as she had spoken her tag phrase, she was embarrassed by its nervous barb.

"Is it loving and peaceful?"

"Why, yes. The families are there. Why?"

"Love is there too, isn't it?"

"... Yes ... I see."

"Well, it could be perpetuated, couldn't it?"

Ann agreed. It was a quiet, strong moment in the consultation. I was reaching into Ann to bring out feelings that surely had to be there somewhere underneath all the symptomatic anxieties reflecting her own personal torment.

"If you divorce your husband, do you think your problems ... as we understand them together thoroughly ... *do you think your problems will end*?"

"No, Mr. Tyl ... Noel ... they won't end. But I won't be emotionally deteriorating."

"But will you be *growing*, Ann?"

Ann understood. An hour had gone by, so much had been covered within the organization of the horoscope, within the manifestation in her life, and Ann understood so much. Her point of view was clarified: her pains, her conceptualization, her fears, the connections among them all, and the challenge to do something about growth.

Her face lit up beautifully when I sat back from my desk and started to review the whole situation objectively, from the point of view we now shared: "Ann, just think of the problems your parents were facing when you were growing up! Your father had to work so hard to earn a living. Your mother ran the show. But together they were facing horrible racist problems in the community. Is it any wonder, really, that you got caught in a terrific traffic pattern?" I spoke casually in great relaxation, in a "matter-of-fact" way.

Ann laughed in recognition. She was also resting comfortably as I reviewed our discussion. She was participating with the objectification perfectly; helpfully, objectivity always can expose humor.

"Sure, you were neglected; sure, your mother had a special bond with your older sister. But there wasn't then and isn't now any real animosity or favoritism. You've said so yourself! And look how careful your mother was in picking your husband for you!" This bit of humor was welcome to us both. Ann agreed wholeheartedly with the retrospective I provided.

"And, you don't hate them do you?"

"Oh no. I love . . . I *know* they did the best they could for me."

"But you were oh so vulnerable! Your specific needs, those deep sensitivities that needed very special attention . . . well, your parents just didn't know how to handle them! And, they were busy with lots of other 'stuff'! So, you latched on to this young man, whom you had high hopes about—first love excitement, independence, someone who could love you and pay you attention, if you would cooperate sexually. Ann, it's a perfectly normal, natural pattern. I hear it all the time. But this doesn't mean it's not painful or important to *your* growth. It most certainly *is*. I just want you to know that many, many, many people work it out, and they're the better off for doing so.

"That first child has become a difficult reminder of all of that back there. But you've raised him well, undoubtedly giving him more love in overcompensation. (Ann nodded enthusiastically.) Well, I think you should take all that we've talked about today, all that 'stuff' back there (intentionally, I was still speaking off-handedly to preserve objectivity and keep emotions out of the recapitulation) *and put it in a box*. (I pretended I had a shoe-box between my hands.) Put it in the box and put it on your living room shelf. (I put the imaginary box on an imaginary shelf.) Whenever your mind starts churning up those thoughts, those routinized fears we've discussed, *catch yourself. Tell yourself* that those things are in the box over there, outside of you, and they can't get at you unless you open up the box. (I pointed to the box on the shelf.)

"Remember, *two* thoughts can't occupy the same circuit at the same time. For example, I'll sing you a phrase of a song, and I bet it will haunt you all the way home today, and tomorrow, and the next day. It'll make you smile. (I sang the refrain of 'The Twelve Days of Christmas' ... 'a partridge in a pear tree'.) That's an example of what I'm talking about: put some new thoughts into your mind, a new point of view, and give it a try."

Ann was all ears. I used the catching song fragment as a mnemonic for her; *it* would come back to her mind, and so would our objective view.

"Now, you've been looking for 'freedom froms' for too long. Freedoms from your mother, your memories, your husband. I think we've got to concentrate now on freedoms 'period'; just freedom to grow and to be. There is love in you for your husband; there's compassion in you about your past; there's professional attention on your job, and we've seen that it is going well; there's *everything but confidence*; but the *understanding* we're sharing today *gives you that*! Let's talk about how you can try to get *growth freedom* going. After all, you can't 'get back to that peaceful place' in your fantasy anymore! Alright?"

Ann agreed wholeheartedly to try. We had come a long way from her assertion that she was losing her mind because of her marriage!

I outlined many things with her, things that she readily knew were natural, normal, and within her ... and several things that were innovative but that had crossed her mind and experience over the years. We covered how her husband's patterns of response would probably stay the same for a while, since they were so routined, and that she shouldn't misinterpret *the way* he said things. We talked about how she could touch him more, sit next to him, listen creatively to his thoughts, serve dinner with a flair, create intimacy at times other than Christmas. We talked about how to answer his observations (probably initially callous) about her changed demeanor. We talked about how to open up sexuality by incorporating reliable masturbation into sexual intercourse positions, about exploring new sensations and intimacy with her husband, to release shared energy. (She had already bought a book on sex techniques.) We built a frame of mind to protect her *and* her husband within *gradual* exploration of change and growth.

"And most important, Ann, is what you've got to do to reward yourself." Within remediation through self-help, it is essential for the person to enjoy reward to reinforce new behavior patterns. Working from within the inner environment, the rewards necessarily have to begin from the self.

"What do you like to buy yourself most?"

"What do you mean?"

"Well if you were a man and, say, you beat your wife (I was still keeping humor and off-handedness within objectification for obvious reasons in support of a new point of view). Say, you resolved to stop beating your wife. You loved good wine. I would suggest that you reward yourself with two bottles of Chateau Margaux, for example, after one week of perfect behavior! You buy the wine as a reward . . . and you share it with your wife!"

"Oh, I see! Well, I'd like to buy myself a dress or two!" Ann enjoyed the idea.

"Fine. That's it. Promise yourself a subtle new routine now. Set up a new pattern. Start using your understanding and appreciate what you and your husband share with each other." While saying this, I changed posture to exert some authority. We had been together an hour and twenty-minutes. The long time of emotional sharing had to end with strategic strength.

Ann resolved "to do my best, I promise." Her words were music to my ears. My eyes and hers met in agreement. A contract was made. *A choice had been clarified.*

I quickly changed the subject: "And Ann, are you thinking about going back to school for more specialized credits?" The next month, she had Solar Arc Uranus trine her natal Mercury, with transiting Jupiter conjunct Jupiter. Her conceptualization axis (III-IX) was not only manifested within our consultation together but probably within advanced schooling as well.

"Why yes! You see that too?"

"Yes indeed! That's great. Do it. It will be fine for you. Share it with your husband as much as you can."

We concluded our time together with some details about her professional situation and exercise program. As we rose together and gave each other a hug, I felt the need for a final word. Everything would not be "roses" for Ann in her adjustment challenge. I wanted to extend our togetherness further and eliminate any collapse of resolve should some of her new behaviors meet with rejection or misunderstanding.

"Ann, please feel free to call me at any time. I'm here. I believe in you and appreciate you. You're a fine lady."

"I'm going to do the best I can. I promise."

"That's a promise to yourself. Let's meet again in, say, three months . . . or tomorrow if you need a shot in the arm! (Transiting Saturn would square its natal position in three months, and would help stabilize Ann's circumstances one way or another.) And, Ann, one more thing: If you give this new effort all you've got, and it doesn't work somehow, I'm here to help you into another direction."

My closing words to her allied us full circle with acknowledgement of her very real years of torment and upset and her initial reason for coming to an astrologer. She now had a way into her positive freedom through marriage, and she would have a way out, if necessary, through her growth and strength in having faced the challenge to get to a loving place *outside* herself.

Time

Time embraces life development. We can most comfortably assign the concept of fate to the dimension of time. Within the structure of inexorable time, our choices reflect will and individuation and, along with sociological awareness (environmental overview), determine the Level of Naturalness of individuated life. Time represents outer structure to which gradually developed behavioral patterns of inner expression cling. Astrology is the only introspective discipline that holistically measures and articulates all of this: fate and will, outer environment and inner environment, victimization and change.

Every astrologer learns with excitement and, hopefully, respect the structural verities of transit cycles, progressions, and arc projections. [29] This framework of time articulates the past, the immediate present, and the near future. Potential meanings within this framework can be outlined generally through experience in fine astrological texts, but these meanings can only be precisely defined in terms of the client's individual life development. The manifestation of any measurement is directly related, almost in-variably, *to the individual's mode and degree of interaction with the outer environment*, focusing the thesis of this entire book.

Two recent telephone calls dramatize this important observa-tion: the first call was from a young mother, "Mr. Tyl, I've just had a baby. She is now five weeks old, and I would like you to do her horoscope."

My careful answer to her was phrased as a warning. I told her that I would not do the child's horoscope, but that other astrolo-gers could be found who would. I pointed out how any horoscope delineation of her child now, no matter how crude or sophisti-cated, would unalterably condition the instinctive love and atten-tion she would give to the child throughout its development time. The chemistry would be upset. The child's freedom to learn, make mistakes, and learn again would be confined.

I asked the mother when she thought the child would reach an age of independence. The mother said, "about 20, I guess." I pointed out that that would be the year 2000! I showed easily how conditions now, the essence of astrology's symbolisms in re-flection of present times, could not ever reliably project a human being's position within the environmental conditions of the year 2000. My point was well made.

The mother observed well-meaningly that she had learned that her daughter had the Sun, Moon, and Ascendant in all three of the Water signs, and that the child would be so sensitive. In acknowledging this possibility, I suggested that there were many options within such sensitivity, if it were indeed extreme: drug addiction, alcoholism, religious ecstacy, artistic talent, prostitu-tion, nursing, etc. I pointed out how the child could only grow by making choices in terms of the love and encouragement shared between mother and child, father and child, initially totally depen-dent upon the parents and gradually more dependent upon herself. I concluded with the observation that hope encourages life and control confines it.

The mother understood and concluded most tellingly: "Well, thank you very much, Mr. Tyl. *I'll take your advice, for the mo-ment.*" I had not said what she wanted to hear. The child's envi-ronment was already being conditioned at five weeks of age. Some astrologer's measurements *would* fit the *mother's* needs.

The second call came from an extremely intelligent female client who has lived a life of deep trauma. She has isolated herself as much as possible from the world around her. She acknowledges functional cooperation with the environment, but she will not allow anything to reach inside her inner environment while she tries "to work things out for herself."

Most interestingly, her entire horoscope pattern is above the horizon (potential victimization by the environment; please recall page 44) with the Sun conjunct Uranus in the VIIIth and the Moon conjunct Neptune in the XIIth. At the time of the call, this young woman was in the closing period of a four-month Pluto transit of her Ascendant, Pluto ruling her IInd and square her Mercury natally. We had anticipated this deep gradual demand within her to alter her life perspective, to remediate her self-worth anxieties. We had discussed it thoroughly during her consultation.

She had had a dream the night before her call. The dream had pointed importantly to the time period two weeks ahead. Astrologically, this time period concluded the Pluto transit of her Ascendant and revealed the transit conjunction of Saturn upon her natal Jupiter (fear and hope), simultaneous with the transit of Neptune square her Jupiter. Here was the juxtaposition of necessary controls absorbed within her life (Saturn), her hope for reward, to be of value (Jupiter in an Earth Sign), and her sense of sacrifice (Neptune) which was so strong within her through natal conjunction with her Moon in the XIIth.

This strong time was closely followed up with transiting Pluto squaring her Midheaven and transiting Jupiter square her Sun and semisquare her Midheaven. —It was clearly a way out for her, a change of personal perspective (she had even changed her name legally!), a final confrontation with her defensive ideals and self-isolation, and obviously an accentuation of her professional hopes (status/identity).

Her question about this time period was simply whether or not such advancement could occur *without her going out to seek it*. Neptune was ignoring Pluto.

My answer simply abbreviated all the things we had discussed in consultation about the vital necessity for the human being to interact with the outer environment, to gather, exchange, and refine resources, to adjust personal point of view constantly. I said, "Please remember that it takes two to tango."

In the first call, we see the need *to establish pattern*, and in the second call we see the need *to preserve pattern*, the forces of social existence.

Questions contain answers. A question of the outer environment—a question put to the astrologer—invariably has the answer within it, within the human being asking the question. For example, an acquaintance whom I have not seen for a long time asked me for some *advice*: "Since my divorce, I've really enjoyed myself living in my mountain house. Do you think I should keep on being a recluse or should I move and get back into things?" She was answering her own question, just as the two telephone call questioners had.

A person says, "I've come to see you because I want to know the best time to divorce my wife." The question is buying time . . . time to clarify personal point of view. In all my practice, I have never seen actual divorce emerge from such a question. Indeed, divorces have occurred thereafter, but they took place conclusively, and usually amicably, because of a concretized point of view and an effort to solve the causative problems underneath the symptoms.

When the client projects the decision making process upon the astrologer, i.e., "I need a miracle; will you give me one?", the astrologer must reflect it back upon the client through analysis, "You do need a miracle; let's help you create one."

Similarly, *questions of time contain the answers of personal value judgements*. Time measures developmental response; the growth process establishes values through the individual. The careful view of times past punctuates accumulated value judgements and points of view that help human beings know of what they are capable in the present and near future.

A female client has a career of long standing within the government in foreign service. Everything she has done in her life reflects perfectly her tight Sun-Jupiter conjunction in Leo in the IXth trine her Moon in Sagittarius in the Ascendant, with the Moon ruling her IXth. She "does her own thing" (Moon in the Ascendant), demands recognition, and gets it, all within terms of internationalism. Venus rules her VIIth, opposes Saturn retrograde in her IInd, and that axis is squared by Uranus in the Vth. Keyed by Saturn retrograde, we know so much, so incredibly much about her parental patterns and the problems therefrom focused within self-worth anxiety, love concerns and relationships. Holistically, we know, and we are sure.

The woman has sacrificed relationships and love concerns in favor of the easier fulfillment of self through foreign service (Pluto oriental adding the dimension of status through affiliation). She came to me in agitation: she had been relieved of foreign duty and felt confined in her "stateside routine job." She was awaiting retirement but was going "crazy" from confinement.

Going into her past problems of parents, self-worth, relationships, etc. revealed the developmental steps that had built this busy life of overcompensation externally, far away from the home country and home concerns, the sacrifice of intimate relationships. Every touch of Saturn by transit and Solar Arc to her Sun-Jupiter conjunction in the IXth and/or her Moon in Sagittarius in the Ascendant throughout her life revealed a threat to the freedoms that powerful trine pattern demanded: there were education problems when her mother would not let her go to a very special school that she wanted to attend. There was religious guilt and oppression put upon her by the Catholic mother. In overviewing the framework of her life development through the timing of these significators alone, we could see together the imbalance of it all. We worked to modify the temperamental frustration of the present confinements within her lifelong pattern by improving the balance through relationship remediation.

Within objective analysis of her job concerns of the moment, there was *no* astrological measurement that corresponded to the present time confinement of her *wanderlust*, as had been so reliably demonstrated throughout her life history. Quite the contrary: in time, she was a month away from transiting Saturn conjunct her Midheaven then square her Moon, with transiting Jupiter conjunct her Sun-Jupiter conjunction, closely followed the next month by Solar Arc Moon conjunct Saturn and transiting Uranus conjunct her Ascendant! She was due for powerful focus on her ambition and reward, undoubtedly through foreign relocation.

In conversation, I had checked the cycles of Jupiter transits to her natal Sun-Jupiter conjunction. Within her adult life, they had always corresponded with rewards within her life. There was absolutely every reason to anticipate a further correspondence and a rewarding freedom.

The only thing that could get in the way, it appeared, was her temperamental upset, her difficulty with relationships, her impatience. This was where remediation was focused. The two of us worked for patience and a balance of inner needs with outer circumstances, especially within the subtleties possible to create job change inside government structure and timeframe.

The client called me frequently as she developed her strategies within tactful relationships. She was not flying off the handle, trying to tell everyone how to do their jobs. Instead, she was facing each day as a tremendous strategic gambit. It paid off. She made her longed for change possible. She was relocated to the Middle East precisely as the projected measurements fulfilled themselves astrologically. She had tuned in to a balance, and *she had made her life happen. She* made it happen, not astrology or astrologer, although she now deified both!

We have seen time and time again how, during development, a human being organizes cognition of personal resources as they are clarified within interaction and exchanges with many different environments. Prescriptive demands embodie the selection forces of the worlds in which we live. Our individual choices to meet those prescriptions, to be chosen in turn for environmental reward, determine our level of fulfillment. Anxiety to live keeps us going and becomes specified in fears which, in turn, are balanced by hope. We have seen so often how the mind controls every process of cognition through awareness, evaluation, and conceptualization. Fantasy facilitates hope. Fortified hopes and, often, fantastic hopes all seek fulfillment in time.

We know that impractical hopes transcend resources, and that remediation must improve practicality in terms of objective understanding of the social maturation process. Similarly, astrological predictions into future time easily ignore practical potential by not appreciating the individual client's developmental process. Therefore, I suggest that the concept of *projection*, instead of prediction, is more helpful and efficacious not only for the client's sensibilities but for the dignity of astrologer and astrology as well.

Just as the level of identity at any time is established within a human being in relation to his or her holistic development from birth to that particular time, so a discussion of the future must similarly project from the birth, through holistic development, and further. The key to the process of understanding future time is to find meaning in the individual's life expression within the past, see it refined within the individual's life present, and *find within the individual* a projection into the future. The individual human being will know best what is possible since he or she lives the patterns that will make the future happen. Again, in this way, the astrological measurements for the future will be brought *to* life by the individual living that life.

Within my own personal consultation organization, projections into future time are discussed only with the last 20 to 25% of the consultation period, after the past and present have corroborated full understanding of the psychodynamics of holistic development. I began with the simplest of questions, "Now, would you please share with me what you project for yourself within the next six or seven months?" The client will (should) answer in full awareness of the point of self-view that has been balanced, refined, and made meaningful by the sharing throughout the earlier portions of the consultation. As the client speaks, the astrologer's projected measurements will be illuminated as punctuation of possible developmental times within the future. Common sense about life strategies will add plausibility, and objective holistic awareness of the past will aid client and astrologer in visualization and anticipation of actual behavior in the future.

The astrologer must have this holistic awareness ever in mind. He or she must have the poise to know and acknowledge with the client that, if little has happened in life, little can be expected to occur. A visit to an astrologer does not change a life pattern *except in terms of the understanding gained of the patterns already established*. As we know so well, the past holistically supports the present. It also stimulates and conditions the future. This understanding awakens self-objectification, and strategy emerges from the balance of resources achieved through objectification and sensitive remediation.

Patterns of defensiveness, guilt, overcompensation through fantasy are weighty. They weigh us down as we approach the future. They weigh us down, depress us throughout time. Even physical posture reflects the burden. We must come up with something, release the depressed spring, and ready ourselves for action. The process must be facilitated mentally, physically, and spiritually. We must do this for ourselves and help our clients to do this for themselves.

A good illustration of this process can be adapted from the physio-spiritual movements of T'ai-Chi.[30] Ask the client to do exactly as you do. Explain that the exercise may look silly, but that it does teach an important principle.

Hold both your forearms vertically in front of your shoulders, with the wrists broken limply. Elbows should be close to the torso. The wrists will be at rest, limply hung forward at about shoulder level. Both you and your client will be doing the same thing.

To ease the awkwardness of the postures, talk to your client about the weightiness of behavioral patterns, the defenses that so easily continue over-fortified long after they're needed, the energies wasted within routinized behavior. Talk just enough to fill about thirty seconds of time.

Then ask your client to lift his hands so that both hands are beautifully and gracefully alined with the vertical forearm axis. Do the same with him. As the hands are lifted, the wrist joints feel enormous relief. The sensation is natural and free; the posture is prepared for action.

The wrists obviously had been weighted down by gravity. The right angle was developmental tension being absorbed by the system. Lifting the hands released energy and defensive depression and defined preparedness for activity. The process occurred within time, through change. The process was understood by the mind and appreciated by the body.

In relation to the T'ai-Chi philosophy, we can learn even more from the expression of *T'ai* within the *I Ching*. T'ai represents peace achieved through union of the receptive earth and the creative heaven. The following description from the *Book of Changes* distills beautifully the holistic premise of our study in this volume and the philosophical goal we keep in mind as we remedially help others to balance subjective position within objective time:

"T'ai: A time in nature when heaven seems to be on earth. Heaven has placed itself beneath the earth, and so their powers unite in deep harmony. The peace and blessing descend upon all living things.

"In the world of man it is a time of social harmony; those in high places show favor to the lowly, and the lowly and inferior in their turn are well disposed toward the highly placed. There is an end to all feuds.

"In this way, each receives his due. When the good elements of society occupy a central position and are in control, the evil elements come under their influence and change for the better.

"... But should we persevere in trying to resist the evil in the usual way, our collapse would only be more complete, and the humiliation would be the result."[31]

As we astrologers look to our heavens in terms of the world of man and his efforts to achieve social harmony, we must know that each receives his due. What is above is below, and what is without is within. We are in control through our understanding. We must *work* to achieve and appreciate constant growth and change. The process is given value by our minds, supported by our bodies, appreciated by our spirits, and framed by our times.

Chapter Eight
SPECIFIC REMEDIATION
TECHNIQUES

The word "therapy" etymologically presumes treatment of disease or disorder. The word "remedy" or the process of "remediation" presumes cure, healing, correction. The nuances are difficult. It is always too easy for a separation to be implied between one person who is doing something and another person who is receiving or needing the "doing". I am personally uncomfortable with this concept, chiefly because it immediately credits the "doer" with authority, skill, responsibility, and rightness, regardless of personal attitude and motivation. The input of the "doing" process does not involve clearly enough the human *subject* of the doing. I have chosen the word "remediation" for this book to introduce and emphasize the concept of *reciprocal process*, to bring astrologer and client together in awareness of the potentials of adjustment. This word recognizes the concept of "help" within process. Astrologers are helpers (that would be the best word). All counselors are. Astrology helps others to know that they have life purpose, the right to fulfillment, and that they are not alone.

But there are countless doctors, lawyers, ministers, and consultants in all fields of human knowledge who are poor helpers. They may have credentials and knowledge of their craft, but they isolate themselves in terms of status, money, and information at the expense of their service in terms of identity, love, and perspective. They lose the major source of their potentials, *caring*, by not appreciating the fundamental focus of their work: the human being they serve; the relationship and resource exchange with that human being. Beyond credentials and knowledge of technique, there is the fundamental demand to relate humanly and to help others to help themselves. This demand frames the reason why there are so many poor, demoralizing astrologers, and the reason why there are so many excellent, helpful ones.

Astrology presents us with the gift of insight, but every gift while living and understanding life is dangerous. Gifts rebalance value judgements within the whole sphere of personal resources. Gifts emphasize the inner environment; they can fortify defenses or grace growth. We hoard concomitants of status, redefine value judgements, and fortify our new information perspective. We easily forget that our gifts become meaningful only in that they increase the personal resources *we have to share*. They must help us relate to the outer environment. If this is not observed, any gift isolates the gifted, and subjective success becomes objective failure.

Indeed, our astrological gifts have a starting point within our self-awareness. We try out every technique we learn upon our own lives. But are we ourselves reliable models for the rest of the world, for the others around us? Do we seek corroboration of our technical gifts in terms of *what has happened* in our lives or do we seek corroboration in terms of *what is developing*? Are we seeing what *we ourselves had to do with what transpires*? Do we see our technique as *an inventory or a guide*?

Our astrological gifts gain fulfillment only in orientation outside ourselves. If we share our gifts in terms of what has happened to us, we limit another person's life to the scope of our own. If we share our gifts in terms of the developmental principles we have experienced and observe continuously all around us, we bring our gift to another's life. When the astrologer knows that astrologer and astrology are guides, the client will know it instantly as well, from the very beginning of the consultation, and he or she will be trusting and open, free for productive relationship through intimate disclosure. Resources will be shared, help will be illuminated, and both astrologer and client will be enriched.

The techniques that follow are offered to help hone the astrologer's skills in helping clients help themselves. They are to be used when the astrologer knows through analytical organization where remediation is to be directed. The principle of objectification is dominant. These techniques of remediation work for holistic reorientation of the client within his or her general area of concerns as outlined in preparatory astrological analysis, corroborated in the connections made through creative communication with the client during the consultation, and framed with time strategies for behavioral modification in the future. They help with an adjusted life point of view.

Status/Identity Concerns: One of the great luxuries of introspection, and perhaps one of the most difficult challenges, is to see ourselves as others see us. This objectification is most difficult to accomplish alone. During astrological consultation, such objectification is indispensible. The client reviews the subjective content of life development, is guided by the astrologer in making meaningful connections within routine behavior patterns and value judgements, and finally is prepared to view the entire process objectively. The final state of objectification through understanding works mightily to stabilize assessment without incrimination and to make plans without fear.

We have seen throughout this book that a major counseling insight to be shared with a client suffering from identity anxiety (and status insecurity that evolves from this anxiety), related to residual parental tension, is that the parents were human beings themselves with their own individual problems and that their child got caught in their "traffic pattern." This view engenders respect and compassion through understanding. In that understanding, there is a separation of self from parents, of effect from cause. To a great degree, the routined connection between present and past is adjusted. The client can see his or her life development through a new lens. Explored sensitively, it is extremely helpful.

Anyone who has ever looked through the lens of a fine camera has experienced the powerful objectification that occurs as self is separated from others. The camera is a powerful protection, insulation, and intervening medium. The inner environment is somehow given safety to study the outer environment. Photographers are urged in the study of their technique to analyze the values and the points of view that dominate and typify their photographs. These values and points of view can be alarmingly revealing.[3][2]

The camera can be used dramatically during a consultation to protect the client during deep status/identity concerns. I have often given a camera to a client, after focusing it perfectly to the distance between us, and asked the client to study me through it. While the client watches me through the camera, I reinforce the seemingly avant garde situation with reference to the intriguing separation, objectification, and different point of view the client is experiencing. The lens of the camera separates the client from the immediacy of feeling.

In one case, during this process, I was portraying the client's father ("Pretend that I am your father, and you are photographing me.") and I asked quietly into the camera, "Have you really forgiven me, David?" In that moment, the client's anxieties dissolved. The relief brought quiet tears, and the understanding brought light to a new point of view. Honesty prevailed since the self was out of the way; the weight of lifelong routine was lifted. He had not forgiven, and he now knew he had to, should.

The process —this one or any process the astrologer can create to help with objectification— helps the client to see the parents as individuals with their own problems. It balances the selfish instincts we have about our parents (necessarily for our own nurturance) with the altruistic feelings that come with mature separation from them. Ideally as adults, we must appreciate ourselves as distinct individuals in contrast to our parents. We must be thankful to them for the developmental experience, and we must have compassionate perspective back into time.

One remediation technique offered to the young self-isolated woman of Case 2 (page 101) was to explore her hobby of photography, not in photographing just flowers, but in photographing people. It was a way for her to begin building her value awarenesses of life outside herself, without putting her emotional naiveté into jeopardy. —The idea intrigued her.

Another fine objectification technique is the use of parables, short stories that teach a point or establish an instructive point of view. The lesson is taught through someone else's experience. As the story is told engagingly, the client rests and welcomes the shift of focus from self to others.

I often use this true story: "We're talking about depression, and I want to assure you that I can really identify with that. I become so depressed sometimes, you wouldn't believe it! You think YOU'RE depressed —well you should see me! (This is relaxing humor as well as a strongly engineered shift of focus off the client.)

"Although I know academically that depression is really self-indulgent (an important thought that the client will store away, and at which he or she will usually smile in recognition), I sometimes can't shake it. One day, I was really moping around, terribly depressed. I got a telephone call from a woman in the Southwest somewhere. She was really distraught. She began to talk to me about her daughter.

"Curiously, while she was talking, she would occasionally start to spell certain words. She would say, 'And when she s-h-e had to talk to h-e-r t-e-a-c-h-e-r-s, s-h-e would have a terrible time.' Then, she would say in hushed tones, 'I'm sorry Mr. Tyl, my daughter just came into the room; now she's gone.' So, I asked how old her daughter was and learned that the daughter was seventeen!

"The problem was that the daughter was severely retarded. She had been traumatized at age five. She had been playing with an electric broiler; the machine locked and turned on while her hands were caught, and her fingers were melted off!"

At this point the client will be completely engrossed in the story and register feelings about this sad situation.

"I talked with this mother for almost an hour, discussing the years of tension that had hurt the family's life —and strengthened it—in many ways. The focus now was upon an important change of schools for the daughter. The mother and father had different views about it. Somehow, we worked much of this out by getting values out into the open and organizing them into a *practical hierarchy*.

"At the end of the call, the woman was most grateful. She asked my charge, and I said that there was none, that I simply wished her well and would help in any way I could in the future.

"Now the important point of this story is that, when I hung up the phone, *I realized I was no longer depressed!*"

This powerful story establishes dramatically the self-isolation within depression, the patterned indulgence of intellect, and the eventual freedom of self in sharing resources within relationship.

In helping others, we help ourselves.

Another technique is equally simple. Clients will often say, "I am depressed, I am afraid, I *am* so damn insecure, I *am* really unhappy, etc." Objective remediation can begin effectively like this: "This may sound absurd to you Henry Kostos, but you are 'Henry'; you are not 'Mr. Depressed'. For example, see if you think that there is any value in looking at it this way: I, Henry Kostos, am aware of who I am —especially with the understanding we are sharing in our time together today— and I am aware of something within me called 'depression'. It's trying to get *at* me. It is not who I am, but it's coming on strong!"

This is an important first step to objectify the specification process of anxiety. The client is led to think of self as *separate* from the intrusion of specific problems. In this objective separation, the anxiety can be clearly specified, acknowledged, *and confronted*.

Confrontation not only acknowledges the difficulty but acknowledges *the self's separate position*. With this distance, the self's position is clarified, defenses can be rested or economically adjusted, and management resources are alerted and strategized. The individual can plan resolution, detour, or escape. Values are clarified without routinized self-indulgent complications. Overdescription of problems is dispensed with in order to establish that time and life continue. Then, thorough study of solutions is possible.

This process is part of the technique of "Focusing", conceived by the psychologist Eugene T. Gendlin. It emerged after Gendlin researched the problem of why therapy does not succeed more often than it does, in the sense that it too often made little difference in people's lives: "We found that it is not the therapist's technique —differences in methods of therapy seem to mean surprisingly little. Nor does the difference lie in what the patients talk about. The difference is in *how* they talk. And that is only an outward sign of the real difference: *what the successful patients do inside themselves*."

Gendlin is not talking about facing personal feelings, which he calls painful self-torment. (And in this book, when we discuss confrontation of anxiety, we are not talking about facing patterned feelings, wallowing in their descriptive recall, either. Instead, we are seeing the values of acknowledging difficulty in order to adjust new feelings within new perspective. The astrologer urges the client to get on with life resourcefully.) Gendlin distills an awareness of a "felt sense". He points out that no one can intellectually figure out all the details of a personal problem. He suggests that we must look further, and he finds that these details are *stored in the body* and revealed often *through* the body.

We can all identify with Gendlin's inspired deduction: when we discover an understanding or a resolution, our bodies shift, subtly or dramatically. Hidden knowledge emerges with a rush; feelings and thoughts release their cramped position. We *jump* for joy, we *relax* in peace, we *spring* into action; we can *exercise* away accumulated tensions, we *shudder* in remembrance, we *tense* in anticipation. Our bodies are telling us details of psychodynamic awareness. Every sensitive astrologer knows the value of body language awareness during every moment of consultation.

In Gendlin's structured technique of Focusing, a guide is used (the astrologer) to help the client objectify and confront problematic concerns. The body's response keys the insights achieved. The process is conducted in relaxed conversation, encouraging the client's visualization and introspection through the body more than the mind.

The astrologer sets a scene that will establish objectification. Throughout conversation, the astrologer presses the client to find deeper feelings, physically more than intellectually. These feelings are guided by simple, artful questioning. The astrologer waits patiently for the client's body to corroborate a meaningful insight.

Please recall Case 3, page 109, and the important insight about that case on page 115. "Leslie" is extremely intelligent, as we have seen, and has every educational opportunity ahead of her, but she is routinely anxious about everything. She focuses at one moment upon her romantic relationships and, in the next moment, upon her fear about going on with her specialized education. We met for a special session of remediation, using a personal adaptation of the technique of focusing.

"Leslie, just relax, please. Take your glasses off, your shoes, if you wish; feel free to do anything that will make you comfortable. You don't have to look at me, and I don't have to look at you. There's no formality. We just want to have a relaxed discussion.

I've turned off the telephone. We've got a nice time to ourselves, to explore some of those feelings deep inside, the ones we have trouble understanding.

"Picture yourself in a room . . . I guess it's a storeroom. Yes, let's make it a storeroom. (This is reinforcement of the visualization process, as if I am participating in it with her.) Now, over there along the side of the room are stacks of boxes. Lots of them. If they weren't so neatly stacked, you wouldn't have a clear place to stand in. But, now we've got them stacked up there neatly so we *can* step back and take a look at them all. —Can you see that?

"Fine. Now, those boxes stacked up over there are your problems, your anxieties. They're safely up against the wall. Look them over. Now, *pick one*. You're going to inspect that box. Which one feels the worst right now?"

Leslie replied, "I feel old. I'm past the time of challenge." (Leslie was planning a major career program into an exciting field of communications. She had received every opportunity in clear synchronization with astrological projections. There was little question she was on the right track, but she could not easily enjoy the whole process of endeavor. Her keen intelligence constantly unnerved her, caused self-doubt, and discomfort.)

"Where does that self-doubt feeling, being old, afraid of challenge . . . where does it come from?"

"My mother."

"Now, forget your mind, Leslie. Just feel your body. What does your *body* say about your mother?"

"Ugh! I'd like to throw her off the roof!"

"What's behind that? How does that feel?"

"Well, I don't really have to please her . . . but I guess I need to in order not to be rejected."

Leslie and I chatted, still in objective visualization, about her relationships with her father and her mother (please recall page 113). Gradually, the deepest feelings were distilled.

"Leslie, again, what's the worst of those feelings? What does your body tell you?"

"It's . . . it's fear of failure."

"But, we know that you are smarter than so many people around you; you've got so much going for you. We've agreed on that many times. So what's behind this fear of failure? What does your body tell you?" (Leslie was sitting very still, although her eyes were filled with tears.)

".... My body will break down."

"In what way?"

"It won't be able to take care of itself."

"But, Leslie, you're very healthy, young and strong."

"It's that I don't want to be shown up within relationships. But I've had that with everybody. I don't want to disappoint others."

"Everybody needs relationships. But you've also got a job to do to set up your adult life on your own."

Leslie didn't respond.

"Now, Leslie, hang in there! *What's really so bad about all this?* What's behind the fears? What does your body tell you?"

And here came the telling body reaction: Leslie stretched her arms and shifted her position, the tension was being released, "My mother will be jealous of how pretty I am, and my smartness!"

Leslie was deeply caught within the parental anxieties her mind had created within the circumstances of her early development, the patterns that were so very clearly indicated within her horoscope. If she achieved her educational goals, she felt she would lose her bid to please her mother.

Our discussion eased out of Focusing (thirty minutes had gone by): *"What does this situation need,* Leslie? *What should happen?"*

"I've got to get rid of the hang-up. But it's hard because I'm lazy." (Leslie is everything *but* lazy!)

"Maybe you're avoiding the challenge because you fear being alone with your new responsibilities to yourself?"

"... That's right."

This observation we shared together became the pivot for objective understanding and practical strategy. Leslie feared being alone because it pushed her back into parental reliance. She specified the parental anxiety in terms of a painful romantic break-up she had had two years earlier, at the time when she was planning her education for her future. She was caught in the middle, and she felt alone.

Leslie could laugh now, saying "My mother is a saint! She'll be canonized next year!" (Recall the power of her Uranus, ruling the Midheaven and only twenty-three minutes of arc off exact conjunction with the nodal axis.) We discussed her whole parental situation with great objectivity, her youth and potential, her pride, her future, her need for her own values and priorities.

"Let your mother *be* canonized! Let her enjoy that while you enjoy *your* own life!"

Leslie would not easily be free of these deep, anxious connections within her development, but she had focused rewardingly upon further understanding of them.[33]

Money/Love Concerns: Throughout this book, we have seen how money/love concerns embrace and articulate the broad and vitally important concerns of self-worth. The spill over potentials from this focus of personal resources is enormous. There is a tremendous split between references to the outer environment and the inner environment. Problematic symptoms within the former often overshadow the problematic causes within the latter, and both affect organization of all other resources. Pablo Picasso, living in self-exile from his native land, said this thought eloquently: "I'd like to live like a poor man with lots of money." He captured perfectly the ordering of personal values within the demands of a materialistic environment: the poor man is forced to create meaningful life values within himself and, *with that security*, it would be ideal to have the money to relate that security to the outer environment on its terms.

A client telephoned me from the Midwest. He is a young, talented, struggling artist. He has just absorbed a long transit of Pluto opposed his Sun, a tremendous challenge to his life perspective. His Aries Sun is in his Ascendant and is opposed by Neptune retrograde in the VIIth, and this axis is squared by Uranus in the IVth. This is a powerful T-square of status/identity concerns and potential power because of them. His Saturn is retrograde on his Descendant.

Immediately, within the guidelines of this book, "Paul's" life development pattern in the early years is so clear, especially with Saturn retrograde ruling his Capricorn Midheaven. Additionally, Mars, ruler of his Aries Ascendant, is retrograde and also in the VIIth. He has easy access to the defense of withdrawal for his status/identity concerns; he has enormous creative imagination through his art; and a sensitive dedication to perfectionism (idealized delay of artistic self-presentation within his relationship concerns) that is symbolized perfectly by Venus in Pisces in his XIIth (a private sense of beauty), ruling his VIIth and in mutual reception with Neptune retrograde in the VIIth.

The powerful Pluto transit that opposed his Sun, going on to conjoin his Neptune, called tremendous attention to his creative powers, his plans to market his art work, and also his wife's personal perspective and self-concerns (Pluto transiting the VIIth and ruling his VIIIth, the second House of the VIIth).

Paul was deeply concerned with a major life decision. He told me that he wanted to move far away to a beautiful climate, live in the country, build a house, and do his art work on his own farm. This was his wife's dream.

I suggested that ecological concerns were not necessarily a good reason to abandon the marketplace of urban environment, necessary to his emergent talent. To his response of how low money resources were, how unsuccessful his work appeared to be, I suggested that he was still so very young, in a very demanding profession, and still needed to give the business exposure of his work a real try. It was too easy for him to withdraw; retrospective wondering ("Could I have made it if I stayed?") would plague him forever. He had not yet *earned* the luxury of fleeing his outer environmental problems.

The conversation disclosed that during the powerful transit activity, he had indeed conceived a potentially extremely important new art technique. It was very exciting, and could be extremely marketable. His Cardinal T-square in angles was demanding aggression in terms of the outer environment; his developmental patterns of idealized artistic withdrawal within the inner environment were being reinforced by his wife's dream of getting away to the country, fleeing the hassle.

His wife's horoscope has such similarities to Paul's. She too has an Aries Ascendant. Venus in Aries in the Acendant rules her VIIth and her IInd and opposes Neptune retrograde in the VIIth. Her Moon, ruling the IVth with Uranus there square her Ascendant, is in Gemini in the IIIrd, square the opposition of Mars-Saturn and Jupiter in her VIth and XIIth (her conceptualization resources within information/perspective concerns). So obviously, we see status/identity concerns from the early homelife (Moon rules IV; Saturn rules X; Mars rules Ascendant; Venus rules VIIth) carried over into adult relationships (VIIth House emphasis). So very much of all this residually focuses upon money/love concerns (Venus ruling the IInd, holding Sun-Mercury, which are square Pluto in the Vth, ruled by the Moon).

Her self-worth concerns are deep, nervous, vague, and probably debilitating. Her personal strength, under stress, works to flee relationships. The concerns for money are obviously used as rationale, as she and her husband try to make a go of their art business. She has a country dream, and that dream of idyllic flight is causing problems of choice. The freedom from challenge manifests as a clear negative freedom; the freedom to support her husband's new ideas (conceived perfectly in accord with astrological measurements to that potential) must be positively based upon conviction, unity, and an ordering of hierarchies within the reality of challenge.

In discussion with Paul, I explained all of this concisely and gently, gaining his objective understanding of the real problems involved: his easy withdrawal from challenge, his wife's flight mechanism, the lack of unity to meet a challenge now that could change their lives and clarify choice soon, and that his wife's dominance of the situation was based upon her deep self-worth concerns. To top it off, I suggested to Paul, "Please talk these dimensions over with your wife. I think if you will say to her that her lack of pride in herself and your effort together is at the base of her anxiety, she will cry tears of relief. The two of them had to unlock the energies held within the causes deep beneath the symptoms.

Fifteen minutes later, another telephone call came. It was Paul's wife. She had indeed cried at Paul's words, and the relief of recognition had released objective strength. She showed enormous poise during the telephone call, which concluded so positively to order hierarchies of practical concerns within positive time projections, to put aside patterned defenses from the past and get on with life for the future. Her immediate objective became to bring her husband out from withdrawal. His major objective became to bring her back from flight. Together, their objective was to give the marketing of Paul's art and new technique their very best shot. Hopefully, such inner fortification would allow more productive contact with outer demands; to gain outer recognition that in time would facilitate fulfillment of inner dream; or to become all the richer inside for having tried.

Paul's wife thanked me for caring. We shared a moment of rapport that is extremely rewarding for both astrologer and client; neither is alone; each is significant. I was reminded of the beautiful words of Dr. Willard Gaylin, a psychoanalyst and Clinical Professor of Psychiatry at Columbia University: "Caring and loving we are, and caring and loving we must be —caring and loving we *will be* as long as we so perceive ourselves. In other ways we are free to change, modify, adapt, and move. We are changing the rules of existence. We *should* change the rules of existence. We have a right to do so. Our natures will evolve in yet unanticipated ways, and that is as it should be. But to caring we must cling."[3][4]

When caringly and lovingly we astrologers deal with poignant self-worth concerns within our clients, we are working with feelings of inferiority. The client feels a separation between what he is and what he would like to be or what he is expected to be by parents, spouse, boss, etc. Again, there is a discrepancy between the inner environment within its choices for fulfillment level and the outer environment within its prescriptive selectivity for behaviors to be rewarded. Often, it is helpful for the astrologer to clarify this discrepancy objectively for the client.

The astrologer can have two circles cut out of paper. These two equal circles can overlap perfectly, partially, touch each other at a tangent point, or be separated from each other by any distance. The client assigns to one circle the symbolism of *the actual self* and to the other circle the symbolism of *the self hoped for*. The client then places the two circles into a spatial relationship that objectively symbolizes the relationship between the two psychodynamic concepts.[3][5]

This very simple objectification maneuver determines a distance of discrepancy, and remediation can begin with questions about "what dimensions are within the distance" separating the two circles. Perhaps idealization has pushed the self hoped for too far away so that congruence with the actual self is improbable, impractical within the actual resources and the relationship opportunities for resource exchange. Perhaps routinized defenses within the actual self separate it from potential. Perhaps one circle is positioned by dimensions of the inner environment, and the other circle is positioned by dimensions of the outer environment (what are the key contact potentials between the two?). The entire thesis of this book, communicated by the astrologer and refined by the client within his or her own reality, can fit in between these two circles.

Within the objectification process, the client begins to see himself clearly within development and projection. A tremendous point of view is studied and clarified. So very, very often, the client must be helped *to care and love himself, herself.*

Another remediation technique to achieve this can begin with the astrologer's amiable suggestion that the client make a list, with the astrologer's help if necessary, of ten things about the client "that are terrific!" Having some fun with this project is natural —the astrologer will have to be softly encouraging— but the exercise is extremely serious in its potential.

The client will start off with some obvious things: appearance, conversational ability perhaps, sense of humor, etc. All the while, the astrologer should write down on paper all the dimensions mentioned, and be encouraging and agreeable. Most importantly, the astrologer must be noting, as well, corollaries to any special point, to be discussed later. For example, if the client is obviously diffident in interpersonal relationships (and even in the consultation with the astrologer) as part of a spill over of self-worth concerns into status/identity relationship concerns, he or she will probably list "I'm a good listener". The astrologer should be prepared to question later, "Perhaps too good?" A constructive discussion of communication dynamics could easily follow.

Clients who are hard pressed within self-worth concerns usually find it difficult to list more than three or four "terrific" dimensions about themselves. The astrologer must be prepared to suggest things to complete the list when the client falters.

If the objective of the remediation process is to improve self-security within relationships by bolstering awareness of self-worth resources, and the client has said that he or she is a good cook —or the astrologer asks to determine if he or she is— the astrologer can build the attribute into a resource exchange idea for the client: "Suppose you cooked super meals, even drew up a fancy menu, and turned it all into a marvelous party. This would be giving of yourself most creatively. You would make others happy and easily gain new friends. The party and your resourcefulness would speak so well for you!" If the client has photography for a hobby, the astrologer can suggest that the client take his or her camera to parties to photograph the host and hostess and send prints along later as a unique "thank-you".

Obviously, the whole exercise is one of personal endorsement for the client, and this endorsement is authoritative and important only in relation to the objectivity, caring, and dignity established by the astrologer during the consultation. The process reinforces the identity and self-worth of the client within the matrix of whatever anxiety of resources is being studied during the consultation. Together, cognition of resources is realistically clarified.

A young woman has had a traumatic development in relation to her parents. Her Sun opposes Neptune, and the axis is squared by Uranus. The Sun and Uranus are her parental rulers. She has Saturn retrograde opposed her Venus in the XIIth. Her Moon rules her self-worth IInd and opposes Mars. The difficulties were extreme in her life. In every way, her self-worth concept was heavily pressed through the status/identity concerns inherited from her homelife. I asked her to prepare a list of ten dimensions that were laudable, that were terrific about her. She struggled tremendously with the list, and finally it was prepared:

1. I'm open-minded. *Too flexible? Too easily pushed around?*

2. Affectionate. *Affectionate with clear value judgements?*

3. Curious about everything. *But how practical is your curiosity?*

4. Honest; I'm sincere when it counts. *Are you this way with yourself?*

5. Artistic and appreciative of beauty. *A private sense of beauty? Too few things?*

6. I'm usually able to be strong when needed. *Offensively or defensively?*

7. I like to share knowledge. *Super!*

8. I'm unpretentious about myself. *Are you demeaning as well?*

9. I try to be analytical. *Too damn analytical? Can you laugh at yourself?*

10. I try to make others feel at ease. *Are YOU comfortable?*

After my client had completed the list, with some suggestions from me, we discussed the corollaries listed in italics above. The counterpoint discussion is never intended to destroy a positive attribute, of course; the discussion works to clarify the relationship perspective of each attribute. With reference to item number six, my question "Offensively or defensively?" gained the response, "When I think offensively, I do get a lot done." I asked for an example and then reinforced that example positively, stirring up her pride in having succeeded in an offensive show of strength. When we reviewed item number eight, I pointed out how her list included not one mention about attractiveness, love, or sexuality ("good in bed" is a very incisive dimension to be watched for or suggested, since we know that self-worth concerns within relationship manifest dramatically within sexual expression). Indeed, some of these references were included in items two, five, and ten, but they were not clearly developed within her self-profile. The discussion we shared about the *objective* list did much to reinforce her position of value on the crest of decidedly difficult developmental tension.

As we have studied on page 52, people with self-worth concerns often are unable to give compliments to others. Somehow, they feel that they themselves are diminished if they do so. The astrologer can expect this from preliminary organization of astrological analysis before the client arrives for consultation, and the astrologer can listen and watch carefully for the client to hold back natural compliments during the consultation, to be tightly self-contained within the show of emotional values.

It is perfectly natural for the client to be tense upon arrival to see the astrologer. It is a new environment about which the client knows little. The client will try to discharge some of this tension in casual chatting with the astrologer immediately upon meeting. One of the major ways human beings accomplish this is by giving compliments. The psychodynamic premise is that by showing appreciation the person will be received warmly. We go into someone's home or office and we immediately find something nice to say; a complimentary observation works to guarantee warm reception.

The astrologer in turn arranges to have his or her office or study tidy, attractive, interesting, and comfortable to speak well of the astrologer's personal taste and organization. If there is not something eminently deserving of notice or compliment in the consultation area, there should be. Such a point of notice stimulates casual conversation, helps the client feel accepted, and helps the astrologer measure client poise, sensitivity, conversational skill, and much, much more. If the dimension of compliment is missing, the astrologer must be aware of its significance.

If the astrologer observes during the consultation that the self-worth concept is defended strongly to the point that relationships suffer since the weakened self-worth concept cannot relate comfortably to the self-worth concepts of others (the IInd House is opposite the VIIIth in awareness), this vital point will have to be discussed. So very often this situation accompanies horoscope patterns that highlight in tension the significator(s) of the VIIIth House.

At the appropriate time during the consultation, the astrologer can ask the client to do a simple experiment. The client should stand comfortably in an open space within the room, with no chair, bookshelf, or table nearby to be used as support. The astrologer should stand about four steps away from the client, but at a position near the door to the room. The astrologer says to the client: "Now, I'm simply going to ask you to do two simple things. First one thing, then a second. Please do just as I ask, with no comments. We'll talk about it all later. Alright? Now, the first thing: *please give me a compliment.*"

The astrologer should make the request very simply, warmly, and clearly and wait immobile for the client's reply. The astrologer should concentrate expectantly upon the client's mouth (instead of the client's eyes, in order to keep the astrologer's gaze still and not threaten the client's poise to excess).

The client will be momentarily startled. He or she will search for the "proper" compliment. The client will think that the astrologer is searching for something in particular.

The astrologer may have to prod simply for a response. When the client gives a compliment, regardless of how extraneous, superficial, insightful, or flattering it is, the astrologer should show no facial expression, slowly and silently turn away from the client, and walk a few paces directly away, preferably out of the room but still in view. The astrologer should show no additional value judgment even through posture or in the rear view of back and shoulders. After five seconds (no more), the astrologer should return to the starting position within the room, facing the client. "Fine. Now, the second thing. *Please give me another compliment.*"

The tension is building. The client is bewildered, but he or she will *not* think the process absurd if the seriousness and poise of the astrologer are intact.

As the client speaks the second compliment, the astrologer should release a warm smile and walk slowly and lovingly forward to the client, saying "Thank you, very, very much." As the astrologer reaches the client, he or she should warmly put an arm around the client in appreciation.

The client usually "melts" in recognition of the contrast of the astrologer's reactions, and usually returns the hug. It becomes so powerfully clear *how rewarding in terms of relationship giving a compliment and appreciating a compliment can be.* In the first cold response, the client's compliment was ignored (so many people with self-worth concerns cannot accept compliments easily; not acknowledging compliments is tantamount to ignoring relationship with the person giving them) and in the second warm response, the client's compliment was rewarded with security and warmth of relationship. "Thank you for sharing that experiment with me. That process is what goes on every day, all the time in life, in so many different ways. Look how great it is to relate affirmatively to others by sincerely complimenting them, acknowledging their resources, their position, and by reaching out in appreciation when you are complimented. You can make others so happy . . . and yourself too; you gain so much in the process!"

Information/Perspective Concerns: A favorite parable told by many teachers of the spirit involves two monks on a long foot journey back to their monastery. One monk is very old and the other is very young. They walk along in silence. The heavy rains have turned their path into mud; puddles are everywhere. They proceed directly, stoically.

The two monks pass a rich country home. A beautiful Geisha, in beautiful robes, is at the threshold of the house. She contemplates the large puddle before her. Her dainty white feet and her trailing robes are threatened with soil.

The younger monk leaves the path to assist the Geisha. He lifts her over the puddle to dry ground, and then he returns to his older partner. The older monk shows silent rage within his face.

The two monks continue their journey for three days. They exchange no words.

Finally, safe within the walls of their temple, the older monk releases his anger at the younger monk: "You should be ashamed of yourself! We monks are not permitted to go near females. It is dangerous. Why did you do it?"

The younger monk replied, "I left the woman back there. *Are you still carrying her?*"

The mind carries accumulated information, value judgments, and points of view within a routinized circuitry that directs the process of choice and continuously determines personal perspective. The mutability of the Cadent Grand Cross of information/ perspective resources creates constant spill over into determinations of new status/identity awareness and broad self-worth concerns within the money/love resources. Fantasy idealization and reality conceptualization become intertwined. The circuitry of the mind becomes individualistically patterned, and the patterns work to preserve samenesses, routine, predictability, security. We all too subjectively stick and stay in the mud.

Our behavioral sciences assume à certain conformity among all human beings since all brains are basically and functionally the same: they are twin structures, bilaterally symmetrical (Gemini); the corpus callosum connects the brain hemispheres (horizon); and the spinal cord continues as the brain stem (Midheaven axis). The adult brain constitutes 2 percent of the body weight, but it consumes 20 percent of the body's oxygen (Mercury)!

Behaviorally, we know that the similarities among brains break down as memory records individual experiences and reactions, as identity is stored and developed. This process of individuation is actually the separation between the fact of brain and the concept of mind. As yet, science cannot assimilate this separation, but holistic astrology can. The brain represents outer capacity, and the mind represents inner potential. It is worthwhile for us to explore this to determine how the mind works within self-conceptualization through choice of information to establish perspective.

A stimulus is registered in our human awareness. It is transmitted throughout our system by electrical signals passed along nerves. These signals interact within the brain to produce responses. The interpretive challenge is to distinguish between event (the stimulus) and reaction (the response). The meaning of an event, of a stimulus, is conceived by the mind. It lies not in the event, but in our reaction to it. Again: events have no value until the human being gives value to them.

This is an extremely important remediation concept. I remember a dramatic case: a woman whose horoscope I knew in detail telephoned me one day saying that she had just received news that her mother had been found dead by suicide some four thousand miles away. The daughter was completely calm, factual, uninvolved. Using every astrological means known to me, I was unable to "find" this dramatic event in the daughter's horoscope. After considerable perplexity about this apparent failure of astrology (or astrologer!), it suddenly hit me that *I* thought this event to be terribly significant, that I was culturally conditioned to expect conformity in the daugher's reaction, but that the daughter interpreted it totally individualistically: it meant very, very little—if anything—to her! It was not in the horoscope because it meant nothing to the individual. Because of a lifetime of choices and reactions, entirely individualistic, and because of a temperament and mental organization that was totally individualistic as well, she did not give the expected value to the event, an event that could have been devastating to someone else.

Conversely, many times a specific developmental tension is indicated in the horoscope, in a person's holistic development, and that person's reactions to the corresponding event far exceed normal expectations. Again, we are aware of something happening somewhere within the psyche that confounds the predictably conforming and emphasizes the individualistically expressive.

We know that all behavior patterns anticipated in the individual are analyzed astrologically through the core network of aspect patterns. Significators key vital resource areas and psychodynamically gain behavioral potential through aspect relationships with other significators symbolizing other resource areas. Holistically, the parts articulate the whole. It is very simple and rewarding to relate these astrological aspect patterns to neurological networks in the brain. In studying the two in parallel, we come very close to the determination of how and where the common brain gives over hegemony to the individualistic mind.

The grey matter of the brain (the cortex, 3 to 4mm thick, wrinkled and fissured) is filled with nerve cells. The white region it covers is filled with bundles of nerve fibers. The cells number in the billions and work in clusters. Cell bodies have long branching fingers emanating from their centers, and these fingers are called *dendrites*. One of these long dendrites develops into an *axon*. Myriad axon groups are located in the white matter of the brain.

The axon becomes most important for our understanding since it is the conductor of the electrical nerve impulse identified with the particular cell group. The axon is insulated by a high-fat sheath (myelin) and has the vitally important capability of *conducting in either direction*. Axons have an inherent reaction capacity, regardless of the intensity of stimulation. When an axon is fired with current for reaction, it will seek an all-or-nothing fulfillment.

When something happens and enters our awareness, a stimulus is recorded in varying frequencies, impulses are received and sent out, and somehow the cell groups are organized categorically in terms of specifically patterned objectives. This process readily lends itself to the astrological overlay of aspect patterns, of all horoscopic components: a stimulus occurs (Transit, Solar Arc, Progression) in varying frequencies; impulses are received and sent out (relationships through aspects with other planets), and somehow the cell groups are organized (the aspect groups themselves) in terms of specific objectives (House references registering outer environmental prescriptions and inner environmental resources).

Within the brain/mind reference within information/perspective concerns of the Cadent Grand Cross of Houses, we can begin to see the whole horoscope as analogous to a human being's neurological process. The neurological faculties involved in responses are represented by the plants: how we need to think in order to be most efficient (Mercury), our need to relate aesthetically and emotionally (Venus), how we need to apply energy for maximum efficiency (Mars), the need for a certain kind of reward, enrichment, and exposure (Jupiter), our need to assimilate the controls for efficiency and strategy (Saturn), our potential for high individualization and intensification of self (Uranus), the creative visualization strengths for protection or planning (Neptune), and our personality's sense of personal perspective in the scheme of things (Pluto). The life-energy of the whole system is seen in the blend between the Sun and Moon, with the Moon representing the reigning need of the personality.

With this recapitulation of the symbological core of this book, it is easy and rewarding to imagine that each planet represents innumerable, specific axon groups, swirling in categorically defined units of function, relating with other groups representing other planets. Resources combine as the inner environment prepares developmentally to face the prescriptions of the outer environment. It's easy to picture the confluence of electrical energies among the groups in terms of aspect relationships among the plaents. Through their patterning, we can appreciate the same categorically organized groups relating differently within every individual. We can see the horizon axis differing in each individual and therefore connecting the two brain hemispheres (the corpus callosum) differently; we can see the Midheaven axis differing in each individual just as the neurological components of the spinal cord extend differently into each individual's brain stem. We can see the power of Mercury ("I think, therefore I am") as symbol of the essential and vastly disproportionate oxygen requirements of the brain, with each individual's awareness of self structured upon the symbolism of his or her individual Mercury and patterned within the connections among variegated resources. Within the conformity of the whole among brains, we begin to see the individual divergence of the parts and their interrelationships within the individual.

The final stage of the response mechanism is where we find the seat of the mind. Every axon ends in what is called a *synapse*, a kind of bi-polar grid. Each synapse comes face to face with another synapse, like two two-pronged wire conductors. Two vital discoveries about the synapse can be extremely important for astrology in the study of conceptualization, of choice and reaction. First, *there is a gap between synapses*. Second, *within this gap there is the potential for acceptance or negation*.

Within the gap between synapses, certain chemicals operate as triggers. A "spark" crosses the gap somehow relating the two swirling cell bodies in a condition of acceptance or negation. Astrologically, I suggest that the synapse point is analogous to the juncture between two planets in aspect. In this sense, an aspect indicates a potential that is realized, modified, missed, or overcome depending upon the action of the individual. The synapse gap is the choice gap *filled by* the individual in relating two faculties of behavior in response to an event, in determining value judgment within cognition of behavioral resources.

Now, within the spinal cord, there are neurons going in both directions, and in the spinal cord grey matter there is a high density of *excitatory* interneurons and *inhibitory* interneurons. Are these not translatable astrologically as Mars and Saturn, respectively? Isn't this the behavioral polarity within any reaction: to excite for further growth and survival or to inhibit necessarily for greater control and learning? Isn't this polarity the challenge of choice, the hot/cold struggle that demands the expression of will? Doesn't the whole awareness of choice make us think, make us use our brains in full, evaluate needs in relation to our resources for fulfillment through relationship with the world around us?

In every choice, then, in every reaction that gives individual value to an event, the brain operates in totality: swirls of nerve cells are translated into faculties of individualized behavior (resources) to fulfill individualized needs. Our minds need to react a certain way (Mercury) and must assimilate necessary controls (Saturn) and energy potentials (Mars). I suggest that these three planetary symbols define the Matrix of the Will.[36]

This entire process then is conditioned by our experience within development. We constantly store information for choice. Accumulated choices establish who we are. We gain our own mind in relation to the minds that judge us. The polarities of mind and brain, self and others, needs and prescriptions, being and non-being are as functional for life development as the polarities of day and night, Sun and Moon. The connections within polarities, the gaps between them are the seat of anxiety. Being is a matter of life *and* death.

When a client manifests strong developmental tension within information/perspective concerns, the conceptualization process is the focus of keen anxiety. Case 3, Leslie, is a clear example of this. Interpretive connections have been made by the mind in terms of inner value reactions to external circumstances. These interpretive connections become routinized into beliefs that protect against indecision in future choices and rationalize decisions made in past choices. We know the root cause of such anxiety: the conflict between inner needs and outer prescriptions.

The mind races continuously to make every awareness significant. Every event or circumstance or pressure must be given meaning by an anxious mind. Every bit of information must be converted into strategic significance to establish personal perspective further. This observation was confirmed for me through an intriguing report in Wilder Penfield's *The Mystery of the Mind*.

Brain surgeons Penfield and William Feindel were side by side in
the operating room observing the responses of patients to gentle
electrical current applied to the temporal lobe of the brain. They
found that, in some patients, they were able to produce artifi-
cially a state of automatic response, random movements and
comments. One patient said, "time and space seem occupied."[37]
—What a thought! The synapse gaps seem closed. The entire brain
function seems to work for holistic completion, for full integration, filling subjective time and objective space. Fullness and
completion are conditions of great significance.

In remediation, this instinctive process, this mystery, can be
used upon itself! For example, the astrologer can recommend an
exercise to the client, to be done at home in privacy: "Please, let
me suggest an exercise. It's really absurd, and it's intended to be.
That's the whole point, as I'll explain in a moment. Pick a time
during your schedule when you can be alone and undisturbed for
five minutes. Take the phone off the hook. Protect your privacy.
Turn off your radio or television, and then set a kitchen timer for
five minutes. Now, I'm really asking you to do something absurd:
put a sturdy chair in the middle of a room and stand on it! Just
stand there on the chair and do nothing until the timer rings at
the end of five minutes! *Just listen to your thoughts*. And, please
promise me that you'll try this three times in a row, once each day
for three days. Then, call me, and let's discuss it."[38]

The client can be asked to write down his or her thoughts.
The process can be repeated over a week, whatever. The principle
is that the exercise is absurd, *but the mind will work to make it
significant*. While standing on the chair, the client's mind will
work overtime to occupy itself. The anxiety will focus itself in
layer after layer of introspection. Often, the discoveries for the
client are amazing.

A client of mine has her Pluto in between her Sun and Moon
conjunction in her XIIth House (an arm of the Cadent Grand
Cross of Houses). The triple conjunction is in Leo, as is her Ascendant. All the planets of the horoscope are in the eastern hemisphere (protecting the identity; please recall page 43). Her parental
significators are under tension (Pluto rules her IVth and conjoins
the Sun and Moon; Venus rules her Midheaven and conceptualization IIIrd and squares Neptune. Mercury rules her IInd, holding
Neptune, and is retrograde, squares her Mars in the Xth and semi-

squares her Saturn in the XIth). There is no doubt that her pride lies dormant under an insecure self-worth image conditioned powerfully by her parental environment.

This woman stood on her chair for five minutes several days in a row. She called me excitedly about incredibly rewarding insights about her mother's manipulation of her during childhood. Specific memories were resurrected and then given proper perspective through fresh understanding. Her tensions abated enormously, and she was able to enjoy powerful Jupiter transits of her triple (Sun-Pluto-Moon) conjunction and establish job status and personal identity securely and proudly for the first time in her adult life.

Without the benefits of introspection, naturally or remedially, clients with information/perspective concerns stay stuck in the mud of defense conceptualizations. They will often seek dependence upon others, to have others supply life meaning and direction. Some will *misinterpret* spiritual teachings or espouse *unilluminated* teachings to fit their major problematic focus of concerns. For example, if relationships and sexuality are threatening because of self-worth concerns, a teaching that espouses sublimation (more usually repression) of sexuality might provide a spiritual rationale to protect a person from this broad area of interpersonal resource exchange. This is compounding the problem rather than solving it. Haridas Chaudhuri writes, "Ethical and religious leaders must stop talking of sex as a reprehensible thing. It is just a natural urge with its legitimate function in the creative flow of life and in the psychic growth of personality. The repression of sex can succeed only in driving it into perverse and abnormal channels. The premature suppression of sex in the interest of religious goals eventually proves disastrous in spite of some apparent or real gain. It is bound to undermine one's health and one's will to live. It encourages gradual withdrawal from the social reality. The desexualized person gets passionately set to flee it all—to escape from this dark dungeon of earthly existence."[39]

We may very easily and instructively substitute "money" for "sex" in Chaudhuri's wise statement. No illuminated teaching can practicably establish premature suppression of *any* resource or premature withdrawal of *any* exchange within relationship. Spirituality is not a goal. It is a developmental process, a mode of growth. Withdrawal from the process of relationship within the world in any way interrupts developmental maturation. To avoid a challenge or to avoid the opportunity to fail is to sacrifice growth.

Excessive dependency upon any teaching, belief, dogma, and/or person can easily become a fantasy, a debilitation, a sickness. We lose our own minds to the minds of others. We cannot close our own gaps our own way, so our entire behavioral potentials misfire in terms not our own. Responsibility to avoid such danger belongs to teachers and to students alike.

Psychiatrist Arthur Deikman captures this remediation concept in a startling scenario: "Let us imagine that you see a poster: 'Teacher is in town!' You go to hear him. He's younger than you'd thought or wanted. It bothers you. You say so. This is his reply:

" 'What you're really asking is whether I have the Big Truth. If I had a long white beard you'd think it more likely. You want me to have it in my pocket; then all you have to do is kiss my feet, be a good boy, be a good girl, and I'll finally pat you on your nice little head and give you your reward: Enlightenment! You're afraid I'm not old enough to have it in my pocket, that's your problem. You're a conniver who's looking for an angle you can play and so you come to me—the mark—to rip me off in perfect sanctity with your eyes rolled up to Heaven, counting your beads and muttering your mantra. . . . Well, it won't work, and if I fell for that baloney I'd be a bigger fool than you and all the others like you, with your flattery and coyness and preening and tears and awe and all that damn emotion.'

"He leans forward. 'What do you want? Do you know? Do you want me to take care of you? Well, I won't, it doesn't interest me, I have children of my own. So that's out. Do you want Enlightenment? Why do you want that when you don't even know what it is? What do you think will happen when you get it? Answer me!'

"You manage to reply, 'I don't want to be afraid of Death and I want to be content and happy—like the time I had a mystical experience. The books say you can be that way all the time, once you're Enlightened.'

"He groans in mock pain. 'My God! Didn't it occur to you that solving your problems comes *first*? When you examine all your problems and see what's going on, when you figure out why you're scared of dying, when you start being happy, and when you cut out all this crap, then, perhaps, a Teacher might have something to show you—if you still needed anyone to show it to you.'

" 'Then what's a Teacher for?'

" 'To get you to work on yourself—the last thing you want to do, because you're lazy or you think it's hopeless or it will take too long. ... Look, it's not finding some Big Truth that's the issue, but your growth. You are like a plant in the ground that is growing: if you are three inches high with three leaves poking up out of the ground, you are not going to be an oak tree three months from now. Indeed, the attempt to be an oak tree would destroy you. You must grow from where you are. Furthermore, you may really be some other kind of tree. We need more than oak trees in this world, you have to allow your growth to take place. ... Don't be afraid that you will fail, that you will make a mistake and not guess under which cup the pea is hidden. There is no pea for you to find. There is only the process of becoming more sane, more real, truly alive. If you look, you will see exactly what your eyes are able to see and use at that time, and if you can have some trust in that process, you will enjoy your life and growth and be free from the fear that holds you where you are now.'

" 'So you see, there is nothing to be afraid of, and there is nothing to lose. There is only the experience of learning, of freedom, of interest and wonder at the vast reality, beyond anything you have seen, to which you belong.' "[40]

We must know deeply that *astrologers are teachers* and we must know deeply what this responsibility entails.

On another level of remediation, clients often have to be reminded that, all too easily and all too often, human beings over-dramatize oppressive circumstances in order to clarify status and identity under pressure, in order to make themselves feel all the more important as a focus of attention. Often personal anxieties are projected onto others; resource exchange tensions are tied together with misinterpreted connections. A person may feel that he or she is unloved or unvalued by a mate or a colleague when, in reality, the person feels that way about *himself* within guilt or self-deprecating depression. The personal symptom is more manageable in projection upon another outside the self. Think of the incredible amount of time and energy wasted by the worry that "someone else dislikes me" or "someone is against me"! Here we have the mind and nervous system in high developmental tension about peer group cooperation, the tension between the IIIrd House and the VIth.

Of course, rarely are we so important as to have others—with the same anxiety potentials—concerning themselves as much about us as we fear! This is a sobering thought and a helpful one in remediation. The solution is to solve concerns internally rather than project inner anxiety externally.

The information/perspective resources are the most accessible of all resources during consultation. The client is constantly communicating his or her information/perspective resources in many, many ways. The creative listening of the astrologer records this profile easily. So often, concerns have to do with the actual *style* of communication itself. If the client has exhibited communication problems during the consultation, the astrologer can point these out gently—even imitate them in objectification and humor—and suggest remediation. For example, if the client cannot keep his or her eyes from roving, fearing direct eye contact (and there is every necessity to fear direct contact if one feels insecure; eye-to-eye contact is a powerful challenge), suggest that the client focus his or her eyes on the person's mouth instead. Additionally, the astrologer can use his hand to bring the client's eyes back to person-focus during all conversation.

Voice level, diction, word choice, grooming . . . all these things can be talked about to give the client something to adjust in self-remediation. These are very important dimensions of interpersonal relationships. They are the dimensions that establish status/identity resources during first meetings. They are external symptoms of internal causes, and all human beings learn through life experience to "read" them instinctively.

Discussion may reveal problems in sharing opinions: "No one thinks the way I do; the world doesn't understand me!" (most often the defense of Pluto in the XIIth). The astrologer can ask the client to test a few opinions out during the consultation. The astrologer can then usually detect an approach to the communication of the ideas that puts off any listener; a different approach could make the opinion perfectly "acceptable." Very often, for example, prefacing a suggestion with "What if" and an opinion with "It could be that" allows the statement of substance while keeping other alternatives open. It can be a real grace of communication for many clients with relationship and communication concerns.

When high nervous energies abound, breathing is shallow, thoughts are incomplete, and anxieties cannot easily specify in manageable fears because they are caught in repetitive treadmill rhythms. The mind needs help in being stilled. The astrologer can slow down his or her own communication, warm the sound of his or her voice to set an example of poised composure. Deep breathing can bring some repose to the client. The study of simple Yoga can be a tremendous boon to the client.

Perhaps the significator of the IXth House is under high developmental tension, suggesting, as we have seen, that the client's education was interrupted. Perhaps, for example, in a woman's horoscope, the significators of the VIIth, VIIIth, and IXth are all stressed and interrelated. Perhaps her education was interrupted for her to work to keep her husband in college, i.e., working for his self-worth image (the VIIIth). Perhaps now in adult years, with children grown, she resents that sacrifice (since he maybe never expressed gratitude for it or has not continued to do so). She needs to do something for herself now. This feeling has gotten in the way of their marriage. The stress comes out in many ways. Symptoms cloud causes. The astrologer can suggest how the husband can be made proud of his wife's fortitude. A new perspective to a nagging old problem can be found logically. Adult education courses can bring pride, formalize conceptualization, and give outlet to the woman. They revitalize information/perspective resources, assist catching up with things, and eliminate idleness.

The astrologer must be prepared usually to still and stabilize strategically the nervous dimensions of the Cadent Grand Cross resources so tied to the mind and nervous system. In the main, clarification of a *hierarchy* of values and concerns remediates well the problems of indecision and vacillation, after the root causes within early development are ascertained and appreciated. The astrologer must be prepared to perk things up as well, showing individual potentials that can reinforce ideas, encouraging freer communication and opinionation. Exuberance, enthusiasm, and imagination are indeed contagious attributes and, expressed by the astrologer, can do wonders to reshow the client the energies and zest of life. Constantly the astrologer is working for balance between the defensive poles of imposition and adaptation, overselling and underselling of the self.

I have a young male client who is an insurance salesman. His horoscope shows a strong dimension of sensitivity, but he was not showing this personally in any way during the consultation. When I asked him about it, he had trouble understanding what I meant.

I then suggested the sensitivity was not working within him strongly enough *because his environment was not putting a premium on it*. In his work circle in the Southwest, sensitivity was not a premium trait.

This observation opened up our conversation, and definite but subtle manifestations of this sensitivity were corroborated. At the moment, he was primarily afraid of losing his new insurance sales job because of not meeting a quota. The quota deadline was two days away, and he was withdrawn in private torment. His sensitivity was working against him.

I pointed out how sensitivity can be used by a businessman, a salesman, especially an insurance salesman. I actually dramatized a sales presentation in two ways: one without sensitivity to the potential buyer's needs and one with deep sensitivity. I sold my point! Then, uncannily, transit configurations for the day before the consultation suggested a beneficial meeting, a contact socially. I asked about this: "Now, tell me. Wasn't there some possible contact made for new business within the last two or three days?"

He thought and thought about it. Suddenly, his gloom gave way to enthusiasm and hope. He *had* made a contact for a potential sale, but he had not followed up on it, since he was so "down" about failing his quota.

I immediately capitalized on the dramatization that had just been so effective and the astrological correspondence of the moment that had been corroborated. I stirred him up as dramatically as I could. I stood up, raised my voice a bit. He stood up. As we shook hands with strong energy, I literally shoved him on his way to make the followup. He was excited, hopeful, confident. —It worked. He made the sale and then some; made his quota; and, in his words, "learned a lesson from the best damn sales presentation I have ever seen!"

A final note brings us to an important point within the remediation process. Very often, a client will say to the astrologer after a full, sharing exchange: "You really haven't told me anything I don't know." I personally feel that this is a high compliment. My reply is always, "If I had, I'd probably be wrong! What I do as an astrologer is help you help yourself, reorganize the balance of resources within your life development. Indeed, you know what's best. We clarified it together. There was a spark between us."

We must realize that problems of stress are so very often problems of fragmentation, of aloneness. We are not created un-whole, with developmental space and life time 'unfull'. We simply lose sight of wholeness at our individual level in our individual life development patterns. When we refind our wholeness, we are able to see so much more space and time.

Within the process of remediation, within all of holistic astrological analysis, we must be humble and know that we are powerless without the client; as powerless as a guide without his compass. There can be no intrusion of our own value systems, our own ego needs. There can only be our objectivity, seasoned through caring, understanding, and experience. These are the graceful outlines of common sense given polish by the wisdom of astrology.

Chapter Nine
MEANINGS AND POINTS OF VIEW

At one and the same time, the concept of meaning is catalyst and confinement. We discover meaning, and we learn the elements of choice and behavioral response. This learning can stimulate growth or define status quo. Meanings establish who we are in terms of varying degrees of victimization, reflection of sameness, and the capacity for change. The meanings of points of view, guiding development throughout lifetime, urge growth or confine it in terms of the developmental tension between inner environmental needs and outer environmental prescriptions.

We have seen vividly throughout our studies in this book that events gain value and take on meanings through the individual who gives them value and meaning. Meaning becomes intricately involved with personal individuated awareness. It is instructive to observe that infinitely varied meanings can be assigned to the same point of focus by infinitely varied individual points of view.

For example, a fixed emphasis upon the values of security (a reigning need often powerful within the Moon in Taurus symbolism) conditions the values given the challenge of change. These values (usually the fear of change since change threatens security) will be different from a cardinally emphasized life point of view. Different meanings are given to the challenge of change, and different strategies emerge within the individualized behaviors to fulfill individualized needs. The relationship between inner and outer environments is affected completely.

A person with a fragile self-worth profile might not be able to take a joke about something personal, whereas the joke may be harmless to someone whose self-profile is well fortified. Such individual vulnerabilities are registered in everything we say and do and are instinctively picked up by the sensitivities in others. Recognition of these vulnerabilities need not be articulated overtly or measured consciously; they are registered in the essence of being alive within societally conditioned reactions. The turn of a phrase, the inflection upon a word, shifts of eyes, movements of hands, deviation from anticipated response patterns . . . all of these things and more are registered within some hypersentient awareness all living things share. This awareness is certainly contained within the "aether" that philosophically connects what is above with what is below, what is without with what is within; it is the domain of the mind, of Mercury.

Under developmental pressure, the concept of meanings is stressed. The mind races to make everything significant, as we have seen. We can anticipate the worst, even encourage it, somehow to confirm who and what we think we are. We can avoid introspection because we do not want to be reminded of ourselves; we can create self-images to fool ourselves. The mind can play tricks through conceptualization, and then communication can play further tricks as human beings meet and relate within resource exchange. Through objectivity, the astrologer remedially helps the client clarify analytical connections and modifying points of view.

Even within the formalized learning precepts of astrology, the problems of meaning, points of view, and communication are legion. We are told by texts of varying degrees of sophistication and tyranny exactly what certain measurements in astrology *mean*. Too easily and conveniently, we can take these meanings and arbitrarily transfer them to the life of another individual. We can commit the crime of categorization by confining a life to what we or someone else knows about astrology, by relating the human being's life to the horoscope.

The entire thesis of this book has been to reverse that process by bringing the horoscope to life by relating its symbols *to the substance developed in life by the particular human being it portrays*. Meanings become individualized for individual significance; symbols become individualistically enriched; and astrologer and client learn more together about the individual profile of growth through anxiety. Meanings and wisdom are illuminated through relevant discussion of life patterns of behavior and the values attached to them throughout development.

When we analyze the tension between astrology and the world of scientific methodology (astrology's inner and outer environments), we again see the problems of meanings: the scientific community expects that astrology still embraces fate as it did for millennia, in reflection of the social predicament, and that there is an absolutism about astrology which must stand up to measurement and predictability in order to have integrity. Too easily, we can work to comply with those prescriptions, taking astrology to scientific task in the terms of science. But we are not expected to do this with religion, love, aesthetics, or even psychology, which are not "scientific". I submit that, if astrology *were* scientifically methodological, science would have found this out long ago and usurped the insights of astrology in the name of science and enforced them upon mankind in another layer of societal prescriptions. Life would be even less individualistic than it is.

Astrology is an artform of individualized interpretation that blends social fact with individual fact, that views the individual as a majority, and that changes its essential significance with every essentially different individual. When *this* point of view is presented to science, science has no rebuttal; not presuming categorized knowledge avoids attack by the knowledgeably categorized.

The eminent psychologist Carl R. Rogers captures this thought beautifully:

"There is no special virtue attached to the policy of limiting our theories to observable behaviors. Neither, I would add, is there any *inherent* virtue in basing our theorizing on phenomenological variables. The fundamental question will be settled by the future. There is at least as much reason to believe that theories based upon existential-phenomenological constructs will be successful, as to believe that theories based upon observable behaviors will be successful. A theory which postulates relationships between inner subjective phenomena not directly measurable, may, like theories regarding non-Euclidean space, prove to be more valuable in advancing our knowledge than theories regarding observable behavior."[41]

Just as individuals in any social era develop habits of reaction that stereotype the era and support its science, arts, religion, and astrology, so do any era's institutions reflect the habits of their identity. Prescriptions of any kind define status/identity as they support patterns of behavior and thought. Habits are the enemy of growth although they are essential for existence. Again, we see the precarious balances between symbols and prescribed meanings, between pattern and change, between living and becoming.

On the personal level, each human being faces this dilemma constantly, doing things in remembrance of the precepts of others, doing what's expected, seeking reward by acquiescence, repressing unrewarded behaviors, communicating in the terms prescribed by outer environments, from intimate relationships to social groups.

CASE 10 shows the horoscope of a young woman caught within enormous familial patterning and the pressures to make a decision for radical change. The Sun-Moon blend (Capricorn-Gemini) promises powerful intellectual, creative, or scientific outlet. Conservatism and innovation can clash or stimulate behavioral vacillation between these two poles. The vacillation potential is powerfully reinforced by the Mars-Saturn conjunction upon the Ascendant.

The Houses of the Angular Grand Cross are powerfully keyed: the Mars-Saturn conjunction at the Ascendant, with Saturn square Pluto, ruler of the Ascendant, which is conjunct the Midheaven; Uranus, ruler of the IVth is opposed by Venus, ruler of the VIIth, and this axis is squared by Neptune in the XIIth. There is no doubt that there is developmental status/identity tension that must be carefully discussed so that individualized meanings can amplify the symbols of the horoscope. At the same time, the Sun in the IInd rules the Midheaven and is beautifully trine Jupiter in the Xth. Similarly the Sun trines Pluto in the Midheaven and sextiles Neptune. Within the "feel" of cross-pressures, within vacillation suggested by the Gemini Moon in relation to the Capricorn Sun and by the conjunction upon the Ascendant, we can see that the home environment is extremely supportive (trines) but probably confining at the same time. The important position of Neptune in the XIIth (the third House of the Xth) suggests that the communication of the parent in the Xth is a decisive factor within the general preparatory holistic view of the horoscope. Uranus and

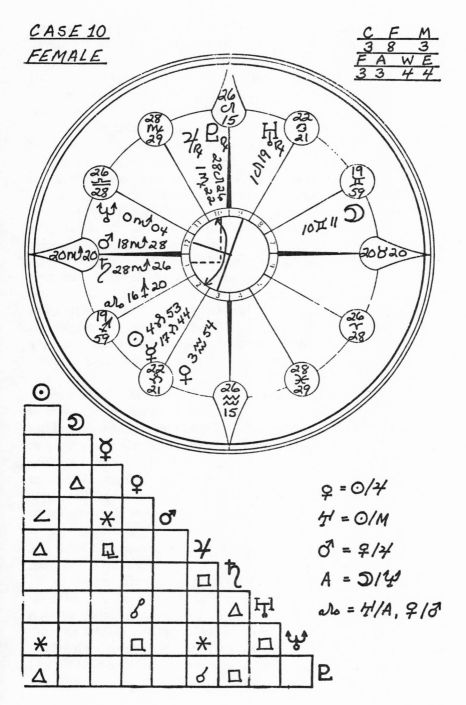

CASE 10
FEMALE

C	F	M
3	8	3

F	A	W	E
3	3	4	4

♀ = ☉/♃

♃ = ☉/M

♂ = ♀/♃

A = ☽/♅

☊ = ♃/A, ♀/♂

333

Neptune are sesquiquadrate and semisquare to the node, respectively, suggesting that the parent of importance within the developmental network is the mother.

With the Venus-Uranus/Neptune configuration occupying Cadent Houses, we can be prepared for an information/perspective tension as well. This is supported by the condition of Venus as ruler of the XIIth, Saturn as ruler of the IIIrd in square to Pluto, and Mars as ruler of the VIth in semisquare with the Sun and rising. The Moon's aspect connections are weak, as are Mercury's. Nervousness, anxiety, conceptual tension must swirl within parental demand as it modifies individual needs. The personal thrust of the inner environment certainly is to professional prominence: Pluto conjunct the Midheaven, Saturn square the Midheaven, Mars conjunct the Ascendant, the Sun semisquare the Ascendant, and the Moon in the VIIth.

The young woman corroborated every detail of the preparatory notes: her mother had been an extreme influence and pressure upon her throughout life; the parents had supported her well financially, as long as she did what the mother expected. The young woman's husband worked for the parents, and they lived in a house next door to the parents, as did other children of the family in homes nearby.

My client trembled with anxiety. She had lost much weight. She was at a crisis decision point in her life which we distilled as the fear of abandoning the pattern of mother dominance and her own patterned reliance upon the mother. The anxiety was a threat of separation, from mother and husband and their support; the threat of their disapproval; the threat of her not being able to go it alone, of not being. The mother had threatened that the daughter would never be supported again if she made the decision to leave.

At the time of consultation, Solar Arc Saturn and Solar Arc Pluto (since they are indeed precisely square natally) had both moved simultaneously into fourth harmonic configuration to the midpoint of Sun/Moon. SA Mars was at the midpoint of Sun/Ascendant. The entire natal construct of status/identity tension was at a breaking point. Additionally, transiting Pluto was semisquare natal Jupiter, and transiting Jupiter was crossing her Midheaven, Pluto, and natal Jupiter. She wanted to leave her husband

and the parental ties, go far away to the west coast (to a new environment) and study law, to practice eventually in the entertainment industry.

There was absolutely no doubt that this break had to take place, that it had to occur for her to grow into her own potentials.

The parents were comfortable and supportive; the young girl had fun as a cheerleader in school. Everything was outwardly "fine." Yet, at every turn of discussion, it was as if the mother were living the daughter's life for herself. The father was ineffective.

To alleviate the anxiety, my client and I were able to specify the feelings in terms of an objective fear, i.e., "I will lose the support of my family." My client feared being alone, separate from the support pattern, regardless of how grievously confining it had been.

Remediation was to establish a point of view that was based upon the young woman's *inner* environment, upon her *own* identity. We worked together to understand the meanings of her life as they were probably conceived by her mother with her own special problems. We worked to understand the meanings life would have if she did not take this educational opportunity she now had. We established the point of view that her parents (her mother) would eventually become proud of their daughter "the lawyer," and that presentation of her decision would have to be made on this basis, away from the hysterical patterns of nerve-rattling communication that had typified confrontations like this throughout her life.

We rehearsed little speeches, each time preserving calm and ordering thoughts upon deep relationship values (taking advantage of the Scorpio sensitivities suggested by the woman's Ascendant). With each repetition of the confrontation scenario, the rational point of view was made stronger, clearer, sturdier. Life took on individual meaning; empathy with the mother seasoned ego awareness; presentation gained nobility; maturity grew; resolve was anchored.

The capacity for change was fighting the habit of pattern; the balance was shifting between victimization and growth. What had life meant? What meanings could it have? From where would new support and approval rewards come? What points of view could clarify a new horizon?

36

In reaction to patterns of behavior, meanings are derived from routined stimulus/response connections. Everyday life privately and in relationships is filled with patterned responses to patterned stimuli: the "How are you's" and the "Fine, thank you's", the images brought to mind by mention of a person's name, the opinions activated by conversations, the feelings animated by sounds, smells, touches, memories, hopes. Remediation within stimulus/response meanings requires conditioning away from pattern; requires *re*conditioning. With the client of Case 10, reconditioning was begun by rehearsing confrontation conversations based upon a fresh point of view. In effect, the tables were being turned knowingly and strategically; patterns were being upset for planned effect within necessary change.

Note how telling stimulus/response reactions can be: at a recent astrology lecture presentation, at the mid-morning break, a rather timid appearing man (already, signals in behavior, dress, appearance had been given meaning by me and are here transmitted in communication by the word "timid") approached me, shaking his head in disbelief. He said, "Wow, are you always like this? You're so powerful!" I placed my hand upon his shoulder and gave him a two-fold answer: "The answer is no; today I'm supposed to be powerful and hopefully helpful. And, may I add, in the spirit of what we're sharing today, that your question reveals more about you than it does me."

In a similar vein, we can hear so often around us people saying, "I really have to hand it to you" as a preface to a compliment. The question here is why is it so difficult to give the compliment? Why does one have to articulate that they "really have to"; why can't it be the most *natural* thing to do?

In both instances, there is a recognition of unexpected stimulus and an effort to understand its meaning in terms of individual response. There is a struggle to break away from patterned reaction and perhaps to come closer to that which is admired in the other person. The other person's quality is such that the normal pattern of criticism or ignoring is loosened. This loosening allows analysis and adjustment of point of view; it allows growth, and the growth point of view is basically acknowledgement of resource exchange, of sharing, of aligning one's self with the impressive quality.

In astrology, if we let stimulus/response considerations involved with symbols intrude upon individualistic analysis of these symbols in terms of a human being's actual life, we can never come close to the person we serve. For example, we understand the principle of Pluto in the VIIIth House (page 151), but its significance, its meaning, can only be known in terms of the individual living it. We understand the juxaposition of Mercury and Neptune as a relationship between the need to think a certain way and the capacity for creative visualization. We abbreviate this idea as "daydreaming," but what is significant, what really has meaning, is how the individual employs daydreaming within holistic development and what the actual individualistic content of the daydreaming is. Stimulus/response meanings must give way to *ideational* meanings, meanings based within ideas, within concepts. In this way, astrological symbolisms grow continuously and differently in each individual's life richness.

In communicating ideational structures to modify stimulus/response patterns, we have the problems of words, which in turn also affect meanings. No astrologer can be helpful to another human being without communication power, a facility with vocabulary, concept, and nuance. But how difficult it can be to cultivate this flexible power when the rest of the astrologer's life is confined by the patterns of family, community, society, and generational background to anything *but* sensitive perception and communication! Jargon takes the place of substance since there is no established way to comprehend or articulate substance. Conventional attitudes are presumed because of a blindness to all but one's own station in life. The lost gather around the lost and reinforce the patterns further. Cliques of astrologers band together to espouse and perpetuate the fruitless patterns of arbitrary meanings. As one's own astrology reflects one's own life, so one's own astrology all too easily and naturally extends to confine the life of another.

The answer to this complex dilemma of meaning and points of view is within objectification as we have seen: astrologers must remain completely objective. During horoscope analysis, the astrologer's personal behavior patterns cannot exist. All value judgments, all personal anxieties, fears, subjective insecurities must be suspended. Objectification allows the astrologer to direct the traffic of stimulus/response behaviors revealed within client dialogue, to illuminate ideas, make connections analytically, and sort out fresh points of view. Experience accumulated through objectivity supports the astrologer's interpretive authority.

Yesterday morning, I received a client into my office. He was a young man of twenty-two, tall, very soft-spoken, even reticent. His Capricorn Ascendant was sharply accentuated by Mars in Capricorn in the Ist House, but his Sun-Mercury conjunction in Pisces opposed by Pluto seemed to dominate as manifested in his sensitive demeanor. Jupiter, Neptune, and the node were in extremely close conjunction with his Scorpio Midheaven. I had expected an extremely sensitive, academic-spiritualist person, perhaps wanting to be a teacher of religious or philosophical subjects (Moon in Gemini in the Vth). The young man was studying retailing.

As we talked in the early part of our time together, I worked hard to alert some enthusiasm within him. I asked him for his projections into the near future, some eight months to a year from now. Very quietly and unemotionally, he told me, "Mr. Tyl I will be dead in February, according to my doctor. I have leukemia; I've just begun Cobalt treatments as a last hope."

Every sensibility in me as a human being was startled, jarred. I felt helpless. For a split second, I was totally shocked by the apparent futility of his life. My objectification endured, and before the split second had elapsed I had staved off the patterns of commiseration and feelings that are naturally patterned within me as a human being. (This was particularly difficult since several personal friends in my life history had died of leukemia.)

What was I to do? Would a planet rescue this young man? Would a magic measurement give me the authority to say, "Well, you're not going to die" or "Well, your doctor's right. These things happen, you know"? Was I to give meaning to death or meaning to life? Objectively, was there something that could keep him meaningfully alive in whatever time he had left? Was there something to fill whatever time and space remained?

I told the young man that astrology is a celebration of life, and that life would be what we would talk about in the face of his mortal challenge. I suggested that his study of retailing was not his end goal, but that it could be an important adjunct, a strong resource in his work in a different field. I then asked him if his mind had ever or recently turned to spiritual concerns.

He replied in surprise: "Why, yes! A friend of mine has recently given me some books on the subject!" He said the books were sensitive works on death, dying, and the hereafter. I coun-

339

tered with, "What about studies concerned with life?" I was doing my best to help him establish a different point of view, to give different meaning to his challenge.

I explored the Jupiter, node, Neptune conjunction upon his Scorpio Midheaven. I suggested boldly that he could become a spiritual teacher, eventually run a school, with his business acumen giving the effort sound fiscal security. I told him of spiritual teachers who had become powerful and effective through life and death challenges. I asked him to visualize himself ten or twenty years from now: standing before an audience, stating his spiritual discovery and strength in the face of a threat to his life.

Gradually, this new point of view filled his life space and time. He became fascinated with the thought. Energy began to glow. That evening and the next he went to lectures and met with spiritual teachers to get a start within his new work. Together we hoped for new meaning in new life.

The body heals itself. People help themselves. Others help in the process.

The concept of an adjusted point of view has spatial connotations. We can note how the role oriented emphasis of the identity society is placed upon concepts of space in order to define personal perspective: "give me some space", "spaced out", "on a trip", "that's a real high", "I need more space". The concept of space certainly defines the tension zone between inner and outer environments, between individual needs and societal prescriptions. In complement to this horizontal sense of space, there is the vertical sense: one is exhilarated by a "high", depressed by a "downer"; well-being puts a spring into one's step, a lift into one's life; frustration, being down and out, takes someone out of the picture.

Astrologically, we know that the emphasis of life is upwards, toward a high, toward the Midheaven, our place in the sun. We know that preparation within the early homelife is designed to prepare us with resources with which to rise above the horizon in cooperation and relationship with others and eventually to achieve public status and fulfilled personal identity. With the necessary developmental tensions en route, fantasy can create such highs that progress is difficult, and objective astrological remediation must adjust those fantasy projections to practicability. Environmental prescriptions can create patterns of underachievement that must be elevated through enlivened visualization and newly alerted strategy.

In his fine book, *The Book of Highs*, Edward Rosenfeld studies 250 methods of altering consciousness (refreshing personal point of view with new awareness) without drugs. In the preface to this book, Andrew Weil, author of *The Natural Mind*, makes an observation that parallels the thrust of our study in this book perfectly: "Highs come from within the individual; they are simply released, or not, by the drug, which always acts in combination with expectations and environment—set and setting." [42]

The drug induced high is artificial. The chemically induced high is an illusion of a temporary nature; the down is as intensive as the up. This is an easy parallel with fantasy frustration, where the conceptualization gets so high in defensive projection away from pain in status/identity or money/love concerns that improper information is fed dysfunctionally into the sense of personal perspective.

Weil continues: "If we look over an extensive catalog of methods for getting high, one common trait stands out: they all are techniques of focusing awareness, of shaking us out of habitual modes of perception and getting us to concentrate on something, whether a sound, a sight, an unusual sensation. And possibly, when our ordinary consciousness is focused on anything, we can become aware of what is ordinarily unconsciously perceived." [43]

I suggest that a natural, enduring high comes from focused understanding and focused commitment. Time and time and time again in astrological practice, I have seen understanding of analytical connections release defensive overcompensations and the overworked anxiety connected to them. I have seen new connections formed in terms of commitment, fortified by understanding. I have seen hope come alive in terms of the understanding of the necessary controls that had shaped development. With focused commitment, potentially disruptive concerns become peripheral; the high of commitment transcends upset. In a very real sense, potential upset is sacrificed (Neptune) within the creative visualization dimension of focused plan.

Rosenfeld himself states, "Concentration means learning to focus; it means training ourselves, through practice, to 'stay with' the object of our attention despite distraction; it means staying with a subject and 'mastering' our relationship with the subject.

(This does not mean mastering the subject! Real concentration indicates a relationship of equality, an I-Thou relationship with the subject.)" [44]

These concepts are high points of meaning during discussion with the client. Remediation proceeds with awareness of developmental connections throughout life time and then focuses commitment within a fresh point of view. Problems make life vital; anxiety stimulates personality growth and life itself. Suffering forces awareness of values, adjustment of response, and change of attitude. Ritualistic maintenance of inherited behavior patterns seek to placate the gods of societal prescription, until the portion of godliness within every human being's inner environment is alerted.

Commitment begins—as does love—with one's self: enjoying one's self, believing that one is created to be fulfilled, appreciating one's resources, understanding the meaning of one's personal development, projecting further developmental potential. Remediation within these considerations can begin with the simple—though powerful—suggestion for the client to study himself or herself naked before a mirror, to learn to appreciate personal beauty, to smile at the work that may need to be done to please personal aesthetic, to get rid of the tightness of embarrassment that is put upon us when we don the clothing and restrictions of our outer environment. *Commitment begins with reinforcement of the inner environment.* Its space is defined and appreciated; its development through time is analyzed and appreciated. Space and time catch up with one another and form a base of pride and resourcefulness.

As a guide to meaning, points of view, and commitment, the astrologer's objective position of analysis is strategically placed upon the client's personal continuum of life space and life time. As we have seen throughout this book, the dynamic interrelationship between inner and outer environments takes place in life development time. The entire concept of individual fact (and blunder) and social fact (and truth) are merged within the time and space defined by the horoscope and given meaning by the human being's life.

The analytical rationale of holistic astrology is to study the intricate patterns of inner and outer environmental interaction as they develop within the past in order to glean meaning as a base for strategic projection into the future. This is a disciplined process as rational as the time conundrum of the heavens in which it is grounded through our study: as we measure the position of the Sun, we are looking back into the past, seeing the Sun's light as it was eight minutes earlier. We see the nearest star as it was four years ago; galaxies as they were millions of years before. The speed of light, the fastest measure we know, ties us throughout space to times past. The grander conundrum of the precession of the equinoxes then gives us relativity measures of zodiacal reference that again relate any now with every past. Times to come are times that were.

In his *The Tao of Physics*, Fritjof Capra quotes Louis De Broglie:

"In space-time, everything which for each of us constitutes the past, the present, and the future is given en bloc . . . Each observer, as his time passes, discovers, so to speak, new slices of space-time which appear to him as successive aspects of the material world, though in reality the ensemble of events constituting space-time exist prior to his knowledge of them."[45]

We see this process within the miracle of every horoscope life.

A 49 year-old man came to see me. He was casual, unassuming, and average in self-presentation. That he could have a grievous conceptual problem was suggested by his Sun-Venus conjunction in Pisces in the IXth, opposed by Neptune retrograde in the IIIrd. Two arms of the Cadent Grand Cross were powerfully accentuated. The Sun ruled the IIIrd.

Additionally, the Moon in Capricorn, ruling his Cancer Ascendant, was conjoined with Saturn in the VIth, another arm of the information/perspective concerns based within the Cadent Grand Cross. Status/identity concerns were equally indicated, especially through the Moon's rulership of the Ascendant and its conjunction with Saturn, ruler of the VIIth, by Neptune's rulership of the Midheaven and its opposition with Sun-Venus.

Our discussion revealed a homelife pattern of paternal coercion and maternal support. Gradually, the development pattern we discussed blandly revealed my client's homosexuality.

Immediately, the man was startled. He shifted forward in his chair, rolled up his shirt's short sleeve, and dramatically and aggressively revealed a large tattoo on his shoulder: "Yes, I'm a homosexual. I'm sick. You see this? This is the formula of my sickness. Dr. _____, the greatest psychoanalyst in the world taught me this formula. Here it is!"

The air was electrified by this man's thrust of body and speech. The tattoo revealed two large crossed streaks of orange lightning, over which were inked a series of letters in the style of a chemical formula. The letters were an acronym of something like, "obsessive maternal oral fixation equals homosexual sickness."

What was I to do? Would a planet rescue my client —or me? Would a magic measurement give me the authority to say, "Well, he's right; you are sick" or "Look, homosexuals are not necessarily sick people. They're really just like anyone else; sexuality is sexuality"? Was I to give meaning to sickness or meaning to health? Objectively, was there something that could erase this tattoo from his mind? Was there something to erase the time and space of his psychoanalytic encounter?

I calmly asked two short questions about how long ago he had seen the "greatest psychoanalyst in the world" and how old the psychoanalyst was at that time. The answers confirmed my hunch: the psychoanalyst had gotten his degree probably in the 1930's during the era of militant Freudianism and, probably, judging from the Austrian-Jewish name of the doctor, in Vienna itself.

My client was completely swamped with the psychoanalyst's information. Information and perspective resources were completely anchored to a time some fifteen years earlier. Prescriptions of an authoritative external environment had been dramatically emblazoned upon the man's body, deep into his inner environment. The doctor had either created this point of view or had confirmed it. My client had convinced his doctor and himself of his "sickness". My client's victimization was there to stay. The psychoanalyst had done a fine job representing another era and invading the time/space continuum of another individual. His past still lived as confinement.

Like some of the Jews going to showers to prepare for a new life, my client believed victimization by the environment was right. —*Astrologer, lament*!

The next day, a woman in her mid-forties came to see me. Her life was incredibly routined—and normal. She had had a routined upbringing soaked in Catholic regimen. She had married for better or worse and had worked at the same menial job for a quarter-century. She and her husband had become bored with each other: sex was non-existent, they went to bed every night after the evening television news, took the same turns in the bathroom, entered their double bed at precisely the same time and at the same angle, and the same "good-night's" were exchanged as the same person turned off the same light.

This woman was all smiles. Even when I asked her what she thought her IQ was, she smiled broadly as she replied, "Probably very, very low."

Very powerful transits and Solar Arc measurements suggested most reliably that her love life was being awakened. There had been no improvement on the homefront, and I asked gently if there were any possibility of an affair. She was indeed having an affair, but she was steeped in guilt and fear because of the lifetime of prescriptions she had taken on and nurtured within routine. Her past still lived as confinement. She reflected it now within the first glimmer of something personal and new.

The horoscopic measurements showed the potential that her life would change because of this affair, that the routine would be broken if this woman could find the courage to live for herself after a lifetime of dedication to others' prescriptions. I explained ways to improve the homelife and explained the problems she would have to face there or in her other eventual option, marrying the lover.

Like the Junior High School students reflecting the attitudes of their parents when hearing of presidential assassination, my client reflected the patterns of her life development to an extreme. Now, in the face of challenge —*astrologer, guide and hope*!

The next client was a woman near sixty. She and her husband had worked a lifetime of constant effort to meet adversity, raise children, and hope for retirement. They loved and supported one another throughout many, many challenges. Now, upon retirement, they had found excitement and commitment to a spiritual teaching through which they could help others. They wanted to teach others the potential of change through the fruits of their life.

Like the thousands championing solar energy, acting upon the environment, my client was seeking to do the same. Now, sharing the light of her sun —*astrologer, be joyful*!

*　　　*　　　*　　　*

As I finished writing this book, I left my office/apartment to take a short walk and to be thankful. As I approached the elevator, my next door neighbor—Mrs. Henderson, alone, pretty, middle-fifties, lonely—emerged with the bored "Hello, Mr. Tyl, how are you" I hear from her sometimes four times a day. In my preoccupation with thought and the press of the elevator door, I did not reply. As the door closed, as my neighbor walked to her apartment, I heard, as usual, her bored "Fine, thank you." I knew again Mrs. Henderson's life pattern.

I left the elevator on the first floor and made my way out to the swimming pool area to walk on the grass. My time and space were still occupied with fulfillment. A cheerful voice interrupted me: "*Good* morning, isn't it, sir?"

A boy about 10 years of age, dressed in white tennis clothes, sat on a bench beside his parked bicycle. I could feel his life pattern. —"It sure is, young man. Thank you!"

We were obviously both proud to be alive.

Footnotes and Bibliography

1. Uriel G. and Edna B. Foa, *Societal Structures of the Mind*, Charles C. Thomas Publisher, Springfield, Illinois, 1974, p. 380.
2. Sidney M. Jourard, *The Transparent Self*, D. Van Nostrand Company, New York, 1971, pp. 104-105.
3. Alan Watts, *Psychotherapy East and West*, Pantheon Books (Random House), New York, 1961, p. 9.
4. See reference 2, p. 11.
5. William Glasser, *The Identity Society*, Harper Colophon Books, New York, Revised Edition, 1975, p. 9.
6. In my twelve volume series, *The Principles and Practice of Astrology* (Llewellyn Publications, St. Paul, MN), I introduced the concept of Pluto's symbolism as "perspective," an adverbial measure of man's position within his world. On the personal level, this sense of perspective allies behavioral faculties with intensity, scope, and maximum potential through Pluto's aspect relationship with planets. Here in this discussion, Pluto's sense of environmental perspective is clear. It does not infringe upon the inner cognitive sense of personal perspective within the Cadent Grand Cross of information/perspective resources.
7. Male insecurities within sexuality will be discussed in Chapter Six.
8. When internal tensions are too great and have no direct outlet within relationships, illness often develops as a more manageable focus of the inner tensions. An illness can become a companion. A person's world shrinks down in size to focus on the self and a specific ailment. On the other hand, health is the freedom and responsibility for the human being to realize potentials in cooperation with others. Illness is a part of "body language".
9. Rollo May, *The Meaning of Anxiety*, Pocket Books, New York, 1977, foreword, p. xx.
10. See reference 9, p. 57.
11. Haridas Chaudhuri, *Mastering the Problems of Living*, Citadel Press, New York, 1975, p. 63.
12. Jeff Jawer, "The Discoveries of Uranus, Neptune, and Pluto", *Astrology Now* magazine, #26, Vol. 4, No. 2, p. 22, Llewellyn Publications, St. Paul, Minnesota.

13. Please see development and presentation of the matrix of the unconscious: Noel Tyl, *The Principles and Practice of Astrology*, Volume V, *Astrology and Personality*, Chapter 5.

14. Noel Tyl, *The Principles and Practice of Astrology*, Volume IV: *Aspects and Houses in Analysis*, Llewellyn Publications, St. Paul, Minnesota, 1974, pp. 139-140.

15. Birth Data: Ralph Nader, February 27, 1934, 04:52 AM, EST, Winsted, Connecticut, 73W04-41N55, according to Birth Certificate as reported in *2001: The Penfield Collection*, Marc Penfield; Vulcan Books, Seattle, WA, 1979.

16. Birth Data: Merv Griffin, July 6, 1925, 04:45 AM, PST, San Mateo, CA, 122W19-37N34, according to birth certificate as reported in *Contemporary Sidereal Horoscopes*, presented in *2001: The Penfield Collection*.

    An additional note in reference to the outlined analysis of Mr. Griffin's horoscope: a book, by Melba Colgrove, Harold H. Bloomfield, and Peter McWilliams (Bantam Books, New York, 1977) carries an endorsement by Griffin: "One of the loveliest books ever written ... It should be in everybody's library." The book's title: *How to Survive the Loss of a Love*.

17. Birth Data: Howard Hughes, December 24, 1905, 11:00 PM, CST, Houston, Texas, 95W23-29N45, according to personal statement to Mr. Hughes' astrologer as reported in *2001: The Penfield Collection*.

18. Noel Tyl, "Beginners' Improvement Column: The Elements", *Astrology Now* magazine, Vol. 3, No. 21, p. 49, Llewellyn Publications, St. Paul, Minnesota.

19. Noel Tyl, *The Principles and Practice of Astrology*, Volume III: *The Planets: Their Signs and Aspects*, p. 154.

20. See reference 13.

21. Marian Christy interview with Mike Wallace, *The Washington Post* newspaper, June 10, 1979.

22. Avodah K. Offit, *The Sexual Self*, J. B. Lippincott Company, Philadelphia and New York, 1977, p. 11.

23. Homosexuality specifically has not been studied within this volume. The insights into sexual concerns apply to homosexuals and heterosexuals alike. Sexuality is sexuality within the purvue of this discussion. For specific study of homosexuality, please see Noel Tyl, *The Guide to the Principles and Practice of Astrology* (Llewellyn Publications, St. Paul, Minnesota), Chapter 9.

24. See reference 22, p. 219.

25. I conceived this complementary axis to the Hermetic Doctrine in 1976 and have developed it throughout my works. Three years later, I discovered that Goethe had conceived the same, as reported by J. E. Cirlot, *A Dictionary of Symbols*, Philosophical Library, Inc., New York, 1962, p. 278.

26. George Mora, "Recent American Psychiatric Developments," *American Handbook of Psychiatry*, 2 volumes, Basic Books, New York, 1960, p. 32.

27. Please see the fine presentation of the Sun-Moon blends in *Heaven Knows What* by Grant Lewi (Llewellyn Publications, St. Paul, Minnesota), and the adaptations of Lewi's work in *The Principles and Practice of Astrology*, Volume III by Noel Tyl.

28. B. F. Skinner, *Beyond Freedom & Dignity*, Bantam Books, New York, 1972, p. 13.

29. Recommended references for these studies: Robert Hand, *Planets in Transit* (Para Research, Gloucester, Massachusetts, 1976); Noel Tyl, *The Principles and Practice of Astrology*, Volume VII, *Integrated Transits*; Grant Lewi, *Astrology for the Millions* (Llewellyn Publications, St. Paul, Minnesota, revised edition, 1970); Noel Tyl, *The Principles and Practice of Astrology*, Volume VI, *The Expanded Present*; Dane Rudhyar, *The Lunation Cycle*; Noel Tyl, *The Guide to the Principles and Practice of Astrology* Llewellyn Publications, St. Paul, Minnesota).

30. T'ai-Chi is an abbreviated name for T'ai-chi Ch'uan (pronounced "tie-jee chwan"). The formal extra word means "fist" or "boxing". The more familiar term, "T'ai-Chi" is derived from a concept of Chinese philosophy meaning "supreme ultimate." T'ai-Chi is a philosophically conceived, spiritually aware, and physically demanding sport-dance exercise of grace, control, and wholeness. A fine reference for T'ai-Chi is Cheng Man-ch'ing and Robert W. Smith, *T'AI-CHI*, Charles E. Tuttle Co., Rutland, Vermont, 1967, eighteenth printing, 1978.

31. "T'ai" is the eleventh hexagram of the *I Ching*; The Receptive, Earth are above the Creative, Heaven. See Wilhelm/Baynes, *The I Ching or Book of Changes*, Princeton University Press, Princeton, New Jersey, revised edition 1969, pp. 48-52.

32. Any reader in photography must be aware of the spiritual and psychodynamic insights of writer Ralph Hattersley. See especially his *Discover Your Self Through Photography*, Morgan & Morgan Inc., Dobbs Ferry, New York, 1976.

33. For a full and inspiring orientation within this technique, please see Eugene T. Gendlin's *Focusing*, Everest House, New York, 1978.

34. Willard Gaylin, *Caring*, Avon Books, New York, 1976, p. 178.

35. This experiment is an adaptation of the insights and technique of J. M. Shlein, "Toward What Level of Abstraction in Criteria?", *Research in Psychotherapy*, Volume II, Washington, D.C., American Psychological Association.

36. Please see Noel Tyl, *The Principles and Practice of Astrology*, Volume XII, Chapter 2.

37. Wilder Penfield, *The Mystery of the Mind*, Princeton University Press, Princeton, New Jersey, 1975, introduction, p. xxvii.

38. This is an adaptation of exercises developed to strengthen the will that are credited to Boyd Barrett and presented by Roberto Assagioli in his *The Act of Will*, Penguin Books, New York, 1974, pp. 36-45.

39. See reference 11, pp. 58-59.

40. Arthur Deikman, *Personal Freedom: On Finding Your Way to the Real World*, Grossman Publishers (Viking Press), New York, 1976, pp. 88-91.

41. Carl R. Rogers, *Readings in Humanistic Psychology*, The Free Press, New York, (division of the MacMillan Company), 1969, pp. 44-45.

42. Edward Rosenfeld, *The Book of Highs*, Quadrangle/The New York Times Book Company, New York, 1973, foreword.

43. See reference 42.

44. See reference 42, section 1.

45. Fritjof Capra, *The Tao of Physics*, Shambhala Publications, Inc., Berkeley, California, 1975, p. 185.

Additional Bibliography

Assagioli, Roberto, *Psychosynthesis*, Penguin Books, New York, 1976.

Bentov, Itzhak, *Stalking the Wild Pendulum*, E. P. Dutton, New York, 1977.

Colgrove, Bloomfield, and McWilliams, *How to Survive the Loss of a Love*, Bantam Books, New York, 1977.

Fensterheim, Herbert and Baer, Jean, *Stop Running Scared!*, Dell, New York, 1977.

Glasser, Ronald J., *The Body is the Hero*, Random House, New York, 1976.

Hall, Calvin S. and Lindzey, Gardner, *Theories of Personality*, John Wiley & Sons, New York, 1957.

Murphy, Gardner, *Human Potentialities*, The Viking Press, New York, 1975.

Ouspensky, P.D., *In Search of the Miraculous*, Harcourt Brace & World, Inc., New York, 1949.

Puharich, Andrija, *Beyond Telepathy*, Anchor Press/Doubleday, New York, 1973.

Rose, Steven, *The Conscious Brain*, Vintage Books (Random House), New York, 1976.

Schwartz, David J., *The Magic of Thinking Big*, Simon and Schuster, New York, reprint 1979.

Selzer, Richard, *Mortal Lessons: Notes on the Art of Surgery*, Simon and Schuster, New York, 1974.

Smith, Adam, *Powers of Mind*, Random House, New York, 1975.

Tillich, Paul, *The Courage to Be*, Yale University Press, New Haven, Conn., 1959.

Tompkins, Peter, *Mysteries of the Mexican Pyramids*, Harper & Row, New York, 1976.

van Pelt-Roemer, "The Cadent Houses," *Astrology Now* magazine, Vol. IV, No. 4, whole number 28, Llewellyn Publications, St. Paul, MN.

Watts, Alan, *Nature, Man, and Woman*, Pantheon Books (Random House), New York, 1961.

INDEX

H

I

J

Resources, personal 12, 26, 27, 31, 33, 47, 180
    exchange 39, 46–52, 54, 61, 81, 82, 181, 209, 263, 309
    in sexuality 222–226
Retrogradation 68–72, 172
Rewards 11, 15, 28, 35, 217–222, 286
    through the Elements 218
Rogers, Carl R. 331
Role orientation 55
Rosenfeld, Edward 340

S

Sacrifice 44, 65, 140, 142, 144, 154–157, 186, 340
Sameness
    maintaining 8, 9, 11, 12, 17, 24, 32
    preserving 7
Saturn
    and fear 174
    and Mars 319
    as need 18, 317
    as necessary control 68
    in fantasy 25
    in XI, V 221
    oriental 163
    retrograde 68–72, 113, 183, 212, 252, 277
Science 331
Security 18
Self-appreciation 243, 310
Self-assertion 53, 54, 65
Self-disclosure 50, 51, 81, 82, 85, 222
Self-worth 10, 19, 20, 27, 40, 44, 51, 63–77, 70, 75, 147
Sexuality 27, 74–76, 123, 127, Ch 6, 268, 280, 311, 321
    and dependency 213
Signification 21
Significator 18
Sin 145
Skinner, B.F. 273, 274
Societal structure 4, 12, 34
Spill over of Houses 44, 45, 47, 48, 50, 51, 53, 54, 60, 75, 77,
    137, 147, 192, 252, 265

V

W

XYZ